Access™ 2007 VBA Bible

Access™ 2007 VBA Bible

For Data-Centric Microsoft® Office Applications

Helen Feddema

Wiley Publishing, Inc.

Access™ 2007 VBA Bible: For Data-Centric Microsoft® Office Applications

Published by
Wiley Publishing, Inc.
10475 Crosspoint Boulevard
Indianapolis, IN 46256
www.wiley.com

Copyright © 2007 by Wiley Publishing, Inc., Indianapolis, Indiana

Published by Wiley Publishing, Inc., Indianapolis, Indiana

Published simultaneously in Canada

ISBN: 978-0-470-04702-6

Manufactured in the United States of America

10 9 8 7 6 5 4 3 2 1

For general information on our other products and services or to obtain technical support, please contact our Customer Care Department within the U.S. at (800) 762-2974, outside the U.S. at (317) 572-3993 or fax (317) 572-4002.

Library of Congress Cataloging-in-Publication Data:

Feddema, Helen Bell.
 Access 2007 VBA Bible: For Data-Centric Microsoft Office Applications / Helen Feddema.
   p. cm.
 Includes index.
 ISBN 978-0-470-04702-6 (paper/website)
 1. Microsoft Access. 2. Database management. 3. Microsoft Visual Basic for applications. I. Title.
 QA76.9.D3F435 2007
 005.75'65--dc22

2007007061

About the Author

Helen Feddema is an independent developer specializing in Microsoft Office applications, concentrating on Access, Word, and (since 1996) Outlook. She has written or co-authored many books on Access and other Office applications, including *Inside Microsoft Access* (New Riders, 1992), *Power Forms for Microsoft Access* and *Power Reports for Microsoft Access* (Pinnacle, 1994), *Access How-Tos* (Waite Group Press, 1995), *MCSD: Access 95 Study Guide* (Sybex, 1998), *DAO Object Model: The Definitive Guide* (O'Reilly, January 2000), and *Access 2002 Inside-Out* (Microsoft Press, 2001), which was judged #1 in the Desktop and Office Applications book category at the Waterside 2004 conference. Her most recent book is *Expert One-on-One Microsoft Access Application Development* (Wiley/Wrox, 2003).

She has also contributed chapters to a number of multi-author Office books, including *Special Edition: Using Microsoft Outlook 97* (Que, 1997), *Office Annoyances* (O'Reilly, 1997), *Outlook Annoyances* (O'Reilly, 1998), *Special Edition: Using Microsoft Project 98* (Que, 1997), *Teach Yourself Project* (Sams, 1998), and *Special Edition: Outlook 2000* (Que, 2000). Helen has been a regular contributor to Pinnacle's *Smart Access* and *Office Developer* journals, Informant's *Microsoft Office and VBA Programming* (now *Office Solutions*), and *Woody's Underground Office* newsletter, and she is currently the editor of the *Access Watch* ezine (formerly *Woody's Access Watch*), for which she writes the Access Archon column.

Credits

Executive Editor
Bob Elliott

Development Editor
Kelly Talbot

Technical Editor
Mary Hardy

Production Editor
Eric Charbonneau

Copy Editor
Kim Cofer

Editorial Manager
Mary Beth Wakefield

Production Manager
Tim Tate

Vice President and Executive Group Publisher
Richard Swadley

Vice President and Executive Publisher
Joseph B. Wikert

Project Coordinator
Adrienne Martinez

Graphics and Production Specialists
Sean Decker
Jennifer Mayberry
Heather Pope
Amanda Spagnuolo

Quality Control Technicians
Melanie Hoffman
Robert Springer
Brian Walls

Proofreading and Indexing
Aptara

Anniversary Logo Design
Richard Pacifico

Contents

Contents

Acknowledgments

Many thanks to my technical editor, Mary Hardy, for catching errors and making many valuable suggestions that improved the quality of the book (and sample databases), and to editors Kelly Talbot and Brian Hermann for their suggestions and support.

Introduction

Welcome to the *Access 2007 VBA Bible*. Like all books in the Bible series, you can expect to find both hands-on tutorials and real-world practical application information, as well as reference and background information that provides a context for what you are learning. This book is a fairly comprehensive resource on writing VBA code to exchange data among the main Office applications (Access, Word, Excel, and Outlook), using Access as the central application for storing data, and using the other applications for producing attractively formatted documents of various types. By the time you have completed the *Access 2007 VBA Bible,* you will be well-prepared to write VBA Automation code that uses your Access data to produce Word letters, mailing labels and other documents (without the overhead of mail merge), to create Excel worksheets and PivotCharts, and to create Outlook appointments, mail messages, contacts, and journal items, with or without attachments. Additionally, you will be able to synchronize contact data (both ways) between Access and Outlook.

Who Should Read This Book

The book is written for the Access/Office developer or power user who is familiar with working with Office applications (particularly Access) in the interface, and has at least a basic familiarity with writing VBA code, but needs more information on how to write Automation code to work with Word, Excel, and Outlook objects, so as to be able to use each Office application for creating the documents that are its specialty, while storing most of the data in Access databases.

How This Book Is Organized

The book starts out in Part I with a description of the Office components (Access, Word, Excel, and Outlook) and what they do best, as a guide to selecting the appropriate Office component for a specific task.

In Part II, more specific coverage is provided for each Office component, with sample databases that illustrate working with Access data, Word documents and templates, Excel worksheets, and Outlook items. This part also includes a chapter on working with files and folders using the FileSystemObject, and another on synchronizing Access contacts with Outlook contacts. This allows you to maintain your contacts in a set of properly normalized linked tables in Access, while also having the ability to reference and use Outlook contacts, without having to do dual entry or manually update contact information. Finally, the last chapter in the part deals with several advanced topics, working with Word and Excel objects.

Part III covers topics that add more functionality to Office, including the creation of COM add-ins with VB 6, Access add-ins, and Visual Studio 2005 Shared add-ins. It also covers customizing the Office 2007 Ribbon with XML in Access databases and with add-ins of various types. Additionally, there is a chapter on creating standalone scripts with Windows Script Host, and another chapter on using Access as a front end for working with SQL Server data.

Conventions and Features

There are many different organizational and typographical features throughout this book designed to help you get the most of the information.

Whenever the authors want to bring something important to your attention, the information will appear in a Tip, Note, or Caution.

CAUTION   This information is important and is set off in a separate paragraph with a special icon. Cautions provide information about things to watch out for, whether simply inconvenient or potentially hazardous to your data or systems.

TIP   Tips generally are used to provide information that can make your work easier—special shortcuts or methods for doing something easier than the norm.

NOTE   Notes provide additional, ancillary information that is helpful, but somewhat outside of the current presentation of information.

NEW FEATURE   New features introduce components or functionality that are new or improved in the software compared to earlier versions.

What's on the Companion Web Site

On the companion web site you will find sample code. Each chapter has its own subfolder on the web site. You'll in subfolders find all the sample databases and other files (such as Word and Excel templates, or Windows Script Host scripts) that were discussed in each chapter.

Minimum Requirements

To run the sample code in this book, you need a computer capable of running at least Windows XP, and of course you need Office 2007. Because Office 2007 runs fine on Windows XP, you don't need Windows Vista, but Office 2007 works even better on Vista. If you intend to run Vista, you need a Vista-ready computer. If you buy a new computer, look for the "Windows Vista Capable" sticker; however, an older computer may support Vista even if it doesn't have the sticker (though probably not the Aero Glass interface, which requires a high-powered video card).

Where to Go from Here

You should take away from this book the ability to select the Office component that does the best job for the task at hand. You should also take away how to write VBA Automation code to transfer data from Access to documents created with other Office components and format the documents as needed; this will let you create procedures that can be run from form events or toolbar buttons to automate any Office-related tasks you need to do on a regular basis.

My web site (`www.helenfeddema.com`) has pages with code samples and Access Archon articles, many of which deal with exchanging various types of data among Office applications. Check them out—you may find that the solution you are looking for is already there, ready to download and use.

Part I

The Office Components and What They Do Best

Chapter 1

Storing and Displaying Data in Access

Since its earliest days — about 14 years ago — Access has been a relational database program, storing data in tables and using its own queries, forms, and reports to sort, filter, display, and print data. With successive Office versions, moving data among Office components (especially Word, Excel, and Outlook) has become so much easier that it is now often more efficient to use another Office component rather than an Access report for a task such as printing letters or analyzing numeric data.

Additionally, using other Office components to display or print data from Access makes the data stored in Access tables more widely accessible. Many Office users have an edition of Office that doesn't include Access — but they all have Word and Excel, and many also have Outlook, so they can easily work with Word documents, Outlook messages or appointments, and Excel worksheets, filled with data from Access tables.

Whether you plan to present your data as an Access report, PivotChart, or PivotTable; or a Word document or Excel worksheet, the data is stored in Access tables, and entered and edited in Access forms.

A Brief History of Office Data Exchange

As the Windows operating system has progressed from Windows 3.0 to Windows XP and Vista, data transfer techniques have improved, from simple cut and paste using the Windows 3.0 clipboard, to Dynamic Data Exchange (DDE) and Open Database Connectivity (ODBC), to Automation (originally called Object Linking and Embedding [OLE], then OLE Automation) and Extensible Markup Language (XML).

In early Windows and Office versions, DDE and ODBC were difficult to use, cranky and unreliable in operation, and ODBC in particular often required elaborate setup. I know — I used both DDE and ODBC, when they were the only connectivity tools available. But I gladly dropped them when OLE became available in Windows 95/Office 95, because it offered a much simpler way to connect Office applications, though at first only in a limited manner.

Before Office 97, there was a distinction between Office components that were OLE servers, which could be manipulated by code running from other applications, and OLE clients, which could work with objects in OLE server applications' object models. Back in the days of Access 1.0 or even 2.0, Access developers had few tools available for connecting to other Office applications such as Word or Excel. Access, for example, was only a client, whereas Word was only a server.

In Office 95 AccessBasic was upgraded to standard Office VBA, and Access became an OLE server (previously it was only an OLE client). By Office 2000, all the major Office applications (Access, Word, Excel, Outlook, and PowerPoint) had been upgraded to support Automation both as clients and servers, so the OLE server/client distinction is no longer significant.

You can write Automation code in any major Office application to connect to any other Office application's data and functionality (and some third-party applications as well).

Storing Data in Access

Access was designed from the start to store data, so (if you have a choice — which is not always the case) it is the place where you should store your data. You may need to use that data to produce Word letters, SharePoint lists, Excel worksheets, or Outlook mail messages, but the data itself should be kept in Access tables, unless there is a very strong reason to store it elsewhere.

CROSS-REF One valid exception is storing data in SQL Server back-end databases, using Access as the front end. SQL Server is usually the choice for huge corporate databases, not small- to medium-sized databases used by individuals or small companies, where Access can easily handle the number of records. See Chapter 18 for more information on this option.

Data entry and editing, too, should be done in Access, for the most part, because you can create Access forms that offer an attractive interface for entering and editing data. You can write VBA code that runs from form and control events for purposes of error handling, and create functions that automate repetitive data-processing operations.

In my earlier book, *Expert One-on-One Microsoft Application Development*, I discussed creating Access applications, with details on using queries, forms, reports, and code. I won't duplicate this information here, but instead in this chapter I concentrate on new or improved features in Access 2007, which enhance the utility of Access forms and reports.

Displaying Data in Access Forms and Reports

Sometimes you don't need to go outside of Access to present your data — if you are designing an Access application, displaying data in forms and printing it in reports may be all you need.

NEW FEATURE Over the years, Access forms and reports have been significantly upgraded. In Access 2007, one long-requested feature has finally arrived in a workable form (I recall an early and unreliable implementation that made a brief appearance in Access 95). Memo fields can now store and display rich text, using the Text Align property, which takes a value of either Plain Text or Rich Text. When you select Rich Text for this property, you can apply various fonts, colors, and other attributes to selected portions of text in a table field or a control bound to that field.

In earlier versions of Office, if you wanted to generate a letter or other document including a block of text with color, bolding, or other attributes applied to selected words or phrases within the block, you had to create a Word letter and use Word's formatting features. In Access 2007, you can produce Access reports with varied formatting within text blocks, displaying text entered into Access memo fields in a textbox on a form.

NOTE The sample database for this section is RichText.accdb.

To create a field that can store data in Rich Text format (behind the scenes, this is done using HTML code, but you don't have to worry about writing the code), start by creating a table field of the Memo data type, and selecting Rich Text as the Text Format value (see Figure 1.1).

FIGURE 1.1

Creating a Memo field to hold Rich Text data.

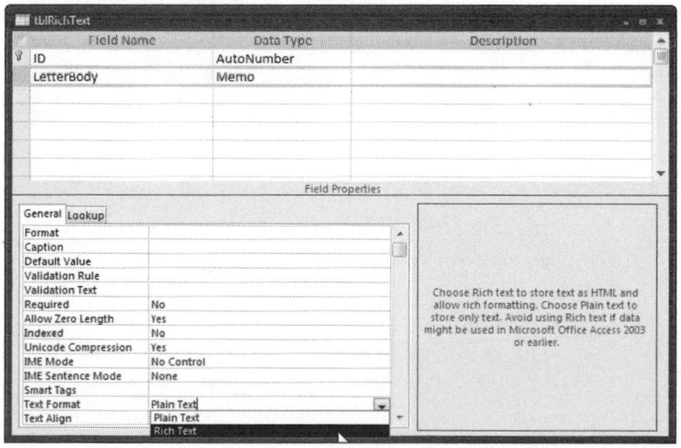

WARNING If you select a block of text in a Rich Text–enabled Memo field, you will see a floating toolbar that lets you apply some formatting, including indenting or outdenting, similar to Word (this works fine; see Figure 1.2). However, if you apply bullets or numbering from this toolbar, you will get the bullets or numbers, but the text that runs over one line won't be indented properly, as shown in Figure 1.3. For this reason, I recommend against using these features, unless all the items on your lists are no more than one line in length.

FIGURE 1.2

Indenting text from the floating toolbar in a Rich Text field.

Please turn off the heat upon rising on the morning of the project (pipes, boilers, or hot water heaters).
Times New Roman
10

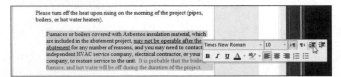

FIGURE 1.3

Incorrect indentation of an item in a numbered list in a Rich Text field.

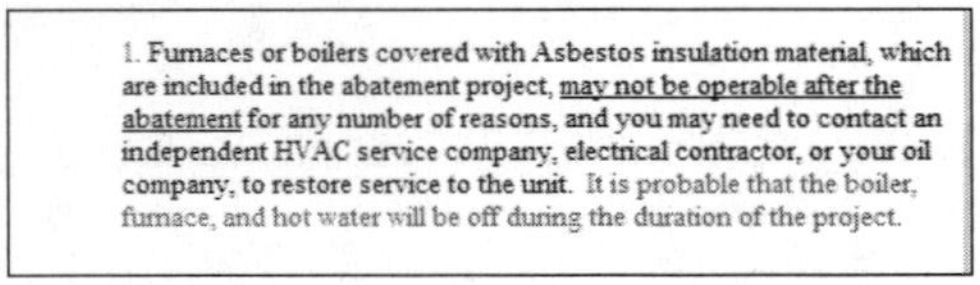

1. Furnaces or boilers covered with Asbestos insulation material, which are included in the abatement project, may not be operable after the abatement for any number of reasons, and you may need to contact an independent HVAC service company, electrical contractor, or your oil company, to restore service to the unit. It is probable that the boiler, furnace, and hot water will be off during the duration of the project.

Create a form bound to the table with the Memo field; you can now enter data into this textbox control and format it with different fonts, color, bolding, and other attributes, as you would while working in a Word document. When you place the cursor into a control with Rich Text enabled, a formatting group on the Form Ribbon is enabled, with a variety of formatting selections, as shown in Figure 1.4.

Figure 1.5 shows the form with a variety of formatting attributes applied to the text in the textbox.

FIGURE 1.4

Selecting formatting for a portion of text in a Rich Text–enabled textbox on a form.

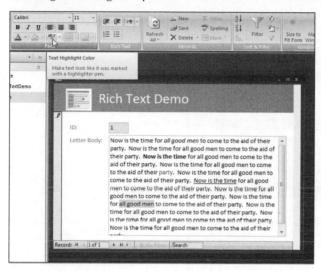

FIGURE 1.5

A Rich Text–enabled textbox with a variety of formatting applied to portions of its text.

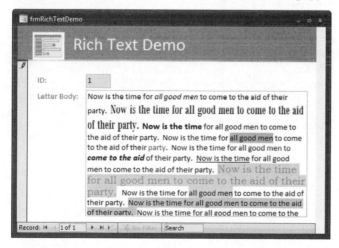

Once you have applied formatting to the text on a form, you can create a report based on the table, and the formatting will display on the report as well (see Figure 1.6).

FIGURE 1.6

A report showing Rich Text formatting applied in a textbox on a form.

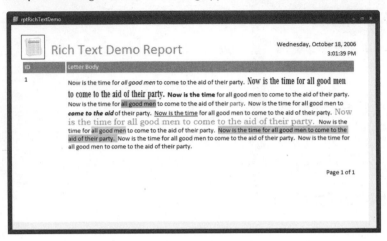

Creating Access Form Letters

A more realistic example of Rich Text formatting would be a form letter report, with the body of the letter text coming from a Rich Text–enabled field, and the name and address information from a table of contacts or customers. I created a table called tblLetterText in the sample database, with a Rich Text–enabled Memo field to hold the letter body text, and an ID and a LetterType text field. The LetterBody field holds formatted text, as shown in Figure 1.7 (the Rich Text formatting can be seen directly in the table, though you will find it easier to create and edit the rich text in a textbox control on a form).

TIP You can copy and paste formatted text from a Word document into a Memo field with Rich Text enabled (or a textbox bound to such a field), and the formatting will be preserved. However, bullets and numbered lists won't be aligned correctly, so it is best to turn off those features before copying text to Access.

I also created a one-row table to hold information to use in the database; in this case, it has two Rich Text–enabled Memo fields for the letter header and signature information. The form fdlgSelectLetter (bound to the information table, zstblInfo) lets you edit the header and signature (Figure 1.8) and select a letter type and a contact.

FIGURE 1.7

A table with formatted letter body text.

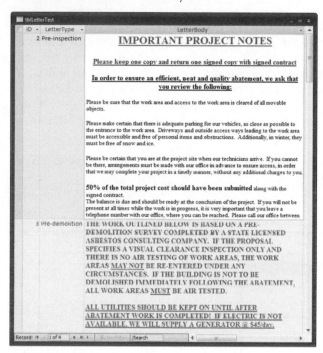

FIGURE 1.8

A dialog form for editing header and signature block information and selecting a letter and contact.

Clicking the Create Letter button opens a filtered Access report displaying name and address data from the selected Contact record, and the letter body from the selected letter type, as depicted in Figure 1.9.

With Rich Text formatting now supported in Access forms and reports, you may not need to produce a Word letter to get the look you want in printed documents. However, compared with Word, Access reports using Rich Text–enabled Memo fields have one significant limitation. In Word, you can place merge fields or DocProperty fields within a block of text, so that merged data or data stored in document properties will print at a certain point in the text, with the surrounding text wrapping as needed, depending on the length of the text in the fields. This is not possible with a Memo field on an Access report, so if you need to embed merge fields or DocProperty fields within the letter body text, you still need to create Word documents.

CROSS-REF See Chapter 2 for information on creating Word documents of various types filled with Access data.

FIGURE 1.9

A report with formatted text.

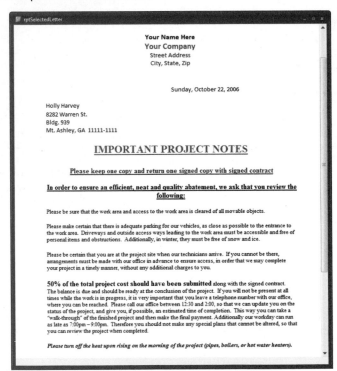

Using a Naming Convention

I first realized what a problem it is to work in a database with no naming convention when I took over a database created by another programmer. The database had a table, a query, a form, a report, a function, and five or six variables (of different data types) all called Sales (this was only one of a number of sets of objects with the same name). This meant that when I encountered the word "Sales" in VBA code, I had no idea whether it was a reference to a table, form, query, function, or variable, unless the context made it clear. There were numerous errors because of the use of the same name for different types of objects, because (among other possible sources of errors) you can set the value of a field with a variable, or with a function — and if several variables and a function are all called Sales, the code may use the wrong one.

You can also get circular reference errors when a control has the same name as the field to which it is bound — which is still the case in Access 2007, when you create a form bound to a table using the Form Wizard. To prevent these reference errors, it is an excellent idea to use a naming convention for database objects, controls, and variables. Using a naming convention also makes your database self-documenting (to some extent, at least), and prevents confusion when selecting an object from a drop-down list.

About 10 years ago, I wrote an Access 97 add-in (LNC Rename.mda) to automate the process of giving the appropriate tags to database objects and controls on forms and reports, using the Leszynski Naming Convention (LNC). This add-in was updated for Access 2000, and that version still works in Access 2007; it is available as Code Sample #10 (for Access 2000 or higher databases) from the Code Samples page of my web site, www.helenfeddema.com.

Creating Worksheet-type Reports in Access

If you need to produce a report formatted in familiar worksheet-type rows and columns, you can do this with an Access report. Access 2007 reports have some new features, letting you sort and filter interactively — and if you want full interactivity, you can create a PivotTable or PivotChart form. To demonstrate these features, I used a variation of the Northwind sample database, with objects renamed according to the Leszynski Naming Convention.

Plain Datasheet Reports

 The sample database for this section is Modified Northwind.accdb.

The query qryNorthwindAll links all the tables in the Modified Northwind database. To produce a plain datasheet report, start by selecting qryNorthwindAll, and selecting Report Wizard in the Reports group on the Create tab of the Ribbon, as shown in Figure 1.10.

FIGURE 1.10

Selecting the Report Wizard to create a report.

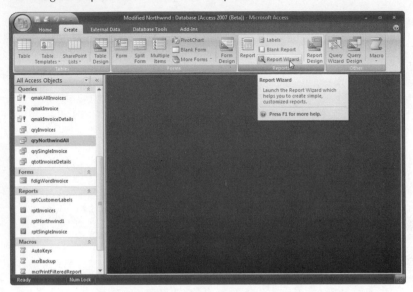

Select the fields to include on the report (see Figure 1.11) and click Next.

FIGURE 1.11

Selecting fields for a report.

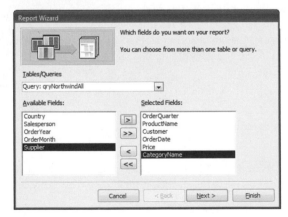

On the next screen of the wizard (see Figure 1.12), select the top-level grouping you want for the report (in this case, I accepted the default selection of OrderQuarter, Customer, OrderDate).

FIGURE 1.12

Selecting a major grouping level for a report.

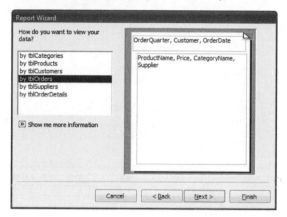

The next screen lets you select sub-groups, if desired; I accepted the default (no further sub-grouping, as shown in Figure 1.13).

FIGURE 1.13

Select sub-grouping levels for a report.

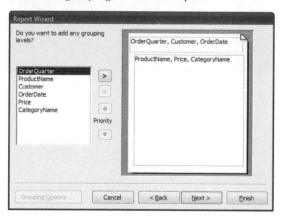

Next, select sorting and summarizing options; I selected ProductName for sorting, as shown in Figure 1.14.

Selecting sorting and summarizing options for a report.

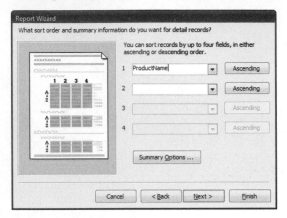

On the report layout screen, depicted in Figure 1.15, I selected the Block option.

Selecting the Block report layout option.

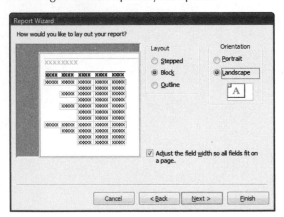

Select a style on the next screen, shown in Figure 1.16 (bear in mind that some of the more artistic styles won't look good when printed on a black-and-white printer). I selected None for a plain report.

FIGURE 1.16

Selecting a report style.

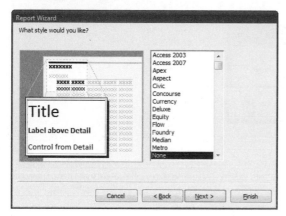

Give the report a name on the Finish screen (Figure 1.17) — I called it rptNorthwindSales. Select the "Modify the report's design" option to open the report in design view, and click Finish.

FIGURE 1.17

The Finish screen of the Report Wizard.

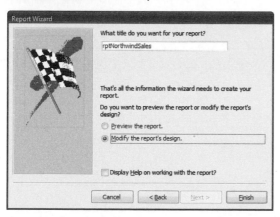

> **TIP** You will need to make some adjustments to the report's design in the property sheet; if it is not open, click the Property Sheet button in the Tools group on the Design tab of the Ribbon, as shown in Figure 1.18.

Opening the property sheet.

By default, in the Block report layout only the cells with values have visible borders, so to create an overall worksheet-type layout, select all the controls in the Detail section of the report, and turn off display of duplicate data values by setting the Hide Duplicates property to No on the Format tab of the properties sheet, as shown in Figure 1.19.

FIGURE 1.19

Setting the Hide Duplicates property to No to eliminate duplicate data on a report.

Although it is generally not a problem for report controls to have the same names as their bound fields (because they are rarely, if ever, referenced in code), I like to give the appropriate tags to the bound controls at least. To do this manually, give the textboxes the prefix txt. (On a report created by the Report Wizard, labels are named with the non-standard suffix _Label.)

NEW FEATURE The Report Wizard generally applies the default alignment to each column label, which may result in inconsistent alignment. That doesn't look good, so (if necessary) adjust the alignment of the column headings labels as desired (generally they should be either all left-aligned or all centered); on the sample report I made them all centered.

If you need to adjust an individual column width, it may be necessary to turn off control grouping (a new feature in Access 2007). To accomplish this, first select the controls in the Detail section and click the yellow group anchor that should now be visible (though not very visible — Microsoft should have selected a color with more contrast than dull mustard yellow) at the upper-left corner of the group, then right-click any control in the group and select Remove from the Layout submenu (see Figure 1.20).

FIGURE 1.20

Turning off control grouping.

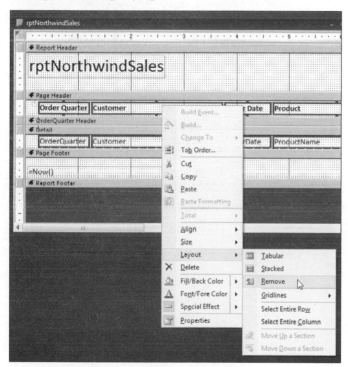

Figure 1.21 shows the finished worksheet-type report.

You can interactively sort and filter a report in report view — for example, when you want to view records from only one customer, as shown in Figure 1.22.

FIGURE 1.21

A worksheet-type Access report.

Order Quarter	Customer	Order Date	Product	Price	Category
Q1, 1995	Around the Horn	16-Jan-95	Gnocchi di nonna Alice	$608.00	Grains/Cereals
Q1, 1995	Queen Cozinha	04-Jan-95	Mozzarella di Giovanni	$291.90	Dairy Products
Q1, 1995	Ernst Handel	23-Jan-95	Mozzarella di Giovanni	$66.72	Dairy Products
Q1, 1995	Frankenversand	27-Jan-95	Mozzarella di Giovanni	$583.80	Dairy Products
Q1, 1995	Consolidated Holdings	07-Mar-95	Mozzarella di Giovanni	$278.00	Dairy Products
Q1, 1995	Victuailles en stock	30-Mar-95	Mozzarella di Giovanni	$1,112.00	Dairy Products
Q1, 1995	Consolidated Holdings	07-Mar-95	Gustaf's Knäckebröd	$201.60	Grains/Cereals
Q1, 1995	Frankenversand	27-Jan-95	Tunnbröd	$288.00	Grains/Cereals
Q1, 1995	Ernst Handel	02-Feb-95	Tunnbröd	$432.00	Grains/Cereals
Q1, 1995	Magazzini Alimentari Riuniti	03-Feb-95	Singaporean Hokkien Fried Mee	$22.40	Grains/Cereals
Q1, 1995	Seven Seas Imports	19-Jan-95	Filo Mix	$22.40	Grains/Cereals
Q1, 1995	Toms Spezialitäten	17-Mar-95	Filo Mix	$8.40	Grains/Cereals
Q1, 1995	Hungry Owl All-Night Grocers	12-Jan-95	Nord-Ost Matjeshering	$37.26	Seafood
Q1, 1995	Split Rail Beer & Ale	02-Jan-95	Gnocchi di nonna Alice	$136.80	Grains/Cereals
Q1, 1995	Ricardo Adocicados	17-Mar-95	Fløtemysost	$34.40	Dairy Products
Q1, 1995	Rattlesnake Canyon Grocery	01-Feb-95	Gnocchi di nonna Alice	$2,128.00	Grains/Cereals
Q1, 1995	Galería del gastrónomo	27-Feb-95	Gnocchi di nonna Alice	$152.00	Grains/Cereals
Q1, 1995	Ernst Handel	02-Mar-95	Gnocchi di nonna Alice	$912.00	Grains/Cereals
Q1, 1995	Princesa Isabel Vinhos	06-Mar-95	Gnocchi di nonna Alice	$851.20	Grains/Cereals

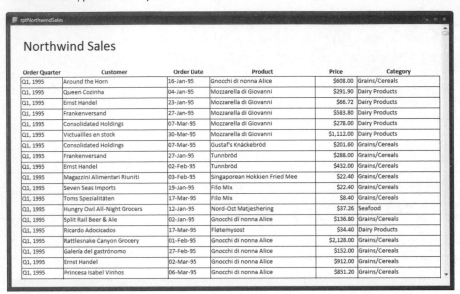

FIGURE 1.22

Filtering a report by a selected value in the Customer field.

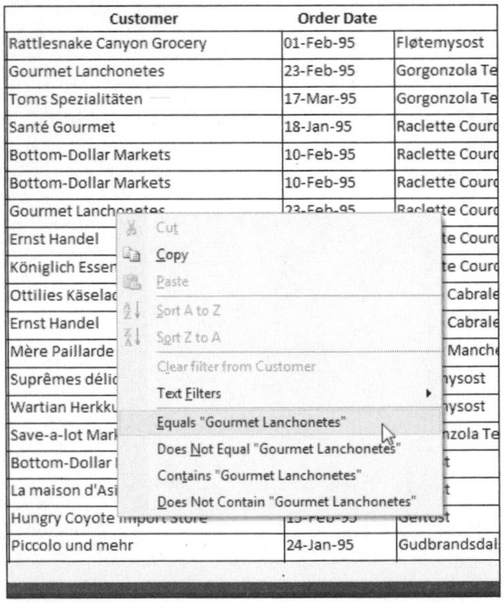

After making the selection, the report shows only Gourmet Lanchonetes records (Figure 1.23).

FIGURE 1.23

A report filtered by a Customer value.

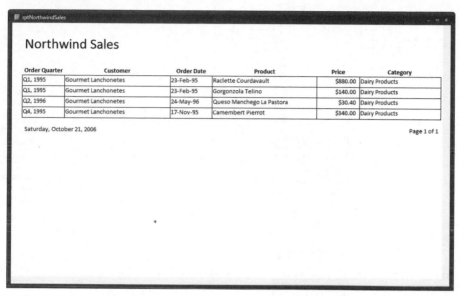

PivotTables

If you need more advanced interactivity, you can make a PivotTable based on the same `qryNorthwindAll` query. In Access 2007, the process of creating a PivotTable has been simplified; just select the data source query or table, then, as depicted in Figure 1.24, select PivotTable from the More Forms menu of the Forms group in the Create tab of the Ribbon.

FIGURE 1.24

Creating a PivotTable.

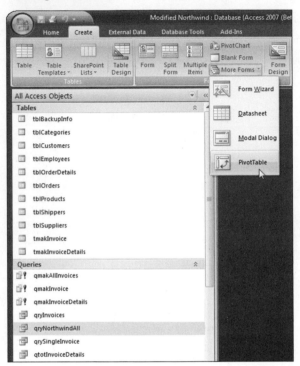

A new form based on the data source opens in PivotTable view (see Figure 1.25), with the Field List open so you can drag fields to the drop zones of the PivotTable, one field each to the Row Fields, Column Fields, and (optionally) Filter Fields drop zones, which are indicated in gray text at the upper-left corner of the form. The data field to be displayed in the body of the table is dragged to the drop zone in the center of the form; Access will automatically create a Count or Sum field when appropriate.

CROSS-REF See Chapter 5 of my book, *Expert One-on-One Microsoft Application Development,* for more information on creating and using PivotTables and PivotCharts.

Figure 1.26 shows the PivotTable with Salesperson selected as the Row field and CategoryName as the Column field, with Price as the Totals field.

FIGURE 1.25

A newly created PivotTable, ready to select fields.

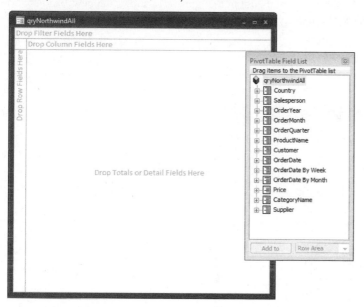

FIGURE 1.26

A completed PivotTable.

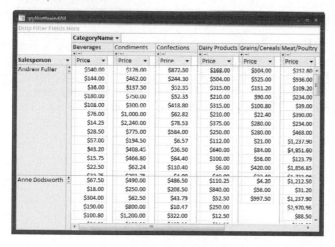

PivotCharts

Making a PivotChart is even easier: select the data source query or table and click the PivotChart button in the Forms group in the Create tab of the Ribbon. Figure 1.27 shows the new, blank PivotChart with drop zones at the top and right sides of the form.

FIGURE 1.27

A new, blank PivotChart.

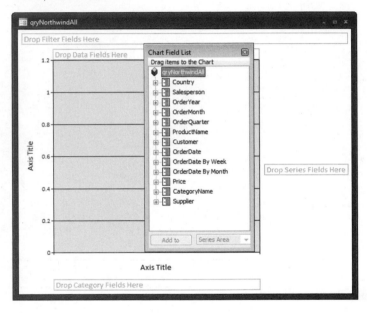

As with a PivotTable, you simply drag fields from the field list to the appropriate drop zones. I dragged the OrderQuarter field to the Category field drop zone, the Supplier field to the Series drop zone, the CategoryName to the Filter drop zone, and the Price field to the Data drop zone, and I selected the Dairy Products category for filtering the data. Figure 1.28 shows the PivotChart at this point.

The PivotChart with fields assigned to its drop zones.

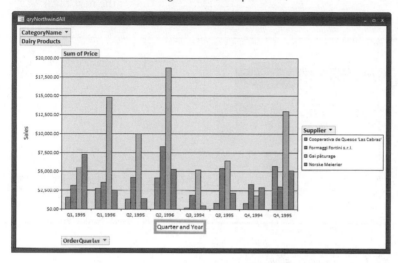

The next step is to give names to the chart's vertical and horizontal axes. To name the axes, select an Axis Title label, open the property sheet, and select its Format tab; enter the name you want to display for that axis in the Caption property, as shown in Figure 1.29. Repeat for the other axis label.

Naming the vertical axis of a PivotChart.

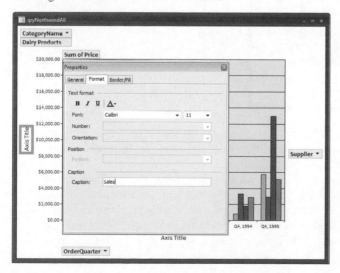

To make the chart's Legend visible (generally a good idea), click the Legend button in the Show/Hide group of the Design tab of the Ribbon, as shown in Figure 1.30.

FIGURE 1.30

Making the PivotChart's Legend visible.

The finished Pivot Chart is shown in Figure 1.31.

FIGURE 1.31

A completed PivotChart.

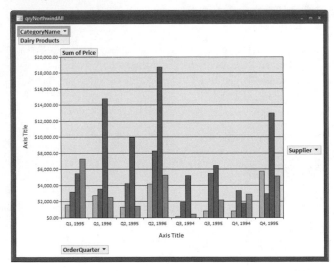

Access 2007 reports have some interactivity, and PivotTables and PivotCharts have almost unlimited interactivity, but both have a serious limitation: the interactivity is available only when you are working in the Access database; when you send an Access report, PivotTable, or PivotChart to someone else who doesn't have Access, say as a PDF file, the recipient gets a read-only image of the report, PivotTable, or PivotChart, with no interactivity. This may be what you want in some cases; but if you need to deliver data in a worksheet or chart format that users can interact with, you need to create an Excel worksheet or chart from your Access data, rather than a report, PivotTable, or PivotChart.

 See Chapter 3 for information on creating Excel worksheets and charts filled with Access data, and Chapter 12 for information on creating Excel PivotCharts filled with Access data.

Summary

In this chapter you have learned about some new features of Access 2007, especially those related to producing Access reports to display data stored in Access tables. But sometimes you need to display your data in Word documents or Excel worksheets, rather than Access reports; or you may need to create Outlook appointments, tasks, contacts, or mail messages, using Access as a control center for working with Office documents.

When you need to produce Word documents, Excel worksheets, or Outlook items, either to make use of the special features of these Office components or to distribute your data in formats that can be used by everyone who has Office, you have two options: use the built-in Export selections on the Ribbon, or write VBA code to create the Office documents and fill them with Access data. The next three chapters describe how to create Word documents, Excel worksheets or charts, and Outlook items, and fill them with Access data.

Chapter 2

Creating Word Documents from Access

I f you need to produce documents with more sophisticated formatting than is available in an Access report, your best option is to create Word documents and fill them with data from Access. There are many ways to export data from Access to Word; which one to use depends on the circumstances, the type of data to export, and user preferences. This chapter discusses the various types of Word documents you can create and the methods you can use to fill them with data, with basic examples.

CROSS-REF For more complex and realistic examples of exporting Access data to Word documents, see Chapters 6 and 12.

NOTE The sample database for this chapter is Access to Word.accdb.

Filling Word Documents with Access Data Using the TypeText Method

You can create a blank Word document (based on the default Word template) with two lines of code:

```
Set appWord = GetObject(, "Word.Application")
Set doc = appWord.Documents.Add
```

NOTE   In most of my Automation code working with other Office applications (Word, Excel, and Outlook), I use the `GetObject` function in the body of a procedure, to set a reference to the running instance of the application, if there is one; the procedure's error handler runs `CreateObject` if the application is not already running (see the code samples later in this chapter for examples). This prevents creation of multiple instances of Word, Excel, or Outlook.

If you don't need any fancy formatting, just a plain text document, you can fill a blank Word document with text using the `TypeText` method. The `FillWithTypeText` procedure listed next creates a blank Word document, then enters a document heading, then reads text from fields in an Access table and writes it directly to the Word document, and finally applies some simple formatting, using Word commands:

```
Private Sub FillWithTypeText ()

On Error GoTo ErrorHandler

    Dim appWord As Word.Application
    Dim doc As Word.Document
    Dim dbs As DAO.Database
    Dim rst As DAO.Recordset

    Set appWord = GetObject(, "Word.Application")
    Set doc = appWord.Documents.Add
```

Insert and format document title:

```
With appWord.Selection
   .TypeText "Current Contacts as of " _
      & Format(Date, "Long Date")
   .TypeParagraph
   .MoveLeft Unit:=wdWord, Count:=11, _
      Extend:=wdExtend
   .Font.Size = 14
   .Font.Bold = wdToggle
   .MoveDown Unit:=wdLine, Count:=1
End With
```

Insert a two-column table to hold contact data (one column for contact names, the other for user comments):

```
doc.Tables.Add Range:=Selection.Range, _
   NumRows:=1, _
   NumColumns:=2, _
   DefaultTableBehavior:=wdWord9TableBehavior, _
   AutoFitBehavior:=wdAutoFitFixed
With appWord.Selection.Tables(1)
   If .Style <> "Table Grid" Then
      .Style = "Table Grid"
   End If
```

```
            .ApplyStyleHeadingRows = True
            .ApplyStyleLastRow = False
            .ApplyStyleFirstColumn = True
            .ApplyStyleLastColumn = False
            .ApplyStyleRowBands = True
            .ApplyStyleColumnBands = False
        End With
```

Insert contact data from Access table into Word table:

```
        Set dbs = CurrentDb
        Set rst = dbs.OpenRecordset("tblContacts")
        Do While Not rst.EOF
            With appWord.Selection
                .TypeText rst![LastName] & ", " & rst![FirstName]
                .MoveRight Unit:=wdCell, Count:=2
            End With
            rst.MoveNext
        Loop
```

Delete the last, blank row:

```
        appWord.Selection.Rows.Delete
```

Sort contact names alphabetically:

```
        doc.Tables(1).Select
        appWord.Selection.Sort ExcludeHeader:=False, _
            FieldNumber:="Column 1", _
            SortFieldType:=wdSortFieldAlphanumeric, _
            SortOrder:=wdSortOrderAscending

    ErrorHandlerExit:
        Set appWord = Nothing
        Exit Sub

    ErrorHandler:
        If Err = 429 Then
```

Word is not running; open Word with `CreateObject`:

```
        Set appWord = CreateObject("Word.Application")
        Resume Next
    Else
        MsgBox "Error No: " & Err.Number _
& "; Description: " & Err.Description
        Resume ErrorHandlerExit
    End If

    End Sub
```

> **TIP** If you don't know the VBA syntax for an operation, you can record a Word macro to create a procedure containing the code, though you may have to trim out the excess — recorded macros generally set every single argument of a method, whether or not they are needed.

The finished contact list document is shown in Figure 2.1.

FIGURE 2.1

A Word document filled with Access data using the TypeText method.

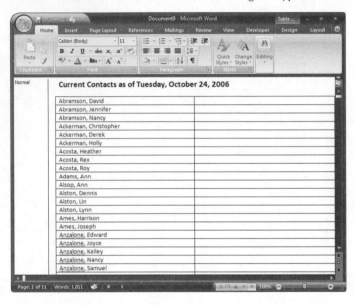

Using Word Templates for Creating Formatted Word Documents

The `TypeText` method used in the previous section is only suitable for creating very simple Word documents. If you need to produce fully formatted Word documents, with headers, footers, and sections with different margins, or if you need to place Access data at various points within blocks of text, it's best to prepare one or more Word templates in advance, formatting them as needed. Then you can create new documents from the templates and fill them with Access data as needed, using either bookmarks or (my preferred method) Word document properties.

The first step is to create the Word templates, with headers, footers, logo, and different fonts as needed. Depending on the method you want to use, either place bookmarks in the template where you want the Access data to appear or create document properties to accept the Access data, and place DocProperty fields in the template where you want the Access data to appear.

Bookmarks

As an example of using bookmarks in a Word template, I created a template designed to print on a certain type of paper (Paper Direct Milano), with a header and footer, several fonts, and two sections, the first for the letter itself and the second for a matching COM 10 envelope. I placed several bookmarks in the letter portion of the template, where the letter date, name and address, and salutation should print, and cross-reference fields in the envelope portion, to print the name and address there, as well as a PostNet ZIP bar code.

WARNING This chapter uses the new .dotx Word 2007 template format, which creates a document of the .docx type. Documents in this new Word format can only be used by people running Office 2007, so if you need to distribute Word documents to people running older versions of Office, it is best to use the .dot template format, and create .doc documents, which are usable in Office 97 through 2007.

Working with Word User Information Fields

You can place Word UserName and UserAddress fields in the document header to print your name and address. If you have used these fields in previous versions of Word, you may have difficulty locating them in the new Word 2007 interface, especially because Microsoft has chosen to put them in different places (in Word 2003, they were all conveniently located on the User Information tab of the Options dialog). In Word 2007, the user name is entered in the User Name field on the Personalize page of the Word Options dialog, which is opened from the Word Options button on the File menu.

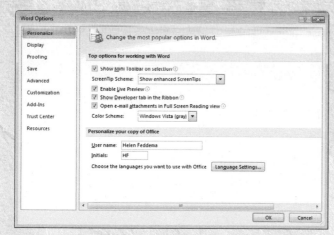

Entering the user name in the Word Options dialog.

continued

continued

Curiously, the user address information is entered in a different location, as "Mailing address" at the bottom of the Advanced page of the Word Options dialog.

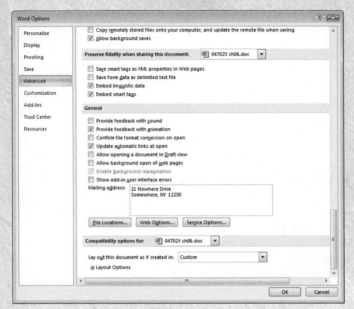

Entering the mailing address (user address) in the Word Options dialog.

To place a field with the user name or user address into a template, select Field from the Quick Parts list in the Text group of the Insert menu.

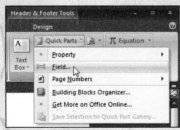

Inserting a field into a template.

This opens the Field dialog (similar to the one in Word 2003), where you can select the User Name or User Address field for insertion.

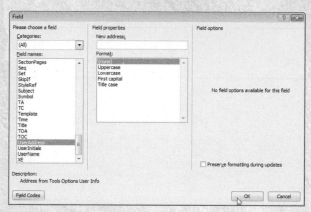

Inserting the UserAddress field on a template.

The following figure shows the user name and address information in a template header.

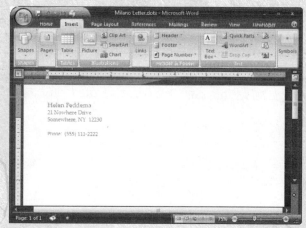

A template header with user name and address information from Word user information fields.

To insert a bookmark in a document or template, select Bookmark from the Links group on the Insert tab, as in Figure 2.2.

 It is advisable to uncheck the "Preserve formatting during updates" checkbox when inserting fields, as otherwise you can get different fonts or sizes for the text displayed in the fields.

FIGURE 2.2

Opening the Bookmark dialog.

Type the bookmark name in the Bookmark dialog and click Add (Figure 2.3).

FIGURE 2.3

Creating a bookmark.

 By default, you won't see the I-beam markers that indicate bookmarks in a Word document; to see them, check the "Show bookmarks" checkbox on the Advanced page of the Word Options dialog, as depicted in Figure 2.4.

FIGURE 2.4

Turning on bookmark display in the Word Options dialog.

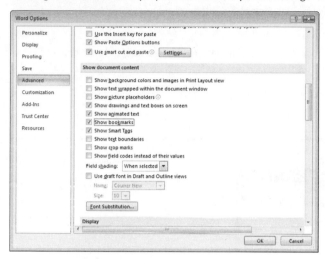

Figure 2.5 shows the second (envelope) page of the Milano Word template, with user information fields, bookmarks, and a BarCode field (to see these fields, press Alt+F9).

FIGURE 2.5

Fields and bookmarks on a Word template.

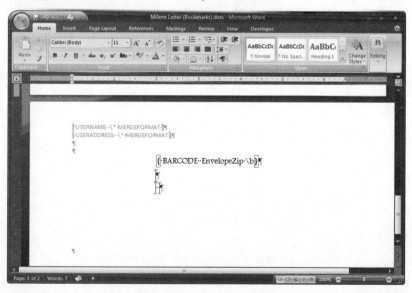

CROSS-REF In code for this chapter's sample database, the assumption is that the Word templates are located in the default folder, which is C:\Users*User Name*\AppData\Roaming\ Microsoft\Templates for Windows Vista or C:\Documents and Settings*User Name*\Application Data\Microsoft\Templates for Windows XP. For a more flexible method of setting the Templates folder, see Chapter 6.

The form frmContacts in the sample Access to Word database displays contacts located in the U.S.A. The form, shown in Figure 2.6, has three buttons, each of which creates a letter to the selected contact using a different method.

FIGURE 2.6

The Contacts form with buttons to create Word letters.

The code for creating a document using bookmarks is listed as follows:

```
Private Sub cmdBookmarks_Click()

On Error GoTo ErrorHandler

    Dim appWord As Word.Application
    Dim doc As Word.Document
    Dim dbs As DAO.Database
    Dim rst As DAO.Recordset
    Dim strTemplatePath As String
    Dim strTemplateName As String
    Dim strTemplateNameAndPath As String
    Dim lngContactID As Long
    Dim strRecipientName As String
    Dim strRecipientAddress As String
```

```
        Dim strRecipientZip As String
        Dim strPrompt As String
        Dim strTitle As String
        Dim strSalutation As String
        Dim fso As New Scripting.FileSystemObject
        Dim fil As Scripting.File


        lngContactID = Nz(Me![ContactID])
        If lngContactID = 0 Then
           strPrompt = "No contact selected"
           strTitle = "Problem"
           MsgBox strPrompt, vbOKOnly + vbExclamation, strTitle
           GoTo ErrorHandlerExit
        Else
           strRecipientName = Nz(Me![FirstNameFirst])
           strRecipientAddress = Nz(Me![RecipientAddress])
           strSalutation = Nz(Me![FirstName])
           strRecipientZip = Nz(Me![PostalCode])
        End If

        Set appWord = GetObject(, "Word.Application")
```

Get the default User Template path from the Word Options dialog (it is still available in code, though it has disappeared from the Word 2007 interface):

```
        strTemplatePath = _
           appWord.Options.DefaultFilePath(wdUserTemplatesPath) _
           & "\"
        Debug.Print "Templates folder: " & strTemplatePath
        strTemplateName = "Milano Letter (Bookmarks).dotx"
        strTemplateNameAndPath = strTemplatePath & strTemplateName

    On Error Resume Next
```

Try to locate the template in the default Templates folder, and put up a message if it is not found:

```
        Set fil = fso.GetFile(strTemplateNameAndPath)
        If fil Is Nothing Then
           strPrompt = "Can't find " & strTemplateName _
              & " in " & strTemplatePath & "; canceling"
           MsgBox strPrompt, vbCritical + vbOKOnly
           GoTo ErrorHandlerExit
        End If

    On Error GoTo ErrorHandler

        Set doc = appWord.Documents.Add(strTemplateNameAndPath)
```

Write information to Word bookmarks in the document:

```
With appWord.Selection
    .Goto what:=wdGoToBookmark, Name:="LetterDate"
    .TypeText Text:=Format(Date, "Long Date")

    .Goto what:=wdGoToBookmark, Name:="RecipientName"
    .TypeText Text:=strRecipientName

    .Goto what:=wdGoToBookmark, Name:="RecipientAddress"
    .TypeText Text:=strRecipientAddress

    .Goto what:=wdGoToBookmark, Name:="RecipientZip"
    .TypeText Text:=strRecipientZip

    .Goto what:=wdGoToBookmark, Name:="Salutation"
    .TypeText Text:=strSalutation

    .Goto what:=wdGoToBookmark, Name:="EnvelopeName"
    .TypeText Text:=strRecipientName

    .Goto what:=wdGoToBookmark, Name:="EnvelopeAddress"
    .TypeText Text:=strRecipientAddress

    .Goto what:=wdGoToBookmark, Name:="EnvelopeZip"
    .TypeText Text:=strRecipientZip
```

Reinsert the EnvelopeZip bookmark so the zip code will be available for use by the bar code field on the envelope:

```
    .MoveLeft Unit:=wdWord, Count:=3, Extend:=wdExtend
    doc.Bookmarks.Add Range:=Selection.Range, _
        Name:="EnvelopeZip"

    .Goto what:=wdGoToBookmark, Name:="LetterText"
    strPrompt = "Ready to enter letter text"
    strTitle = "Access data imported"
    MsgBox strPrompt, vbOKOnly, strTitle
    appWord.Visible = True
    appWord.Activate

End With

ErrorHandlerExit:
    Set appWord = Nothing
    Exit Sub

ErrorHandler:
    If Err = 429 Then
```

Word is not running; open Word with `CreateObject`:

```
        Set appWord = CreateObject("Word.Application")
        Resume Next
    Else
        MsgBox "Error No: " & Err.Number _
            & "; Description: " & Err.Description
        Resume ErrorHandlerExit
    End If

    End Sub
```

Document Properties

When you use Word document properties rather than bookmarks to write Access data to a Word document, you don't need to have two (or more) sets of bookmarks, one for each place you want to display a piece of data (for example, displaying the recipient's name and address on the letter and the envelope). You can write the data to a document property once and display it in multiple places in the Word document with DocProperty fields.

To create the properties, first select Finish from the File menu in the template, and select Properties, as shown in Figure 2.7.

FIGURE 2.7

Opening the Document Information panel.

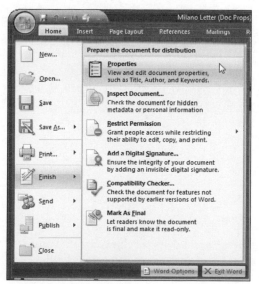

This opens the Document Information panel, with a few of the more common document properties displayed (see Figure 2.8).

The Document Information panel.

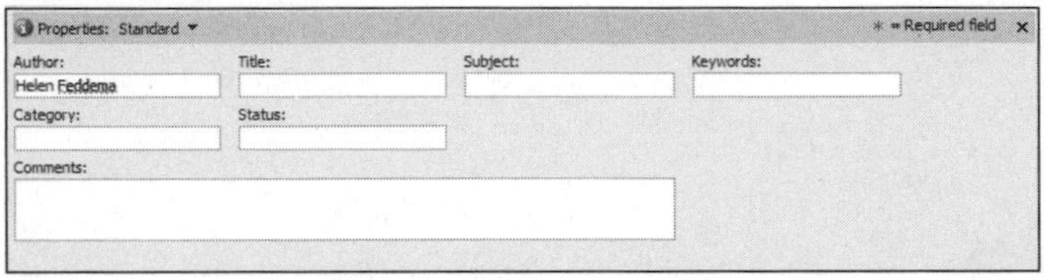

To get to the Properties sheet, select Advanced from the Properties drop-down at the top of the panel; this opens the Properties sheet, which looks much the same as in Word 2003. Click the Custom tab (Figure 2.9) to start creating document properties.

The Custom page of the Word Properties sheet.

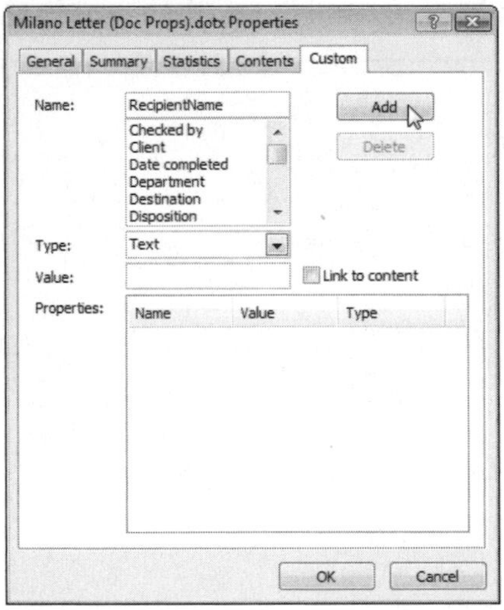

To create a document property, enter its name (no spaces), select the type, enter a value (a space will do for a Text property), and then click Add. Figure 2.10 shows the doc properties for the Milano Letter (Doc Props) template.

FIGURE 2.10

The Doc properties for the Milano Letter (Doc Props) template.

Next, place DocProperty fields in the template where you want the values in the doc properties to display.

> **NOTE** One bookmark is still needed, even if you are using doc properties to display data from Access: The BarCode field needs to reference a bookmark in order to create the PostNet bar code. Therefore, after placing a DocProperty field for the zip into the template, select that field and create a bookmark for it.

To insert a DocProperty field, select QuickParts from the Text group on the Insert tab of the Ribbon, select DocProperty as the field type, and then select the doc property from the Property list (see Figure 2.11).

> **TIP** Don't give your doc properties the same names as any built-in properties, although Word lets you do this, because this will make it difficult to select the correct property from the list of properties, which includes both built-in and custom doc properties.

Figure 2.12 shows the first page of the template, with DocProperty fields displayed, and one bookmark to indicate the place where the letter text is to be typed.

FIGURE 2.11

FIGURE 2.11

Inserting a DocProperty field.

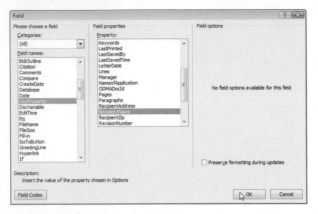

FIGURE 2.12

The first page of the Milano Letter (DocProps) template, with User information and DocProperty fields.

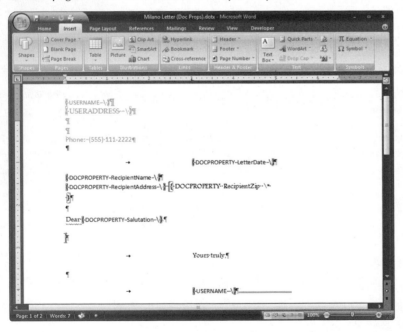

The code that creates the document with text written to doc properties is listed as follows:

```
Private Sub cmdDocProps_Click()

On Error GoTo ErrorHandler

    Dim appWord As Word.Application
    Dim doc As Word.Document
    Dim dbs As DAO.Database
    Dim rst As DAO.Recordset
    Dim strTemplatePath As String
    Dim strTemplateName As String
    Dim strTemplateNameAndPath As String
    Dim lngContactID As Long
    Dim strRecipientName As String
    Dim strRecipientAddress As String
    Dim strRecipientZip As String
    Dim strPrompt As String
    Dim strTitle As String
    Dim strSalutation As String
    Dim fso As New Scripting.FileSystemObject
    Dim fil As Scripting.File
    Dim prps As Object

    lngContactID = Nz(Me![ContactID])
    If lngContactID = 0 Then
        strPrompt = "No contact selected"
        strTitle = "Problem"
        MsgBox strPrompt, vbOKOnly + vbExclamation, strTitle
        GoTo ErrorHandlerExit
    Else
        strRecipientName = Nz(Me![FirstNameFirst])
        strRecipientAddress = Nz(Me![RecipientAddress])
        strSalutation = Nz(Me![FirstName])
        strRecipientZip = Nz(Me![PostalCode])
    End If

    Set appWord = GetObject(, "Word.Application")
```

Get the default User Templates path from the Word Options dialog:

```
    strTemplatePath = _
        appWord.Options.DefaultFilePath(wdUserTemplatesPath) _
        & "\"
    Debug.Print "Templates folder: " & strTemplatePath
    strTemplateName = "Milano Letter (Doc Props).dotx"
    strTemplateNameAndPath = strTemplatePath & strTemplateName

On Error Resume Next
```

Try to locate the template in the default Templates folder, and put up a message if it is not found:

```
Set fil = fso.GetFile(strTemplateNameAndPath)
If fil Is Nothing Then
    strPrompt = "Can't find " & strTemplateName _
        & " in " & strTemplatePath & "; canceling"
    MsgBox strPrompt, vbCritical + vbOKOnly
    GoTo ErrorHandlerExit
End If

On Error GoTo ErrorHandler

Set doc = appWord.Documents.Add(strTemplateNameAndPath)
```

Write information to Word doc properties:

```
Set prps = doc.CustomDocumentProperties
prps.Item("LetterDate").Value = Format(Date, "Long Date")
prps.Item("RecipientName").Value = strRecipientName
prps.Item("RecipientAddress").Value = strRecipientAddress
prps.Item("RecipientZip").Value = strRecipientZip
prps.Item("Salutation").Value = strSalutation
```

Update fields:

```
With appWord
    .Selection.WholeStory
    .Selection.Fields.Update
    .Selection.HomeKey unit:=wdStory
End With

appWord.Selection.Goto what:=wdGoToBookmark, _
    Name:="LetterText"
strPrompt = "Ready to enter letter text"
strTitle = "Access data imported"
MsgBox strPrompt, vbOKOnly, strTitle
appWord.Visible = True
appWord.Activate

ErrorHandlerExit:
    Set appWord = Nothing
    Exit Sub

ErrorHandler:
    If Err = 429 Then
```

Word is not running; open Word with `CreateObject`:

```
Set appWord = CreateObject("Word.Application")
Resume Next
```

```
    Else
        MsgBox "Error No: " & Err.Number _
            & "; Description: " & Err.Description
        Resume ErrorHandlerExit
    End If

End Sub
```

Form Field Documents

Sometimes you need to create documents that display some data from Access and also allow users to enter more data in a controlled fashion. This can be done using either bookmarks or doc properties to display the Access data, and Word content controls (called form fields in earlier versions of Word) for the user-entered data.

The third button on frmContacts creates a letter filled with data from Access, using doc properties; additionally, the template has two form fields, to be filled in by the user when creating the document. Of course, users can just type text into a document, but form fields allow the developer to limit the information to a selection of appropriate values, perhaps in a protected document section that does not allow free-form entry.

To insert a content control into a template, select the control type from the Controls group on the Developer tab of the Ribbon, as shown in Figure 2.13.

FIGURE 2.13

Inserting a dropdown-type content control.

 If you don't see the Developer tab, turn it on by checking the "Show Developer tab in the Ribbon" checkbox on the Personalize page of the Word Options dialog (Figure 2.14).

To add the choices for a drop-down or combo box list, switch to Design mode by clicking the Design button in the Controls group, select the control, and then select Properties from the Controls group on the Developer tab, as depicted in Figure 2.15.

FIGURE 2.14

Turning on the Developer tab on the Word Ribbon.

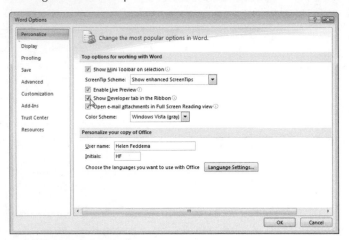

FIGURE 2.15

Opening a control's Properties sheet.

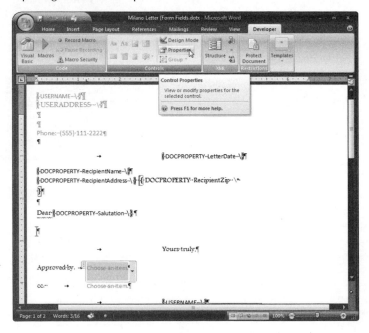

Add the choices for the drop-down list in the Properties sheet (see Figure 2.16). To add a choice, click the Add button, enter the display name and value, and click OK; repeat for each selection you want to add to the list.

FIGURE 2.16

Adding choices for a drop-down list content control.

> **TIP** Don't check the "Contents cannot be edited" checkbox; if you do, selections can't be made from the drop-down list.

When a new document is created from a template with content controls, when you hover the mouse over a content control, the title appears over the control, and you can click the drop-down arrow to open the list and select an item (Figure 2.17).

FIGURE 2.17

Selecting an item from a drop-down content control.

Summary

This chapter covered three methods that you can use to write Access data to Word documents (TypeText, bookmarks, and doc properties). With the aid of these techniques, and a set of preformatted Word templates, you can make use of the superior data storage and editing capabilities of Access and the superior document formatting properties of Word.

Chapter 3

Analyzing Data with Excel

You can print Access data directly, using Access reports, as described in Chapter 1, or you can present the data interactively in PivotTables or PivotCharts. But, as mentioned in Chapter 1, these options have some limitations, because you can only work interactively with PivotTables and PivotCharts within an Access database. If you (or others) want to be able to manipulate and analyze Access data without the need to have Access installed, Excel worksheets are an excellent choice.

Rather than preparing Access reports, PivotTables, or PivotCharts (or in addition to them), you can export data to Excel, and allow users to analyze the data with Excel's tools. This option is available to everybody who has Office installed, because even the most basic editions of Office include Excel, whereas Access is only included in some editions (the more expensive ones).

You can export the Access data to an unformatted worksheet and let the users work with it as they want (this works fine if they just need the data and don't require fancy formatting), or you can create Excel templates and export the data to a new worksheet made from a template; this technique allows you to do some of the formatting in advance.

A third alternative is to export the Access data into either a default worksheet or a worksheet created from a template, and sort the data, create totals, or apply formatting using Excel commands in VBA code. The following sections describe using these three methods to export Access data to Excel.

NOTE The sample database for this chapter is Access to Excel.accdb.

IN THIS CHAPTER

Exporting Access data to Excel using a Ribbon command

Creating new Excel worksheets from templates

Formatting Access data exported to an Excel worksheet

Exporting Access Data to an Unformatted Worksheet

If you just need to move a chunk of data from Access to Excel, and you don't need fancy format-ting, you can use the Excel command in the Export group on the External Data tab of the Ribbon to export the Access data to a plain, unformatted worksheet. The sample database, based on the Northwind sample database, has a query that links all the data tables, `qryNorthwindAll`. A query of this type is very useful for doing data exports, because it contains all the data you might want to export. (Figure 3.1 shows this query selected in the Object Bar.)

FIGURE 3.1

Exporting to Excel from a Ribbon command.

Clicking the Excel command with a database object selected opens the Export dialog, where you can browse for the folder where the worksheet should be saved, and select a worksheet file format. This dialog is shown in Figure 3.2. You can check the "Export data with formatting and layout" selection if desired, but it doesn't make much of a difference when exporting data from tables or queries, and I don't recommend exporting data from forms or reports, because the formatting you need in Excel isn't the same as the formatting you need in an Access form or report.

FIGURE 3.2

The Export dialog opened from the Excel command.

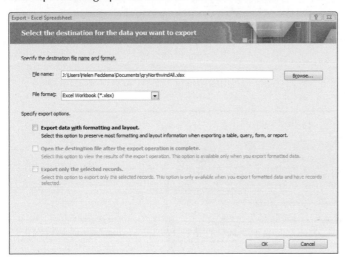

Using `qryNorthwindAll` as the data source, you get the plain worksheet shown in Figure 3.3.

FIGURE 3.3

An Excel worksheet created from data in the qryNorthwindAll Access query.

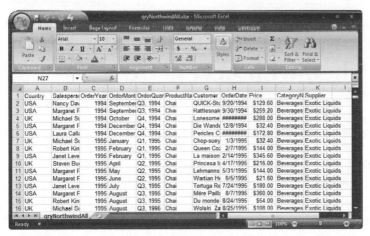

> **TIP**   Using a query as a data source allows you to combine data from multiple tables and also to format data as you want it to appear in the target worksheet, using data type conversion functions such as `CDate`, `CCur`, or `CStr`.

With a few clicks, you can resize the worksheet columns as needed, edit the column headers as needed, and make the column header row bold, and a plain but serviceable worksheet (Figure 3.4) is ready for use.

FIGURE 3.4

The exported worksheet with a little formatting applied manually.

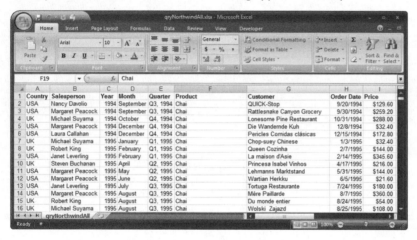

Using Excel Templates to Create Formatted Worksheets Filled with Access Data

If you want to produce a more formatted worksheet, you can prepare an Excel template and format it as needed — for example, adding a large, centered title and column headings with appropriate text, perhaps in a larger or bolder font than the data area. Then, instead of using the Excel command on the Ribbon, use VBA code to export the Access data row by row to the data area of a new worksheet created from the template. I created a set of queries for archiving data, again using the sample Northwind data, and a dialog form (fdlgArchiveOrders) that allows the user to select a date range for archiving Orders data, as shown in Figure 3.5.

> **NEW FEATURE**   Note the calendar icon next to the date controls (it appears when a control bound to a Date field has the focus). Clicking the icon opens a calendar for selecting a valid date, as shown in Figure 3.6. The new calendar pop-up is definitely useful, though selecting a date far in the past can be tedious, because there is no way to move year by year.

A dialog form for selecting Northwind Orders data to archive.

Selecting a date from the calendar pop-up.

Once the start date and end date have been entered or selected, clicking the Archive button runs a procedure that creates a new Excel worksheet from a template (Orders Archive.xltx) in the same folder as the database, fills it with data from tblOrders in the selected date range, and deletes the archived records.

The ArchiveData procedure uses the Start Date and End Date values selected in the dialog as arguments. This procedure is listed as follows, together with the CreateAndTestQuery procedure it uses to create a query programmatically, and another procedure (TestFileExists) that tests whether a file exists in a specific folder:

```
Public Sub ArchiveData(dteStart As Date, dteEnd As Date)

On Error GoTo ErrorHandler

    Dim appExcel As Excel.Application
    Dim intReturn As Integer
    Dim lngCount As Long
    Dim n As Long
```

```
Dim rng As Excel.Range
Dim rngStart As Excel.Range
Dim strDBPath As String
Dim strPrompt As String
Dim strQuery As String
Dim strSaveName As String
Dim strSheet As String
Dim strSheetTitle As String
Dim strSQL As String
Dim strTemplate As String
Dim strTemplateFile As String
Dim strTemplatePath As String
Dim strTitle As String
Dim wkb As Excel.Workbook
Dim wks As Excel.Worksheet
```

Create a filtered query using the dates selected in the dialog:

```
strQuery = "qryArchive"
Set dbs = CurrentDb
strSQL = "SELECT * FROM tblOrders WHERE " _
    & "[ShippedDate] Between #" & dteStart & "# And #" _
    & dteEnd & "#;"
Debug.Print "SQL for " & strQuery & ": " & strSQL
lngCount = CreateAndTestQuery(strQuery, strSQL)
Debug.Print "No. of items found: " & lngCount
If lngCount = 0 Then
```

Exit if no orders are found in the selected date range:

```
    strPrompt = "No orders found for this date range; " _
        & "canceling archiving"
    strTitle = "Canceling"
    MsgBox strPrompt, vbOKOnly + vbCritical, strTitle
    GoTo ErrorHandlerExit
Else
    strPrompt = lngCount & " orders found in this date " _
        & "range; archive them?"
    strTitle = "Archiving"
    intReturn = MsgBox(strPrompt, vbYesNo + vbQuestion, _
        strTitle)
    If intReturn = vbNo Then
        GoTo ErrorHandlerExit
    End If
End If
```

Create a new worksheet from the template and export the Access data to it:

```
strDBPath = Application.CurrentProject.Path & "\"
Debug.Print "Current database path: " & strDBPath
```

```
strTemplate = "Orders Archive.xltx"
strTemplateFile = strDBPath & strTemplate
If TestFileExists(strTemplateFile) = False Then
```

Put up a message and exit if the template is not found:

```
strTitle = "Template not found"
strPrompt = "Excel template 'Orders Archive.xlt'" _
    & " not found in " & strDBPath & ";" & vbCrLf _
    & "please put template in this folder and try again"
MsgBox strPrompt, vbCritical + vbOKOnly, strTitle
GoTo ErrorHandlerExit
Else
    Debug.Print "Excel template used: " & strTemplateFile
End If
```

Template found; create a new worksheet from it:

```
Set appExcel = GetObject(, "Excel.Application")
Set rst = dbs.OpenRecordset("qryRecordsToArchive")
Set wkb = appExcel.Workbooks.Add(strTemplateFile)
Set wks = wkb.Sheets(1)
wks.Activate
appExcel.Visible = True
```

Write the date range to title cell:

```
Set rng = wks.Range("A1")
strSheetTitle = "Archived Orders for " _
    & Format(dteStart, "d-mmm-yyyy") _
    & " to " & Format(dteEnd, "d-mmm-yyyy")
Debug.Print "Sheet title: " & strSheetTitle
rng.Value = strSheetTitle
```

Go to the first data cell:

```
Set rngStart = wks.Range("A4")
Set rng = wks.Range("A4")
```

Reset lngCount to the number of records in the data source query:

```
rst.MoveLast
rst.MoveFirst
lngCount = rst.RecordCount

For n = 1 To lngCount
```

Write data from the recordset to the data area of the worksheet, using the columnoffset argument to move to the next cell:

```
        rng.Value = Nz(rst![OrderID])
        Set rng = rng.Offset(columnoffset:=1)
        rng.Value = Nz(rst![Customer])
        Set rng = rng.Offset(columnoffset:=1)
        rng.Value = Nz(rst![Employee])
        Set rng = rng.Offset(columnoffset:=1)
        rng.Value = Nz(rst![OrderDate])
        Set rng = rng.Offset(columnoffset:=1)
        rng.Value = Nz(rst![RequiredDate])
        Set rng = rng.Offset(columnoffset:=1)
        rng.Value = Nz(rst![ShippedDate])
        Set rng = rng.Offset(columnoffset:=1)
        rng.Value = Nz(rst![Shipper])
        Set rng = rng.Offset(columnoffset:=1)
        rng.Value = Nz(rst![Freight])
        Set rng = rng.Offset(columnoffset:=1)
        rng.Value = Nz(rst![ShipName])
        Set rng = rng.Offset(columnoffset:=1)
        rng.Value = Nz(rst![ShipAddress])
        Set rng = rng.Offset(columnoffset:=1)
        rng.Value = Nz(rst![ShipCity])
        Set rng = rng.Offset(columnoffset:=1)
        rng.Value = Nz(rst![ShipRegion])
        Set rng = rng.Offset(columnoffset:=1)
        rng.Value = Nz(rst![ShipPostalCode])
        Set rng = rng.Offset(columnoffset:=1)
        rng.Value = Nz(rst![ShipCountry])
        Set rng = rng.Offset(columnoffset:=1)
        rng.Value = Nz(rst![Product])
        Set rng = rng.Offset(columnoffset:=1)
        rng.Value = Nz(rst![UnitPrice])
        Set rng = rng.Offset(columnoffset:=1)
        rng.Value = Nz(rst![Quantity])
        Set rng = rng.Offset(columnoffset:=1)
        rng.Value = Nz(rst![Discount])
```

Go to the next row in the worksheet, using the `rowoffset` argument:

```
        rst.MoveNext
        Set rng = rngStart.Offset(rowoffset:=n)

    Next n
```

Save and close the filled-in worksheet, using a workbook save name with the date range selected in the dialog:

```
        strSaveName = strDBPath & strSheetTitle & ".xlsx"
        Debug.Print "Time sheet save name: " & strSaveName
```

```
        ChDir strDBPath

    On Error Resume Next
```

If there already is a saved worksheet with this name, delete it:

```
        Kill strSaveName

    On Error GoTo ErrorHandler
        wkb.SaveAs FileName:=strSaveName, _
            FileFormat:=xlWorkbookDefault
        wkb.Close
        rst.Close
```

Put up a success message, listing the name and path of the new worksheet:

```
        strTitle = "Workbook created"
        strPrompt = "Archive workbook '" & strSheetTitle & "'" _
            & vbCrLf & "created in " & strDBPath
        MsgBox strPrompt, vbOKOnly + vbInformation, strTitle
```

Delete the archived records, processing the "many" table first, because you can't delete a record in the "one" table if there are linked records in the "many" table:

```
        DoCmd.SetWarnings False
        strSQL = "DELETE tblOrderDetails.*, " _
            & "tblOrders.ShippedDate " _
            & "FROM tblOrderDetails INNER JOIN qryArchive " _
            & "ON tblOrderDetails.OrderID = qryArchive.OrderID;"
        Debug.Print "SQL string: " & strSQL
        DoCmd.RunSQL strSQL
        strSQL = "DELETE tblOrders.* FROM tblOrders WHERE " _
            & "[ShippedDate] Between #" & dteStart & "# And #" _
            & dteEnd & "#;"
        Debug.Print "SQL string: " & strSQL
        DoCmd.RunSQL strSQL
```

Put up a message listing the cleared records:

```
        strTitle = "Records cleared"
        strPrompt = "Archived records from " _
            & Format(dteStart, "d-mmm-yyyy") _
            & " to " & Format(dteEnd, "d-mmm-yyyy") _
            & " cleared from tables"
        MsgBox strPrompt, vbOKOnly + vbInformation, strTitle

    ErrorHandlerExit:
        Exit Sub
```

```
ErrorHandler:
    'Excel is not running; open Excel with CreateObject
    If Err.Number = 429 Then
        Set appExcel = CreateObject("Excel.Application")
        Resume Next
    Else
        MsgBox "Error No: " & Err.Number & "; Description: "
        Resume ErrorHandlerExit
    End If

End Sub

Public Function CreateAndTestQuery(strTestQuery As String, _
    strTestSQL As String) As Long
```

This function is called from other procedures to create a filtered query, using a SQL string in its strTestSQL argument:

```
On Error Resume Next

    Dim qdf As DAO.QueryDef

    'Delete old query
    Set dbs = CurrentDb
    dbs.QueryDefs.Delete strTestQuery

On Error GoTo ErrorHandler

    'Create new query
    Set qdf = dbs.CreateQueryDef(strTestQuery, strTestSQL)

    'Test whether there are any records
    Set rst = dbs.OpenRecordset(strTestQuery)
    With rst
        .MoveFirst
        .MoveLast
        CreateAndTestQuery = .RecordCount
    End With

ErrorHandlerExit:
    Exit Function

ErrorHandler:
    If Err.Number = 3021 Then
        CreateAndTestQuery = 0
        Resume ErrorHandlerExit
    Else
        MsgBox "Error No: " & Err.Number & "; Description: " &
Err.Description
        Resume ErrorHandlerExit
    End If
```

```
End Function

Public Function TestFileExists(strFile As String) As Boolean

On Error Resume Next

    TestFileExists = Not (Dir(strFile) = "")

End Function
```

> **NOTE** The code in the sample database requires a reference to the Excel object library; Figure 3.7 shows this reference checked in the References dialog, which is opened from the Tools menu in the Visual Basic window.

FIGURE 3.7

Setting a reference to the Excel object model.

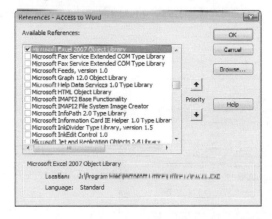

After the worksheet of archived records has been created and saved, you will get a message (depicted in Figure 3.8) listing the location where the archive worksheet was saved.

FIGURE 3.8

A success message after records are archived.

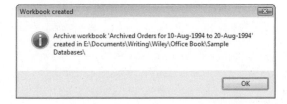

NOTE See Chapter 7 for a more flexible way of specifying a Templates folder and a Documents folder.

After the code deletes the archived records — first the ones in tblOrderDetails (the "many" table) and then those in tblOrders (the "one" table) — a final message appears, as shown in Figure 3.9.

FIGURE 3.9

A final informative message stating that the archived database records have been cleared.

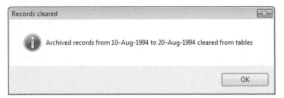

A worksheet filled with archived data is shown in Figure 3.10.

FIGURE 3.10

A worksheet filled with archived Access data.

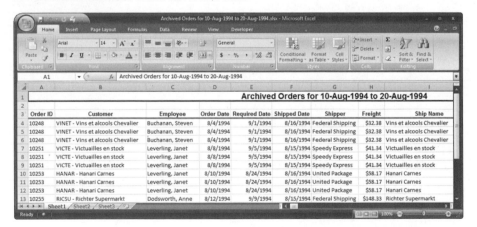

Saving the newly created worksheet with the xlWorkbookDefault value for the FileFormat argument saves it as a standard Excel worksheet. If you need to save the worksheet in another format, perhaps for use by someone running an older version of Excel, you can use one of the other values in the XlFileFormat enum, which are shown in the Object Browser in Figure 3.11. The xlExcel9795 named constant will create a worksheet in a format usable by people running Excel 95 or 97. (The worksheet format choices available in VBA code are much more numerous than those available in the interface, as shown in Figure 3.12.)

FIGURE 3.11

FIGURE 3.11

Viewing the file format choices for saving an Excel workbook.

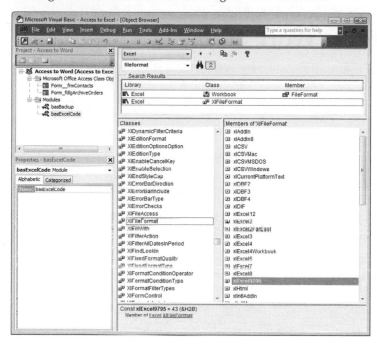

WARNING If you create a worksheet in the new .xlsx format, only Office 2007 users will be able to open it. To create a worksheet that can be opened and edited by users with earlier versions of Office, select one of the other formats. The Excel 97–Excel 2003 Workbook (.xls) format (shown being selected in Figure 3.12) is usable in Office 97 through 2007, so it is generally the most useful worksheet format.

FIGURE 3.12

Selecting a worksheet save format.

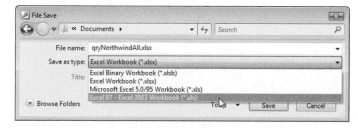

 To open the Object Browser for examining components of an object model, open the Visual Basic window and select Object Browser from the View menu, or press F2.

Formatting Excel Worksheets in VBA Code

If you need to sort, group, indent, or otherwise format exported data in an Excel worksheet, or create a total under the last row of data, you can write VBA code to use Excel commands to do the work in code. You can apply formatting to a worksheet created by the `TransferSpreadsheet` method, or one created from the Ribbon command, or a worksheet created programmatically from a template.

CROSS-REF See Chapter 7 for examples of creating worksheets using the `TransferSpreadsheet` method.

In this section, data from qryOrdersAndDetails is exported to a new worksheet made from a template and is then formatted in code. For convenience, the `ExportNorthwindData` procedure can be run from the macro mcrExportNorthwindData.

The procedure starts by creating a new worksheet from a template (Northwind Orders.xltx), as for the `ArchiveData` procedure. Data from the query `qryOrdersAndDetails` is written to rows in the worksheet, and then a set of Excel commands is used to apply hairline borders to the data area, and a double bottom border to the column headings row.

Next, the worksheet's data area is sorted by the first two columns (Country and Category), and the extra values are removed (the effect is similar to turning on Hide Duplicates in an Access report). Finally, a Grand Total is created under the last row, made large and bold, and enclosed in a box. The procedure is listed as follows:

```
Public Sub ExportNorthwindData()

On Error GoTo ErrorHandler

    Dim appExcel As Object
    Dim i As Integer
    Dim lngCount As Long
    Dim lngCurrentRow As Long
    Dim lngRows As Long
    Dim n As Long
    Dim objFind As Object
    Dim rng As Excel.Range
    Dim rngData As Excel.Range
    Dim rngStart As Excel.Range
    Dim strCategory As String
    Dim strCountry As String
    Dim strCurrAddress As String
    Dim strDBPath As String
    Dim strFormula As String
```

```
Dim strPrompt As String
Dim strDataRange As String
Dim strRange As String
Dim strSaveName As String
Dim strSheetName As String
Dim strStartAddress As String
Dim strTemplate As String
Dim strTemplateFile As String
Dim strTitle As String
Dim wkb As Excel.Workbook
Dim wks As Excel.Worksheet
```

Create a new worksheet from the template and export data to it:

```
strDBPath = Application.CurrentProject.Path & "\"
Debug.Print "Current database path: " & strDBPath
strTemplate = "Northwind Orders.xltx"
strTemplateFile = strDBPath & strTemplate
If TestFileExists(strTemplateFile) = False Then
```

Put up a message and exit if the template is not found:

```
    strTitle = "Template not found"
    strPrompt = "Excel template 'Northwind Orders.xlt'" _
        & " not found in " & strDBPath & ";" & vbCrLf _
        & "please put template in this folder and try again"
    MsgBox strPrompt, vbCritical + vbOKOnly, strTitle
    GoTo ErrorHandlerExit
Else
    Debug.Print "Excel template used: " & strTemplateFile
End If

Set appExcel = GetObject(, "Excel.Application")
Set dbs = CurrentDb
```

Create a recordset based on the Access query:

```
Set rst = dbs.OpenRecordset("qryOrdersAndDetails")
```

Create a new worksheet based on the template:

```
Set wkb = appExcel.Workbooks.Add(strTemplateFile)
    Set wks = wkb.Sheets(1)
    wks.Activate
    appExcel.Visible = True
```

Go to the first data cell in the worksheet:

```
Set rngStart = wks.Range("A4")
Set rng = wks.Range("A4")
```

Reset lngCount to the number of records in the query:

```
rst.MoveLast
rst.MoveFirst
lngCount = rst.RecordCount

For n = 1 To lngCount
```

Write data from the recordset to cells in the current row of the worksheet, using the `columnoff-set` argument to move to the next cell:

```
rng.Value = Nz(rst![ShipCountry])
Set rng = rng.Offset(columnoffset:=1)
rng.Value = Nz(rst![Category])
Set rng = rng.Offset(columnoffset:=1)
rng.Value = Nz(rst![Product])
Set rng = rng.Offset(columnoffset:=1)
rng.Value = Nz(rst![Customer])
Set rng = rng.Offset(columnoffset:=1)
rng.Value = Nz(rst![OrderID])
Set rng = rng.Offset(columnoffset:=1)
rng.Value = Nz(rst![UnitPrice])
Set rng = rng.Offset(columnoffset:=1)
rng.Value = Nz(rst![Quantity])
Set rng = rng.Offset(columnoffset:=1)
rng.Value = Nz(rst![Discount])
Set rng = rng.Offset(columnoffset:=1)
rng.Value = Nz(rst![TotalPrice])
```

Go to the next row of the worksheet, using the `rowoffset` argument:

```
rst.MoveNext
    Set rng = rngStart.Offset(rowoffset:=n)
Next n
```

Determine the number of data rows in the worksheet with the `UsedRange` property:

```
lngRows = wks.UsedRange.Rows.Count
Debug.Print "Number of data rows in worksheet: " & lngRows
```

Define the data range:

```
strRange = "A4:I" & CStr(lngRows)
Set rngData = wks.Range(strRange)
```

Apply hairline borders to the data range:

```
With rngData
    .Borders(xlDiagonalDown).LineStyle = xlNone
    .Borders(xlDiagonalUp).LineStyle = xlNone
```

```
        .Borders(xlEdgeLeft).LineStyle = xlContinuous
        .Borders(xlEdgeLeft).Weight = xlHairline
        .Borders(xlEdgeLeft).ColorIndex = xlAutomatic
        .Borders(xlEdgeTop).LineStyle = xlContinuous
        .Borders(xlEdgeTop).Weight = xlHairline
        .Borders(xlEdgeTop).ColorIndex = xlAutomatic
        .Borders(xlEdgeBottom).LineStyle = xlContinuous
        .Borders(xlEdgeBottom).Weight = xlHairline
        .Borders(xlEdgeBottom).ColorIndex = xlAutomatic
        .Borders(xlEdgeRight).LineStyle = xlContinuous
        .Borders(xlEdgeRight).Weight = xlHairline
        .Borders(xlEdgeRight).ColorIndex = xlAutomatic
        .Borders(xlInsideVertical).LineStyle = xlContinuous
        .Borders(xlInsideVertical).Weight = xlHairline
        .Borders(xlInsideVertical).ColorIndex = xlAutomatic
        .Borders(xlInsideHorizontal).LineStyle = xlContinuous
        .Borders(xlInsideHorizontal).Weight = xlHairline
        .Borders(xlInsideHorizontal).LineStyle = xlContinuous
    End With
```

Apply a double border to the bottom of the column headings row:

```
    wks.Rows("3:3").Select

    With appExcel.Selection
        .Borders(xlDiagonalDown).LineStyle = xlNone
        .Borders(xlDiagonalUp).LineStyle = xlNone
        .Borders(xlEdgeLeft).LineStyle = xlNone
        .Borders(xlEdgeTop).LineStyle = xlNone
    End With

    With appExcel.Selection.Borders(xlEdgeBottom)
      .LineStyle = xlDouble
      .ColorIndex = 0
      .TintAndShade = 0
      .Weight = xlThick
    End With

    With appExcel.Selection
        .Borders(xlEdgeRight).LineStyle = xlNone
        .Borders(xlInsideVertical).LineStyle = xlNone
    End With
```

Sort the data range by country and category:

```
    strDataRange = "A3:I" & CStr(lngRows)
    strKey1Range = "A4:A" & CStr(lngRows)
    strKey2Range = "B4:B" & CStr(lngRows)
    Debug.Print "Data range: " & strDataRange
```

```
wks.Range(strDataRange).Select
wks.Sort.SortFields.Clear
wks.Sort.SortFields.Add Key:=Range(strKey1Range), _
    SortOn:=xlSortOnValues, _
        Order:=xlAscending, _
        DataOption:=xlSortNormal
wks.Sort.SortFields.Add Key:=Range(strKey2Range), _
    SortOn:=xlSortOnValues, _
    Order:=xlAscending, _
    DataOption:=xlSortNormal
With wks.Sort
    .SetRange Range(strDataRange)
    .Header = xlYes
    .MatchCase = False
    .Orientation = xlTopToBottom
    .SortMethod = xlPinYin
    .Apply
End With
```

Remove the duplicate countries:

```
Set rng = wks.Range("A:A")
For i = 4 To lngRows
Debug.Print rng.Cells(i, 1).Address & " contains " _
    & rng.Cells(i, 1).Value
    If rng.Cells(i, 1) = rng.Cells(i - 1, 1) Then
        rng.Cells(i, 1).Font.ColorIndex = 2
    ElseIf rng.Cells(i, 1).Value <> strCountry Then
        Debug.Print "Different data in " _
            & rng.Cells(i, 1).Address
        strCountry = rng.Cells(i, 1).Value
    End If
Next i
```

Remove the duplicate categories:

```
Set rng = wks.Range("B:B")
For i = 4 To lngRows
Debug.Print rng.Cells(i, 1).Address & " contains " _
    & rng.Cells(i, 1).Value
    If rng.Cells(i, 1).Value = rng.Cells(i - 1, 1) Then
        rng.Cells(i, 1).Font.ColorIndex = 2
    ElseIf rng.Cells(i, 1).Value <> strCategory Then
        Debug.Print "Different data in " _
            & rng.Cells(i, 1).Address
        strCategory = rng.Cells(i, 1).Value
    End If
Next i
```

Add a Grand Total, and format its cell:

```
strFormula = "=SUM(R[-" & CStr(lngRows - 2) _
    & "]C:R[-1]C)"
Debug.Print "Formula: " & strFormula
strRange = "I" & CStr(lngRows + 2)
Debug.Print "Range: " & strRange
wks.Range(strRange).FormulaR1C1 = strFormula
wks.Range(strRange).Select

With appExcel.Selection.Font
    .Name = "Calibri"
    .Size = 14
    .Strikethrough = False
    .Superscript = False
    .Subscript = False
    .OutlineFont = False
    .Shadow = False
    .Underline = xlUnderlineStyleNone
    .ThemeColor = 2
    .TintAndShade = 0
    .ThemeFont = xlThemeFontMinor
End With

With appExcel.Selection
    .Font.Bold = True
    .Borders(xlDiagonalDown).LineStyle = xlNone
    .Borders(xlDiagonalUp).LineStyle = xlNone
End With

With appExcel.Selection.Borders(xlEdgeLeft)
    .LineStyle = xlContinuous
    .ColorIndex = 0
    .TintAndShade = 0
    .Weight = xlMedium
End With

With appExcel.Selection.Borders(xlEdgeTop)
    .LineStyle = xlContinuous
    .ColorIndex = 0
    .TintAndShade = 0
    .Weight = xlMedium
End With

With appExcel.Selection.Borders(xlEdgeBottom)
    .LineStyle = xlContinuous
    .ColorIndex = 0
    .TintAndShade = 0
    .Weight = xlMedium
End With
```

```
With appExcel.Selection.Borders(xlEdgeRight)
    .LineStyle = xlContinuous
    .ColorIndex = 0
    .TintAndShade = 0
    .Weight = xlMedium
End With

With appExcel.Selection
    .Borders(xlInsideVertical).LineStyle = xlNone
    .Borders(xlInsideHorizontal).LineStyle = xlNone
End With
```

Save and close the filled-in worksheet, using a workbook save name with the date range:

```
strSheetName = "Northwind Orders as of " _
    & Format(Date, "d-mmm-yyyy")
Debug.Print "Sheet name: " & strSheetName
```

Write the title with the date range to the worksheet:

```
wks.Range("A1").Value = strSheetName
strSaveName = strDBPath & strSheetName & ".xlsx"
Debug.Print "Time sheet save name: " & strSaveName

ChDir strDBPath

On Error Resume Next
```

If there already is a saved worksheet with this name, delete it:

```
Kill strSaveName

On Error GoTo ErrorHandler
    wkb.SaveAs FileName:=strSaveName, _
        FileFormat:=xlWorkbookDefault
    wkb.Close
    rst.Close
```

Put up a success message with the name and path of the new worksheet:

```
strTitle = "Workbook created"
strPrompt = strSheetName & vbCrLf & "created in " _
    & strDBPath
MsgBox strPrompt, vbOKOnly + vbInformation, strTitle

ErrorHandlerExit:
    Exit Sub

ErrorHandler:
    'Excel is not running; open Excel with CreateObject
```

```
    If Err.Number = 429 Then
        Set appExcel = CreateObject("Excel.Application")
        Resume Next
    Else
        MsgBox "Error No: " & Err.Number & "; Description: " _
            & Err.Description
        Resume ErrorHandlerExit
    End If

End Sub
```

A finished worksheet is shown in Figure 3.13.

FIGURE 3.13

A worksheet filled with data and formatted using VBA code.

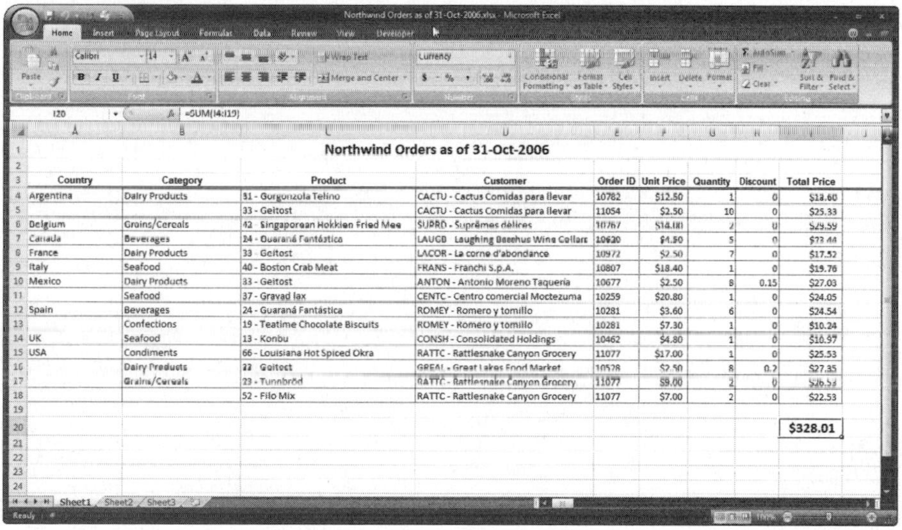

Summary

When you need to export Access data to Excel worksheets so that everyone who has Office can work with them, you can use the techniques discussed in this chapter to export Access data in the interface, or using VBA code, either to a plain default worksheet, or a formatted worksheet created from an Excel template.

Chapter 4

Organizing and Communicating with Outlook

O utlook is the Office component that is used for communicating via email, maintaining a calendar, and storing contact and task information. For email and appointments (a set of appointments in a folder is called a calendar), the Outlook interface is so superior that I recommend not trying to replicate its functionality in Access, but instead to export Access data to Outlook, creating email messages, appointments, or other Outlook items as needed.

Way back in Access 2.0, I created a database to manage tasks, allowing me to assign them priorities, start and due dates, and notes, and order them by any of those priorities or dates. Of course, when Outlook was introduced in Office 97, my Tasks database was no longer needed, because Outlook includes its own Task List (or To Do List, as it is labeled in Office 2007). All the features I wanted were built in to the Outlook Task List, so I moved all my tasks to Outlook and managed them with Outlook's tools. Because Outlook does such a good job with tasks, there is no need to store task data in Access, though in some special circumstances you might need to do this, and then perhaps export the data to Outlook.

Outlook's rarely used Journal component, which records the creation of selected Outlook items, as well as user-entered items, also has little need for connecting to Access. If you find this component useful (I have used it as part of my Time & Expense Billing application, to store time slip data), you can set up the Journal to record various types of Outlook items, and add manual entries to the Journal as needed. However (as with tasks), there may occasionally be circumstances in which you would need to export Access data to Outlook journal items, and I describe one of them later in this chapter.

IN THIS CHAPTER

Creating Outlook appointments and tasks from Access data

Writing Access data to the Outlook Journal

Creating emails to contacts in an Access table

If you store email addresses in a table of contacts, customers, or clients, you can use VBA code to create emails to them from an Access form, either to a single recipient or a group of recipients, without having to switch to Outlook.

Contacts are another matter—although Outlook has a Contacts component, with many useful features (especially the link to email), nevertheless, Outlook contacts are deficient in one very important feature when compared to Access: All Outlook data is stored in a flat-file MAPI table, so you can't set up one-to-many relationships between (for example) companies and contacts, or contacts and phone numbers. If a company moves to another location or changes its name, you have to make the change manually in each contact for that company; if a contact has more than three addresses, or a phone number that doesn't fit into one of the available categories, you are out of luck.

For contacts, you really need both the attractive interface and built-in email connectivity of Outlook contacts, and the relational database capabilities of Access. This means you need a way to synchronize data between Outlook and Access contacts; my Synchronizing Contacts.accdb database does just this.

CROSS-REF   See Chapter 11 for a discussion of the Synchronizing Contacts database. Chapter 8 deals with exporting and importing contacts without synchronization.

This chapter concentrates on exporting tasks, appointments, and journal items from Access to Outlook and creating emails to contacts stored in an Access table.

NOTE   The sample database for this chapter is Access to Outlook.accdb.

Exporting Appointments and Tasks to Outlook

If you have an Access table of employee, contact, or customer information, you may need to create Outlook appointments or tasks based on information in the table records. The tblEmployees table in the sample database has two employee review date fields: LastReviewDate and NextReviewDate. Figure 4.1 shows the frmEmployees form, which is bound to this table.

The next employee review can be scheduled by entering a date in the Next Review Date field and then clicking the Schedule Appointment button. Code on the BeforeUpdate event of txtNextReviewDate (listed next) checks that the date entered (or selected using the Calendar pop-up) is a Tuesday or Thursday (the assumption is that employee reviews are only done on those days):

```
Private Sub txtNextReviewDate_BeforeUpdate(Cancel As Integer)

On Error GoTo ErrorHandler

    Dim strWeekday As String
    Dim intWeekday As Integer
```

An Employees form with review date fields.

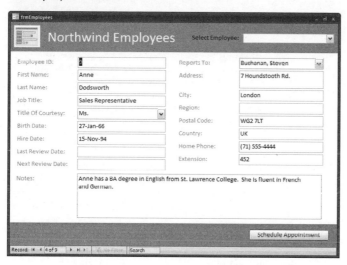

Check that a date has been entered (or selected):

```
If IsDate(Me![NextReviewDate]) = False Then
    GoTo ErrorHandlerExit
Else
    dteNextReviewDate = CDate(Me![NextReviewDate])
    intWeekday = Weekday(dteNextReviewDate)
    Select Case intWeekday
```

Check whether selected date is a weekend day, and put up error message and exit if so:

```
Case vbSunday, vbSaturday
    strTitle = "Wrong day of week"
    strPrompt = _
        "Reviews can't be scheduled on a weekend"
    MsgBox strPrompt, vbOKOnly + vbExclamation, _
        strTitle
    Cancel = True
    GoTo ErrorHandlerExit

Case vbMonday, vbWednesday, vbFriday
```

Check whether selected date is the wrong day of the week, and put up error message and exit if so:

```
    strTitle = "Wrong day of week"
    strPrompt = "Reviews can only be scheduled on " _
        & "a Tuesday or Thursday"
    MsgBox strPrompt, vbOKOnly + vbExclamation, _
```

```
                                strTitle
                         Cancel = True
                         GoTo ErrorHandlerExit

                  Case vbTuesday, vbThursday
```

Date is a Tuesday or Thursday; put up message and continue:

```
                         strTitle = "Right day of week"
                         strPrompt = "Review date OK"
                         MsgBox strPrompt, vbOKOnly + vbInformation, _
                             strTitle

                  End Select

            End If

      ErrorHandlerExit:
            Exit Sub

      ErrorHandler:
            MsgBox "Error No: " & Err.Number _
                  & "; Description: " & Err.Description
            Resume ErrorHandlerExit

      End Sub
```

NOTE   To work with Outlook items in code, you need to set a reference to the Outlook object library (select Tools ⇨ References in the Visual Basic window, as shown in Figure 4.2). To avoid creating multiple instances of Outlook, I like to use an error handler that will open a new instance of Outlook using `CreateObject` if the `GetObject` function fails because Outlook is not running.

FIGURE 4.2

Setting a reference to the Outlook object library.

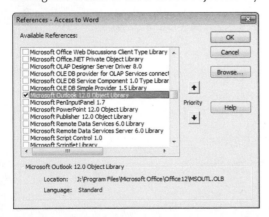

Once a correct Tuesday or Thursday date has been selected or entered, clicking the Schedule Appointment button creates three Outlook items: an appointment for the employee, an appointment for the supervisor (the person the employee reports to), and a task for the supervisor. The button's Click event procedure is listed as follows:

```
Private Sub cmdScheduleAppt_Click()

On Error GoTo ErrorHandler

    Dim appOutlook As Outlook.Application
    Dim strEmployeeName As String
    Dim strSupervisorName As String
    Dim appt As Outlook.AppointmentItem
    Dim fldTopCalendar As Outlook.Folder
    Dim fldContactCalendar As Outlook.Folder
    Dim fldSupervisorCalendar As Outlook.Folder
    Dim fldTasks As Outlook.Folder
    Dim tsk As Outlook.TaskItem
    Dim nms As Outlook.NameSpace

    Set appOutlook = GetObject(, "Outlook.Application")
    Set nms = appOutlook.GetNamespace("MAPI")
```

Set variables for information to be exported to Outlook:

```
    strTitle = "Missing Information"

    If IsDate(Me![txtNextReviewDate].Value) = True Then
        dteNextReviewDate = CDate(Me![txtNextReviewDate].Value)
    Else
        strPrompt = _
            "No next review date; can't create appointment"
        MsgBox strPrompt, vbOKOnly + vbExclamation, strTitle
        GoTo ErrorHandlerExit
    End If

    strEmployeeName = Me![FirstNameFirst]
    strSupervisorName = Nz(Me![cboReportsTo].Column(1))

    If strSupervisorName = "" Then
        strPrompt = "No supervisor selected; can't schedule review"
        strTitle = "No supervisor"
        MsgBox strPrompt, vbOKOnly + vbExclamation, strTitle
        GoTo ErrorHandlerExit
    End If
```

Set reference to (or create) contact's calendar:

```
On Error Resume Next
   Set fldTopCalendar = _
      appOutlook.Session.GetDefaultFolder(olFolderCalendar)
   Set fldContactCalendar = _
      fldTopCalendar.Folders(strEmployeeName)
   If fldContactCalendar Is Nothing Then
      Set fldContactCalendar = _
         fldTopCalendar.Folders.Add(strEmployeeName)
   End If
```

Set reference to (or create) supervisor's calendar:

```
   Set fldSupervisorCalendar = _
      fldTopCalendar.Folders(strSupervisorName)
   If fldSupervisorCalendar Is Nothing Then
      Set fldSupervisorCalendar = _
         fldTopCalendar.Folders.Add(strSupervisorName)
   End If

On Error GoTo ErrorHandler
```

Create appointment in contact's calendar:

```
   Set appt = fldContactCalendar.Items.Add
   With appt
      .Start = CStr(dteNextReviewDate) & " 10:00 AM"
      .AllDayEvent = False
      .Location = "Small Conference Room"
      .ReminderMinutesBeforeStart = 30
      .ReminderSet = True
      .ReminderPlaySound = True
      .Subject = "Review with " & strSupervisorName
      .Close (olSave)
   End With
```

Create appointment in supervisor's calendar:

```
   Set appt = fldSupervisorCalendar.Items.Add
   With appt
      .Start = CStr(dteNextReviewDate) & " 10:00 AM"
      .AllDayEvent = False
      .Location = "Small Conference Room"
      .ReminderMinutesBeforeStart = 30
      .ReminderSet = True
      .ReminderPlaySound = True
      .Subject = strEmployeeName & " review"
      .Close olSave
   End With
```

Create task for supervisor (day before the appointment):

```
Set fldTasks = _
    appOutlook.Session.GetDefaultFolder(olFolderTasks)
Set tsk = fldTasks.Items.Add
With tsk
    .StartDate = DateAdd("d", -1, dteNextReviewDate)
    .DueDate - DateAdd("d", -1, dteNextReviewDate)
    .ReminderSet = True
    .ReminderPlaySound = True
    .Subject = "Prepare materials for " & strEmployeeName _
        & " review"
    .Close (olSave)
End With

strTitle = "Done"
strPrompt = dteNextReviewDate _
    & " appointments scheduled for " _
    & strEmployeeName & " (employee) and " _
    & strSupervisorName _
    & " (supervisor) and a task scheduled for " _
    & strSupervisorName
MsgBox strPrompt, vbOKOnly + vbInformation, strTitle

End Sub
```

The code first attempts to set references to the supervisor's and employee's folders under the default Calendar folder. If there is no folder for the employee (or supervisor), it then creates a new folder for the employee or supervisor, using the Add method of the Calendar folder's Folders collection. Next, the Items collection of the supervisor's folder is used to create a new item of the default item type in that folder, and similarly for the employee's folder. You can also create a new item using the CreateItem method of the Outlook Application object, but that creates the item in the default folder; if you want to create an item in a custom folder, you need to use the Add method instead.

> **NOTE** You can't use the Add method directly with an Outlook folder; this method works with collections, such as the Items collection or the Folders collection.

Finally, you will get a "Done" message (Figure 4.3) reporting on the appointments and task that have been scheduled.

Figure 4.4 shows several employee and manager folders under the default Calendar folder, and a supervisor appointment in the daily calendar.

> **NOTE** If you don't see the employee and manager folders, you are probably in another view; switch to Folder view to see the calendar folders.

FIGURE 4.3

A success message with details about the Outlook items created.

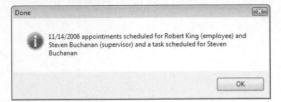

FIGURE 4.4

Employee and supervisor folders and an appointment created from code.

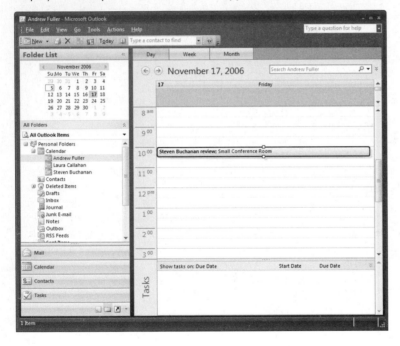

You can double-click the appointment to open it in a separate window.

Exporting Journal Information to Outlook

If you link to or import mainframe transaction or batch processing data into an Access database table, it may be convenient to export that data to Outlook journal items, for quick reference in the Outlook interface. The table tblMainframeData in the sample database is an example of such data. Figure 4.5 shows a portion of this table, with the fields to be exported to Outlook.

A table of mainframe data to export to Outlook journal items.

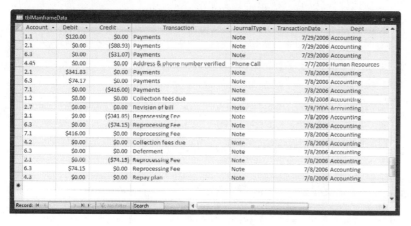

The function that exports the mainframe data to Outlook journal items is listed as follows (for convenience, this function is run from the macro mcrExportTransactions).

```
Public Function ExportTransactions()

On Error GoTo ErrorHandler

    Dim appOutlook As Outlook.Application
    Dim jnl As Outlook.JournalItem
    Dim dbs As DAO.Database
    Dim rst As DAO.Recordset
    Dim strBody As String
    Dim strPrompt As String
    Dim strTitle As String

    Set appOutlook = GetObject(, "Outlook.Application")
    Set dbs = CurrentDb
    Set rst = dbs.OpenRecordset("tblMainframeData")
    Do While Not rst.EOF
        Set jnl = appOutlook.CreateItem(olJournalItem)
```

```
jnl.Subject = rst![Transaction]
jnl.Type = rst![JournalType]
jnl.Companies = rst![Dept]
jnl.Start = rst![TransactionDate]
```

Create a text string with data from various table fields, for writing to the journal item's Body field:

```
strBody = IIf(rst![Debit] > 0, "Debit of " _
    & Format(rst![Debit], "$###,##0.00") _
    & " for ", "") & IIf(rst![Credit] > 0, _
    "Credit of " & Format(rst![Debit], _
    "$###,##0.00") & " for ", "") _
    & "Account No. " & rst![Account]
Debug.Print "Body string: " & strBody
jnl.Body = strBody
jnl.Close (olSave)
rst.MoveNext
Loop

strTitle = "Done"
strPrompt = "All transactions exported to Outlook " _
    & "journal items"
MsgBox strPrompt, vbOKOnly + vbInformation, strTitle

ErrorHandler:
    'Outlook is not running; open Outlook with CreateObject
    If Err.Number = 429 Then
        Set appOutlook = CreateObject("Outlook.Application")
        Resume Next
    Else
        MsgBox "Error No: " & Err.Number _
            & "; Description: " & Err.Description
        Resume ErrorHandlerExit
    End If

End Function
```

 When Outlook 2007 is first installed, the Journal component is turned off; activate it in order to see the journal entries created by the preceding procedure.

This function first sets up a DAO recordset based on tblMainframeData and loops through it, creating a new journal item in the default Journal folder for each record in the table, and setting its properties from data in the table's fields. There is a success message when all the data has been exported. Figure 4.6 shows a journal item created from a transaction record.

To avoid having to create a custom Journal form, the code writes the Dept data to the Companies (Company in the interface) field of a standard Journal item. Data from several fields is concatenated into a String variable, which is written to the Body field (the large textbox at the bottom of the Journal item).

A journal item created from a record in a table of mainframe transaction data.

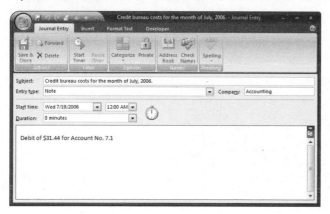

Creating Emails from an Access Table

If you have an Access table (say, of customer, client, or contact information) with email addresses, you can create emails to people in the table directly from an Access form, so you don't need to open Outlook to create an email, which can save time. tblContacts in the sample database has an Email field with the contact's email address, and the form frmEMail (Figure 4.7) lets you send emails to contacts selected from a multi-select ListBox.

A form for selecting contacts as email recipients.

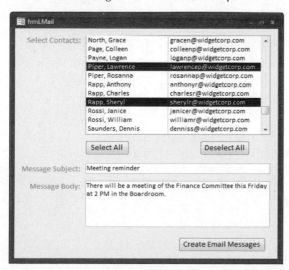

Two buttons let you quickly select (or deselect) all the contacts; once you have selected the email recipients, and entered the message subject and body, you can click the Create Email Messages button to create the set of emails and open them for review before sending. A set of email messages is shown in Figure 4.8.

FIGURE 4.8

A set of email messages created from an Access form.

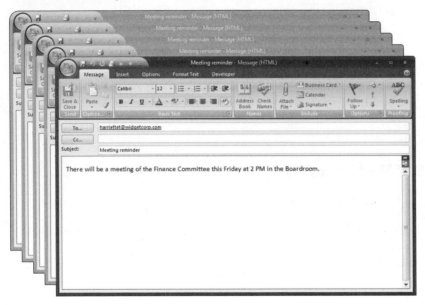

The code that creates the email messages (and also the code that selects or deselects ListBox items) is listed here:

```
Private Sub cmdMergetoEMailMulti_Click()

On Error GoTo ErrorHandler

    Set lst = Me![lstSelectContacts]
```

Check that at least one contact has been selected:

```
If lst.ItemsSelected.Count = 0 Then
    MsgBox "Please select at least one contact"
    lst.SetFocus
    GoTo ErrorHandlerExit
End If
```

Test for required fields, and exit if any are empty:

```
strSubject = Me![txtSubject].Value
If strSubject = "" Then
    MsgBox "Please enter a subject"
    Me![txtSubject].SetFocus
    GoTo ErrorHandlerExit
End If

strBody = Me![txtBody].Value
If strBody = "" Then
    MsgBox "Please enter a message body"
    Me![txtBody].SetFocus
    GoTo ErrorHandlerExit
End If

For Each varItem In lst.ItemsSelected
```

Check for email address:

```
strEMailRecipient = Nz(lst.Column(1, varItem))
Debug.Print "EMail address: " & strEMailRecipient
If strEMailRecipient = "" Then
    GoTo NextContact
End If
```

Create new mail message and send to the current contact:

```
Set appOutlook = GetObject(, "Outlook.Application")
Set msg = appOutlook.CreateItem(olMailItem)
With msg
    .To = strEMailRecipient
    .Subject = strSubject
    .Body = strBody
    .Display
End With

NextContact:
    Next varItem

ErrorHandlerExit:
    Set appOutlook = Nothing
    Exit Sub

ErrorHandler:
```

Outlook is not running; open Outlook with `CreateObject`:

```
If Err.Number = 429 Then
    Set appOutlook = CreateObject("Outlook.Application")
```

```
         Resume Next
      Else
         MsgBox "Error No: " & Err.Number _
            & "; Description: " & Err.Description
         Resume ErrorHandlerExit
      End If

End Sub

Private Sub cmdSelectAll_Click()

On Error GoTo ErrorHandler

    Set lst = Me![lstSelectContacts]
    lngListCount = Me![lstSelectContacts].ListCount

    For lngCount = 0 To lngListCount
       lst.Selected(lngCount) = True
    Next lngCount

ErrorHandlerExit:
    Exit Sub

ErrorHandler:
    MsgBox "Error No: " & Err.Number & "; Description: " _
       & Err.Description
    Resume ErrorHandlerExit

End Sub

Private Sub cmdDeselectAll_Click()

On Error GoTo ErrorHandler

    Set lst = Me![lstSelectContacts]
    lngListCount = Me![lstSelectContacts].ListCount

    For lngCount = 0 To lngListCount
       lst.Selected(lngCount) = False
    Next lngCount

ErrorHandlerExit:
    Exit Sub

ErrorHandler:
    MsgBox "Error No: " & Err.Number & "; Description: " _
       & Err.Description
    Resume ErrorHandlerExit

End Sub
```

 If you prefer to send the email messages automatically (without reviewing them), replace the `.Display` line in the code with `.Send`.

Summary

With the techniques presented in this chapter, you can create tasks, appointments, email messages, or journal items from data in Access tables, allowing you to use Access as a control center, while making use of Outlook items where they offer a superior interface, or are more widely accessible for users.

Part II

Writing VBA Code to Exchange Data between Office Components

Chapter 5

Working with Access Data

I n older versions of Microsoft Office, there were two choices for working with data stored in Access tables. One was the Data Access Objects (DAO) object model, which was developed specifically to work with Access data in recordsets (including form recordsets) and to work with table structure using the Tables (and subsidiary Fields) collections. Because of these customized features, DAO was the best object model for working with Access data.

The other choice for working with Access data was (and is) the ADO object model, introduced with Visual Studio 97, and available for use in Office 2000 and up. This object model is intended for working with data in a wide variety of sources, including Access databases. Although it lacks some of the customized features that make DAO so well suited to Access data, ADO code works fine for basic data manipulation, where you don't need to work with Access form recordsets or create tables and fields (in other words, you are just working with data in Access tables, not with their structure).

Before the release of Office 2007, word was out that Microsoft was dropping support for the DAO object model (and indeed you can see statements to this effect in various online Microsoft documents). I wondered whether ADO would be updated to work with form recordsets, and the Tables (and subsidiary Fields) collection (or some alternate method for creating tables and their fields programmatically), because there are situations when you need these features of DAO, while working in an Access database, or creating an Access add-in.

IN THIS CHAPTER

Using the old and new DAO object models to work with Access data

Working with Access databases in formats from 2000 to 2007

Using the ADO object model to work with Access data

Converting DAO code to ADO code

NOTE   DAO library references older than 3.6 are not supported in Access 2007. This means that if you have references to older DAO versions in any older format databases you want to work with in Access 2007, you will need to reset these references to DAO 3.6. Databases that were created in Access 2000 format with a DAO 3.6 reference, when opened in Access 2007, still have a reference set to the DAO 3.6 object model (as shown in Figure 5.1), and their DAO code compiles and runs. The same is true of Access 2002/2003 format databases opened in Access 2007.

FIGURE 5.1

A reference to the DAO 3.6 object model in an Access 2000 database opened in Access 2007.

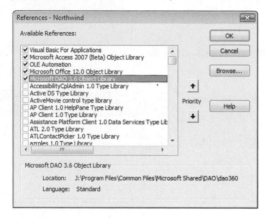

As it turned out, the DAO object model is still supported, though with some changes. If you convert an earlier format database to Access 2007 format, or create a new Access 2007 database, by default it has a reference to the Microsoft Office 2007 Access database engine object model (file name: ACCESS 2007 DAO.DLL). This new object model (which I will hereafter reference as Access 2007 DAO) has the same core functionality as DAO 3.6 (with a few differences, which are discussed in the "New Objects in the Access 2007 DAO Object Model" section), and the same object model abbreviation (DAO) for use in declarations, so Microsoft hasn't really pulled DAO after all — instead, they renamed it, added a new object and a few new attributes, and hid some of the components that are not directly related to working with Access data.

This means that all your old DAO code will run the same as before, so you don't need to convert it to ADO (though of course you can, if you want to use the more modern ADO object model), and if you are working with an Access 2007 database, you will have a few new object model components that represent the new features in Access 2007.

NOTE   The sample database for this chapter is DAO and ADO Sample Code.accdb. In addition, some of the code references the sample database Northwind 2007.accdb, which you can create by double-clicking the Northwind.accdt template in the C:\Program Files\ Microsoft Office\Templates\1033\Access folder.

FIGURE 5.2

The default Access 2007 DAO reference in a new Access 2007 database.

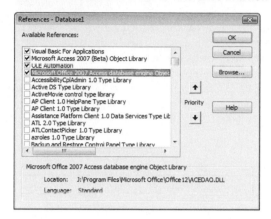

Working with Older Format Databases in Access 2007

Even if you are currently using Access 2007, you may still be working with Access 2002/2003 format databases (or even Access 2000 format databases) for a while. Access 2007 supports working with these older database formats in read/write mode, and you may need to do this — for example, if you are working on a database for a client running an older version of Office. So long as you don't need to use any of the new features introduced in Access 2007 (such as multi-valued lookup fields, or rich text in Memo fields and attachments), you can continue to work with databases in 2000 or 2002/2003 format in Access 2007 without converting them to the new database format.

Disambiguating References to Object Model Components

When DAO was the only object model you could use to work with Access data, when you declared DAO objects there was no need to indicate which object model your objects belonged to — you could just declare a recordset variable as Recordset, or a field variable as Field (as in the following declarations), and your code would work fine:

```
Dim rst as Recordset
Dim fld as Field
```

But since the introduction of the ADO object model, you may run into problems with such declarations, because certain object names are used in both of these object models. This is true of the new Access 2007 DAO object model as well as the old DAO object model. If you compare the DAO (or Access 2007 DAO) and ADO object models, you will see Recordset, Parameter, and Field objects in both.

When your code is compiled, if the declarations don't include the object model, the first reference in the list of references that contains that object name is used, and it may not be the right one. In Access 2000 and XP (perhaps prematurely), new databases had a default reference only to the ADO object model, which led to many problems for users and developers who were working primarily or exclusively with DAO (see Figure 5.3). However, if you create a new database in Access 2003, in the Access 2002/2003 database format, by default it will have references set to both the DAO and ADO object models, in that order, as shown in Figure 5.4.

FIGURE 5.3

The default references for a new Access 2002 (XP) database.

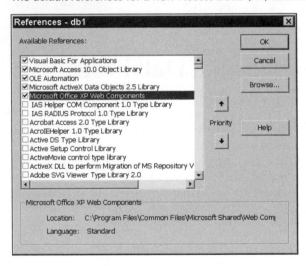

This means that all Recordset, Field, and Parameter variables declared without an object model reference will be interpreted as belonging to the DAO object model, which may not be correct.

If your database was first created in Access 2000 or XP, and you didn't set a reference to the DAO object model, you will have the opposite problem — Recordset, Field, and Parameter variables will be interpreted as belonging to the ADO object model, which could cause problems when working with DAO object properties and methods.

FIGURE 5.4

The default references for a new Access 2003 database.

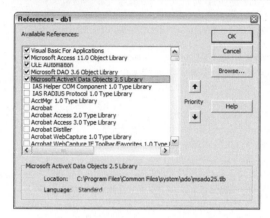

> **TIP**   When using one of the `Find*` search methods (`FindFirst`, `FindNext`, and so forth),
> save the search string to a variable, and display it in the Immediate window using a
> `Debug.Print` statement; this will be very helpful in debugging any problems because it shows you
> exactly what expression is being used for the search.

If you are working on a database originally created several Access versions ago, it might have
ambiguous declarations such as:

```
Dim dbs As Database
Dim rst As Recordset
```

As a demonstration of possible problems, the following procedure sets up a recordset and uses
FindFirst to locate the first match for "Microsoft" in the CompanyID field:

```
Private Sub TestFindFirst()

    Dim dbs As Database
    Dim rst As Recordset
    Dim strSearch As String

    Set dbs = CurrentDb
    Set rst = dbs.OpenRecordset(Name:="tblCompanyIDs", _
        Type:=dbOpenDynaset)
    strSearch = "[CompanyID] = " & Chr$(39) _
        & "Microsoft" & Chr$(39)
    Debug.Print "Search string: " & strSearch
    rst.FindFirst strSearch

End Sub
```

If you have a reference set only to the ADO object model, this code won't even compile, and you will get a "User-defined type not defined" error. If you have references set to both object models, and the ADO reference is first, you will get a different error, this time on the line with the FindFirst method reference: "Method or data member not found." If you have just a DAO reference, or the DAO reference is positioned above the ADO reference, the code will compile and run.

> **TIP**   If you get a "User-defined type not defined" or "Method or data member not found" error message when compiling code, this is almost always an indication of a missing or incorrect object model version reference.

A more subtle problem could result from an ambiguous declaration of the Field object. There is a Field object in both the ADO and DAO object models, but it has different properties and methods in each object model (see Figures 5.5 and 5.6), so a line of code referencing a Field property could lead to an error if that property is not supported in the object model that is being used.

> **NOTE**   Although the Access 2007 interface is very different than the interface you might be used to, which has remained pretty much the same from Access 2000 through Access 2003, the Visual Basic (Modules) window is unchanged, except that the mouse wheel now works (about time!).

Using the Object Browser

The Object Browser is a very useful tool for examining object models and their components. It can be opened from a Visual Basic window in Access, Word, Excel, or Outlook from a command on the View menu or by pressing the F2 key. The drop-down list at the top-left lists the available object libraries (corresponding to the references you have set in the database); the lower drop-down list is a search box where you can enter the name of an object model component or attribute to search for; clicking the binoculars button starts the search, and the results are displayed in the Search Results box, as in the following figure. The Classes list shows the members of the selected object library, and the Members of 'Field' list shows the attributes (properties, methods, and events) of the selected object model component.

If you click the yellow question mark button, you will usually get a Help topic for the selected object or attribute, but you can't depend on this—sometimes all you get is a blank Help window. In the case of ADO, in previous versions of Access, if you set a reference to the most recent version of this library (2.8 at that time), you would get blank Help pages; if you set a reference to ADO 2.5, however, you would get the appropriate Help topic. In Access 2007, if you set a reference to the highest version of ADO (6.0), you will get an "Unable to display Help" error message on clicking the Help button. If you set a reference to ADO 2.5, clicking the Help button opens the "Browse Access Developer Help" screen, rather than the specific Help topic for the selected object model component or attribute.

Figure 5.5 shows the attributes of the ADO Field object in the Object Browser.

FIGURE 5.5

The attributes of the Field object in the ADO object model.

There are many more properties for the Field object in the DAO object model (Figure 5.6), corresponding to specific Access field properties; the ADO Field properties are more generic, because ADO supports data in many different applications.

The solution to the ambiguous reference problems discussed previously is simple: include the object model name in declarations of DAO and ADO variables, as in the following declarations for DAO variables (either DAO 3.6 or Access 2007 DAO). This is called *disambiguating* the declarations:

```
Dim rst as DAO.Recordset
Dim fld as DAO.Field
```

Here is the ADO version (note that the object model name is not ADO, as you might think, but ADODB):

```
Dim rst as ADODB.Recordset
Dim fld as ADODB.Field
```

FIGURE 5.6

The attributes of the Field object in the DAO object model.

I prefer to always include the object model name in declarations, even if the object in question only appears in one object model, for consistency and in case that object name might be used in some other object model I might need to reference in the future.

The DAO Object Model (Old and New)

The DAO 3.6 object model (shown in Figure 5.7) has been listed as deprecated by Microsoft, which generally means that it will soon be obsolete (not supported). Yet DAO 3.6 is still supported in Access 2007, at least for databases created in Access 2000 or Access 2002/2003 format, so it is worth documenting, because you may need to continue working with older format databases for compatibility with other users who have not yet upgraded to Access 2007.

The DAO object model has many components; for purposes of this book, I will examine in detail only the main components used to reference Access data — Databases, QueryDefs, Recordsets, and TableDefs.

The new Access 2007 DAO object model omits (actually, hides) some of the less frequently used components of the DAO 3.6 object model, and adds a few new ones. This object model is now specifically focused on working with data in Access tables, always its strong point.

FIGURE 5.7

The DAO 3.6 object model.

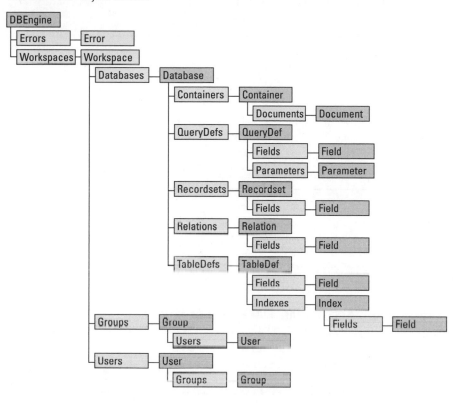

New Objects in the Access 2007 DAO Object Model

There are three new objects in the new object model: ComplexType, Field2, and Recordset2. These objects are described in the following sections.

ComplexType

The ComplexType object represents a multi-valued field and has its own Fields collection to hold the values.

Field2

This object represents a field in an Access 2007 database. It has the new attributes outlined in Table 5.1, as compared with the Field property, representing a field in an Access 2000 or Access 2002/2003 database.

TABLE 5.1

New Attributes of the Field2 Object

Attribute Type	Name	Notes
Property	AppendOnly	Gets or sets a Boolean value that indicates whether the specified field is set to append new values to the existing contents of the field as they are added (Read/Write).
Property	ComplexType	Represents a multi-valued field (Read-only).
Property	IsComplex	Returns a Boolean value that indicates whether the specified field is a multi-valued data type (Read-only).
Method	LoadFromFile	Loads the specified file from disk.
Method	SaveToFile	Saves an attachment to disk.

Recordset2

The `Recordset2` object represents a recordset based on Access 2007 data. Compared with the old `Recordset` object, it has only one new property, `ParentRecordset`, representing the parent Recordset of the specified recordset.

Hidden Objects in the Access 2007 DAO Object Model

The properties and methods listed in Table 5.2 are hidden in the new Access 2007 DAO object model. The Container, DBEngine, and Workspace objects are visible; only the listed properties and methods for these objects are invisible. The Group and User objects and the Groups and Users collections are entirely invisible.

TABLE 5.2

Database Components Hidden in the Microsoft Office 2007 Access Database Engine Object Model

Collection or Object	Properties	Methods	Constants
Container	AllPermissions		
	Inherit		
	Owner		
	Permissions		
	UserName		
DBEngine	SystemDB		

Collection or Object	Properties	Methods	Constants
Group/Groups			
User/Users			
Workspace	Groups	CreateGroup	
	UserName	CreateUser	
	Users		
WorkspaceTypeEnum			dbUseODBC

Databases

When working with Access data, a DAO Database object represents (no surprise!) an Access database. (For working with other types of data, use the ADO object model.) To reference the current database, you can use the `CurrentDb` method of the Access Application object, after declaring the appropriate DAO Database variable, as in the following code:

```
Dim dbs as DAO.Database

Set dbs = CurrentDb
```

If you need to reference an external database, use the `OpenDatabase` method, with the name of an open database as its argument, as in the following code:

```
Dim dbs As DAO.Database
Dim strDBName As String

strDBName = "E:\Documents\Northwind.mdb"
Set dbs = OpenDatabase(Name:=strDBName)
```

Once the database is open, you can proceed to work with it, using the Recordsets, QueryDefs, and TableDefs collections.

Recordsets

Recordsets are used to manipulate data in Access databases; they represent the records in tables or queries in a database. There are five types of DAO recordsets, with different properties, as described in the following sections. Specify the recordset type by using the appropriate constant for the type argument when creating a recordset, as in the following code:

```
Set rst = dbs.OpenRecordset(Name:="tblOrders", _
    Type:=dbOpenDynaset)
```

Table 5.3 lists the named constants corresponding to the five recordset types (and their numeric equivalents). These named constants are used in VBA code; some dialects of Visual Basic, such as

99

VBScript (VBS), don't support named constants, so you need to use the numeric values instead, for example when writing Outlook VBS code or Windows Script Host (WSH) code.

CROSS-REF   See Chapter 17 for examples of WSH code.

TABLE 5.3

DAO Recordset Type Named Arguments

Recordset Type	Named Constant	Numeric Value
Table	dbOpenTable	1
Dynaset	dbOpenDynaset	2
Snapshot	dbOpenSnapshot	4
Forward-only	dbOpenForwardOnly	8
Dynamic	dbOpenDynamic	16

If you don't specify a recordset type, DAO assumes first that you intend to create a table-type recordset, and if that is impossible, then a dynaset, then a snapshot, then a forward-only recordset. The table- and dynaset-type recordsets are the most commonly used types.

Table

Table-type recordsets represent base tables (that is, tables located within the database from which the code is running, as opposed to linked tables). You can add, edit, or delete records from a table using a table-type recordset. These recordsets don't support the Find methods (FindFirst, FindLast, FindNext, FindPrevious); instead they support the Seek method.

NOTE   To run one of the procedures in the DAO and ADO Sample Code database, place your cursor inside the procedure and press F5, or select Run Sub/UserForm from the Run menu in the Visual Basic window.

TIP   If you don't get a response when pressing a function key, function keys may be disabled; some newer keyboards disable function keys by default. To enable function keys, press the F Lock key.

The following code segment searches for the record with a specific value (retrieved from an InputBox) in the CompanyID field and, if it is found, displays the value in the ID/AccountNumber field for that record in a message box:

```
Private Sub ListID()

    Dim dbs As DAO.Database
    Dim rst As DAO.Recordset
```

```
        Dim strValue As String
        Dim strPrompt As String
        Dim strTitle As String

        Set dbs = CurrentDb
        Set rst = dbs.OpenRecordset(Name:="tblCompanyIDs", _
            Type:=dbOpenTable)
        rst.Index = "CompanyID"

    EnterID:
        strValue = InputBox(prompt:="Please enter a company ID", _
            Title:="Company ID", Default:="TEAC")
        rst.Seek Comparison:="=", key1:=strValue
        If rst.NoMatch = True Then
            strPrompt = "Couldn't find " & strValue & _
                "; please try again"
            strTitle = "Search failed"
            MsgBox prompt:=strPrompt, Buttons:=vbCritical _
                + vbOKOnly, Title:=strTitle
            GoTo EnterID
        Else
            strPrompt = "The first ID for " & strValue _
                & " is " & rst![ID/AccountNumber]
            strTitle = "Search succeeded"
            MsgBox prompt:=strPrompt, Buttons:=vbOKOnly _
                + vbInformation, Title:=strTitle
        End If

    End Sub
```

Figure 5.8 shows the message box with the ID for the selected company.

FIGURE 5.8

A message box displaying an ID for a selected company.

Dynaset

Dynaset-type recordsets represent the results of updatable queries, possibly based on more than one table. You can use these recordsets to add, edit, or delete records from one or more base tables. Dynaset-type recordsets support the more flexible Find methods (FindFirst, FindLast,

Argument Styles

When writing VBA code, you have two style choices: using argument names (as I do in most of the procedures in this book), which is more verbose, but allows you to skip arguments without causing syntax errors; or omitting argument names, in which case you have to make sure you have the right number of commas between arguments, with the spaces between commas representing the arguments you aren't using. I prefer using argument names for clarity, even though it makes my code a little longer.

If you use one argument name, you must use argument names for all the arguments of a function or method you use — mix and match is not permitted.

FindNext, FindPrevious); unlike the Seek method for table-type dynasets, you don't need to set an index, and you can search for a value in any field in the recordset. Here is an example in which the code searches for the last record with a matching value in the IDLabel field and displays the Company ID for that record in a message box:

```
Private Sub ListCompany()

    Dim dbs As DAO.Database
    Dim rst As DAO.Recordset
    Dim strValue As String
    Dim strPrompt As String
    Dim strTitle As String
    Dim strSearch As String

EnterID:
    strValue = InputBox(prompt:="Please enter an ID label", _
        Title:="ID Label", Default:="E-Mail Address")
    strSearch = "[IDLabel] = " & Chr$(39) & strValue _
        & Chr$(39)
    Debug.Print "Search string: " & strSearch

    Set dbs = CurrentDb
    Set rst = dbs.OpenRecordset(Name:="tblCompanyIDs", _
        Type:=dbOpenDynaset)
    rst.FindLast strSearch
    If rst.NoMatch = True Then
        strPrompt = "Couldn't find " & strValue & _
            "; please try again"
        strTitle = "Search failed"
        MsgBox prompt:=strPrompt, Buttons:=vbCritical _
            + vbOKOnly, Title:=strTitle
        GoTo EnterID
    Else
```

```
        strPrompt = "The last Company ID for " & strValue _
           & " is " & rst![CompanyID]
        strTitle = "Search succeeded"
        MsgBox prompt:=strPrompt, Buttons:=vbOKOnly _
           + vbInformation, Title:=strTitle
     End If

  End Sub
```

Snapshot

A snapshot-type recordset is a read-only copy of a set of records, useful only for viewing data or generating reports. The following procedure moves through a recordset based on a table, writing the values in several fields to the Immediate window, using the VB constants vbCrLf and vbTab to create line breaks and indents for better readability:

```
  Private Sub ListValues()

     Dim dbs As DAO.Database
     Dim rst As DAO.Recordset

     Set dbs = CurrentDb
     Set rst = dbs.OpenRecordset(Name:="tblCompanyIDs", _
        Type:=dbOpenSnapshot)
     Do While Not rst.EOF
        Debug.Print "Company ID: " & rst![CompanyID] _
           & vbCrLf & vbTab & "ID Label: " & rst![IDLabel] _
           & vbCrLf & vbTab & "ID/Account No.: " _
           & rst![ID/AccountNumber] & vbCrLf
        rst.MoveNext
     Loop

  End Sub
```

The results of running this procedure for two records are listed as follows:

```
  Company ID: MS Office & VBA
     ID Label: CIS ID
     ID/Account No.: 70304,3633

  Company ID: Fisher Consulting
     ID Label: E-Mail Address
     ID/Account No.: Rfisher@RickWorld.com
```

Unlike table-type and dynaset-type recordsets, you can work with a snapshot-type recordset even if the underlying table is open, which can occasionally be useful.

Forward-only

Forward-only recordsets are similar to snapshot-type recordsets, except that you only move through the records in a forward direction.

Dynamic

Dynamic recordsets represent the results of updatable queries, possibly based on more than one table. You can use these recordsets to add, edit, or delete records from one or more base tables, and so can other users.

QueryDefs

QueryDefs correspond to queries in the Access interface. Though you can create dynaset-type recordsets based directly on queries, and for select queries that works fine, QueryDefs offer extra functionality: you can create a query on the fly, in VBA code (for example, to filter by a value entered or selected on a form), and then use that QueryDef as the data source for a recordset. You can even create a make-table query in code, and execute it to create a table, for circumstances where you need a table to work with. This eliminates the need for numerous filtered queries, and also lets you work around various problems with creating recordsets based on parameter queries.

The following procedure creates a QueryDef programmatically, using a SQL string as the data source, and returns the number of records; it is useful in determining whether there are any records in a filtered query, before taking an action. I call this procedure frequently in code in the sample databases for this book:

```
Public Function CreateAndTestQuery(strTestQuery As String, _
   strTestSQL As String) As Long

On Error Resume Next
```

Delete old query:

```
      Set dbs = CurrentDb
      dbs.QueryDefs.Delete strTestQuery

On Error GoTo ErrorHandler
```

Create new query:

```
      Set qdf = dbs.CreateQueryDef(Name:=strTestQuery, _
         sqltext:=strTestSQL)
```

Test whether there are any records:

```
      Set rst = dbs.OpenRecordset(Name:=strTestQuery)
      With rst
```

```
            .MoveFirst
            .MoveLast
            CreateAndTestQuery = .RecordCount
        End With

ErrorHandlerExit:
    Exit Function

ErrorHandler:
    If Err.Number = 3021 Then
        CreateAndTestQuery = 0
        Resume ErrorHandlerExit
    Else
        MsgBox "Error No: " & Err.Number _
            & "; Description: " & Err.Description
        Resume ErrorHandlerExit
    End If

End Function
```

Here is a typical code segment using the CreateAndTestQuery function:

```
strInventoryCode = Me![InventoryCode]
strQuery = "qryTemp"
Set dbs = CurrentDb
strSQL = "SELECT * FROM tblInventoryItemsComponents _
    WHERE [InventoryCode] = " & Chr$(39) _
    & strInventoryCode & Chr$(39) & ";"
Debug.Print "SQL for " & strQuery & ": " & strSQL
lngCount = CreateAndTestQuery(strQuery, strSQL)
Debug.Print "No. of items found: " & lngCount
If lngCount = 0 Then
    strPrompt = "No records found; canceling"
    strTitle = "Canceling"
    MsgBox strPrompt, vbOKOnly + vbCritical, strTitle
    GoTo ErrorHandlerExit
Else
    'Further code here to work with the newly created query
End If
```

The code creates a SQL string filtered by a value picked up from a form, and uses that string and a query name as arguments for the CreateAndTestQuery function. That function returns the number of records; if there are no records (the function returns zero), the code exits; otherwise, it can continue to perform some action on the query created by the CreateAndTestQuery function.

You can also create a QueryDef and use it directly to create a recordset, as in the following line of code:

```
Set rst = qdf.OpenRecordset
```

NOTE Argument names are inconsistently capitalized in VBA code. Regardless of how you type them in, when your cursor leaves the line of code, some argument names are capitalized (such as "Name") and some are not (such as "sqltext"). The capitalization does not match the capitalization of the arguments in their Help topics, where they are usually represented as all lowercase.

You can also create a QueryDef corresponding to an action query and run it directly from code, to create a table for use elsewhere in the code instead of a parameter query, to avoid errors that will occur if a query criterion is looking for a value on a form that is closed when the code runs:

```
strFilter = "[InvoiceDate] = #" & dteDue & "#"
strSQL = "SELECT [InvoiceNo], InvoiceDate, _
    Customer, Employee " _
    & "INTO tmakMatchingRecords " _
    & "FROM tblInvoices " _
    & " WHERE " & strFilter & ";"

Debug.Print "SQL string: " & strSQL
Set qdf = dbs.CreateQueryDef(Name:=strQuery, _
    sqltext:=strSQL)
qdf.Execute
```

TIP You can create a QueryDef without a name, using just double quotes, as in this line of code:

```
Set qdfTemp = dbs.CreateQueryDef(Name:="", _
    sqltext:=strSQL)
```

However, I generally prefer to create a named query, so I can examine it in the interface for debugging purposes, if necessary.

TableDefs and Fields

TableDefs correspond to tables in the interface. Although it is much more common to need to create a query programmatically, sometimes you may need to create a table in code. When you create a new table, you also need to create fields for it. The following code creates a new table in an external database, with several fields of different data types. Each field is created (and its default value set, for two of them), and is then appended to the new table. An error handler returns the user to the input box where the new table name is entered, in case a table of that name already exists in the database. Finally, all the TableDefs in the database are listed to the Immediate window, with the new table as the last entry in the list:

```
Private Sub NewTable()

On Error Resume Next

    Dim dbsNorthwind As DAO.Database
    Dim tdfNew As DAO.TableDef
    Dim fld As DAO.Field
```

```
Dim strDBName As String
Dim strDBNameAndPath As String
Dim strPrompt As String
Dim strTitle As String
Dim strTable As String
Dim strCurrentPath As String
Dim fso As New Scripting.FileSystemObject
Dim fil As Scripting.File

strCurrentPath = Application.CurrentProject.Path & "\"
strDBName = "Northwind 2007.accdb"
strDBNameAndPath = strCurrentPath & strDBName
```

Attempt to find database, and put up a message if it is not found.

```
Set fil = fso.GetFile(strDBNameAndPath)
If fil Is Nothing Then
    strPrompt = "Can't find " & strDBName & " in " _
        & strCurrentPath
            & "; to create this database, double-" _
        & "click the Northwind.accdt template in the " _
        & "C:\Program Files\Microsoft
Office\Templates\1033\Access folder"
    MsgBox strPrompt, vbCritical + vbOKOnly
    GoTo ErrorHandlerExit
End If

On Error GoTo ErrorHandler
    Set dbsNorthwind = OpenDatabase(Name:=strDBNameAndPath)

NameNewTable:
    strPrompt = "Please enter new table name"
    strTitle = "Table name"
    strTable = InputBox(prompt:=strPrompt, Title:=strTitle, _
        Default:="tblNew")

    With dbsNorthwind
```

Create new table.

```
        Set tdfNew = _
            dbsNorthwind.CreateTableDef(Name:=strTable)
```

Create fields and append them to new table.

```
        With tdfNew
            Set fld = .CreateField(Name:="EmployeeID", _
                Type:=dbLong)
```

```
            .Fields.Append fld
            Set fld = .CreateField(Name:="Department", _
               Type:=dbText, Size:=14)
            .Fields.Append fld
            Set fld = .CreateField(Name:="Shift", _
               Type:=dbText, Size:=20)
            .Fields.Append fld
            Set fld = .CreateField(Name:="AnnualBonus", _
               Type:=dbCurrency)
            fld.DefaultValue = 500
            .Fields.Append fld
            Set fld = .CreateField(Name:="ShiftSupervisor", _
               Type:=dbBoolean)
            fld.DefaultValue = False
            .Fields.Append fld
        End With
```

Add the new table to the TableDefs collection.

```
        .TableDefs.Append Object:=tdfNew
    End With
```

List the TableDefs in the database after appending the new table.

```
    Debug.Print "TableDefs in " & dbsNorthwind.Name
        For Each tdf In dbsNorthwind.TableDefs
            Debug.Print vbTab & tdf.Name
        Next tdf
    dbsNorthwind.Close

ErrorHandlerExit:
    Exit Sub

ErrorHandler:
    If Err.Number = 3010 Then
        strPrompt = "Table name already used; " _
            & "please enter another name"
        strTitle = "Duplicate table name"
        MsgBox prompt:=strPrompt, _
            Buttons:=vbExclamation + vbOKOnly, Title:=strTitle
        GoTo NameNewTable
    Else
        MsgBox "Error No: " & Err.Number & "; Description: " _
            & Err.Description
        Resume ErrorHandlerExit
    End If
End Sub
```

Here is the list of tables as printed to the Immediate window by the `NewTable` procedure:

```
MSysAccessStorage
MSysACEs
MSysComplexColumns
MSysNavPaneGroupCategories
MSysNavPaneGroups
MSysNavPaneGroupToObjects
MSysNavPaneObjectIDs
MSysObjects
MSysQueries
MSysRelationships
Order Details
Orders
Products
Shippers
Suppliers
tblNew
```

> **NOTE**   If you open tblNew in datasheet view, you will see a zero in the ShiftSupervisor Boolean field. If you prefer to see True/False or Yes/No values, you will have to select the format of your choice manually; the `CreateField` method does not have an argument for setting the display format for a field.

Other Ways of Creating Tables Programmatically

In addition to the `CreateTableDef` method, there are three other ways to create Access tables in VBA code:

- The `CopyObject` method of the DoCmd object in the Access object model creates a new table based on an existing table.

- Executing a make-table query using the `OpenQuery` or `RunSQL` method of the DoCmd object, or the `Execute` method of QueryDef object, creates a new table as the output of the query.

- A Jet SQL CREATE TABLE statement, as in the following code, can be used to create a table:

```
strSQL = "CREATE TABLE " & "tblForms" & _
    "(FormName TEXT (100), Use YESNO);"
DoCmd.RunSQL strSQL
```

Compared with these techniques, the `CreateTableDef` method gives you the maximum control over the new table's fields and their properties. However you create a table, it will be appended to the TableDefs collection, and it will show up in the Tables group of the database window.

The ADO Object Model

The ADO object model is much simpler than the DAO object model; it is used to connect to a wide variety of data sources, so it is not customized to Access data, as the DAO object model is. However, with a few exceptions (working with form recordsets and creating tables programmatically), you can manipulate Access data with ADO much the same as with DAO.

Connection

Although the ADO object model is not hierarchical (unlike the DAO object model), the Connection object is the foundation object, because connections are the link to data in databases.

 **NOTE** In DAO recordsets, the BOF property represents the beginning of the recordset (Beginning Of File), and the EOF (End Of File) property represents the end.

The handy NoMatch property of DAO recordsets is missing from ADO; instead, you have to determine whether or not a search succeeded by examining where the cursor is. For example, in doing a Find, starting from the beginning of the recordset (BOF) and moving forward, if the cursor ends up at the end of the recordset (EOF), the search was unsuccessful. Here is some sample code to illustrate this technique; if the search is successful, this means that the proposed new category name has already been used, whereas if the cursor ends up at the end of the recordset (EOF), the search was unsuccessful, and the new record can be created using the new category name in the strSearch variable (the code segment is part of the TestKeysetOptimistic procedure, which is listed later in this chapter):

```
rst.Find strSearch
If rst.EOF = False Then
    strPrompt = Chr$(39) & strCategory _
        & Chr$(39) & " already used; " _
        & "please enter another category " _
        & "name"
    strTitle = "Category used"
    MsgBox prompt:=strPrompt, _
        Buttons:=vbExclamation + vbOKOnly, _
        Title:=strTitle
    GoTo CategoryName
```

The Tables collection and form recordsets are not supported in ADO, so you will need to continue to use DAO (either the old DAO 3.6 or the new Access 2007 DAO object model) to work with them.

TIP If you don't close and set to Nothing DAO database or recordset objects, it is extremely unlikely that you will have any problems; however, if you leave ADO connections and recordsets open, the next time you run the code, you may get this error message (with your logon name and computer name), and you will have to close down and reopen the database to get the code working again: "The database has been placed in a state by user 'Admin' on machine 'DELL_DIMEN_8300' that prevents it from being opened or locked." The sample ADO procedures have code to close any open connection or recordset in their error handlers.

The syntax for creating a connection to the current database is simple:

```
Dim cnn As ADODB.Connection

Set cnn = CurrentProject.Connection
```

The ADO syntax for working with a recordset in an external database is a little different; you have to specify the database path and file name, and specify the Microsoft Jet 4.0 provider, as in the procedure listed as follows, which uses a SQL string to create a recordset:

```
Private Sub OpenRecordsetSQL()

On Error Resume Next

    Dim cnn As ADODB.Connection
    Dim rst As ADODB.Recordset
    Dim strDBName As String
    Dim strConnectString As String
    Dim strSQL As String
    Dim strDBNameAndPath As String
    Dim strCurrentPath As String
    Dim fso As New Scripting.FileSystemObject
    Dim fil As Scripting.File
    Dim strPrompt As String
```

Create connection to an external database.

```
    strCurrentPath = Application.CurrentProject.Path & "\"
    strDBName = "Northwind.mdb"
    strDBNameAndPath = strCurrentPath & strDBName
```

Attempt to find the database, and put up a message if it is not found.

```
    Set fil = fso.GetFile(strDBNameAndPath)
    If fil Is Nothing Then
       strPrompt = "Can't find " & strDBName & " in " _
          & strCurrentPath & "; please copy it from the " _
          & "Office11\Samples subfolder under the main " _
          & "Microsoft Office folder " _
          & "of an earlier version of Office"
       MsgBox strPrompt, vbCritical + vbOKOnly
       GoTo ErrorHandlerExit
    End If

On Error GoTo ErrorHandler

    Set cnn = New ADODB.Connection
    Set rst = New ADODB.Recordset
```

Need to specify the Jet 4.0 provider for connecting to Access .mdb format databases.

```
With cnn
    .Provider = "Microsoft.Jet.OLEDB.4.0"
    .Open strDBNameAndPath
    strConnectString = .ConnectionString
End With
```

Use a SQL string to create a filtered recordset.

```
strSQL = "SELECT CompanyName, ContactName, " _
    & "City FROM Suppliers " _
    & "WHERE Country = 'Australia' " _
    & "ORDER BY CompanyName;"
rst.Open Source:=strSQL, _
    ActiveConnection:=strConnectString, _
    CursorType:=adOpenStatic, _
    LockType:=adLockReadOnly
```

Iterate through the recordset, and print values from fields to the Immediate window.

```
With rst
    .MoveLast
    .MoveFirst
    Debug.Print .RecordCount _
        & " records in recordset" & vbCrLf
    Do While Not .EOF
        Debug.Print "Australian Company name: " _
            & ![CompanyName] _
            & vbCrLf & vbTab & "Contact name: " _
            & ![ContactName] _
            & vbCrLf & vbTab & "City: " & ![City] _
            & vbCrLf
        rst.MoveNext
    Loop
End With

ErrorHandlerExit:
```

Close the Recordset and Connection objects.

```
If Not rst Is Nothing Then
    If rst.State = adStateOpen Then
        rst.Close
        Set rst = Nothing
    End If
End If
```

```
        If Not cnn Is Nothing Then
            If cnn.State = adStateOpen Then
                cnn.Close
                Set cnn = Nothing
            End If
        End If

        Exit Sub

    ErrorHandler:
        MsgBox "Error No: " & Err.Number _
            & "; Description: " & Err.Description
        Resume ErrorHandlerExit
    End Sub
```

Command

The ADO Command object represents SQL commands, roughly equivalent to queries in Access databases, or QueryDefs in the DAO object model. You don't need to use this object to query or filter Access data; this can be done using a SQL statement (as in the preceding code segment) or the name of a saved query for the Source argument when opening a recordset. However, the Command object can be useful when you want to reuse a command later in the code, or if you need to pass detailed parameter information with the command.

The procedure uses a Command object to create a recordset, which can be used later in the code:

```
    Private Sub OpenRecordsetCommand()

On Error Resume Next

        Dim cnn As ADODB.Connection
        Dim rst As ADODB.Recordset
        Dim cmdSQL As ADODB.Command
        Dim strDBName As String
        Dim strConnectString As String
        Dim strSQL As String
        Dim strCursorType As String
        Dim strLockType As String
        Dim strDBNameAndPath As String
        Dim strCurrentPath As String
        Dim fso As New Scripting.FileSystemObject
        Dim fil As Scripting.File
        Dim strPrompt As String
```

Create connection to an external database.

```
        strCurrentPath = Application.CurrentProject.Path & "\"
        strDBName = "Northwind.mdb"
        strDBNameAndPath = strCurrentPath & strDBName
```

113

Attempt to find the database, and put up a message if it is not found.

```
Set fil = fso.GetFile(strDBNameAndPath)
If fil Is Nothing Then
    strPrompt = "Can't find " & strDBName & " in " _
        & strCurrentPath & "; please copy it from the " _
        & "Office11\Samples subfolder under the main " _
        & "Microsoft Office folder " _
        & "of an earlier version of Office"
    MsgBox strPrompt, vbCritical + vbOKOnly
    GoTo ErrorHandlerExit
End If

On Error GoTo ErrorHandler

Set cnn = New ADODB.Connection
Set rst = New ADODB.Recordset
```

Need to specify the Jet 4.0 provider for connecting to Access .mdb format databases.

```
With cnn
    .Provider = "Microsoft.Jet.OLEDB.4.0"
    .Open strDBNameAndPath
    strConnectString = .ConnectionString
End With

Set cmdSQL = New ADODB.Command
Set cmdSQL.ActiveConnection = cnn
```

Use a SQL string to create a command.

```
strSQL = "SELECT CompanyName, ContactName, " _
    & "City FROM Suppliers " _
    & "WHERE Country = 'Sweden' " _
    & "ORDER BY CompanyName;"
cmdSQL.CommandText = strSQL
Set rst = cmdSQL.Execute
```

Check cursor and lock type of recordset.

```
strCursorType = Switch(rst.CursorType = _
    adOpenDynamic, _
    "Dynamic (" & adOpenDynamic & ")", _
    rst.CursorType = adOpenForwardOnly, _
    "Forward-only (" _
    & adOpenForwardOnly & ")", _
    rst.CursorType = adOpenKeyset, "Keyset (" _
    & adOpenKeyset & ")", _
    rst.CursorType = adOpenStatic, "Static (" _
    & adOpenStatic & ")")
```

```
strLockType = Switch(rst.LockType = _
   adLockOptimistic, _
   "Optimistic (" & adLockOptimistic & ")", _
   rst.LockType = adLockReadOnly, "Read-only (" _
   & adLockReadOnly & ")", _
   rst.LockType = adLockBatchOptimistic, _
   "BatchOptimistic (" _
   & adLockBatchOptimistic & ")", _
   rst.LockType = adLockPessimistic, _
   "Pessimistic (" _
   & adLockPessimistic & ")")

Debug.Print "Recordset cursor/lock type: " _
   & strCursorType & ", " & strLockType & vbCrLf
```

Iterate through the recordset, and print values from fields to the Immediate window.

```
With rst
   .MoveFirst
   Do While Not .EOF
      Debug.Print "Swedish Company name: " _
         & ![CompanyName] _
         & vbCrLf & vbTab & "Contact name: " _
         & ![ContactName] _
         & vbCrLf & vbTab & "City: " & ![City] _
         & vbCrLf
      rst.MoveNext
   Loop
End With


ErrorHandlerExit:
```

Close the Recordset and Connection objects.

```
If Not rst Is Nothing Then
   If rst.State = adStateOpen Then
      rst.Close
      Set rst = Nothing
   End If
End If

If Not cnn Is Nothing Then
   If cnn.State = adStateOpen Then
      cnn.Close
      Set cnn = Nothing
   End If
End If

Exit Sub
```

```
ErrorHandler:
    MsgBox "Error No: " & Err.Number _
        & "; Description: " & Err.Description
    Resume ErrorHandlerExit
End Sub
```

Recordset

ADO recordsets represent sets of records in a database, much like DAO recordsets, though their attributes are more generic. An ADO recordset can be based on a table, query, SQL statement, or Command object. The `TestForwardReadOnly` procedure listed here uses a saved select query as the recordset source:

```
Private Sub TestForwardReadOnly()

On Error GoTo ErrorHandler

    Dim cnn As ADODB.Connection
    Dim rst As ADODB.Recordset
```

Create a connection to the current database.

```
    Set cnn = CurrentProject.Connection
    Set rst = New ADODB.Recordset
```

Create a recordset based on a select query.

```
    rst.Open Source:="qryCompanyAddresses", _
        ActiveConnection:=cnn.ConnectionString, _
        CursorType:=adOpenForwardOnly, _
        LockType:=adLockReadOnly
```

Iterate through the query, and print values from fields to the Immediate window.

```
    Do While Not rst.EOF
        Debug.Print "Company ID: " & rst![CompanyID] _
            & vbCrLf & vbTab & "Category: " _
            & rst![Category] _
            & vbCrLf & vbTab & "Company Name: " _
            & rst![Company] & vbCrLf
        rst.MoveNext
    Loop

ErrorHandlerExit:
```

Close the Recordset and Connection objects.

```
If Not rst Is Nothing Then
    If rst.State = adStateOpen Then
        rst.Close
        Set rst = Nothing
    End If
End If

If Not cnn Is Nothing Then
    If cnn.State = adStateOpen Then
        cnn.Close
        Set cnn = Nothing
    End If
End If

Exit Sub

ErrorHandler:
    MsgBox "Error No: " & Err.Number _
        & "; Description: " & Err.Description
    Resume ErrorHandlerExit

End Sub
```

ADO recordsets have four types of cursors (cursors in ADO are roughly equivalent to the DAO recordset types), as described in the following two tables. Each cursor type supports different methods depending on the setting of the LockType argument. The two most commonly used lock types are the read-only (named constant: adLockReadOnly) and optimistic (named constant: adLockOptimistic) type. Table 5.4 lists the ADO cursor types, with their numeric equivalents, and Table 5.5 lists the most commonly used cursor and lock type combinations for working with Access data.

TABLE 5.4

ADO Recordset Cursor Type Named Arguments

Cursor Type	Named Constant	Numeric Value
Dynamic	adOpenDynamic	2
Keyset	adOpenKeyset	1
Static	adOpenStatic	3
Forward-only	adOpenForwardOnly	0

TABLE 5.5		

ADO Recordset Lock Type Named Arguments

Lock Type	Named Constant	Numeric Value
Read-only	adLockReadOnly	1
Optimistic	adLockOptimistic	3
Batch Optimistic	adLockBatchOptimistic	4
Pessimistic	adLockPessimistic	2

NOTE Sometimes the ADO recordset that is created is not the type you specify in the CursorType argument, depending on the lock type. In particular, if you specify the `adLockOptimistic` lock type for any cursor type, you will actually get a Keyset cursor. To determine the actual recordset type, use the following statement (see Table 5.4 to convert the numeric type to its matching named constant):

```
Debug.Print "Recordset cursor type: " _
    & rst.CursorType
```

For a more advanced determination of the actual cursor type and lock type of a newly created recordset, run the following procedure, substituting the desired cursor and lock type in the `rst.Open` line:

```
Private Sub TestMethodsSupported()

On Error Resume Next

    Dim cnn As ADODB.Connection
    Dim rst As ADODB.Recordset
    Dim strDBName As String
    Dim strConnectString As String
    Dim strSQL As String
    Dim strCursorType As String
    Dim strLockType As String
    Dim strCurrentPath As String
    Dim fso As New Scripting.FileSystemObject
    Dim fil As Scripting.File
    Dim strDBNameAndPath As String
    Dim strPrompt As String
```

Create a connection to an external database.

```
    strCurrentPath = Application.CurrentProject.Path & "\"
    strDBName = "Northwind.mdb"
    strDBNameAndPath = strCurrentPath & strDBName
```

Attempt to find the database, and put up a message if it is not found.

```
Set fil = fso.GetFile(strDBNameAndPath)
If fil Is Nothing Then
    strPrompt = "Can't find " & strDBName & " in " _
        & strCurrentPath & "; please copy it from the " _
        & "Office11\Samples subfolder under the main " _
        & "Microsoft Office folder " _
        & "of an earlier version of Office"
    MsgBox strPrompt, vbCritical + vbOKOnly
    GoTo ErrorHandlerExit
End If

On Error GoTo ErrorHandler

    Set cnn = New ADODB.Connection
    Set rst = New ADODB.Recordset
```

Need to specify the Jet 4.0 provider for connecting to Access databases.

```
With cnn
    .Provider = "Microsoft.Jet.OLEDB.4.0"
    .Open strDBNameAndPath
    strConnectString = .ConnectionString
End With
```

Use a SQL string to create a filtered recordset.

```
strSQL = "SELECT CompanyName, ContactName, City " _
    & "FROM Suppliers " _
    & "WHERE Country = 'Australia' " _

    & "ORDER BY CompanyName;"
```

Modify the `cursortype` and `locktype` arguments as desired to test what type of recordset is created when the procedure is run.

```
rst.Open Source:=strSQL, _
    ActiveConnection:=strConnectString, _
    CursorType:=adOpenForwardOnly, _
    LockType:=adLockOptimistic

strCursorType = Switch(rst.CursorType = _
    adOpenDynamic, _
    "Dynamic (" & adOpenDynamic & ")", _
    rst.CursorType = adOpenForwardOnly, _
    "Forward-only (" _
    & adOpenForwardOnly & ")", _
    rst.CursorType = adOpenKeyset, "Keyset (" _
    & adOpenKeyset & ")", _
```

```
      rst.CursorType = adOpenStatic, "Static (" _
         & adOpenStatic & ")")

   strLockType = Switch(rst.LockType = _
      adLockOptimistic, _
      "Optimistic (" & adLockOptimistic & ")", _
      rst.LockType = adLockReadOnly, "Read-only (" _
      & adLockReadOnly & ")", _
      rst.LockType = adLockBatchOptimistic, _
      "BatchOptimistic (" _
      & adLockBatchOptimistic & ")", _
      rst.LockType = adLockPessimistic, _
      "Pessimistic (" _
      & adLockPessimistic & ")")

   Debug.Print "Recordset cursor/lock type: " _
      & strCursorType & ", " & strLockType & vbCrLf
   Debug.Print "AddNew supported? " _
      & rst.Supports(adAddNew)
   Debug.Print "Delete supported? " _
      & rst.Supports(adDelete)
   Debug.Print "Find supported? " _
      & rst.Supports(adFind)
   Debug.Print "MovePrevious supported? " _
      & rst.Supports(adMovePrevious)
   Debug.Print "Update supported? " _
      & rst.Supports(adUpdate)


ErrorHandlerExit:
```

Close the Recordset and Connection objects.

```
   If Not rst Is Nothing Then
      If rst.State = adStateOpen Then
         rst.Close
         Set rst = Nothing
      End If
   End If

   If Not cnn Is Nothing Then
      If cnn.State = adStateOpen Then
         cnn.Close
         Set cnn = Nothing
      End If
   End If

   Exit Sub
```

```
ErrorHandler:
    MsgBox "Error No: " & Err.Number _
        & "; Description: " & Err.Description
    Resume ErrorHandlerExit
End Sub
```

Because other types of cursors are converted to keysets when you use optimistic locking for an ADO recordset, you may as well specify the keyset cursor when you create the recordset, because that is what you are going to get. See Table 5.6 for the details.

TABLE 5.6

ADO Recordset Cursor/Lock Type Combinations

Cursor Type Named Constant	Lock Type Named Constant	Available Methods
adOpenDynamic (converts to adOpenKeyset)	AdLockOptimistic	AddNew Delete Find MoveFirst MovePrevious MoveNext MoveLast Update
adOpenDynamic (converts to adOpenStatic)	adLockReadOnly	Find MoveFirst MovePrevious MoveNext MoveLast
adOpenKeyset	AdLockOptimistic	AddNew Delete Find MoveFirst MovePrevious MoveNext MoveLast Update
adOpenKeyset	AdLockReadOnly	Find MoveFirst MovePrevious MoveNext MoveLast

continued

TABLE 5.6	(continued)	
Cursor Type Named Constant	**Lock Type Named Constant**	**Available Methods**
adOpenStatic *(converts to adOpenKeyset)*	AdLockOptimistic	AddNew Delete Find MoveFirst MovePrevious MoveNext MoveLast Update
adOpenStatic	AdLockReadOnly	Find MoveFirst MovePrevious MoveNext MoveLast
adOpenForwardOnly *(converts to adOpenKeyset)*	AdLockOptimistic	AddNew Delete Find MoveFirst MovePrevious MoveNext MoveLast Update
adOpenForwardOnly	AdLockReadOnly	Find MoveFirst MoveNext MoveLast

Dynamic

A dynamic cursor (DAO equivalent: dbOpenDynaset) lets you view additions, changes, or deletions made by other users. All types of movement through the recordset are allowed.

Keyset

In a recordset with a keyset cursor (there is no equivalent DAO recordset type), you can add, change, and delete data in records, but you can't see records that other users add or delete. However, you can see changes made by other users. With an optimistic (adLockOptimistic) lock type, you can modify the data; if you don't need to modify the data, use a read-only lock type (adLockReadOnly) for faster data access.

The following TestKeysetOptimistic procedure adds a new record to the tlkpCategories table, and sets the value of a field from input provided by the user, after checking whether the category name provided by the user has already been used:

```
Private Sub TestKeysetOptimistic()

On Error GoTo ErrorHandler

    Dim cnn As ADODB.Connection
    Dim rst As ADODB.Recordset
    Dim strCategory As String
    Dim strPrompt As String
    Dim strTitle As String
    Dim strSearch As String
```

Create a connection to the current database.

```
    Set cnn = CurrentProject.Connection
    Set rst = New ADODB.Recordset
```

Create a recordset based on a table.

```
    rst.Open Source:="tlkpCategories", _
        ActiveConnection:=cnn.ConnectionString, _
        CursorType:=adOpenKeyset, _
        LockType:=adLockOptimistic

    CategoryName:
```

Add a new record, getting a field value from the user.

```
    strPrompt = "Please enter new category name"
    strTitle = "New category"
    strCategory = Nz(InputBox(prompt:=strPrompt, _
        Title:=strTitle))
    If strCategory = "" Then
        GoTo ErrorHandlerExit
    Else
        strSearch = "[Category] = " & Chr$(39) _
            & strCategory & Chr$(39)
        Debug.Print "Search string: "; strSearch
        With rst
            .MoveLast
            .MoveFirst
            Debug.Print .RecordCount _
                & " records initially in recordset"
```

Check whether this category name has already been used — if the search fails, the cursor will be at the end of the recordset.

```
        rst.Find strSearch
        If rst.EOF = False Then
            strPrompt = Chr$(39) & strCategory _
```

```
                                & Chr$(39) & " already used; " _
                                & "please enter another category " _
                                & "name"
                    strTitle = "Category used"
                    MsgBox prompt:=strPrompt, _
                        Buttons:=vbExclamation + vbOKOnly, _
                        Title:=strTitle
                    GoTo CategoryName
                Else
                    .AddNew
                    ![Category] = strCategory
                    .Update
                    strPrompt = Chr$(39) & strCategory _
                        & Chr$(39) & " added to table"
                    strTitle = "Category added"
                    MsgBox prompt:=strPrompt, _
                        Buttons:=vbInformation + vbOKOnly, _
                        Title:=strTitle
                    Debug.Print .RecordCount _
                        & " records in recordset after adding"
                End If
            End With
        End If

    ErrorHandlerExit:
```

Close the Recordset and Connection objects.

```
        If Not rst Is Nothing Then
            If rst.State = adStateOpen Then
                rst.Close
                Set rst = Nothing
            End If
        End If

        If Not cnn Is Nothing Then
            If cnn.State = adStateOpen Then
                cnn.Close
                Set cnn = Nothing
            End If
        End If

        Exit Sub

    ErrorHandler:
        MsgBox "Error No: " & Err.Number _
            & "; Description: " & Err.Description
        Resume ErrorHandlerExit

    End Sub
```

The code prints the search string (always useful for debugging) and the number of records in the recordset, before and after adding the new record, to the Immediate window:

```
Search string: [Category] = 'Firmware'
29 records initially in recordset
30 records in recordset after adding
```

Static

The static cursor type (DAO equivalent: dbOpenSnapshot) provides a static copy of a set of records, for viewing or printing data. All types of movement through the recordset are allowed. Additions, changes, or deletions made by other users are not shown. For fast access to data that you don't need to modify, where you don't need to view other users' changes and you do need to be able to move both forward and backward in the recordset, use a static cursor and the adLockReadOnly lock type, as in the following TestStaticReadOnly procedure. If you do need to modify the data, but don't need to see other users' changes, use the adLockOptimistic lock type instead (the cursor type will change to keyset, as noted previously).

The TestStaticReadOnly procedure sets up a connection to the Northwind database, opens a filtered recordset based on a table in the database, and then iterates through the recordset, printing information from its fields to the Immediate window. Note that once an ADO recordset has been created, many of the same methods can be used to work with it as for a DAO database (BOF, EOF, Find*, Move*):

```
Private Sub TestStaticReadOnly()

On Error Resume Next

    Dim cnn As ADODB.Connection
    Dim rst As ADODB.Recordset
    Dim strDBName As String
    Dim strDBNameAndPath As String
    Dim strConnectString As String
    Dim strSQL As String
    Dim strCurrentPath As String
    Dim fso As New Scripting.FileSystemObject
    Dim fil As Scripting.File
    Dim strPrompt As String
```

Create a connection to an external database.

```
    strCurrentPath = Application.CurrentProject.Path & "\"
    strDBName = "Northwind.mdb"
    strDBNameAndPath = strCurrentPath & strDBName
```

Attempt to find the database, and put up a message if it is not found.

```
Set fil = fso.GetFile(strDBNameAndPath)
If fil Is Nothing Then
    strPrompt = "Can't find " & strDBName & " in " _
        & strCurrentPath & "; please copy it from the " _
        & "Office11\Samples subfolder under the main " _
        & "Microsoft Office folder " _
        & "of an earlier version of Office"
    MsgBox strPrompt, vbCritical + vbOKOnly
    GoTo ErrorHandlerExit
End If


On Error GoTo ErrorHandler

    Set cnn = New ADODB.Connection
    Set rst = New ADODB.Recordset
```

Need to specify the Jet 4.0 provider for connecting to Access databases.

```
With cnn
    .Provider = "Microsoft.Jet.OLEDB.4.0"
    .Open strDBNameAndPath
    strConnectString = .ConnectionString
End With
```

Use a SQL string to create a filtered recordset.

```
strSQL = "SELECT CompanyName, ContactName, " _
    & "City FROM Suppliers " _
    & "WHERE Country = 'Australia' " _
    & "ORDER BY CompanyName;"
rst.Open Source:=strSQL, _
    ActiveConnection:=strConnectString, _
    CursorType:=adOpenStatic, _
    LockType:=adLockReadOnly
```

Iterate through the recordset, and print values from fields to the Immediate window.

```
With rst
    .MoveLast
    .MoveFirst
    Debug.Print .RecordCount _
        & " records in recordset" & vbCrLf
    Do While Not .EOF
        Debug.Print "Australian Company name: " _
            & ![CompanyName] _
            & vbCrLf & vbTab & "Contact name: " _
            & ![ContactName] _
```

```
                  & vbCrLf & vbTab & "City: " & ![City] _
                  & vbCrLf
              rst.MoveNext
          Loop
      End With

   ErrorHandlerExit:
```

Close the Recordset and Connection objects.

```
      If Not rst Is Nothing Then
          If rst.State = adStateOpen Then
              rst.Close
              Set rst = Nothing
          End If
      End If

      If Not cnn Is Nothing Then
          If cnn.State = adStateOpen Then
              cnn.Close
              Set cnn = Nothing
          End If
      End If

      Exit Sub

   ErrorHandler:
      MsgBox "Error No: " & Err.Number _
          & "; Description: " & Err.Description
      Resume ErrorHandlerExit
   End Sub
```

The following information is printed to the Immediate window:

```
2 records in recordset

Australian Company name: G'day, Mate
   Contact name: Wendy Mackenzie
   City: Sydney

Australian Company name: Pavlova, Ltd.
   Contact name: Ian Devling
   City: Melbourne
```

Forward-only

The forward-only cursor (DAO equivalent: dbOpenForwardOnly) allows only forward movement through a recordset and doesn't show additions, changes, or deletions made by other users.

It is the default cursor type. For the fastest access to data that you don't need to modify, use a forward-only cursor and the `adLockReadOnly` lock type, as in the `TestForwardReadOnly` procedure that follows; if you do need to modify the data, use the `adLockOptimistic` lock type instead:

```
Private Sub TestForwardReadOnly()

On Error GoTo ErrorHandler

    Dim cnn As ADODB.Connection
    Dim rst As ADODB.Recordset
```

Create a connection to the current database.

```
    Set cnn = CurrentProject.Connection
    Set rst = New ADODB.Recordset
```

Create a recordset based on a select query.

```
    rst.Open Source:="qryCompanyAddresses", _
        ActiveConnection:=cnn.ConnectionString, _
        CursorType:=adOpenForwardOnly, _
        LockType:=adLockReadOnly
```

Iterate through the query, and print values from its fields to the Immediate window.

```
    Do While Not rst.EOF
        Debug.Print "Company ID: " & rst![CompanyID] _
            & vbCrLf & vbTab & "Category: " _
            & rst![Category] _
            & vbCrLf & vbTab & "Company Name: " _
            & rst![Company] & vbCrLf
        rst.MoveNext
    Loop


ErrorHandlerExit:
```

Close the Recordset and Connection objects.

```
    If Not rst Is Nothing Then
        If rst.State = adStateOpen Then
            rst.Close
            Set rst = Nothing
        End If
    End If

    If Not cnn Is Nothing Then
        If cnn.State = adStateOpen Then
            cnn.Close
```

```
                Set cnn = Nothing
            End If
        End If

        Exit Sub

    ErrorHandler:
        MsgBox "Error No: " & Err.Number _
            & "; Description: " & Err.Description
        Resume ErrorHandlerExit

    End Sub
```

Data from each record is printed to the Immediate window; the last two records' data is listed here:

```
    Company ID: Yclept Yarbro
        Category: Books
        Company Name: Yclept Yarbro

    Company ID: ZDExpos
        Category: Computer
        Company Name: ZDExpos
```

Record

An ADO Record object represents a set of data, which may be from a recordset or a non-database source. When working with Access data, the Record object is a single row from a recordset, or a one row recordset. There are many specialized uses of Record objects based on non-Access data (in particular, for working with hierarchical data and displaying it in TreeView controls), but when working with Access data in VBA code there is no reason to use the Record object, because you can reference fields as needed on the current record in a recordset without creating a Record object.

Stream

A Stream object represents a stream of data from a text file, XML document, or web page. Because this object doesn't work with Access data, it is dealt with in the chapters on working with text files, specifically Chapters 9 and 17.

Converting DAO Code to ADO Code

If you want to convert your old DAO code to new ADO code — perhaps for consistency with ADO code working with other types of data, or out of concern that DAO will no longer be supported in future versions of Access — you can use Table 5.7 as a guideline. Bear in mind that some types of DAO code can't be converted to ADO, because they have no equivalent in the ADO object model, so you will still need to use DAO for Access form recordsets, or creating tables and their fields programmatically.

 You can't exchange data between ADO and DAO recordsets, even when working in databases with references set to both object models.

TABLE 5.7

ADO Equivalents of DAO Objects

DAO Object	ADO Object	Notes
DBEngine	No equivalent	Not needed
Workspace	No equivalent	Not needed
Database	Connection	
Recordset	Recordset	
Dynaset type	Keyset cursor	
Snapshot type	Static cursor	
Table type	Keyset cursor with acCmdTableDirect option	
Field	Field	Recordset fields only
QueryDef	No direct equivalent, but can use the Command object to get the same functionality	
TableDef	No equivalent	

When using the DAO object model to work with Access data, the following code segment opens a recordset based on a query in an external database:

```
Dim dbs as DAO.Database
Dim strDBName As String
Dim rst As DAO.Recordset

strDBName = "E:\Documents\Northwind.mdb"
Set dbs = OpenDatabase(Name:=strDBName)
Set rst = dbs.OpenRecordset(Name:="qryCurrentOrders", _
Type:=dbOpenDynaset)
```

This ADO code opens an equivalent recordset:

```
Dim cnn As ADODB.Connection
Dim rst As ADODB.Recordset
Dim strDBName As String
Dim strConnectString As String
Dim strQuery As String
```

Create a connection to an external database.

```
strDBName = "D:\Documents\Northwind.mdb"
Set cnn = New ADODB.Connection
Set rst = New ADODB.Recordset
strQuery = "qryCategorySalesFor1997"
```

Need to specify the Jet 4.0 provider for connecting to Access databases.

```
With cnn
    .Provider = "Microsoft.Jet.OLEDB.4.0"
    .Open strDBName
    strConnectString = .ConnectionString
End With
```

Open a recordset based on a saved query.

```
rst.Open Source:=strQuery, _
    ActiveConnection:=cnn, _
    CursorType:=adOpenStatic, _
    LockType:=adLockReadOnly
```

Once the recordset has been created, you can work with it much like a DAO recordset, though there are some differences — see the sections on ADO recordset cursor and lock types for details on the differences.

> **TIP** For further information on converting DAO code to ADO code see Alyssa Henry's article "Porting DAO Code to ADO with the Microsoft Jet Provider," which is available online in the MSDN Library by searching its title or at `http://msdn.microsoft.com/library/default.asp?url=/library/en-us/dndao/html/daotoado.asp`.

Summary

The DAO object model was developed to work with Access data, and (despite rumors of its death, which have been heard for many versions now, and heavy promotion of the alternative ADO object model) DAO is still the best object model for working with data in Access tables. In Access 2007 instead of removing the DAO object model, Microsoft wisely chose to trim it of some rarely used components and rename it the Microsoft Office 2007 Access database engine object model. My recommendation is to use DAO for all tasks involving Access data.

When you need to work with data in other types of databases or data sources, however, ADO is the object model you need to use (no choice there — DAO only works with Access data). ADO can be used to work with Access data as well, though it has some limitations compared to DAO, so in some cases you may want (or need) to use ADO to work with Access data; I have provided information on converting DAO code to ADO for these situations.

Chapter 6

Working with Word Documents and Templates

espite the new and improved report interactive features discussed in the "Report Layout View" sidebar, for full control over the appearance and content of documents filled with Access data, VBA Automation code working with Word documents is the best choice. This chapter discusses producing Word documents by using a Ribbon command to create simple documents, or writing VBA Automation code to create Word documents and fill them with data, using four different methods.

In contrast to Access reports (even in the new Layout view), Word documents have extensive formatting options, including tables, form fields, and other specialized controls not available in Access reports, even in Layout view. Generating Word documents from Access VBA code lets you use all of Word's formatting options and (if desired) to create a separate document for each Access record, instead of a multi-page mail merge document. And the Word documents containing merged Access data can be edited, which is not an option even for Access 2007 reports.

Report Layout View

NEW FEATURE Access 2007 reports have a new view selection, Layout View. Access 2003 had Print Preview, Layout Preview (read-only, no data), and Design View, and you could only modify the report's layout, filtering, or sorting in Design view. In Access 2007, the new Layout view replaces Layout Preview, and there is a new Report view in addition to Print Preview. The following figure shows the View selector on the Access report Ribbon.

Access 2007 report views.

The new Layout view for Access reports has much more functionality than the old Layout Preview, letting users sort and filter from a right-click menu, as shown in the next screenshot, and even resize report columns while looking at the data (a long-requested feature).

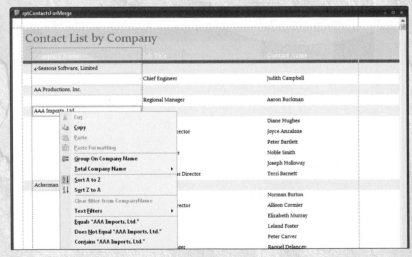

The new Layout view for an Access report.

134

However, even an interactive report still falls far short of the functionality of a Word document, especially if you need to distribute documents containing Access data to people who don't have Access installed.

Built-in Word Export in Office 2007

For many Office versions, it has been possible to export Access data to Word documents from the Access toolbar. The name of the control and toolbar location have changed over Office versions; in Access 2003 it was the OfficeLinks drop-down control on the Database toolbar, offering options to Merge to Word (Mail Merge), Publish to Word (RTF), or Analyze with Excel (XLS). In Access 2007, on the new Ribbon that replaces the old toolbars and menus, the External Data tab (shown in Figure 6.1) has an Export group with a variety of export options, including Excel, SharePoint, Word (RTF), Text File, and More. On the More drop-down menu, there are a number of export selections, including Merge It with Microsoft Office Word.

NOTE   You will see different selections on the More menu (or selections appearing as enabled or disabled) according to the type of object selected in the Object Bar, and whether the object is open or closed. With a form open, for example, you will see the Access Database, XML File, and HTML Document selections (these selections are enabled) and a disabled selection, Merge It with Microsoft Office Word; the Snapshot Viewer selection is only enabled when a report is selected.

FIGURE 6.1

The new External Data tab on the Access 2007 Ribbon, with the More menu dropped down.

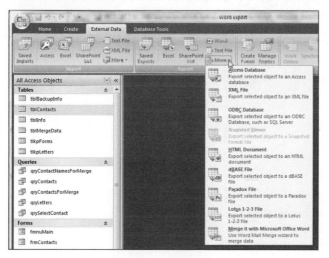

The Word (RTF) and Word Mail Merge features in Access 2007 work much the same as in earlier Office versions. If you select an Access table, query, or other object, and then select the Word (RTF) option, all the data from the entire selected object is automatically exported to a new Word document, with no option for selecting records.

The RTF document created from a table, query, or form is a Word table, which is a good match for data in an Access table or select query, but a very poor match for a form. Reports are created as text documents, not tables (even if they are tabular reports), with footers as text in the body of the document, and without most of their formatting; such a document is barely usable. (This is unchanged for many Office versions now.)

The RTF export option may be useful for creating a quick-and-dirty Word document you can send to someone who doesn't have Access, but it is not useful for creating letters or other formatted Word documents. Figure 6.2 shows an Access table to be exported, and Figure 6.3 shows the Export dialog, with two options enabled and one disabled (because the object being exported is a table, there is no formatting to export).

Figure 6.4 shows the Word table created by the RTF export. It has basically the same appearance as the Access table, but it lacks the alternate-row shading, even though Word 2007 supports this feature.

FIGURE 6.2

An Access table to be exported to Word.

FIGURE 6.3

The Word RTF Export dialog when exporting an Access table.

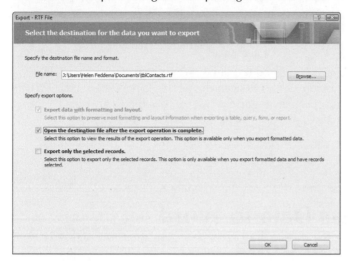

FIGURE 6.4

A Word document created by exporting an Access table, using the Word (RTF) option.

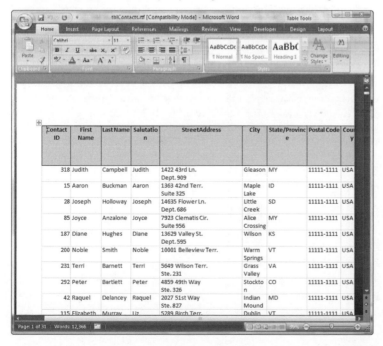

The Word Mail Merge option runs a wizard, which is generally similar to the one in the last two Office versions. It offers you a choice of deselecting some records from the data source before performing the merge, and you can create a new merge letter on the fly, so this interface choice can be useful when you need to create a set of minimally formatted Word letters to recipients from an Access table or query — but it may not be any easier to go through the six steps of the wizard, compared with just creating a simple Access letter report based on a filtered query.

My conclusion, after reviewing the new data export features in Access 2007, is that (just as with previous versions of Access) if you want to be able to select the records for an export of Access data to Word, and to produce great looking documents that can be opened and possibly edited by all Office users, you're still best off writing VBA code to merge Access data to Word documents.

 The Word Export.accdb sample database contains the tables, queries, forms, and code used in this chapter.

Exporting Access Data to Word Using Automation Code

Automation code is the tool you need to use when creating or working with Word documents in Access VBA. Automation code is not a special programming language, just a set of functions used in VBA code to work with the object models of other applications.

All Automation code starts with one of the two functions described as follows, either of which sets a reference to a high-level Automation object. When working with Word, this is generally the Word Application object.

The CreateObject function with "Word.Application" as the Class argument creates a new Word instance; it works whether or not Word is already open. The GetObject function with "Word.Application" as the Class argument attempts to set a reference to an existing instance of Word. GetObject succeeds in setting a reference only if Word is already running.

To avoid creating multiple instances of Word, I use the GetObject function in the body of a procedure, which sets a reference to an existing Word Application object, if Word is running, in combination with an error handler that uses CreateObject to create a new Word Application object if GetObject fails with Error 429, "ActiveX component can't create object":

```
Set appWord = GetObject(Class:="Word.Application")
```

[body of procedure here]

```
ErrorHandlerExit:
    Set appWord = Nothing
    Exit Sub
```

```
ErrorHandler:
   If Err = 429 Then
      'Word is not running; open Word with CreateObject
      Set appWord = CreateObject(Class:="Word.Application")
      Resume Next
   Else
      MsgBox "Error No: " & Err.Number _
         & "; Description: " & Err.Description
      Resume ErrorHandlerExit
   End If
```

NOTE In the error handler in the preceding code segment, the appWord Application object variable is set to Nothing. If you want to close down Word when your code has run, this is appropriate; but if you want to preserve the Word Application object for future use (generally a good idea), either comment out this line or delete it, as I have done in most of the procedures in the Word Export sample database.

To work with objects in an object model, first you need to set up a reference to the Application object, or some other object that can be used with the CreateObject or GetObject function. Although you use CreateObject or GetObject to set a reference directly to a Word Document object, generally it is best to create (or set a reference to) a Word Application object, and then use the appWord variable to get at other Word objects below the Application object, because many of the properties and methods you need to use in Automation code belong to the Application object, and you can access all the other objects through the Application object..

The Word Object Model

An object model is a representation of application components that are available for control by Automation code. Typically, most (but not all) of an application's functionality is represented by objects in the object model, letting you do almost anything you can do in the interface, and perhaps a few things that can't be done in the interface. The Word object model is very extensive, but fortunately, in order to work with Word documents and templates, and fill them with data from Access, you need to work with only a few components of the object model — in particular the Application object, Documents collection and Document object, the Tables collection and Table object, and the Bookmarks collection and Bookmark object. These object model components are the ones used in the procedures described in the following sections.

You can use the Object Browser to examine the properties and methods of the Word object model's components. Press F2 in the Visual Basic window to open the Object Browser, and select Word in the Libraries drop-down list at the top-left of its window. Figure 6.5 shows the Object Browser with the MailMerge object selected in the Classes list, so you can examine its properties and methods.

The following sample procedures use Automation code to perform some common tasks when working with the Word object model.

FIGURE 6.5

Examining the Word MailMerge object in the Object Browser.

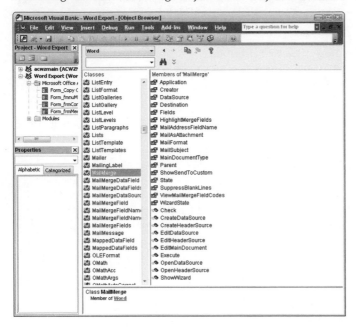

Creating a New, Blank Word Document

The NewDoc function creates a new, blank Word document based on the default Word template:

```
Public Function NewDoc()

On Error GoTo ErrorHandler

    Dim appWord As Word.Application
    Dim docs As Word.Documents
    Dim doc As Word.Document

    Set appWord = GetObject(Class:="Word.Application")
    Set docs = appWord.Documents
    docs.Add
    Set doc = appWord.ActiveDocument

ErrorHandlerExit:
    Exit Function
```

```
ErrorHandler:
    If Err = 429 Then
        'Word is not running; open Word with CreateObject
        Set appWord = CreateObject(Class:="Word.Application")
        Resume Next
    Else
        MsgBox "Error No: " & Err.Number _
            & "; Description: " & Err.Description
        Resume ErrorHandlerExit
    End If

End Function
```

Creating a Word Document Based on a Template

The functions in this section (and later sections) pick up the Contact Templates folder path, and the Contact Documents folder path, from the main menu. Each path has a command button and a TextBox bound to a field in tblInfo; clicking the command button opens a FolderPicker dialog for selecting the path. The selected path is displayed in the TextBox, as shown in Figure 6.6.

FIGURE 6.6

The main menu of the Word Export sample database.

If you click the Contact Templates Path or Contact Documents Path button, a Browse dialog opens, where you can select the folder for storing templates or documents (see Figure 6.7).

CROSS-REF The procedures that pop up these Browse dialogs are discussed in Chapter 9.

FIGURE 6.7

Selecting a folder as the Contact Documents folder.

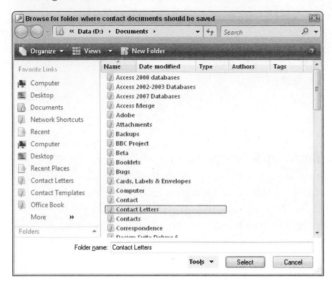

The NewDocFromTemplate function listed next creates a new document based on a template in the Contact Templates folder, using Word document properties to hold the data from Access. The document properties method is the most common technique I use for creating documents to fill with Access data. In the NewDocFromTemplate procedure, after creating the new document, the names of its document properties are printed to the Immediate window.

NOTE   As with previous versions of Word, although there is a CustomProperties collection in the Word 2007 object model, and a CustomProperty object, this collection and object actually belong to the Smart Tags, so if you declare variables of these data types, you will get a compile error; therefore, they must be declared as Object.

```
Public Function NewDocFromTemplate()

On Error GoTo ErrorHandler

    Dim appWord As Word.Application
    Dim docs As Word.Documents
    Dim strLetter As String
    Dim strTemplateDir As String
    Dim doc As Word.Document
```

Must declare this variable as Object because declaring it as Word.CustomProperties doesn't work:

```
Dim prps As Object
```

Must declare this variable as Object because declaring it as Word.CustomProperty doesn't work:

```
Dim prp As Object

Set appWord = GetObject(Class:="Word.Application")

strTemplateDir = GetContactsTemplatesPath()
Debug.Print "Templates directory: " & strTemplateDir
strLetter = strTemplateDir & "DocProps.dot"
Debug.Print "Letter: " & strLetter

Set docs = appWord.Documents
docs.Add strLetter
Set doc = appWord.ActiveDocument
Set prps = doc.CustomDocumentProperties
For Each prp In prps
    Debug.Print "Property name: " & prp.Name
Next prp

ErrorHandlerExit:
    Exit Function

ErrorHandler:
    If Err = 429 Then
        'Word is not running; open Word with CreateObject
        Set appWord = CreateObject(Class:="Word.Application")
        Resume Next
    Else
        MsgBox "Error No: " & Err.Number _
            & "; Description: " & Err.Description
        Resume ErrorHandlerExit
    End If

End Function
```

Using a Query to Concatenate Data for Export

I like to create a select query to use as the data source for merging Access data to Word, concatenating data from various fields as needed for best results when working with Word documents. One field concatenates name, job title, and company name information, using the IIf function to avoid creating blank lines, and another creates a single field with address information. This technique ensures that you won't see blank lines in the address block in a letter, or on a label, even if some fields lack data. I also create a separate ZipCode field for use in creating U.S. PostNet bar codes on envelopes or labels.

In the sample database, this query is `qryContactsForMerge`. The calculated field expressions I used to concatenate data from the simple flat-file tblContacts are listed next. Depending on the fields in your table(s), these expressions will need to be customized — for example, to deal with multi-field addresses or name prefixes and suffixes:

```
ContactName:
[FirstName] & " " & [LastName]

NameTitleCompany:
[FirstName] & " " & [LastName] & Chr(13) & Chr(10) &
[JobTitleCompany]

JobTitleCompany:
IIf(Nz([JobTitle])="" And
Nz([CompanyName])="","",IIf(Nz([JobTitle])<>"",[JobTitle] &
IIf(Nz([CompanyName])<>"",Chr(13) & Chr(10) &
[CompanyName]),[CompanyName]))

CityStateZip:

[City] & ", " & [StateOrProvince] & "  " & [PostalCode]

WholeAddress:
[StreetAddress] & Chr(13) & Chr(10) & [CityStateZip] &
IIf(Nz([Country])<>"" And Nz([Country])<>"USA", Chr(13) & Chr(10)
& [Country],"")

ZipCode:
IIf([Country]="USA" Or Nz([Country])="",[PostalCode],"")

LastNameFirst
[LastName] & IIf([FirstName],", " & [FirstName],"")
```

> **TIP**   In VBA code, you can use the VB named constant **vbCrLf** to indicate a CR + LF (carriage return plus linefeed) to start a new line in a text string, but named constants can't be used in query field expressions, so I use the Chr(13) & Chr(10) syntax instead, using the numeric values of the CR and LF characters.

Using a query to do the concatenating (rather than creating expressions in VBA code) makes it much easier to verify that the expressions are returning the correct data, and to fix any problems before doing the merge. After creating the expressions, just switch to datasheet view to inspect the results, and then switch back to design view to fix any problems you see.

Choosing a Method for Merging Access Data to Word

The `NewDocFromTemplate` procedure listed in the previous section lists Word document properties that can be filled with Access data. This is my preferred method for exporting Access data to Word documents, but it is not the only method. You can also export Access data to Word bookmarks, or simply insert data into a Word document using the TypeText method. And then there is mail merge, which is most suitable for merging data from very large numbers of records. Table 6.1 compares the advantages and disadvantages of these methods.

TABLE 6.1

Comparison of Four Ways to Merge Access Data to Word

Method	Advantages	Disadvantages
Bookmarks	There is no need to open the properties sheet; bookmarks are inserted directly into the template. Bookmarks are more familiar to Word users than document properties. Creates a separate document for each record, which allows easy customization of specific documents. There is no link to the Access database, so documents can be opened even on another computer.	You can't insert the same bookmark twice in a template; to display the same information in two or more places, you either need to create another bookmark or use a cross-reference field that references the first bookmark. Users may inadvertently type into the text inside a bookmark, overwriting the exported value.
Document Properties	Data from a document property can be displayed in multiple locations, using fields. Creates a separate document for each record, which allows easy customization of specific records. There is no link to the Access database, so documents can be opened even on another computer.	Requires creating document properties in the template, in the custom tab of the properties sheet.

continued

TABLE 6.1	(continued)	
Method	**Advantages**	**Disadvantages**
TypeText	No advance preparation of any kind is needed; this method works with a document created from the default Word template, or a default labels document. There is no link to the Access database, so documents can be opened even on another computer.	Suitable only for very simple documents, such as mailing labels or tabular lists.
Mail Merge	Suitable for merging very large numbers of records, too large to create an individual document for each record.	Customization of individual records is difficult, because all data is merged to a single document. Creating a mail merge labels document is more complex than creating a labels document for use with the TypeText method.

NOTE You can work with Word 97/2003 documents in Word 2007, as well as create new documents in the new Word 2007 format, so you don't need to redo all your templates just to get them to work in Office 2007. Some of the templates used for Word merge in the sample Word Export database are in Word 2007 format, and others are in Word 97/2003 format. The extensions differ for these two formats; new documents have the .docx extension, and new templates have the .dotx extension, whereas older ones have the .doc or .dot extensions, as shown in Figure 6.8. When you open a document or template in the older format, the title bar says "(Compatibility Mode)" after the file name.

TIP The new Type column in the Windows Vista Explorer shows the contents of a Word 2007 document's Keywords field, so you can use this built-in Word property to display relevant information in the Explorer.

Working with Word Document Properties

In previous versions of Word, document properties were accessed in a straightforward manner, through the Properties dialog, opened from the File menu. The process is now more complicated; in Word 2007 you click the Office button, select Prepare, and then Properties (see Figure 6.9).

FIGURE 6.8

Word templates and documents in Word 2002/2003 and Word 2007 formats.

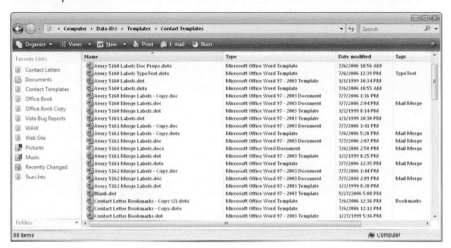

FIGURE 6.9

The Properties selection on the new Word Prepare menu.

NEW FEATURE The Properties command on the Office menu opens a new feature of Word 2007, the Document Information Panel (see Figure 6.10), where you can modify a few of the more common built-in document properties.

FIGURE 6.10

The Word 2007 Document Information Panel.

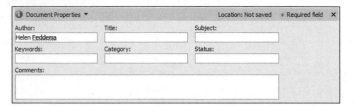

Next, click the drop-down Properties button in the title bar (the initial selection is Standard) and select Advanced Properties. At last, the familiar Word properties sheet opens, to the General tab (see Figure 6.11).

FIGURE 6.11

The General tab of the Word properties sheet.

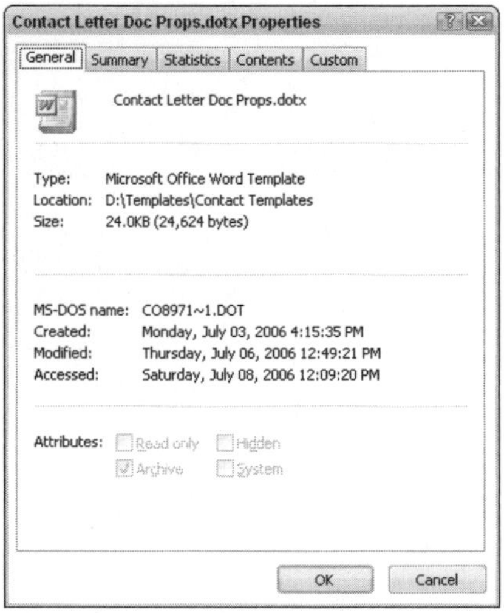

Click the Custom tab to see the custom document properties; these are the ones that are most commonly filled with data from Access fields. Figure 6.12 shows the Custom tab of a Word 2007 template properties sheet, with several custom document properties that are useful for creating letters and other documents filled with data from an Access select query.

FIGURE 6.12

The Custom tab of the Word properties sheet.

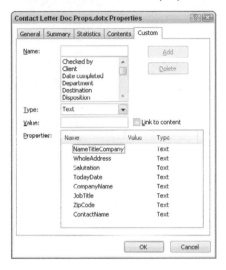

You may also want to use some of the fields on the Summary tab (see Figure 6.13), in particular the Keywords field, which is displayed in the Type column in the Windows Vista Explorer.

To create a new Word document property, enter its name in the Name field (no spaces, and you should avoid using the same name as a built-in property, although Word allows this), select the data type (Text, Numeric, Date, or Yes/No), enter a default value if desired, and click the Add button. Over years of working with Word document properties, I have discovered some limitations of Word document properties and developed some workarounds to deal with them:

- If you don't specify a default value for a Text property, Word won't let you save it; instead, use a space (which is permitted) as the default value.

- Date fields should generally be avoided, except for the rare cases where you actually need a default date value, because there is no way to give them a blank default value. You can format a Text value as a date, using Word field switches.

- Numeric fields should also be avoided, both because you can't make them blank (you may not want a zero appearing in your document when the field has no data from Access), and, more importantly, because all numbers are truncated to integers. A value of 49.21 in Access will be truncated to 49 in the Word document property. As with Date values, it's best to save numeric values to a Text document property (Text values are not truncated), and then format them with the appropriate numeric format in Word.

- Yes/No properties require you to select either Yes or No as the default value; if that is unacceptable, use a Text field, possibly converting the True or False values in an Access Yes/No field to "Yes," "No," or a zero-length string ("").

FIGURE 6.13

The Summary tab of the Word properties sheet.

> **TIP** Sometimes, in Word 2007, after delving down a few levels from the new Ribbon, you will see a familiar Word 2003 dialog box. If you see a tiny diagonal arrow in the lower-right corner of a group on a Ribbon, click the arrow, then the image of the dialog, to open the familiar Word 2003 dialog box for that feature (see Figure 6.14).

Sending a Word Letter to a Single Access Contact

You may have a Contacts or Customers form in an Access database, and it would be convenient to have a quick way to create a letter to the current contact, using a command button on the form. The sample Word Export database has a form for browsing contacts, frmContacts, shown in Figure 6.15.

If you click the Word button in this form's header, a letter to the selected contact is created, filling Word document properties with data from that record.

FIGURE 6.14

Opening the old Paragraph dialog box from the new Ribbon.

FIGURE 6.15

A form for browsing contacts, with a button for creating a Word letter.

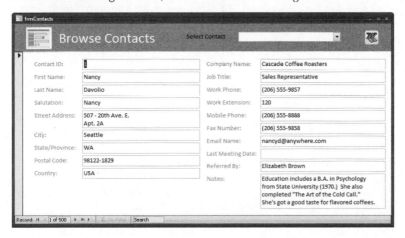

Using Word Field Switches to Format Text Data in DocProperty Fields

When you use Word document properties to merge Access data to Word documents, the values written to the document properties are displayed on the Word document in DocProperty fields. You can use field switches to format the data displayed in the DocProperty field in a variety of ways, which is going to be necessary if you follow my advice and use mostly (if not exclusively) Text document properties. The field switches needed to produce some commonly used formats are listed in the following table.

Raw Access Data	Desired Word Format	Field Code Switches
11523.75	$11,523.75	DOCPROPERTY "DollarAmount" \# $###,##0.00
2/2/2001	February 2, 2001	DOCPROPERTY "DueDate" \@ "MMMM d, yyyy"
282839898	28283-9898	DOCPROPERTY "ZipCode" \# "00000'-'0000"
829887445	829-88-7445	DOCPROPERTY "SSN" \# "000'-'00'-'0000"
150250.50	one hundred fifty thousand two hundred fifty and 50/100	DOCPROPERTY "DollarAmount" * DollarText
150250.25	ONE HUNDRED FIFTY THOUSAND TWO HUNDRED FIFTY AND 25/100	DOCPROPERTY "DollarAmount" * DollarText * Upper
150250.50	one hundred fifty thousand two hundred fifty	DOCPROPERTY "EntryAmount" * CardText
11/13/2005	Thirteenth	DOCPROPERTY "StartDate" \@ "d" * OrdText *FirstCap
11/13/2005	November	DOCPROPERTY "StartDate" \@ "MMMM"

TIP   You can create PostNet bar codes for U.S. zip codes on an envelope or label by adding a ZipCode DocProperty field to the Word template and applying a ZipCode bookmark to it. Because the WholeAddress field includes the zip code (or postal code, depending on the country), you should make the ZipCode DocProperty field invisible. To do this, select the field, open the Font Dialog by clicking the tiny arrow in the lower right of the Font group on the Word Ribbon, and check the Hidden checkbox. Next, position your cursor above the address block, select Insert ⇨ Quick Parts ⇨ Field, select the BarCode field, and then the ZipCode bookmark; leave the POSTNET bar code checkbox checked, and click OK to insert the bar code field (see the next figure).

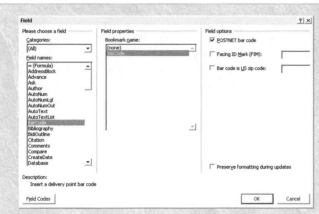

Inserting a U.S. PostNet BarCode field on a Word document.

TIP   When placing DocProperty fields in a template, make sure that the "Preserve formatting during updates" checkbox is not checked — if it is checked, and the text displayed from a doc property is longer than one word, the first word may have (probably will have, in my experience) a different font or size than the other words.

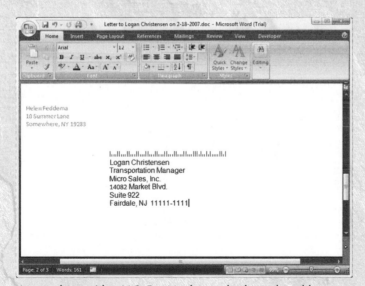

An envelope with a U.S. PostNet bar code above the address.

CROSS-REF   See the previous table for a listing of Word field switches used to format values in DocProperty fields.

The cmdWord_Click() event procedure first saves information to variables, for use later in the code, then checks that the template is found in the templates folder, sets a Word Application variable, and creates a new Word document based on the template. Next, it sets a reference to the Word CustomDocumentProperties collection of the newly created document and sets each document property to either a variable or the value in a field from the current record. The segment of code that creates a save name for the document (used in most of my export procedures) uses a Do...Loop statement to create a save name for the document containing the merged data, picking up the contact name from a field on the form, adding today's date, in a format that uses dashes to create an acceptable file name:

```
Private Sub cmdWord_Click()

On Error GoTo ErrorHandler

    Dim appWord As Word.Application
    Dim strCompanyName As String
    Dim strContactName As String
    Dim strWholeAddress As String
    Dim strJobTitle As String
    Dim docs As Word.Documents
    Dim doc As Word.Document
    Dim strWordTemplate As String
    Dim strDocsPath As String
    Dim strTemplatePath As String
    Dim prps As Object
    Dim strShortDate As String
    Dim strLongDate As String
    Dim strTest As String
    Dim strAddress As String
    Dim strCountry As String
    Dim strSaveName As String
    Dim strTestFile As String
    Dim intSaveNameFail As Boolean
    Dim i As Integer
    Dim strSaveNamePath As String
```

Check for required address information:

```
    strTest = Nz(Me![StreetAddress])
    If strTest = "" Then
        MsgBox "Can't send letter -- no address!"
        GoTo ErrorHandlerExit
    End If

    strContactName = _
        Nz(Me![ContactName])
    strCompanyName = _
        Nz(Me![CompanyName])
    strWordTemplate = "Contact Letter Doc Props.dotx"
```

```
strLongDate = Format(Date, "mmmm d, yyyy")
strShortDate = Format(Date, "m-d-yyyy")
strSaveName = "Letter to " & strContactName
strSaveName = strSaveName & " on " & strShortDate _
    & ".doc"
strDocsPath = GetContactsDocsPath()
Debug.Print "Docs path: " & strDocsPath
strTemplatePath = GetContactsTemplatesPath()
Debug.Print "Template path: " & strTemplatePath
strWordTemplate = strTemplatePath & strWordTemplate
Debug.Print "Word template and path: " _
    & strWordTemplate
```

Check for the template in the selected Contact Templates folder, and exit if it is not found:

```
strTestFile = Nz(Dir(strWordTemplate))
Debug.Print "Test file: " & strTestFile
If strTestFile = "" Then
    MsgBox strWordTemplate _
        & " template not found; can't create letter"
    GoTo ErrorHandlerExit
End If
```

Set the Word Application variable; if Word is not running, the error handler defaults to CreateObject:

```
Set appWord = GetObject(Class:="Word.Application")
Set docs = appWord.Documents
Set doc = docs.Add(strWordTemplate)
Set prps = doc.CustomDocumentProperties
```

Turn off error handler because some of the templates may not have all of the doc properties:

```
On Error Resume Next
    prps.Item("NameTitleCompany").Value = _
        Nz(Me![NameTitleCompany])
    prps.Item("WholeAddress").Value = _
        Nz(Me![WholeAddress])
    prps.Item("Salutation").Value = _
        Nz(Me![Salutation])
    prps.Item("TodayDate").Value = strLongDate
    prps.Item("CompanyName").Value = _
        strCompanyName
    prps.Item("JobTitle").Value = _
        Nz(Me![JobTitle])
    prps.Item("ZipCode").Value = _
        Nz(Me![ZipCode])
    prps.Item("ContactName").Value = strContactName

On Error GoTo ErrorHandler
```

155

Check for a previously saved letter in the documents folder, and append an incremented number to the save name if one is found:

```
i = 2
intSaveNameFail = True
Do While intSaveNameFail
    strSaveNamePath = strDocsPath & strSaveName
    Debug.Print "Proposed save name and path: " _
        & vbCrLf & strSaveNamePath
    strTestFile = Nz(Dir(strSaveNamePath))
    Debug.Print "Test file: " & strTestFile
    If strTestFile = strSaveName Then
        Debug.Print "Save name already used: " _
            & strSaveName
```

Create a new save name with the incremented number:

```
        intSaveNameFail = True
        strSaveName = "Letter " & CStr(i) & " to " & _
            Me![FirstName] & " " & Me![LastName]
        strSaveName = strSaveName & " on " & strShortDate _
            & ".doc"
        strSaveNamePath = strDocsPath & strSaveName
        Debug.Print "New save name and path: " _
            & vbCrLf & strSaveNamePath
        i = i + 1
    Else
        Debug.Print "Save name not used: " & strSaveName
        intSaveNameFail = False
    End If
Loop

With appWord
    .Visible = True
    .Selection.WholeStory
    .Selection.Fields.Update
    Debug.Print "Going to save as " & strSaveName
    .ActiveDocument.SaveAs strSaveNamePath
    .Activate
    .Selection.EndKey Unit:=wdStory
End With

ErrorHandlerExit:
    Exit Sub

ErrorHandler:
    If Err = 429 Then
        'Word is not running; open Word with CreateObject
        Set appWord = CreateObject(Class:="Word.Application")
        Resume Next
```

```
      Else
          MsgBox "Error No: " & Err.Number _
              & "; Description: " & Err.Description
          Resume ErrorHandlerExit
      End If

  End Sub
```

Figure 6.16 shows the resulting letter.

TIP   When creating Word documents in VBA code, I save the current date to the TodayDate document property in the export code, rather than inserting a date code into the Word template, to ensure that the date on the letter will always be the date the letter was created; a Date field will show the current date (the date the letter is reopened).

If the name has already been used, the code loops back and adds a number to the end of the save name, and keeps trying until an unused number is reached. This technique means that you won't overwrite documents created the same day, but instead will create a series of documents with incrementing numbers.

FIGURE 6.16

A Word letter filled with Access data from a single contact record.

If you don't want to create multiple documents, you can eliminate the Do...Loop statement and overwrite an existing file with the same name, if there is one.

Sending a Word Letter to Multiple Access Contacts

When you need to select a group of recipients for a Word letter, set of labels, or another document, you need a different interface. The form frmMergeToWord has a combo box for selecting a Word template, and a multi-select ListBox for selecting one or more contacts as recipients (see Figure 6.17).

FIGURE 6.17

A form for selecting a document and recipients for creating Word documents filled with Access data from multiple contact records.

The Select Document combo box list shows the merge type in the second column (see Figure 6.18).

The procedure on the cmdMerge button's Click event first determines that a template has been selected, and that the template can be found in the Contact Templates folder (this folder is set on the database's main menu). Next, the merge method is picked up from the third column of the combo box's list (the first column is not displayed; it contains the file name of the selected document, for use in code).

Because some of the merge documents are Word documents, and some are templates, and some are in Word 2007 format and others in Word 97/2003 format, there is an If...Then statement in the procedure that examines the original document's extension, and creates the appropriate save document extension for use as an argument for the called procedures.

A combo box for selecting a Word template for merging data from Access.

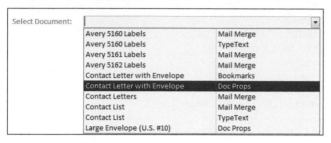

Avery 5160 Labels	Mail Merge
Avery 5160 Labels	TypeText
Avery 5161 Labels	Mail Merge
Avery 5162 Labels	Mail Merge
Contact Letter with Envelope	Bookmarks
Contact Letter with Envelope	Doc Props
Contact Letters	Mail Merge
Contact List	Mail Merge
Contact List	TypeText
Large Envelope (U.S. #10)	Doc Props

The procedure then calls one of four procedures with the document file name (including path) and extension as arguments, depending on the merge type.

The cmdCreateDocuments_Click procedure is listed as follows:

```
Private Sub cmdCreateDocuments_Click()

On Error GoTo ErrorHandler

    Dim cbo As Access.ComboBox
    Dim strCompanyName As String
    Dim strContactName As String
    Dim strJobTitle As String
    Dim strTestFile As String
    Dim strWordTemplate As String
    Dim strTest As String
    Dim strDocType As String
    Dim strMergeType As String
    Dim strExtension As String
```

Check that a document has been selected:

```
    Set cbo = Me![cboSelectDocument]
    strWordTemplate = Nz(cbo.Value)
    If strWordTemplate = "" Then
       MsgBox "Please select a document"
       cbo.SetFocus
       cbo.Dropdown
       GoTo ErrorHandlerExit
    End If

    strTemplatePath = GetContactsTemplatesPath()
    Debug.Print "Template path: " & strTemplatePath
    strWordTemplate = strTemplatePath & strWordTemplate
```

Check for the template in the selected template folder, and exit if it is not found:

```
strTestFile = Nz(Dir(strWordTemplate))
Debug.Print "Test file: " & strTestFile
If strTestFile = "" Then
   MsgBox strWordTemplate & " template not found; " _
      & "can't create document"
   GoTo ErrorHandlerExit
End If
```

Call the appropriate procedure depending on the selected merge type:

```
strMergeType = Nz(Me![cboSelectDocument].Column(2))
If Right(strWordTemplate, 1) = "x" Then
   strExtension = ".docx"
Else
   strExtension = ".doc"
End If

Select Case strMergeType

   Case "Doc Props"
      Call MergeDocProps(strWordTemplate, strExtension)

   Case "Bookmarks"
      Call MergeBookmarks(strWordTemplate, strExtension)

   Case "TypeText"
      Call MergeTypeText(strWordTemplate, strExtension)

   Case "Mail Merge"
      Call MailMerge(strWordTemplate, strExtension)

End Select

ErrorHandlerExit:
   Exit Sub

ErrorHandler:
   MsgBox "Error No: " & Err.Number _
      & "; Description: " & Err.Description
   Resume ErrorHandlerExit

End Sub
```

If a document of the Doc Props merge type is selected, the MergeDocProps procedure is called. This procedure first sets a reference to the handy ItemsSelected collection of the ListBox (this collection includes only the rows selected in the ListBox), then iterates through the collection, creating a new Word document for each contact record.

The code then sets a reference to the Word CustomDocumentProperties collection of the newly created document, and sets each document property to the value in a column of the current row from the ListBox. A save name is created, including the document title, contact name, company name, and date, and the document is saved:

```
Private Sub MergeDocProps(strWordTemplate As String, _
    strExtension As String)

On Error GoTo ErrorHandler

    strLongDate = Format(Date, "mmmm d, yyyy")
    strShortDate = Format(Date, "m-d-yyyy")
    strDocsPath = GetContactsDocsPath()
    Debug.Print "Docs path: " & strDocsPath
```

Check that at least one contact has been selected:

```
    Set lst = Me![lstSelectContacts]

    If lst.ItemsSelected.Count = 0 Then
        MsgBox "Please select at least one contact"
        lst.SetFocus
        GoTo ErrorHandlerExit
    End If

    intColumns = lst.ColumnCount
    intRows = lst.ItemsSelected.Count

    For Each varItem In lst.ItemsSelected
```

Check for required address information:

```
        strTest = Nz(lst.Column(5, varItem))
        Debug.Print "Street address: " & strTest
        If strTest = "" Then
            Debug.Print "Skipping this record -- no address!"
            GoTo ErrorHandlerExit
        End If

        strTest = Nz(lst.Column(1, varItem))
        Debug.Print "Contact name: " & strTest
        If strTest = "" Then
            Debug.Print _
                "Skipping this record -- no contact name!"
            GoTo ErrorHandlerExit
        End If

        strContactName = _
            Nz(lst.Column(1, varItem))
        strCompanyName = _
            Nz(lst.Column(7, varItem))
```

Open a new document based on the selected template:

```
Set appWord = GetObject(Class:="Word.Application")
appWord.Documents.Add strWordTemplate
```

Write information to Word custom document properties:

```
Set prps = _
    appWord.ActiveDocument.CustomDocumentProperties
```

Turn off error handler because some templates don't have all of the doc properties:

```
On Error Resume Next
    prps.Item("NameTitleCompany").Value = _
        Nz(lst.Column(2, varItem))
    prps.Item("WholeAddress").Value = _
        Nz(lst.Column(5, varItem))
    prps.Item("Salutation").Value = _
        Nz(lst.Column(10, varItem))
    prps.Item("TodayDate").Value = strLongDate
    prps.Item("CompanyName").Value = _
        strCompanyName
    prps.Item("JobTitle").Value = _
        Nz(lst.Column(8, varItem))
    prps.Item("ZipCode").Value = _
        Nz(lst.Column(6, varItem))
    prps.Item("ContactName").Value = strContactName

On Error GoTo ErrorHandler
```

Check for a previously saved document in the documents folder, and append an incremented number to the save name if one is found:

```
strDocType = _
    appWord.ActiveDocument. _
        BuiltInDocumentProperties(wdPropertyTitle)
strSaveName = strDocType & " to " _
    & strContactName & " - " & strCompanyName
strSaveName = strSaveName & " on " _
    & strShortDate & strExtension
i = 2
intSaveNameFail = True
Do While intSaveNameFail
    strSaveNamePath = strDocsPath & strSaveName
    Debug.Print "Proposed save name and path: " _
        & vbCrLf & strSaveNamePath
    strTestFile = Nz(Dir(strSaveNamePath))
    Debug.Print "Test file: " & strTestFile
    If strTestFile = strSaveName Then
        Debug.Print "Save name already used: " _
            & strSaveName
```

Create a new save name with the incremented number:

```
                    intSaveNameFail = True
                    strSaveName = strDocType & " " & CStr(i) _
                        & " to " & strContactName & " - " _
                        & strCompanyName
                    strSaveName = strSaveName & " on " _
                        & strShortDate & strExtension
                    strSaveNamePath = strDocsPath & strSaveName
                    Debug.Print "New save name and path: " _
                        & vbCrLf & strSaveNamePath
                    i = i + 1
                Else
                    Debug.Print "Save name not used: " & strSaveName
                    intSaveNameFail = False
                End If
        NextContact:
            Loop
```

Update fields in Word document and save it:

```
        Re-hide ZipCode field
            With appWord.Selection
                .GoTo What:=wdGoToBookmark, Name:="ZipCode"
                .Find.ClearFormatting
                .Font.Hidden = True
            End With
                With appWord
                    .Selection.WholeStory
                    .Selection.Fields.Update
                    .Selection HomeKey unit:=wdStory
                    .ActiveDocument.SaveAs strSaveNamePath
                End With
            Next varItem

        With appWord
            .ActiveWindow.WindowState = wdWindowStateNormal
            .Visible = True
            .Activate
        End With

    ErrorHandlerExit:
        Exit Sub

    ErrorHandler:
        If Err = 429 Then
            'Word is not running; open Word with CreateObject
            Set appWord = CreateObject(Class:="Word.Application")
            Resume Next
```

```
    Else
       MsgBox "Error No: " & Err.Number _
           & "; Description: " & Err.Description
       Resume ErrorHandlerExit
    End If

End Sub
```

> **TIP**   For a list of the built-in Word named constants that can be used as arguments for functions or methods, or set as the values of properties, look up the appropriate enumeration (enum) in the Object Browser. Word enums start with Wd and are at the bottom of the Classes list. For example, to see what named constants can be used for the WindowState property of the ActiveWindow property, look up the WdWindowState enum, which is shown in Figure 6.19.

FIGURE 6.19

Examining the WdWindowState enum in the Object Browser.

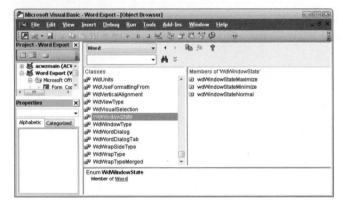

The cmdDeselectAll_Click procedure, run from the Clear All Selections command button, deselects all the rows in the listbox, even the ones you can't see, so you can start fresh:

```
Private Sub cmdDeselectAll_Click()

On Error GoTo ErrorHandler

    Set lst = Me![lstSelectContacts]

    intRows = lst.ListCount - 1
```

```
    For intIndex = 0 To intRows
        lst.Selected(intIndex) = False
    Next intIndex

ErrorHandlerExit:
    Exit Sub

ErrorHandler:
    MsgBox "Error No: " & Err.Number _
        & "; Description: " & Err.Description
    Resume ErrorHandlerExit

End Sub
```

The cmdSelectAll_Click procedure, run from the Select All Names command button, selects all the rows in the listbox; its code is similar, setting the Selected value to True instead of False.

Clicking the Clear All Selections command button clears any selections you have made in the list-box; clicking the Create Documents command button starts the merge, calling one of four procedures, depending on the merge type.

Word Bookmarks

If you select the Contact Letter with Envelope (Bookmarks) template from the Select Document combo box on frmMergeToWord, you will get a set of individual letters, one to each selected contact, with bookmarks filled with Access data. One of these letters is shown in Figure 6.20 (I made bookmarks visible so you can see their locations; note the gray I-bars).

The MergeBookmarks procedure (listed next) is basically similar to the MergeDocProps code listed in an earlier section; the difference is that instead of working with the CustomDocumentProperties collection, it works with the Bookmarks collection, writing information from either variables or the listbox to named bookmarks in the newly created Word document:

```
Private Sub MergeBookmarks(strWordTemplate As String, _
    strExtension As String)

On Error GoTo ErrorHandler

    strLongDate = Format(Date, "mmmm d, yyyy")
    strShortDate = Format(Date, "m-d-yyyy")
    strDocsPath = GetContactsDocsPath()
    Debug.Print "Docs path: " & strDocsPath
```

FIGURE 6.20

A Word document with Access data displayed in bookmarks.

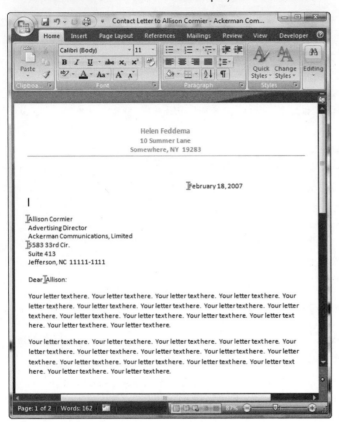

Check that at least one contact has been selected:

```
Set lst = Me![lstSelectContacts]

If lst.ItemsSelected.Count = 0 Then
   MsgBox "Please select at least one contact"
   lst.SetFocus
   GoTo ErrorHandlerExit
End If

intColumns = lst.ColumnCount
intRows = lst.ItemsSelected.Count

For Each varItem In lst.ItemsSelected
```

Check for required address information:

```
strTest = Nz(lst.Column(5, varItem))
Debug.Print "Street address: " & strTest
If strTest = "" Then
   Debug.Print "Skipping this record -- no address!"
   GoTo NextContact
End If

strTest = Nz(lst.Column(1, varItem))
Debug.Print "Contact name: " & strTest
If strTest = "" Then
   Debug.Print _
      "Skipping this record -- no contact name!"
   GoTo NextContact
End If

strContactName = _
   Nz(lst.Column(1, varItem))
strCompanyName = _
   Nz(lst.Column(7, varItem))
strNameTitleCompany = _
   Nz(lst.Column(2, varItem))
strWholeAddress = _
   Nz(lst.Column(5, varItem))
```

Open a new document based on the selected template:

```
Set appWord = GetObject(Class:="Word.Application")
appWord.Documents.Add strWordTemplate
```

Write information to Word bookmarks, first turning off the error handler because some templates
don't have all of these bookmarks:

```
On Error Resume Next
   With appWord.Selection
      .GoTo what:=wdGoToBookmark, _
         Name:="NameTitleCompany"
      .TypeText Text:=strNameTitleCompany
      .GoTo what:=wdGoToBookmark, _
         Name:="WholeAddress"
      .TypeText Text:=strWholeAddress
      .GoTo what:=wdGoToBookmark, Name:="Salutation"
      .TypeText Text:=Nz(lst.Column(10, varItem))
      .GoTo what:=wdGoToBookmark, Name:="TodayDate"
      .TypeText Text:=strLongDate
```

```
        .GoTo what:=wdGoToBookmark, _
            Name:="EnvelopeNameTitleCompany"
        .TypeText Text:=strNameTitleCompany
        .GoTo what:=wdGoToBookmark, _
            Name:="EnvelopeWholeAddress"
        .TypeText Text:=strWholeAddress
        .GoTo what:=wdGoToBookmark, Name:="ZipCode"
        .TypeText Text:=Nz(lst.Column(6, varItem))
    End With
```

Re-insert bookmark:

```
With appWord.Selection
        .MoveLeft _
            unit:=wdWord, Count:=3, _
            Extend:=wdExtend
        .Font.Hidden = True
    End With
```

```
Re-hide zip code.
        With ActiveDocument.Bookmarks
            .Add Range:=Selection.Range, Name:="ZipCode"
            .DefaultSorting = wdSortByName
            .ShowHidden = False
        End With
```

```
    On Error GoTo ErrorHandler
```

Check for a previously saved document in the documents folder, and append an incremented number to the save name if one is found:

```
        strDocType = _
            appWord.ActiveDocument.
                BuiltInDocumentProperties(wdPropertyTitle)
        strSaveName = strDocType & " to " _
            & strContactName & " - " & strCompanyName
        strSaveName = strSaveName & " on " _
            & strShortDate & strExtension
        i = 2
        intSaveNameFail = True
        Do While intSaveNameFail
            strSaveNamePath = strDocsPath & strSaveName
            Debug.Print "Proposed save name and path: " _
                & vbCrLf & strSaveNamePath
            strTestFile = Nz(Dir(strSaveNamePath))
            Debug.Print "Test file: " & strTestFile
            If strTestFile = strSaveName Then
                Debug.Print "Save name already used: " _
                    & strSaveName
```

Create a new save name with the incremented number:

```
                intSaveNameFail = True
                strSaveName = strDocType & " " & CStr(i) _
                    & " to " & strContactName & " - " _
                    & strCompanyName
                strSaveName = strSaveName & " on " _
                    & strShortDate & strExtension
                strSaveNamePath = strDocsPath & strSaveName
                Debug.Print "New save name and path: " _
                    & vbCrLf & strSaveNamePath
                i = i + 1
            Else
                Debug.Print "Save name not used: " & strSaveName
                intSaveNameFail = False
            End If
    NextContact:
        Loop
```

Update fields in Word document and save it:

```
        With appWord
            .Selection.WholeStory
            .Selection.Fields.Update
            .Selection.HomeKey unit:=wdStory
            .ActiveDocument.SaveAs strSaveNamePath
        End With

    Next varItem

    With appWord
        .ActiveWindow.WindowState = wdWindowStateNormal
        .Visible = True
        .Activate
    End With

ErrorHandlerExit:
    Exit Sub

ErrorHandler:
    If Err = 429 Then
        'Word is not running; open Word with CreateObject
        Set appWord = CreateObject(Class:="Word.Application")
        Resume Next
    Else
        MsgBox "Error No: " & Err.Number _
            & "; Description: " & Err.Description
        Resume ErrorHandlerExit
    End If

End Sub
```

The TypeText Method

For simple documents such as mailing labels, where you just need to insert a block of text from Access, without fancy formatting, the TypeText method of the Word Selection object can be useful. If you select the Avery 5160 (TypeText) selection from the Select Document combo box on frmMergeToWord, you will get a Word document in the form of a table with cells of the right size to print on the label sheets, as shown in Figure 6.21.

FIGURE 6.21

An Avery 5160 labels document filled with data from Access.

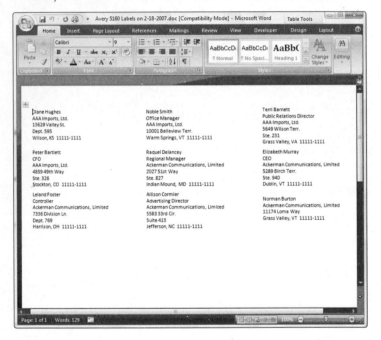

NEW FEATURE   You can also create a list-type document using the TypeText method, filling a table with data from Access records, one record per row. Figure 6.22 shows such a document, using one of the new Word 2007 table themes and the new banded rows feature.

The `MergeTypeText` procedure (listed as follows) writes data from variables directly to cells in a table, moving to the next cell using the `MoveRight` method:

```
Private Sub MergeTypeText(strWordTemplate As String, _
    strExtension As String)

On Error GoTo ErrorHandler
```

170

```
Dim intMod As Integer
Dim lngCount As Long
Dim lngSkip As Long
Dim doc as Word.Document

strLongDate = Format(Date, "mmmm d, yyyy")
strShortDate = Format(Date, "m-d-yyyy")
strDocsPath = GetContactsDocsPath()
Debug.Print "Docs path: " & strDocsPath
```

Open a new document based on the selected labels template:

```
Set appWord = GetObject(Class:="Word.Application")
Set doc = appWord.Documents.Add(strWordTemplate)
```

FIGURE 6.22

A Contact list filled with data from Access, showing new Word 2007 formatting features.

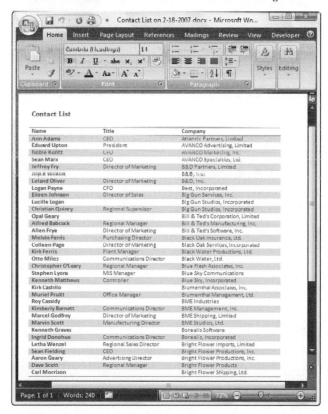

Determine whether the template is for labels or list, and move to the first data cell in table if needed:

```
If Nz(InStr(strWordTemplate, "List")) > 0 Then
   appWord.Selection.GoTo what:=wdGoToTable, _
      which:=wdGoToFirst, _
      Count:=1
   appWord.Selection.MoveDown unit:=wdLine, _
      Count:=1
End If
```

Set the `intMod` value depending on the number of cells per row:

```
strDocType = _
     doc.BuiltInDocumentProperties(wdPropertyTitle)
   Select Case strDocType

      Case "Avery 5160 Labels"
         intMod = 3

      Case "Avery 5161 Labels"
         intMod = 2

      Case "Avery 5162 Labels"
         intMod = 2

   End Select
```

Check that at least one contact has been selected:

```
Set lst = Me![lstSelectContacts]

If lst.ItemsSelected.Count = 0 Then
   MsgBox "Please select at least one contact"
   lst.SetFocus
   GoTo ErrorHandlerExit
End If

intColumns = lst.ColumnCount
intRows = lst.ItemsSelected.Count

For Each varItem In lst.ItemsSelected
```

Check for required information:

```
strTest = Nz(lst.Column(1, varItem))
Debug.Print "Contact name: " & strTest
If strTest = "" Then
   Debug.Print _
      "Skipping this record -- no contact name!"
   GoTo NextContact
```

```
End If

strNameTitleCompany = _
    Nz(lst.Column(2, varItem))
strWholeAddress = _
    Nz(lst.Column(5, varItem))
strContactName = _
    Nz(lst.Column(1, varItem))
strCompanyName = _
    Nz(lst.Column(7, varItem))
strJobTitle = Nz(lst.Column(8, varItem))
```

Process differently depending on whether the template is for labels or a list:

```
If Nz(InStr(strWordTemplate, "List")) > 0 Then
```

Insert data into list:

```
With appWord.Selection
    .TypeText Text:=strContactName
    .MoveRight unit:=wdCell, Count:=1
    .TypeText Text:=strJobTitle
    .MoveRight unit:=wdCell, Count:=1
    .TypeText Text:=strCompanyName
    .MoveRight unit:=wdCell, Count:=1
End With

ElseIf Nz(InStr(strWordTemplate, "Labels")) > 0 Then
    lngCount = lngCount + 1
```

Insert data into labels, skipping narrow spacer columns:

```
With appWord.Selection
    .TypeText Text:=strNameTitleCompany
    .TypeParagraph
    .TypeText Text:=strWholeAddress
    .TypeParagraph
```

Use the Mod operator to handle every second or third record differently, in order to write data only to valid cells:

```
    lngSkip = lngCount Mod intMod
    If lngSkip <> 0 Then
        .MoveRight unit:=wdCell, Count:=2
    ElseIf lngSkip = 0 Then
        .MoveRight unit:=wdCell, Count:=1
    End If
End With
End If
```

```
NextContact:
   Next varItem

   If Nz(InStr(strWordTemplate, "List")) > 0 Then
```

Delete redundant last (blank) row:

```
      With appWord.Selection
         .SelectRow
         .Rows.Delete
         .HomeKey unit:=wdStory
      End With
   End If
```

Check for the previously saved document in the documents folder, and append an incremented number to the save name if one is found:

```
   strDocType = _
appWord.ActiveDocument.BuiltInDocumentProperties(wdPropertyTitle)
   strSaveName = strDocType & " on " _
      & strShortDate & strExtension
   i = 2
   intSaveNameFail = True
   Do While intSaveNameFail
      strSaveNamePath = strDocsPath & strSaveName
      Debug.Print "Proposed save name and path: " _
         & vbCrLf & strSaveNamePath
      strTestFile = Nz(Dir(strSaveNamePath))
      Debug.Print "Test file: " & strTestFile
      If strTestFile = strSaveName Then
         Debug.Print "Save name already used: " _
            & strSaveName
```

Create a new save name with the incremented number:

```
         intSaveNameFail = True
         strSaveName = strDocType & " " & CStr(i) & " on " _
            & strShortDate & strExtension
         strSaveNamePath = strDocsPath & strSaveName
         Debug.Print "New save name and path: " _
            & vbCrLf & strSaveNamePath
         i = i + 1
      Else
         Debug.Print "Save name not used: " & strSaveName
         intSaveNameFail = False
      End If
   Loop
```

Save Word document:

```
appWord.ActiveDocument.SaveAs strSaveNamePath

With appWord
   .ActiveWindow.WindowState = wdWindowStateNormal
   .Visible = True
   .Activate
End With
```

```
ErrorHandlerExit:
   Exit Sub
```

```
ErrorHandler:
   If Err = 429 Then
```

Word is not running; open Word with `CreateObject`:

```
      Set appWord = CreateObject(Class:="Word.Application")
      Resume Next
   Else
      MsgBox "Error No: " & Err.Number _
         & "; Description: " & Err.Description
      Resume ErrorHandlerExit
   End If
End Sub
```

Word Mail Merge

You can link a Word merge document directly to an Access table or query; however, there are some drawbacks to this method. The merge document won't open unless the Access database is available and is in the same location as when the merge data source was selected. Because of this limitation, when using mail merge I prefer to export the Access data to a text file, and assign the newly created text file as the merge document's data source. This means that the document can be opened without Access being available, and without the need to establish a link to a database.

Mailing Labels

Sheets of mailing labels are very suitable for mail merge; you can select three types of Avery mailing labels (Mail Merge type) from the Select Document combo box on frmMergeToWord. If you select the Avery 5160 Labels (Mail Merge) document, you will get a Word document like the one shown in Figure 6.23.

The Avery labels documents look (and work) exactly the same whether produced by mail merge or the `TypeText` method, so I prefer to use the `TypeText` method, because it is much simpler to set up a plain labels document than a mail merge document; all you have to do is create a labels-type document in Word, whereas creating a mail merge document requires manually linking to a data source and inserting merge fields.

FIGURE 6.23

An Avery 5161 mailing labels merge document filled with Access data.

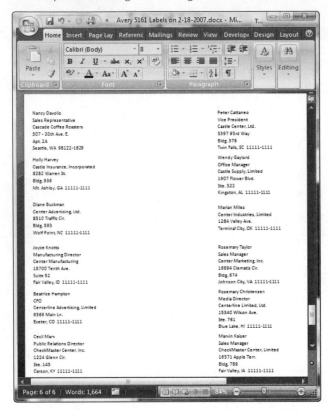

Lists

The Word Catalog-type merge is very useful for producing lists of merged data. Selecting the Contact List (Mail Merge) document (this is a Word 97/2003 document, used in Compatibility mode) from the Select Document combo box on frmMergeToWord creates a list in tabular form, shown in Figure 6.24.

Documents

You can use mail merge to create a merge document, where each page displays data from one contact record. I prefer to use the document properties or bookmarks method, in order to have a separate document for each contact, but if you have many hundreds (or thousands) of documents to generate, this is not practical. The Contact Letters (Mail Merge) selection in the Select Document combo box creates a mail merge document with a letter on each page; Figure 6.25 shows one page of this merge document.

FIGURE 6.24

The Contact List filled with merged data from Access.

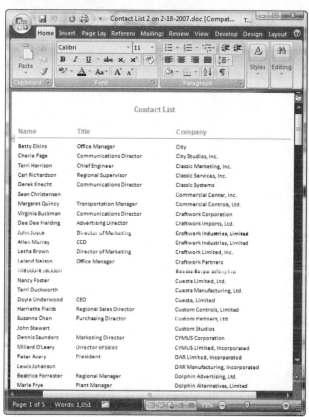

If a merge document with the Merge Data.txt data source is open, if you try to create another merge document bound to the same data source, you will get an error message saying that `Merge Data.txt` already exists, and you won't be able to continue. To prevent this from happening, the mail merge code closes the original merge document after merging the data to a new document.

The `MailMergeTextFile` procedure is listed as follows. This procedure first fills an Access table with data from the ItemsSelected collection of the ListBox, and then exports the data from that table to a text file, `Merge Data.txt`, which is used as the data source for the mail merge document. The merge is executed to a new document (so the document can be opened later, without needing the data source) and saved to a name picked up from the template's Title field and the date, formatted with dashes to avoid file name problems:

FIGURE 6.25

The third page of a mail merge form letters document.

```vba
Private Sub MailMergeTextFile(strWordTemplate As String, _
    strExtension As String)

On Error GoTo ErrorHandler

    Dim rst As DAO.Recordset
    Dim dbs As DAO.Database
    Dim strDBPath As String
    Dim strTextFile As String
    Dim strDocName As String
    Dim strSalutation As String
    Dim strZipCode As String
    Dim strSQL As String
    Dim strTable As String
```

```
strLongDate = Format(Date, "mmmm d, yyyy")
strShortDate = Format(Date, "m-d-yyyy")
strDocsPath = GetContactsDocsPath()
Debug.Print "Docs path: " & strDocsPath
strTemplatePath = GetContactsTemplatesPath()
```

Check that at least two contacts have been selected, because there is no point of doing a mail merge to only one contact:

```
Set lst = Me![lstSelectContacts]

If lst.ItemsSelected.Count < 0 Then
   MsgBox "Please select at least one contact"
   lst.SetFocus
   GoTo ErrorHandlerExit
End If
```

Clear the merge data table of old data:

```
DoCmd.SetWarnings False
strTable = "tblMergeData"
strSQL = "DELETE * FROM " & strTable
DoCmd.RunSQL strSQL
```

Create a recordset based on the table of merge data:

```
Set dbs = CurrentDb
Set rst = dbs.OpenRecordset(Name:=strTable)

intColumns = lst.ColumnCount
intRows = lst.ItemsSelected.Count

For Each varItem In lst.ItemsSelected
```

Check for required address information:

```
strTest = Nz(lst.Column(5, varItem))
Debug.Print "Street address: " & strTest
If strTest = "" Then
   Debug.Print "Skipping this record -- no address!"
   GoTo NextContact
End If

strTest = Nz(lst.Column(1, varItem))
Debug.Print "Contact name: " & strTest
If strTest = "" Then
   Debug.Print _
      "Skipping this record -- no contact name!"
   GoTo NextContact
End If
```

```
strContactName = _
    Nz(lst.Column(1, varItem))
strCompanyName = _
    Nz(lst.Column(7, varItem))
strNameTitleCompany = _
    Nz(lst.Column(2, varItem))
strWholeAddress = Nz(lst.Column(5, varItem))
strSalutation = Nz(lst.Column(10, varItem))
strJobTitle = Nz(lst.Column(8, varItem))
strZipCode = Nz(lst.Column(6, varItem))
```

Add records to the table from the selected items in the ListBox:

```
With rst
    .AddNew
    ![NameTitleCompany] = strNameTitleCompany
    ![WholeAddress] = strWholeAddress
    ![Salutation] = strSalutation
    ![TodayDate] = strLongDate
    ![CompanyName] = strCompanyName
    ![JobTitle] = strJobTitle
    ![ZipCode] = strZipCode
    ![ContactName] = strContactName
    .Update
End With

NextContact:
    Next varItem
    rst.Close
```

Export the merge table data to a text file, to be used as the mail merge document's data source:

```
strTextFile = strTemplatePath & "Merge Data.txt"
Debug.Print "Text file for merge: " & strTextFile
DoCmd.TransferText transfertype:=acExportDelim, _
    TableName:=strTable, _
    FileName:=strTextFile, _
    HasFieldNames:=True
```

Open a new merge document based on the selected template:

```
Set appWord = GetObject(Class:="Word.Application")
appWord.Documents.Add strWordTemplate
appWord.Visible = True
strDocName = appWord.ActiveDocument.Name
Debug.Print "Initial doc name: " & strDocName
```

Check for a previously saved document in the documents folder, and append an incremented number to the save name if one is found:

```
strDocType = _
   appWord.ActiveDocument.
      BuiltInDocumentProperties(wdPropertyTitle)
strSaveName = strDocType & " on " _
   & strShortDate & strExtension
i = 2
intSaveNameFail = True
Do While intSaveNameFail
   strSaveNamePath = strDocsPath & strSaveName
   Debug.Print "Proposed save name and path: " _
      & vbCrLf & strSaveNamePath
   strTestFile = Nz(Dir(strSaveNamePath))
   Debug.Print "Test file: " & strTestFile
   If strTestFile = strSaveName Then
      Debug.Print "Save name already used: " _
         & strSaveName
```

Create a new save name with the incremented number:

```
      intSaveNameFail = True
      strSaveName = strDocType & " " & CStr(i) & " on " _
         & strShortDate & strExtension
      strSaveNamePath = strDocsPath & strSaveName
      Debug.Print "New save name and path: " _
         & vbCrLf & strSaveNamePath
      i = i + 1
   Else
      Debug.Print "Save name not used: " & strSaveName
      intSaveNameFail = False
   End If
Loop
```

Set the merge data source to the text file just created, and do the merge:

```
With appWord
   .ActiveDocument.MailMerge.OpenDataSource _
      Name:=strTextFile, _
      Format:=wdOpenFormatText
   .ActiveDocument.MailMerge.Destination = _
      wdSendToNewDocument
   .ActiveDocument.MailMerge.Execute
```

Save the newly created merge document:

```
.ActiveDocument.SaveAs strSaveNamePath
```

Close the master merge document:

```
.Documents(strDocName).Close _
    SaveChanges:=wdDoNotSaveChanges
End With

ErrorHandlerExit:
    Exit Sub

ErrorHandler:
    If Err = 429 Then
```

Word is not running; open Word with `CreateObject`:

```
    Set appWord = CreateObject(Class:="Word.Application")
    Resume Next
Else
    MsgBox "Error No: " & Err.Number _
        & "; Description: " & Err.Description
    Resume ErrorHandlerExit
End If

End Sub
```

Summary

Now you know how to export Access data to various types of Word documents, both in the interface and in VBA code, you can produce highly formatted Word documents filled with Access data. Microsoft promotes mail merge, but in my opinion it is best to avoid this method (especially in Office 2007 and Windows Vista), because of the problems it has with security features. With the three other techniques covered in this chapter, you will know how to produce almost any type of document using other methods, and avoid the problems with locked or unavailable databases when using mail merge when it is needed.

Chapter 7

Working with Excel Worksheets

Just as you might want to export Access data to Word documents to take advantage of their superior formatting and transportability, you may also want (or need) to export Access data to Excel worksheets, so users can review, edit, or add data, or perform various numerical calculations, in a familiar and widely used format (all Office users have Excel, whereas only some have Access). Excel worksheets are often used for entering and analyzing numerical (and text) data, such as timesheets, applications, and other forms. Or you may want to export Access data to a simple rows-and-columns worksheet, so that users can manipulate the data in various ways and produce charts based on the data, using the tools in Excel.

This chapter describes how you can export data to Excel spreadsheets for a variety of purposes. You can export Access data to Excel using a command on the new Ribbon, or use the `TransferSpreadsheet` method in a single line of code to do a basic export of all the data in a table or query to a plain worksheet, or write more complex VBA Automation code to create a fully formatted worksheet filled with Access data.

IN THIS CHAPTER

The Excel object model

Creating worksheets from the Ribbon

Creating worksheets from templates

Formatting worksheets in VBA code

Filling Excel worksheets with Access timesheet data

> **NOTE** Strictly speaking, an .xls (or the new .xlsx) file is a *workbook*; each workbook contains one or more *worksheets*. However, in general parlance you will hear (and read) *worksheet* used to reference an .xls file, a practice carried over from the earliest days of Excel, before workbooks were added to the interface. I will follow that usage except when it is necessary to distinguish between a workbook and a worksheet, such as in describing how a procedure works.

Simply Exporting Access Data to Excel

Just as in earlier Office versions, Access offers two ways to do a quick-and-dirty export of table or query data to an Excel worksheet. You can use the Excel button in the Export group of the External Data tab of the Ribbon to export Access data without worrying about formatting, for an Office 2007 user who just wants the data. If you need to create worksheets that can be opened and edited by users running older versions of Office, or using a handheld device such as a BlackBerry, you can use the `TransferSpreadsheet` method to export data, selecting the desired output worksheet format. This can be useful when you work for an organization that has upgraded its software and you need to send a worksheet with client contact information to a sales representative who has not updated her laptop yet.

For a quick export to the new .xlsx worksheet format, use the Excel button in the Export group of the External Data tab of the new Access Ribbon, as shown in Figure 7.1.

FIGURE 7.1

Exporting a table to an Excel worksheet from the Ribbon.

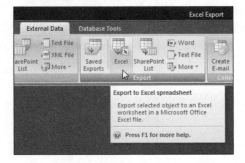

Clicking the Excel button opens a dialog where you can browse for the location for saving the worksheet. This dialog has an option for preserving the layout and formatting of the original Access object, which (curiously) is only available if a table or query is selected (see Figure 7.2).

Tables and queries don't have much in the way of formatting and layout, but if you check the "Export data with formatting and layout" checkbox your Excel worksheet will use the same font as the table or query (though not the alternate row shading), and it will show data from a linked table instead of the linking ID field. Figure 7.3 shows two worksheets made from the same table; the top one displays the customers' company name in the CustomerID column (picking it up from the linked table) and uses the Calibri 11 font; the second worksheet displays the CustomerID in that column and uses the Arial 10 font.

FIGURE 7.2

The options when exporting a table to an Excel worksheet.

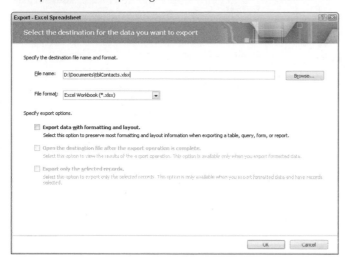

FIGURE 7.3

Excel worksheets exported with and without checking the "Export data with formatting and layout" option on the export dialog.

The Excel button on the Ribbon (with or without the layout and formatting preserved) is a useful option when you need to create a quick-and-dirty Excel worksheet in Excel 2007 format (the new extension is .xlsx). If you need to export to an older Excel format, but you don't need fancy formatting, you can do an export with a single line of VBA code, using the `TransferSpreadsheet` method, which has been available since the earliest days of Access.

The `TransferSpreadsheet` method allows you to select the Excel version for creating your worksheet filled with Access data, so you can create worksheets that will be usable by recipients who have older versions of Office. The procedure listed as follows exports tblContacts to an Excel 97-2003 worksheet called Contacts.xls (the named constant for this worksheet version is `acSpreadsheetTypeExcel7`):

```
Public Function TransferToExcel()

On Error GoTo ErrorHandler

    Dim strTable As String
    Dim strWorksheetPath As String

    strWorksheetPath = GetWorksheetsPath
    strWorksheetPath = strWorksheetPath & "Contacts.xls"
    strTable = "tblContacts"
    strWorksheetPath = GetWorksheetsPath()
    strWorksheetPath = strWorksheetPath & "Contacts.xls"
    Debug.Print "Worksheet path: " & strWorksheetPath
```

Export table data to a new worksheet:

```
    DoCmd.TransferSpreadsheet transfertype:=acExport, _
        spreadsheettype:=acSpreadsheetTypeExcel7, _
        TableName:=strTable, FileName:=strWorksheetPath, _
        hasfieldnames:=True


ErrorHandlerExit:
    Exit Sub

ErrorHandler:
    MsgBox "Error No: " & Err.Number _
        & "; Description: " & Err.Description
    Resume ErrorHandlerExit

End Sub
```

The exported worksheet looks just like the unformatted worksheet exported from the Ribbon selection, but it is in the older format, as you can see from the "(Compatibility Mode)" after the worksheet name in its title bar (see Figure 7.4).

FIGURE 7.4

An Access table exported to an Excel 97-2003 worksheet.

The Excel Object Model

The two export options described in the previous section are fine for creating a simple, minimally formatted or unformatted worksheet filled with data from an Access table or query, but if you need to create fully formatted worksheets, such as personnel forms, timesheets, sales reports, factory production data reports, and so forth, you will need to work with the Excel object model to create worksheets using Automation code, fill them with Access data, and then apply formatting, using components of the Excel object model.

NOTE The Excel Export.accdb sample database contains the tables, queries, forms, and code used in this chapter.

The `CreateObject` and `GetObject` functions are used to either create a new Excel object, or set a reference to an existing instance of Excel. Using `GetObject` to retrieve a reference to an existing workbook avoids creating extra instances of Excel, which uses up system resources. To open a worksheet within a workbook, first set a reference to the Workbook object, then add a new workbook to the Workbooks collection. By default, the new workbook will have three worksheets. The `CreateNewWorkbook` procedure creates a new, blank workbook from the default Excel template, with three worksheets:

```
Public Function CreateNewWorkbook ()

On Error GoTo ErrorHandler

    Dim appExcel As Excel.Application
    Dim bks As Excel.Workbooks

    Set appExcel = GetObject(, "Excel.Application")
    Set bks = appExcel.Workbooks
```

Create and open a new, blank workbook:

```
bks.Add
```

Make the workbook visible:

```
appExcel.Application.Visible = True

ErrorHandlerExit:
    Exit Sub

ErrorHandler:
    If Err = 429 Then
```

Excel is not running; open Excel with `CreateObject`:

```
        Set appExcel = CreateObject("Excel.Application")
        Resume Next
    Else
        MsgBox "Error No: " & Err.Number & "; Description: " & _
Err.Description
        Resume ErrorHandlerExit
    End If

End Sub
```

NOTE   The procedures in this section can be run from macros; each procedure has a macro whose name is `mcr` plus the procedure name.

The error handler in the preceding procedure is similar to the one used in the Word Automation code in Chapter 6; sets a reference to the current Excel instance if Excel is running and otherwise creates a new Excel Application instance using the `CreateObject` function from a line in the procedure's error handler. If you run the `CreateNewWorkbook` procedure repeatedly, each time it runs a new workbook is created within the Excel window, named Book1, Book2, and so forth, as shown in Figure 7.5.

FIGURE 7.5

Three workbooks in the Excel window.

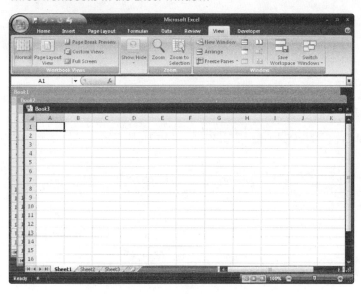

To open a specific saved workbook, use a procedure like the one listed next, which opens a saved workbook using the Worksheets collection's Open method and the file name and path:

```
Public Function OpenSpecificWorkbook()

On Error GoTo ErrorHandler

    Dim appExcel As Excel.Application
    Dim bks As Excel.Workbooks
    Dim sht As Excel.Worksheet
    Dim strWorkbook As String

    Set appExcel = GetObject(, "Excel.Application")
    strPrompt = "Enter path and title of workbook"
    strTitle = "Workbook Name"
    strDefault = "D:\Documents\tblContacts2.xls"

    strWorkbook = InputBox(prompt:=strPrompt, _
        Title:=strTitle, Default:=strDefault)
    appExcel.Workbooks.Open (strWorkbook)
    Set sht = appExcel.ActiveWorkbook.Sheets(1)
```

```
        sht.Activate
        appExcel.Application.Visible = True


ErrorHandlerExit:
    Exit Sub

ErrorHandler:
    If Err = 429 Then
```

Excel is not running; open Excel with `CreateObject`:

```
        Set appExcel = CreateObject("Excel.Application")
        Resume Next
    Else
        MsgBox "Error No: " & Err.Number & "; Description: " &
Err.Description
        Resume ErrorHandlerExit
    End If

End Sub
```

If Excel is open, the workbook will be opened in the same window, as shown in Figure 7.6.

FIGURE 7.6

Opening a saved workbook in an existing Excel window.

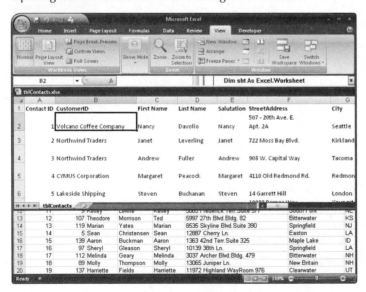

If Excel is not running, the workbook will open in a new Excel window.

As with exporting Access data to Word, when writing Automation code to work with Excel, you only need a few components of the Excel object model: Workbooks, Worksheets, the Range object, Rows, and Columns. These objects are used in the more complex Excel Automation procedures in the following sections.

Minimally Formatted Worksheets

If you need to create a simple tabular worksheet listing the contacts in qryContacts, with minimal formatting, you can create a new workbook in VBA code, from a saved workbook template with a title, correctly sized columns, and the font and other layout of your choice, and fill it with Access data. The `ExportContactsToExcel` procedure creates a recordset based on qryContacts, and exports selected fields from each record in that query to a workbook created from a template, with a title, column headings, and some minimal formatting:

```
Public Function ExportContactsToExcel()

On Error GoTo ErrorHandler

    Dim dbs As DAO.Database
    Dim rst As DAO.Recordset
    Dim strWorksheetPath As String
    Dim appExcel As Excel.Application
    Dim strTemplatePath As String
    Dim bks As Excel.Workbooks
    Dim rng As Excel.Range
    Dim rngStart As Excel.Range
    Dim strTemplateFile As String
    Dim wkb As Excel.Workbook
    Dim wks As Excel.Worksheet
    Dim lngCount As Long
    Dim strPrompt As String
    Dim strTitle As String
    Dim strTemplateFileAndPath As String
    Dim prps As Object
    Dim strSaveName As String
    Dim strTestFile As String
    Dim strDefault As String

    Set appExcel = GetObject(, "Excel.Application")
    strTemplatePath = GetWorksheetTemplatesPath
    strTemplateFile = "Access Contacts.xltx"
    strTemplateFileAndPath = strTemplatePath _
        & strTemplateFile
```

Check for the template in the selected template folder, and exit if not found:

```
strTestFile = Nz(Dir(strTemplateFileAndPath))
Debug.Print "Test file: " & strTestFile
If strTestFile = "" Then
    MsgBox strTemplateFileAndPath _
        & " template not found; " _
        & "can't create worksheet"
    GoTo ErrorHandlerExit
End If

strWorksheetPath = GetWorksheetsPath
Debug.Print "Worksheet template and path: " _
    & strTemplateFileAndPath
```

Set a reference to the workbook and worksheet, and activate the worksheet:

```
Set bks = appExcel.Workbooks
Set wkb = bks.Add(strTemplateFileAndPath)
Set wks = wkb.Sheets(1)
wks.Activate
```

Set a reference to the query:

```
Set dbs = CurrentDb
Set rst = dbs.OpenRecordset("qryContacts", _
    dbOpenDynaset)
rst.MoveLast
rst.MoveFirst
lngCount = rst.RecordCount
If lngCount = 0 Then
    MsgBox "No contacts to export"
    GoTo ErrorHandlerExit
Else
    strPrompt = "Exporting " & lngCount _
        & " contacts to Excel"
    strTitle = "Exporting"
    MsgBox strPrompt, vbInformation + vbOKOnly, strTitle
End If
```

Go to the first data cell:

```
Set rngStart = wks.Range("A4")
rngStart.Activate
```

Loop through the recordset, importing each record to a cell in the worksheet:

```
With rst
    Do Until .EOF
```

Write Access data from a record directly to cells in the worksheet:

```
rngStart.Activate
rngStart.Value = Nz(![ContactID])
Set rng = _
    appExcel.ActiveCell.Offset(columnoffset:=1)
rng.Value = Nz(![CompanyName])
Set rng = _
    appExcel.ActiveCell.Offset(columnoffset:=2)
rng.Value = Nz(![FirstName])
Set rng = _
    appExcel.ActiveCell.Offset(columnoffset:=3)
rng.Value = Nz(![LastName])
Set rng = _
    appExcel.ActiveCell.Offset(columnoffset:=4)
rng.Value = Nz(![Salutation])
Set rng = _
    appExcel.ActiveCell.Offset(columnoffset:=5)
rng.Value = Nz(![StreetAddress])
Set rng = _
    appExcel.ActiveCell.Offset(columnoffset:=6)
rng.Value = Nz(![City])
Set rng = _
    appExcel.ActiveCell.Offset(columnoffset:=7)
rng.Value = Nz(![StateOrProvince])
Set rng = _
    appExcel.ActiveCell.Offset(columnoffset:=8)
rng.Value = Nz(![PostalCode])
Set rng = _
    appExcel.ActiveCell.Offset(columnoffset:=9)
rng.Value = Nz(![Country])
Set rng = _
    appExcel.ActiveCell.Offset(columnoffset:=10)
rng.Value = Nz(![JobTitle])
```

Go to the first column of the next row:

```
rngStart.Activate
Set rngStart = _
    appExcel.ActiveCell.Offset(rowoffset:=1)
.MoveNext
        Loop
End With

MsgBox "All Contacts exported!"
```

193

Get the save name from workbook's Title property:

```
Set prps = _
    appExcel.ActiveWorkbook.BuiltinDocumentProperties

strSaveName = strWorksheetPath & prps("Title") _
    & " - " & Format(Date, "d-mmm-yyyy")
Debug.Print "Worksheet save name: " & strSaveName
```

```
On Error Resume Next
```

If there already is a saved worksheet with this name, delete it:

```
    Kill strSaveName
```

```
On Error GoTo ErrorHandler
```

```
    strPrompt = "Enter file name and path for saving worksheet"
    strTitle = "File name"
    strDefault = strSaveName
    strSaveName = InputBox(prompt:=strPrompt, _
        Title:=strTitle, Default:=strDefault)

    wkb.SaveAs FileName:=strSaveName, _
        FileFormat:=xlWorkbookDefault
    appExcel.Visible = True

ErrorHandlerExit:
    Exit Sub

ErrorHandler:
    If Err = 429 Then
```

Excel is not running; open Excel with `CreateObject`:

```
        Set appExcel = CreateObject("Excel.Application")
        Resume Next
    Else
        MsgBox "Error No: " & Err.Number _
            & "; Description: " & Err.Description
        Resume ErrorHandlerExit
    End If

End Sub
```

The procedure first picks up the worksheet template path from the main menu, checks that the template is to be found in that location, and then creates a new workbook from the template. It then sets up a recordset based on an Access query, goes to the first data cell in the worksheet, and starts iterating through the records in the recordset, using the `Offset` method of the active cell to place data from each field in the correct column.

When all the contacts have been exported to the worksheet, a save name is constructed from the template's Title property and the current date, and displayed in an InputBox so it can be edited, if desired; finally, the worksheet is saved with the save name and made visible.

 **NOTE** The `ExportContactsToExcel` procedure in this section can be run from the macro `mcrExportContactsToExcel`.

The resulting worksheet is shown in Figure 7.7.

FIGURE 7.7

A minimally formatted worksheet filled with Access data.

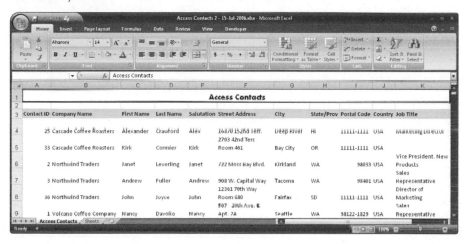

Tabular Worksheets Formatted from Code

Many companies store data on customer or client accounts in an Access database and need to export that data to Excel for further analysis or distribution. For example, an insurance company might need to export data on the companies it insures, including the account number, account type, policyholder, and account executive for use by their employees in the field. The `ExportAccountSummary` procedure (listed as follows) exports this data, using a different approach than the previous procedure. Instead of using a preformatted Excel template, all the formatting and sizing is applied directly from VBA code, to an Excel 9 worksheet filled with Access data by the `TransferSpreadsheet` method:

```
Public Function ExportAccountSummary()

    Dim strWorksheet As String
    Dim strWorksheetPath As String
    Dim appExcel As Excel.Application
```

```
        Dim sht As Excel.Worksheet
        Dim wkb As Excel.Workbook
        Dim rng As Excel.Range
        Dim strTable As String
        Dim strRange As String
        Dim strSaveName As String
        Dim strPrompt As String
        Dim strTitle As String
        Dim strDefault As String

    On Error GoTo ErrorHandler
```

Re-create table for export:

```
        strTable = "tmakAccountSummary"
        DoCmd.SetWarnings False
        DoCmd.OpenQuery "qmakAccountSummary"
```

Create worksheet save name:

```
        strWorksheetPath = GetWorksheetsPath()
        strWorksheet = "Account Summary"
        strSaveName = strWorksheetPath & strWorksheet & ".xls"
        Debug.Print "Worksheet save name" & strSaveName

    On Error Resume Next
```

Delete existing worksheet (if there is one):

```
        Kill strSaveName

    On Error GoTo ErrorHandler
```

Export query data to a new worksheet in Excel 9 format:

```
        DoCmd.TransferSpreadsheet transfertype:=acExport, _
            spreadsheettype:=acSpreadsheetTypeExcel9, _
            TableName:=strTable, FileName:=strSaveName, _
            hasfieldnames:=True
```

Open the newly created worksheet and insert title material:

```
        Set appExcel = GetObject(, "Excel.Application")
        appExcel.Workbooks.Open (strSaveName)
        Set wkb = appExcel.ActiveWorkbook
        Set sht = appExcel.ActiveSheet
        sht.Activate

        With sht
```

Apply the Calibri 9 pt font to the entire worksheet:

```
.Range("A:F").Font.Name = "Calibri"
.Range("A:F").Font.Size = 9
```

Apply hairline borders to the entire worksheet:

```
.Range("A:F").Borders(xlDiagonalDown).LineStyle = _
   xlNone
.Range("A:F").Borders(xlDiagonalUp).LineStyle = xlNone
.Range("A:F").Borders(xlEdgeLeft).LineStyle = _
   xlContinuous
.Range("A:F").Borders(xlEdgeLeft).Weight = xlHairline
.Range("A:F").Borders(xlEdgeLeft).ColorIndex = _
   xlAutomatic
.Range("A:F").Borders(xlEdgeTop).LineStyle = _
   xlContinuous
.Range("A:F").Borders(xlEdgeTop).Weight = xlHairline
.Range("A:F").Borders(xlEdgeTop).ColorIndex = _
   xlAutomatic
.Range("A:F").Borders(xlEdgeBottom).LineStyle = _
   xlContinuous
.Range("A:F").Borders(xlEdgeBottom).Weight = _
   xlHairline
.Range("A:F").Borders(xlEdgeBottom).ColorIndex = _
   xlAutomatic
.Range("A:F").Borders(xlEdgeRight).LineStyle = _
   xlContinuous
.Range("A:F").Borders(xlEdgeRight).Weight = _
   xlHairline
.Range("A:F").Borders(xlEdgeRight).ColorIndex = _
   xlAutomatic
.Range("A:F").Borders(xlInsideVertical).LineStyle = _
   xlContinuous
.Range("A:F").Borders(xlInsideVertical).Weight = _
   xlHairline
.Range("A:F").Borders(xlInsideVertical).ColorIndex = _
   xlAutomatic
.Range("A:F").Borders(xlInsideHorizontal).LineStyle = _
   xlContinuous
.Range("A:F").Borders(xlInsideHorizontal).Weight = _
   xlHairline
.Range("A:F").Borders(xlInsideHorizontal).LineStyle = _
   xlContinuous
```

Set the widths of the columns:

```
.Range("A:A").ColumnWidth = 25
.Range("B:B").ColumnWidth = 15
.Range("C:C").ColumnWidth = 15
```

```
.Range("D:D").ColumnWidth = 20
.Range("E:E").ColumnWidth = 15
.Range("F:F").ColumnWidth = 20
```

Insert blank rows at top of worksheet:

```
.Range("1:1").Insert Shift:=xlDown
.Range("1:1").Insert Shift:=xlDown
.Range("1:1").Insert Shift:=xlDown
.Range("1:1").Insert Shift:=xlDown
```

Format the column headings row:

```
With .Range("5:5")
    .Font.Size = 10
    .Font.Bold = True
    .Borders(xlEdgeTop).Weight = xlMedium
    .Borders(xlEdgeBottom).Weight = xlMedium
    .Interior.ColorIndex = 15
    .Interior.Pattern = xlSolid
    .Interior.PatternColorIndex = xlAutomatic
    .RowHeight = 15
    .VerticalAlignment = xlBottom
    .HorizontalAlignment = xlCenter
    .WrapText = True
End With
```

Insert and format title text:

```
.Range("A1:F1").HorizontalAlignment = xlCenter
.Range("A1:F1").VerticalAlignment = xlBottom
.Range("A1:F1").WrapText = False
.Range("A1:F1").Orientation = 0
.Range("A1:F1").ShrinkToFit = False
.Range("A1:F1").MergeCells = True
.Range("A1:F1").Borders(xlDiagonalDown).LineStyle = _
    xlNone
.Range("A1:F1").Borders(xlDiagonalUp).LineStyle = _
    xlNone
.Range("A1:F1").Borders(xlEdgeLeft).LineStyle = xlNone
.Range("A1:F1").Borders(xlEdgeTop).LineStyle = xlNone
.Range("A1:F1").Borders(xlEdgeBottom).LineStyle = _
    xlNone
.Range("A1:F1").Borders(xlEdgeRight).LineStyle = _
    xlNone
.Range("A1:F1").Borders(xlInsideVertical).LineStyle = _
    xlNone
.Range("A2:F2").HorizontalAlignment = xlCenter
```

```
.Range("A2:F2").VerticalAlignment = xlBottom
.Range("A2:F2").WrapText = False
.Range("A2:F2").Orientation = 0
.Range("A2:F2").ShrinkToFit = False
.Range("A2:F2").MergeCells = True
.Range("A2:F2").Borders(xlDiagonalDown).LineStyle = _
   xlNone
.Range("A2:F2").Borders(xlDiagonalUp).LineStyle = _
   xlNone
.Range("A2:F2").Borders(xlEdgeLeft).LineStyle = xlNone
.Range("A2:F2").Borders(xlEdgeTop).LineStyle = xlNone
.Range("A2:F2").Borders(xlEdgeBottom).LineStyle = _
   xlNone
.Range("A2:F2").Borders(xlEdgeRight).LineStyle = xlNone
.Range("A2:F2").Borders(xlInsideVertical).LineStyle = _
   xlNone
.Range("A3:F3").HorizontalAlignment = xlCenter
.Range("A3:F3").VerticalAlignment = xlBottom
.Range("A3:F3").WrapText = False
.Range("A3:F3").Orientation = 0
.Range("A3:F3").ShrinkToFit = False
.Range("A3:F3").MergeCells = True
.Range("A3:F3").Borders(xlDiagonalDown).LineStyle = _
   xlNone
.Range("A3:F3").Borders(xlDiagonalUp).LineStyle = _
   xlNone
.Range("A3:F3").Borders(xlEdgeLeft).LineStyle = xlNone
.Range("A3:F3").Borders(xlEdgeTop).LineStyle = xlNone
.Range("A3:F3").Borders(xlEdgeBottom).LineStyle = _
   xlNone
.Range("A3:F3").Borders(xlEdgeRight).LineStyle = xlNone
.Range("A3:F3").Borders(xlInsideVertical).LineStyle = _
   xlNone
.Range("A4:F4").MergeCells = True
.Range("A4:F4").Borders(xlDiagonalDown).LineStyle = _
   xlNone
.Range("A4:F4").Borders(xlDiagonalUp).LineStyle = _
   xlNone
.Range("A4:F4").Borders(xlEdgeLeft).LineStyle = xlNone
.Range("A4:F4").Borders(xlEdgeTop).LineStyle = xlNone
.Range("A4:F4").Borders(xlEdgeRight).LineStyle = xlNone
.Range("A4:F4").Borders(xlInsideVertical).LineStyle = _
   xlNone
.Range("A1:A4").Font.Size = 14
.Range("A1:A4").Font.Bold = True
.Range("A3").Value = "As of " & Date
.Range("A2").Value = "Account Services"
.Range("A1").Value = "Nation-wide Summary of"
```

Adjust worksheet print setup and margins:

```
    .PageSetup.PrintTitleRows = "$5:$5"
    .PageSetup.LeftFooter = "&F"
    .PageSetup.CenterFooter = ""
    .PageSetup.CenterHeader = ""
    .PageSetup.RightFooter = "Page &P"
    .PageSetup.Orientation = xlLandscape
    .PageSetup.PrintGridlines = False
    .PageSetup.Zoom = 90
End With
```

Make worksheet visible and save it:

```
    appExcel.Application.Visible = True

    strPrompt = _
        "Enter file name and path for saving worksheet"
    strTitle = "File name"
    strDefault = strSaveName
    strSaveName = InputBox(prompt:=strPrompt, _
        Title:=strTitle, Default:=strDefault)

    wkb.SaveAs FileName:=strSaveName, _
        FileFormat:=xlWorkbookDefault
    appExcel.Visible = True

ErrorHandlerExit:
    Exit Function

ErrorHandler:
    If Err = 429 Then
```

Excel is not running; open Excel with `CreateObject`:

```
    Set appExcel = CreateObject("Excel.Application")
    Resume Next
Else
    MsgBox "Error No: " & Err.Number _
        & "; Description: " & Err.Description
    Resume ErrorHandlerExit
End If

End Function
```

 **NOTE** Because the workbook was created in an older format, you will see "(Compatibility Mode)" in its title bar.

The procedure starts by running a make-table query to create a table for export to Excel, then creates a save name for the worksheet, and deletes the old worksheet file, if it exists. The data in the table created by the make-table query is then exported to a new Excel worksheet, using the `TransferSpreadsheet` method. The new worksheet is opened and activated, and various ranges in the worksheet are formatted, applying the Calibri font, hairline borders, and appropriate column widths for each column.

TIP I like to give tables created by make-table queries the prefix `tmak`, with the same base name as the query. This lets me know that a table was created by a make-table query, so I know that if I want to change it, I need to modify the query, not the table.

Next, the procedure inserts blank rows at the top of the worksheet, and title text is inserted at the top; these header lines are then formatted with a gray background and upper and lower lines. Several print setup and margin settings are done next, and finally the worksheet is saved, with an InputBox so you can modify the save name, if desired. The finished worksheet is shown in Figure 7.8.

FIGURE 7.8

An Excel worksheet formatted in VBA code.

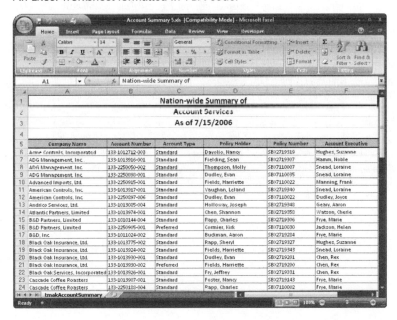

As a quick way to find out the syntax for various Excel commands, open an Excel worksheet, turn on the macro recorder, perform the actions, and then save the macro. Open the saved macro and copy the code to your Access procedure; with a little trimming of redundant arguments and editing to insert your variable names, it should work fine.

Timesheets

Almost any type of business (other than a one-person operation) needs a form for recording employees' work hours and a way to print or electronically distribute the timesheet data. Often a company has used a paper form to record work hours for many years, and the electronic form needs to replicate the paper form. In some cases, there are specific government or industry standard formats that must be used, or the data must be produced in a format that can be imported by a mainframe computer. You can use a preformatted Excel worksheet template to produce timesheets in the exact format you need and fill them with data from Access.

One example of using timesheets in such a fashion is an engineering firm whose employees work on various projects for the company's clients. Because the employees' work hours (except for those assigned to internal projects) will be billed back to the clients, in this case a separate worksheet is needed for each employee's work on a specific project per week, so a single employee might have several timesheets in a week. In the case of (for example) a scientific research establishment, where hours are not billed out to clients, one timesheet per employee, listing multiple projects in a week, would be more appropriate.

The form frmWeeklyTimesheet (shown in Figure 7.9) is an Access front end for entering timesheet data that will be exported to Excel timesheets. This form lets you select an employee, client, and project, and fill in a timesheet for that employee. The assumption is that a separate timesheet is done for each client/project combination, so an employee can have multiple timesheets for a given week.

The cboEmployeeID combo box's row source is a union query that combines data from two queries: qryThisWeeksTimesheets, which lists the timesheets that have been filled in so far this week, and qryNeedTimesheets, which lists the employees who have not yet filled out a timesheet for this week. The resulting list displays all the employees, showing the timesheets that have been filled out so far, as illustrated in Figure 7.10.

FIGURE 7.9

An Access form for entering timesheet data for export to Excel.

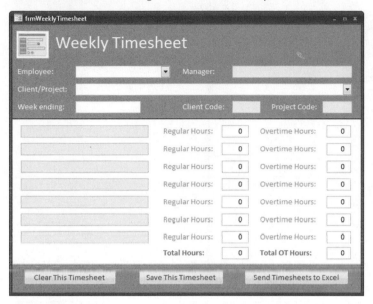

FIGURE 7.10

A combo box list showing timesheets for employees.

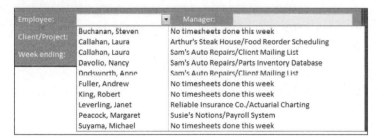

After selecting an employee, the `CurrentWeekEnding` procedure calculates the week ending date (today, if it is Sunday, otherwise last Sunday) and fills the captions of the seven date labels on the form with the correct day of the week; the Manager name is also displayed in the Manager field (the light blue back color indicates that the text box is locked). (See Figure 7.11.)

NOTE I give locked controls a light blue background (as opposed to a white background for editable controls) to give users a visual cue that they can't enter or edit text in these controls.

203

FIGURE 7.11

Date information automatically filled in after selecting an employee.

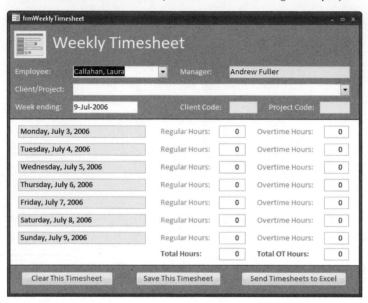

The `CurrentWeekEnding` and `FillDateControls` procedures are listed as follows:

```
Public Function CurrentWeekEnding() As Date

On Error GoTo ErrorHandler

    Dim dteToday As Date

    dteToday = Date
    Do While Weekday(dteToday) <> vbSunday
        dteToday = dteToday - 1
        Debug.Print "Testing " & dteToday
    Loop

    CurrentWeekEnding = dteToday

ErrorHandlerExit:
    Exit Function

ErrorHandler:
    MsgBox "Error No: " & Err.Number & "; Description: " &
Err.Description
    Resume ErrorHandlerExit

End Function
```

```
Private Sub FillDateControls()

On Error GoTo ErrorHandler

    Dim strFormattedDate As String
```

Fill week ending and weekday controls with text:

```
    Me![txtWeekEnding].Value = CurrentWeekEnding
    strFormattedDate = Format(DateAdd("d", -6, _
        CDate(Me![WeekEnding])), "dddd, mmmm d, yyyy")
    Me![lblMondayDate].Caption = strFormattedDate
    strFormattedDate = Format(DateAdd("d", -5, _
        CDate(Me![WeekEnding])), "dddd, mmmm d, yyyy")
    Me![lblTuesdayDate].Caption = strFormattedDate
    strFormattedDate = Format(DateAdd("d", -4, _
        CDate(Me![WeekEnding])), "dddd, mmmm d, yyyy")
    Me![lblWednesdayDate].Caption = strFormattedDate
    strFormattedDate = Format(DateAdd("d", -3, _
        CDate(Me![WeekEnding])), "dddd, mmmm d, yyyy")
    Me![lblThursdayDate].Caption = strFormattedDate
    strFormattedDate = Format(DateAdd("d", -2, _
        CDate(Me![WeekEnding])), "dddd, mmmm d, yyyy")
    Me![lblFridayDate].Caption = strFormattedDate
    strFormattedDate = Format(DateAdd("d", -1, _
        CDate(Me![WeekEnding])), "dddd, mmmm d, yyyy")
    Me![lblSaturdayDate].Caption = strFormattedDate
    strFormattedDate = Format((Me![WeekEnding]), _
        "dddd, mmmm d, yyyy")
    Me![lblSundayDate].Caption = strFormattedDate

ErrorHandlerExit:
    Exit Sub

ErrorHandler:
    MsgBox "Error No: " & Err.Number _
        & "; Description: " & Err.Description
    Resume ErrorHandlerExit

End Sub
```

Additionally, the code runs a make-table query that creates a table for use in the query that is the row source of cboClientProject (see Figure 7.12); initially, the combo box's row source is blank, because otherwise the query could not be run. The row source query is a FindUnmatched query created with the Query Wizard that excludes client/project combinations for worksheets that have already been filled out for the selected employee, so you can't accidentally select the same one twice.

205

FIGURE 7.12

Selecting a client and project for a timesheet.

If you need to modify the data on an existing timesheet, you can do this later, in the review stage, from fdlgTimesheets.

After the client and project has been selected, the hours can be entered; the totals will recalculate automatically (see Figure 7.13).

FIGURE 7.13

Entering hours on a timesheet.

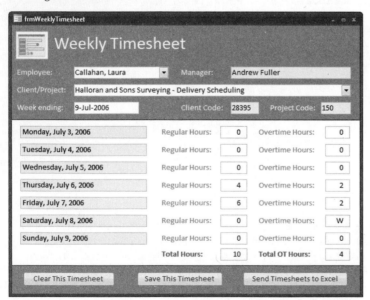

In the form footer there are three command buttons: the first ("Clear This Timesheet") clears the timesheet so you can start over; the second ("Save This Timesheet") saves the current timesheet and starts a new record for entering another timesheet; and the third ("Send Timesheets to Excel") opens a dialog form listing the timesheets that have been completed for the current week, for review. The three command button event procedures are listed as follows:

```
Private Sub cmdClearTimesheet_Click()

On Error Resume Next
```

Delete record in temp table:

```
    DoCmd.SetWarnings False
    DoCmd.RunCommand acCmdSelectRecord
    DoCmd.RunCommand acCmdDeleteRecord
    Me![cboClientProject].RowSource = ""

End Sub

Private Sub cmdSendToExcel_Click()

On Error GoTo ErrorHandler

    DoCmd.OpenForm FormName:="fdlgTimesheets"
    DoCmd.Close acForm, Me.Name

ErrorHandlerExit:
    Exit Sub

ErrorHandler:
    MsgBox "Error No: " & Err.Number _
        & "; Description: " & Err.Description
    Resume ErrorHandlerExit

End Sub
```

The frmWeeklyTimesheet form is bound to a temp table, tblWeeklyTimesheetTemp, to ensure that data won't be saved to the regular table (tblWeeklyTimesheet) until the user chooses to save it, and required fields have been filled in:

```
Private Sub cmdSaveTimesheet_Click()

On Error GoTo ErrorHandler
```

Check that required fields have values, and exit if not:

```
    strTitle = "Value required"

    If Nz(Me![cboEmployeeID].Value) = "" Then
        strPrompt = "Please select an employee"
```

```
    MsgBox prompt:=strPrompt, Buttons:=vbExclamation _
        + vbOKOnly, Title:=strTitle
    Me![cboEmployeeID].SetFocus
    GoTo ErrorHandlerExit
End If

If Nz(Me![cboClientProject].Value) = "" Then
    strPrompt = "Please select a client and project"
    MsgBox prompt:=strPrompt, Buttons:=vbExclamation _
        + vbOKOnly, Title:=strTitle
    Me![cboClientProject].SetFocus
    GoTo ErrorHandlerExit
End If
```

Save data from temp table to regular table:

```
Set dbs = CurrentDb
Set rst = dbs.OpenRecordset("tblWeeklyTimesheet")
With rst
    .AddNew
    ![EmployeeID] = Nz(Me![cboEmployeeID].Value)
    ![ClientCode] = Nz(Me![cboClientProject].Value)
    ![ProjectCode] = Nz(Me![txtProjectCode].Value)
    ![WeekEnding] = Nz(Me![txtWeekEnding].Value)
    ![ManagerID] = Nz(Me![cboEmployeeID].Column(2))
    ![MondayHours] = Nz(Me![txtMondayHours].Value)
    ![TuesdayHours] = Nz(Me![txtTuesdayHours].Value)
    ![WednesdayHours] = Nz(Me![txtWednesdayHours].Value)
    ![ThursdayHours] = Nz(Me![txtThursdayHours].Value)
    ![FridayHours] = Nz(Me![txtFridayHours].Value)
    ![SaturdayHours] = Nz(Me![txtSaturdayHours].Value)
    ![SundayHours] = Nz(Me![txtSundayHours].Value)
    ![MondayOTHours] = Nz(Me![txtMondayOTHours].Value)
    ![TuesdayOTHours] = Nz(Me![txtTuesdayOTHours].Value)
    ![WednesdayOTHours] = _
        Nz(Me![txtWednesdayOTHours].Value)
    ![ThursdayOTHours] = Nz(Me![txtThursdayOTHours].Value)
    ![FridayOTHours] = Nz(Me![txtFridayOTHours].Value)
    ![SaturdayOTHours] = Nz(Me![txtSaturdayOTHours].Value)
    ![SundayOTHours] = Nz(Me![txtSundayOTHours].Value)
    .Update
    .Close
End With
```

Delete record in temp table:

```
DoCmd.SetWarnings False
DoCmd.RunCommand acCmdSelectRecord
```

```
DoCmd.RunCommand acCmdDeleteRecord

Me![cboEmployeeID].Requery
Me![cboClientProject].RowSource = ""

ErrorHandlerExit:
    Exit Sub

ErrorHandler:
    MsgBox "Error No: " & Err.Number _
        & "; Description: " & Err.Description
    Resume ErrorHandlerExit

End Sub
```

The dialog form opened from the Send Timesheets to Excel button is shown in Figure 7.14.

FIGURE 7.14

A dialog form for reviewing this week's timesheets.

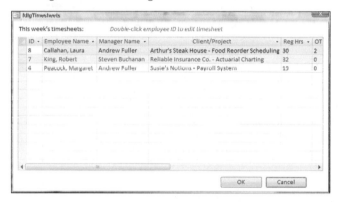

The txtEmployeeID textbox on the datasheet subform on the dialog form has a DblClick event procedure, so you can double-click an employee name to open that timesheet for editing, if necessary:

```
Private Sub txtEmployeeID_DblClick(Cancel As Integer)

On Error GoTo ErrorHandler

    Dim lngID As Long
    Dim strClientCode As String
```

```
        Dim strProjectCode As String
        Dim strSearch As String
        Dim strSQL As String
        Dim frm As Access.Form
        Dim strForm As String
```

Create a filtered query and run it to create the form's record source:

```
        strForm = "frmSelectedTimesheet"
        lngID = Nz(Me![EmployeeID])
        strClientCode = Nz(Me![ClientCode])
        strProjectCode = Nz(Me![ProjectCode])
        strSQL = "SELECT tblWeeklyTimesheet.*, " _
            & "qryEmployees.EmployeeName, " _
            & "qryEmployees.ManagerName, " _
            & "qryClientsAndProjects.ClientProject " _
            & "INTO tmakSelectedTimesheetTemp " _
            & "FROM qryClientsAndProjects " _
            & "INNER JOIN (tblWeeklyTimesheet " _
            & "INNER JOIN qryEmployees " _
            & "ON tblWeeklyTimesheet.EmployeeID = " _
            & "qryEmployees.EmployeeID) " _
            & "ON (qryClientsAndProjects.ProjectCode = " _
            & "tblWeeklyTimesheet.ProjectCode) " _
            & "AND (qryClientsAndProjects.ClientCode = " _
            & "tblWeeklyTimesheet.ClientCode) " _
            & "WHERE tblWeeklyTimesheet.EmployeeID=" _
            & lngID & " AND tblWeeklyTimesheet.ClientCode=" _
            & Chr$(39) & strClientCode & Chr$(39) _
            & " AND tblWeeklyTimesheet.ProjectCode=" _
            & Chr$(39) & strProjectCode & Chr$(39) _
            & " AND tblWeeklyTimesheet.WeekEnding = " _
            & "CurrentWeekEnding();"
        Debug.Print "SQL string: " & strSQL
        DoCmd.SetWarnings False
        DoCmd.RunSQL strSQL
```

Open form for editing selected timesheet:

```
        DoCmd.OpenForm FormName:=strForm
        Set frm = Forms![frmSelectedTimesheet]
        frm.Caption = "Weekly Timesheet for " _
            & Me![EmployeeName]
        DoCmd.Close acForm, Parent.Name

    ErrorHandlerExit:
        Exit Sub
```

```
ErrorHandler:
    MsgBox "Error No: " & Err.Number _
        & "; Description: " & Err.Description
    Resume ErrorHandlerExit

End Sub
```

The frmSelectedTimesheet form is a simplified version of the frmWeeklyTimesheet (see Figure 7.15).

FIGURE 7.15

A form for editing a selected timesheet.

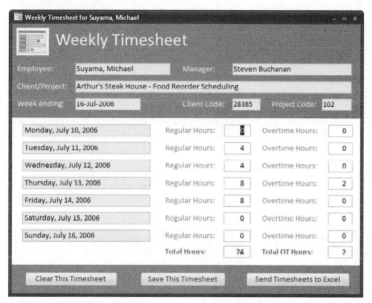

The hours can be edited on this form, and when you are done you can either delete this timesheet record by clicking the "Clear This Timesheet" button, or save the record to the regular tblWeeklyTimesheets table. Clicking the "Send Timesheets to Excel" button reopens the fdlgTimesheets dialog, with updated data.

Clicking the OK button on fdlgTimesheets runs the CreateExcelTimesheets procedure, which creates one Excel worksheet for each timesheet listed in the dialog; one of these timesheets is shown in Figure 7.16.

FIGURE 7.16

An Excel timesheet filled with data from Access.

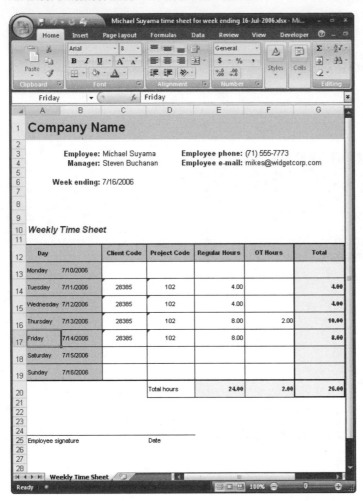

The `CreateExcelTimesheets` procedure listed as follows first sets up a DAO recordset of the current week's timesheets, and another recordset for that employee's hours. The employee information is entered on the worksheet first, then the code iterates through the Hours recordset, processing the hours for each project and day, both regular hours and overtime, until all have been filled in, and then loops to the next employee record:

```
Function CreateExcelTimeSheets()

On Error GoTo ErrorHandler
```

212

```
Dim appExcel As Excel.Application
Dim dteWeekEnding As Date
Dim lngCount As Long
Dim lngEmployeeID As Long
Dim n As Long
Dim rngCC As Excel.Range
Dim rngDay As Excel.Range
Dim rngOT As Excel.Range
Dim rngPC As Excel.Range
Dim rngRH As Excel.Range
Dim rngTotal As Excel.Range
Dim rngTotalAbove As Excel.Range
Dim rstAll As DAO.Recordset
Dim rstOne As DAO.Recordset
Dim strDocsPath As String
Dim strEmployeeName As String
Dim strPrompt As String
Dim strQuery As String
Dim strSaveName As String
Dim strSheet As String
Dim strSQL As String
Dim strTemplate As String
Dim strTemplateFile As String
Dim strTemplatePath As String
Dim strTitle As String
Dim wkb As Excel.Workbook
Dim wks As Excel.Worksheet
Dim lbl As Access.Label

Set dbs = CurrentDb
Set rstAll = _
   dbs.OpenRecordset("qryCurrentTimesheetInfo", _
   dbOpenDynaset)
rstAll.MoveLast
rstAll.MoveFirst
lngCount = rstAll.RecordCount
If lngCount = 0 Then
  MsgBox "No current time sheet records to export"
   GoTo ErrorHandlerExit
Else
   Set lbl = _
      Forms![fdlgTimesheets]![lblCreatingWorksheets]
   Debug.Print lngCount _
      & " current time sheet records to transfer to Excel"
   lbl.Visible = True
End If
```

8

Get the template path that was selected on the main menu:

```
strTemplate = _
    "Weekly time sheet by client and project.xlt"
strTemplatePath = GetWorksheetTemplatesPath()
strTemplateFile = strTemplatePath & strTemplate
If TestFileExists(strTemplateFile) = False Then
    strTitle = "Template not found"
    strPrompt = "Excel template " _
        & "'Weekly time sheet by client and project.xlt'" _
        & " not found in " & strTemplatePath & ";" _
        & vbCrLf _
        & "please put template in this folder and try again"
    MsgBox strPrompt, vbCritical + vbOKOnly, strTitle
    GoTo ErrorHandlerExit
Else
    Debug.Print "Excel template used: " _
        & strTemplateFile
End If
```

Get the path for saving workbooks:

```
strDocsPath = GetWorksheetsPath()
```

Set a reference to the Excel Application object for use in creating workbooks:

```
Set appExcel = GetObject(, "Excel.Application")

Do While Not rstAll.EOF
```

Create a recordset of hours for this employee:

```
lngEmployeeID = rstAll![EmployeeID]
strEmployeeName = rstAll![EmployeeName]
dteWeekEnding = CDate(rstAll![WeekEnding])
strQuery = "qfltHours"
strSQL = "SELECT * FROM qryCurrentTimesheetInfo " _
    & "WHERE [EmployeeID] = " & lngEmployeeID & ";"
Debug.Print "SQL for " & strQuery & ": " & strSQL
lngCount = CreateAndTestQuery(strQuery, strSQL)
Debug.Print "No. of items found: " & lngCount
If lngCount = 0 Then
    MsgBox "No items found; canceling"
    GoTo ErrorHandlerExit
End If

Set rstOne = dbs.OpenRecordset(strQuery, _
    dbOpenDynaset)

With rstOne
```

Count the number of records for this employee:

```
.MoveLast
.MoveFirst
lngCount = .RecordCount
```

Create a new workbook from the template to enter hours:

```
Set wkb = appExcel.Workbooks.Add(strTemplateFile)
Set wks = wkb.Sheets(1)
wks.Activate
appExcel.Visible = True
wks.Range("C3") = ![EmployeeName]
wks.Range("C4") = ![ManagerName]
wks.Range("F3") = Nz(![HomePhone])
wks.Range("F4") = Nz(![Email])
wks.Range("C6") = ![WeekEnding]

For n = 1 To lngCount
    Debug.Print "Record " & n & " for " _
        & strEmployeeName

    If n = 1 Then
```

Process hours for first project.

Check for hours worked on Monday:

```
If Nz(![MondayHours]) _
    + Nz(![MondayOTHours]) > 0 Then
    appExcel.GoTo _
        Reference:=wks.Range("Monday")
    Set rngCC = _
        appExcel.ActiveCell.Offset(columnoffset:=2)
    Set rngPC = _
        appExcel.ActiveCell.Offset(columnoffset:=3)
    Set rngRH = _
        appExcel.ActiveCell.Offset(columnoffset:=4)
    Set rngOT = _
        appExcel.ActiveCell.Offset(columnoffset:=5)
    rngCC.Value = ![ClientCode]
    rngPC.Value = ![ProjectCode]
    rngRH.Value = ![MondayHours]
    rngOT.Value = ![MondayOTHours]
End If
```

[Similar code for processing Tuesday through Sunday hours omitted.]

```
ElseIf n > 1 Then
```

Process different project hours for the same employee on the same worksheet.

Check for extra hours worked on Monday:

```
If Nz(![MondayHours]) + _

    Nz(![MondayOTHours]) > 0 Then
```

Determine whether any hours were added for this day:

```
appExcel.GoTo _
    Reference:=wks.Range("Monday")
Set rngCC = _
    appExcel.ActiveCell.Offset(columnoffset:=2)


If rngCC.Value <> "" Then
```

Go to next day and insert a new row above:

```
appExcel.GoTo _
    Reference:=wks.Range("Tuesday")
appExcel.ActiveCell.Select
appExcel.Selection.EntireRow.Insert
Set rngCC = _
    appExcel.ActiveCell.Offset(columnoffset:=2)
Set rngPC = _
    appExcel.ActiveCell.Offset(columnoffset:=3)
Set rngRH = _
    appExcel.ActiveCell.Offset(columnoffset:=4)
Set rngOT = _
    appExcel.ActiveCell.Offset(columnoffset:=5)
rngCC.Value = ![ClientCode]
rngPC.Value = ![ProjectCode]
rngRH.Value = ![MondayHours]
rngOT.Value = ![MondayOTHours]
Set rngTotalAbove = _
    appExcel.ActiveCell.Offset(rowoffset:=-1, _
    columnoffset:=6)
Set rngTotal = _
    appExcel.ActiveCell.Offset(columnoffset:=6)
rngTotalAbove.Select
```

Copy Total formula from cell above:

```
appExcel.Selection.Copy
rngTotal.Select
wks.Paste
appExcel.CutCopyMode = False
Else
```

Enter hours in regular Monday row:

```
                Set rngPC = _
                   appExcel.ActiveCell.Offset(columnoffset:=3)
                Set rngRH = _
                   appExcel.ActiveCell.Offset(columnoffset:=4)
                Set rngOT = _
                   appExcel.ActiveCell.Offset(columnoffset:=5)
                rngCC.Value = ![ClientCode]
                rngPC.Value = ![ProjectCode]
                rngRH.Value = ![MondayHours]
                rngOT.Value = ![MondayOTHours]
             End If
          End If
```

[Similar code for processing Tuesday through Sunday hours omitted.]

```
          .MoveNext
       Next n
```

Save and close filled-in worksheet.

Create workbook save name from employee name and week ending date:

```
       strSaveName = strDocsPath & strEmployeeName _
          & " time sheet for week ending " _
          & Format(dteWeekEnding, "d-mmm-yyyy")
       Debug.Print "Time sheet save name: " _
          & strSaveName
```

```
   On Error Resume Next
```

If there already is a saved worksheet with this name, delete it:

```
          Kill strSaveName
```

```
On Error GoTo ErrorHandler
```

```
          wkb.SaveAs FileName:=strSaveName, _
             FileFormat:=xlWorkbookDefault
          wkb.Close
```

```
       End With
       rstAll.MoveNext
    Loop
```

```
    rstAll.Close
    rstOne.Close
```

```
    appExcel.Visible = False
```

217

```
    Set appExcel = Nothing
    MsgBox "All time sheet workbooks created in " _
        & strDocsPath

ErrorHandlerExit:
    Exit Function

ErrorHandler:
```

Excel is not running; open Excel with `CreateObject`:

```
    If Err.Number = 429 Then
        Set appExcel = CreateObject("Excel.Application")
        Resume Next
    Else
        MsgBox "Error No: " & Err.Number _
            & "; Description: "
        Resume ErrorHandlerExit
    End If

End Function
```

This procedure creates a new Excel worksheet from a template for each record. This template is pre-filled with standard text, colors, and other features; all it needs is to have the timesheet data filled in from the Access record.

Summary

With the techniques described in this chapter, you can export data in Access tables to Excel worksheets in a variety of formats, for compatibility with older Office versions or handheld devices. You can use the Excel button on the Ribbon to do a quick-and-dirty export to the new .xlsx format, or create a worksheet in an older format that can be synchronized with a PDA, using the `TransferSpreadsheet` method. And finally, when you need to output your data to an Excel worksheet in a specific format, you can use a preformatted worksheet template, or format a plain worksheet using VBA Automation code to get the exact results you want.

Chapter 8

Working with Outlook Items

O utlook has a great interface for working with calendars, contacts, and tasks, as well as for sending email messages. But Outlook is a relative newcomer to Office (it was first introduced in Office 97), which means that if you have been using Access for longer than that, you probably have calendar, contact, or task data stored in Access tables in databases that were created many Office versions ago. (I have some that were originally created in Access 1.0!)

In the case of contact information, there is another reason that many users prefer storing data in Access: Access is a relational database, allowing you to set up one-to-many links between companies and contacts, contacts and phones, contacts and addresses, and so forth. Outlook, in contrast, isn't a relational database; it stores all of its data in a flat-file MAPI database. That's why you will see slots for three addresses on an Outlook contact, and a large (but finite) selection of Phone and ID slots. If you need to enter four addresses for a contact, you are out of luck. If you need to enter a type of phone number or ID that is not one of the available items, you can't do it.

But if you store your contact data in Access, you can create linked tables of addresses, phone numbers, and IDs, letting you enter as many phones and IDs as you need per contact, and you can give them whatever identifiers you wish. And with a one-to-many link between companies and contacts, you can change a company's address or main phone number once, and the changed information will be picked up through the link for all of that company's contacts. In Outlook, by contrast, if you have 10 contacts for a company, and the company's address or main phone number changes, you have to make the change separately on all 10 contacts.

As an example, the Microsoft record in my personal Access Contacts database has 30 phone numbers, many with non-standard descriptions — I couldn't do that in Outlook!

However, despite the advantages of a relational database, Outlook is undeniably attractive and convenient, so much so that you may want (or need) to export your Access contact data to Outlook contact items, so you can quickly look up a phone number or email address (or at least those that correspond to standard Outlook slots). And if you have tasks or calendar items stored in an Access table (perhaps created before Office 97), you may wish to permanently move them to Outlook, which offers a superior interface for working with these types of items.

CROSS-REF   See Chapter 11 for a detailed treatment of synchronizing a set of linked Access tables with matching Outlook contacts.

Exporting Access Data to Outlook Items

Apart from exporting whole contact, task, or appointment records to Outlook, you may need to create new Outlook items on the fly, as the data in your Access tables changes, using code running from event procedures or macros. For example, if you have a database of project-related information, you can create project task reminders in the form of email messages filled with data from an Access table, or Outlook tasks or appointments triggered by changes in data stored in the Access tables.

You can use the legacy `SendObject` command to create email messages (it's in some of the embedded macros on the forms imported from the new Microsoft sample databases discussed later on in the chapter), but `SendObject` only allows you to set a few properties of a standard Outlook mail message, and thus won't do the job if you need to create a mail message based on a custom form, or you want to set built-in properties that are not arguments of the `SendObject` command.

Alternatively, the Export group on the External Data tab of the new Ribbon offers many choices for exporting Access data, but curiously, as you can see in Figure 8.1, there is no selection for exporting to Outlook.

Using the Collect Data Group

In Access 2007, there is a new choice for interacting with Outlook: The Collect Data group on the External Data tab of the Ribbon has two buttons, one to create emails for gathering data to import into Access tables and the other to manage the replies (see Figure 8.2).

FIGURE 8.1

Ribbon choices for exporting Access data.

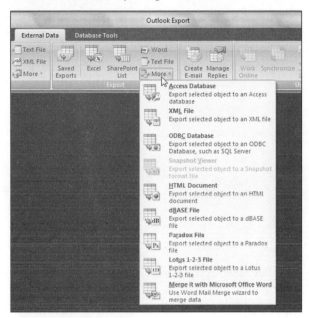

FIGURE 8.2

The Collect Data group on the Access Ribbon.

Using the Import Group to Import or Link to Outlook Data

There is also a familiar choice for linking Access tables to Outlook, now updated to a selection on the More menu of the Import group on the Ribbon. You can see this selection in Figure 8.3.

FIGURE 8.3

The Outlook Folder selection in the Import group on the Ribbon.

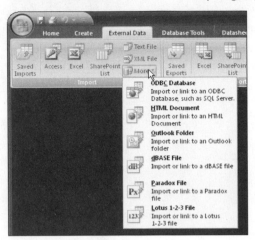

Selecting the Outlook Folder selection on the More menu opens a dialog box offering you three choices (shown in Figure 8.4): importing Outlook data into a new Access table, appending the data to an existing table, or linking the folder to a newly created Access table.

FIGURE 8.4

The Import/Link selections for Outlook folders.

After selecting the "Link to the data source by creating a new table" option (shown in Figure 8.5) and clicking OK, the Link Exchange/Outlook Wizard opens, much the same as in previous versions of Office, letting you select a folder to link to an Access table.

FIGURE 8.5

Selecting the Tasks folder for linking to an Access table.

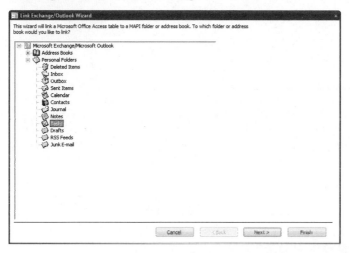

On the next screen of the wizard, you can give the table a name; I use the "ol" prefix to indicate that the table is linked to Outlook. I made linked tables for tasks, contacts, and appointments (located in the calendar folder, and named as such). Figure 8.6 shows three linked Outlook tables in the Tables list; note the arrow indicating a linked table, and the distinctive icon for Outlook.

FIGURE 8.6

Access tables linked to Outlook folders.

As with earlier versions of Office, the Link option has serious limitations. The linked olTasks table (shown in Figure 8.7) has a great many fields, but it lacks the crucial Subject field, making it all but useless.

FIGURE 8.7

A linked Outlook Tasks folder, lacking the Subject field.

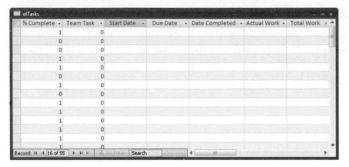

The linked olCalendar table (shown in Figure 8.8) does include the Subject field, as well as many mysterious and irrelevant fields such as MessageToMe and MessageCCToMe, but it lacks the crucial Start and End dates and times, so it is also useless.

FIGURE 8.8

A linked Outlook calendar.

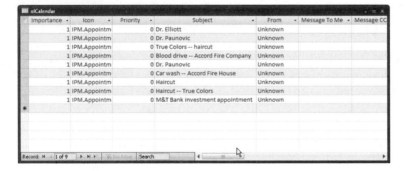

Of the three, the linked olContacts table provides the best match for Outlook contacts: it does have most (but not all) of the standard contact item fields (though not the Customer ID field, which could be useful in linking records). However, the promise of linking Access tables to Outlook—specifically that changes made in Access will be saved to Outlook, and vice versa—is not completely fulfilled. For example, though I made changes to both the contact name and company name for a contact record in Access, only the company change was reflected back to Outlook. However, both contact and company name changes in Outlook were reflected to Access. Figure 8.9 shows the linked olContacts table.

FIGURE 8.9

A linked Contacts folder.

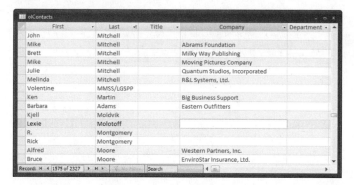

Creating a Database from a Template

To create a database from one of the new templates, first select New from the Access File menu, as shown in the following figure.

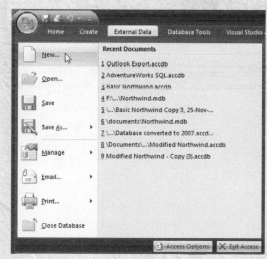

The New item on the Access File menu.

continued

continued

If the template you want to use is displayed in the next screen, select it directly.

Selecting the Contacts database template.

If the template you want to use is not shown, you can browse for it (or just take a look at what is available) by clicking the Templates link at the bottom of the screen.

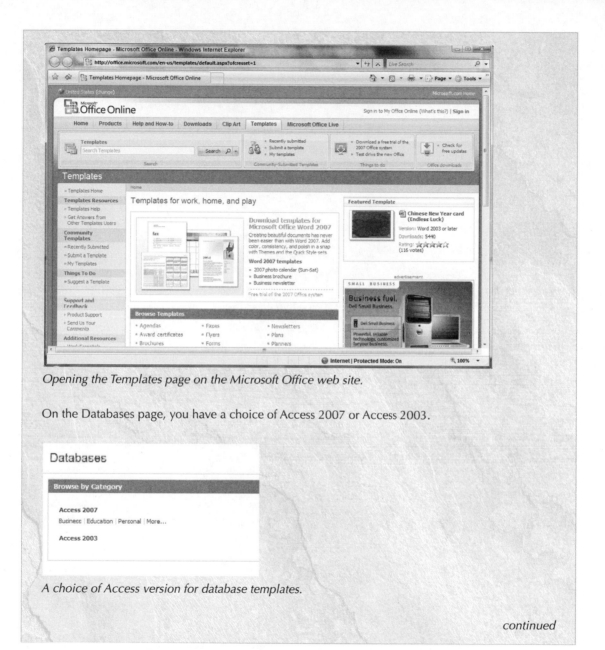

Opening the Templates page on the Microsoft Office web site.

On the Databases page, you have a choice of Access 2007 or Access 2003.

A choice of Access version for database templates.

continued

continued

In the Access 2007 group, you'll see several categories.

Access 2007

Browse by Category

Business

Education

Personal

Sample

Categories of Access 2007 database templates.

On selecting the Business category, you'll see the templates I used in this chapter.

Issues New!
Version: Access 2007
Downloads: 5940
Rating: ★★★★☆ (13 votes)

Assets New!
Version: Access 2007
Downloads: 12780
Rating: ★★★★☆ (11 votes)

Sales pipeline New!
Version: Access 2007
Downloads: 8460
Rating: ★★★★☆ (11 votes)

Tasks New!
Version: Access 2007
Downloads: 6180
Rating: ★★★★☆ (6 votes)

Projects New!
Version: Access 2007
Downloads: 10260
Rating: ★★★★☆ (9 votes)

Database templates in the Business category.

Click the template you want to use to open a page with a Download link.

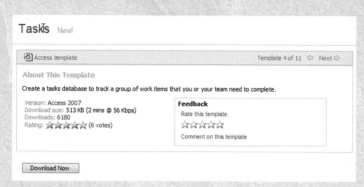

A download link for the Tasks database template.

Click the Download Now button to proceed (you may get a message about installing an ActiveX control for Office Online). After installing the ActiveX control (if necessary), Access will open to the Create Database screen, with Tasks1.accdb as the proposed database name.

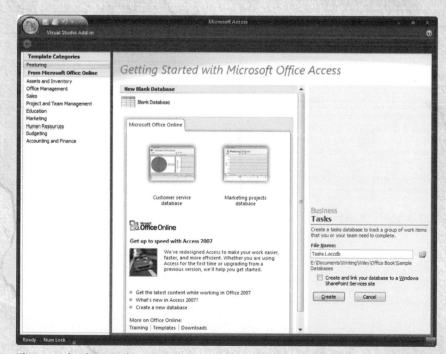

The new database to be created from a database template.

Click Create to create the new database from the template.

Using Sample Databases and Forms

I created Events and Tasks databases from the new templates and imported the relevant tables and forms from these databases into the sample database for this chapter, Outlook Export.accdb, and then renamed the objects and controls with appropriate prefixes.

NEW FEATURE Microsoft has created several new database templates for Access 2007; one of them creates an Events database, and another creates the Tasks database. See the "Creating a Database from a Template" sidebar for full details on how to locate a database template and create a database from it.

Personally I prefer to maintain my calendar and task list in Outlook, because it has the richest interface for working with appointments and tasks. However, if you want (or need) to maintain a simple calendar or task list in Access, you might want to use these new sample databases, or import objects from them, into your database. You can examine the forms I imported from the sample databases by selecting them from the Forms section on the main menu of the Outlook Export database, as shown in Figure 8.10 (the imported forms end with "List").

Selecting a form from the main menu.

Figure 8.11 shows the Task List form, and Figure 8.12 shows the Event List form.

FIGURE 8.11

The Task List form, imported from a database created from the new Tasks database template.

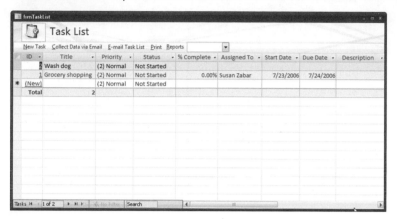

FIGURE 8.12

The Event List form, imported from a database created from the new Events database template.

NOTE The Outlook Export.accdb sample database contains the tables, queries, forms, and code used in this chapter.

There is also a Contact List form (in the Tasks sample database), shown in Figure 8.13. This form is only suitable for maintaining a simple flat-file contact list, and it lacks most of the special features Outlook provides for working with contacts, but again there are circumstances where you might want (or need) to keep contact information in a single Access table, such as when you need to regularly export basic contact data to a text file or worksheet for distribution via email, or for export to a mainframe flat-file database.

FIGURE 8.13

The Contact List form, imported from a database created from the new Tasks database template.

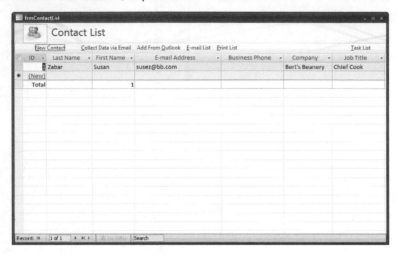

These forms from the new templates have buttons with embedded macros. The Add from Outlook button, which uses a new command argument, `acCmdAddFromOutlook`, opens a Select Names dialog for selecting a contact from Outlook, as shown in Figure 8.14.

FIGURE 8.14

Selecting a contact from Outlook.

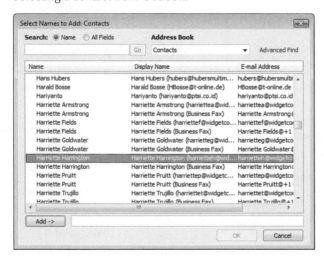

 **NEW FEATURE** All of these forms from the new database templates use the new embedded macros instead of VBA code for various purposes. Using macros instead of code seems to me to be a step back to the earliest days of Access, but embedded macros do have the advantage of avoiding security problems that can occur if you try to run code that is not signed with a digital signature (or even when you run signed code, in Windows Vista). For simple tasks, such as closing a form or running a command or two, embedded macros work fine, but for more complex tasks, they won't do the job; you still need to write VBA code to perform complex tasks such as iterating through a recordset or creating new objects in other Office applications.

I also imported reports from the Tasks and Events databases, which you can view by selecting the report name from the Reports section of the sample database's main menu, shown in Figure 8.15.

FIGURE 8.15

Selecting a report from the main menu.

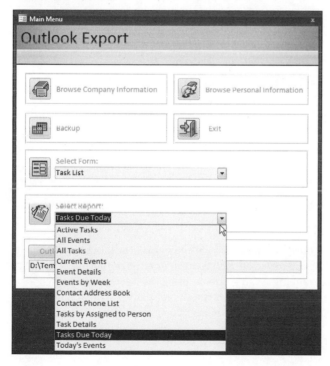

NOTE Depending on what type of printer you have, you may have to adjust the margins on some of these reports to avoid error messages when opening them.

The Outlook Object Model

Because of the limited options for exporting Access data to Outlook, I prefer to use VBA Automation code to export Access data to Outlook objects. To export Access data to Outlook, you need to understand the Outlook object model.

The Outlook 2007 object model has a number of new components; they are listed in the MSDN article "What's New for Developers in Microsoft Office Outlook 2007 (Part 1 of 2)," which you can download from the following link: `http://msdn2.microsoft.com/en-us/library/ms772422.aspx#officeoutlook2007whatsnewdeveloperspart1_enhancements`.

The Outlook object model doesn't represent the Outlook interface as closely as the object models of other Office components; instead of representing contacts, mail messages, tasks, appointments, and other familiar Outlook objects directly in the object model, these components must be accessed indirectly, via the Items collection of a Folder object, using specific named constants to reference or create the specific item types. Folders are accessed through the curiously named `NameSpace` object (representing the data stored in Outlook folders), which makes for some very unintuitive code.

Explorer, Inspector, and other Outlook Objects

When working with Outlook objects in VBA code, you will mostly be working with folders and items; occasionally you may also need to use an Explorer or Inspector object. The Explorer object represents a folder, as displayed in a pane in the interface; the Inspector object represents an item, as displayed in a window in the interface. Explorers and Inspectors are used to work with the currently open item or folder; if you just need to create and save items, you don't need to use these objects in your code.

In Figure 8.16, the Outlook Contacts folder is displayed in an Explorer pane, and an Outlook task item is displayed in an Inspector window.

You can use the `CreateObject` or `GetObject` functions with the `"Outlook.Application"` argument (with the quotes) to either create a new Outlook instance, or retrieve a reference to the current Outlook instance, if Outlook is running. With Outlook, using the `New` keyword when declaring an Outlook Application variable is also a useful method, especially if you want to work with an instance of Outlook other than the one currently in use in the interface.

If your code makes use of Explorer or Inspector objects, it is generally best to use the `New` keyword when declaring the Outlook Application object, and then set the variable to `Nothing` at the end of the procedure, because the user may be opening and closing various folders and windows, which could cause code errors if you are working with the currently running instance of Outlook.

FIGURE 8.16

Outlook Explorer and Inspector objects.

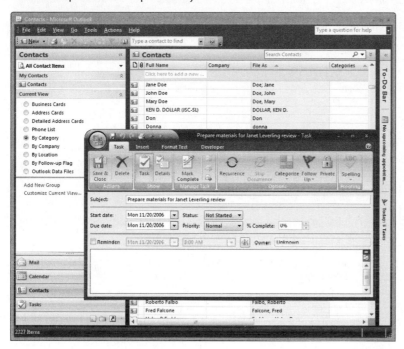

The NameSpace, Explorer, and Inspector objects, in addition to the Application object itself, are the key to most of the Outlook components you need to work with, such as folders and items. To work with a folder, for example, you must first set a reference to the Outlook Application object, then the NameSpace object, and then you can retrieve one of the default local folders using the GetDefaultFolder method, or a custom folder by referencing it as a member of the top-level Folders collection, or some folder underneath that folder. (Note that the singular of Folders is now Folder—apparently Microsoft realized that the previous name of MAPIFolder was causing confusion.)

NOTE Although the MAPIFolder object has been replaced with the more intuitive Folder object in the Object Browser, you can still declare a folder object as MAPIFolder without causing a compile error. This means you don't need to go through all your old Outlook code and change MAPIFolder declarations to Folder.

Syntax for Referencing Outlook Objects

The Items collection for a Folder represents all the separate Outlook items in that folder, which may be of different types. There is no such thing as a singular Item object in Outlook—a pitfall that has caught many beginning Outlook programmers. Thus when you need to work with items in a folder, you also need to declare a variable as Object. This is because a variable of the Object type may represent items of different types; each item can be inspected, and if it is of the appropriate type, further action can be taken, as in my following code samples.

To create an item of a specific type, use the Add method with a folder's Items collection (this creates a standard item of the folder's default item type), or use the Application object's CreateItem method with the appropriate constant (see Table 8.1 for lists of these constants). If you want to use custom objects, use the Application object's CreateItemFromTemplate object, with the name of the saved Outlook custom form. The code samples in the following sections illustrate uses of these methods.

The following code fragments show you how to set a reference to an Outlook folder or item, with a number of variations. You can declare the Application variable using the New keyword, in which case you don't need to set the variable. Or you can declare it without the New keyword, and then set the variable later with GetObject or CreateObject, as I generally do in my complete procedures.

A procedure generally starts with declaring a number of variables of different types; the following list of declarations covers the most commonly used high-level Outlook objects:

```
Dim appOutlook As New Outlook.Application
Dim nms As Outlook.NameSpace
Dim flds As Outlook.Folders
Dim fld As Outlook.Folder
Dim exp As Outlook.Explorer
Dim ins As Outlook.Inspector
```

Declare a variable as Object so it can be used for any type of item. This is necessary if you need to reference the current item in a folder that may contain items of different types:

```
Dim itm As Object
```

Declare variables as specific item types, for use when you are creating or working with items of specific types:

```
Dim msg As Outlook.MailItem
Dim con As Outlook.ContactItem

Set nms = appOutlook.GetNamespace("MAPI")
```

The flds variable references the folders under the top-level folder:

```
Set flds = nms.Folders("Personal Folders").Folders
```

Create an item using the Add method of the Items collection of a folder. The item will be of the folder's default item type:

```
Set appt = fldCalendar.Items.Add
```

Create a standard item using the `CreateItem` method of the Application object:

```
Set msg = appOutlook.CreateItem(olMailItem)
```

Create a custom mail message item from a saved Outlook template:

```
strTemplate = "D:\Templates\Outlook\Personnel.oft"
Set msg = appOutlook.CreateItemFromTemplate(strTemplate)
```

 **In previous versions of Office, you could open a saved Outlook template (.oft file) by simply double-clicking it in an Explorer window. This no longer works, because of more rigorous Microsoft security measures. In Office 2007 running on Windows Vista, if you try to open an Outlook template directly, you will get the warning message shown in Figure 8.17.**

FIGURE 8.17

A warning message when opening a saved Outlook template file.

After clicking OK, the file will then open as a standard item, not your custom form. To get around this annoying security feature, select Tools ➪ Forms ➪ Choose Form in the main Outlook window, as shown in Figure 8.18.

FIGURE 8.18

Selecting a custom form in the Outlook interface.

In the Choose Form dialog, select "User Templates in File System" from the "Look in" drop-down list, as shown in Figure 8.19.

FIGURE 8.19

Selecting the "User Templates in File System" option to open a saved template file.

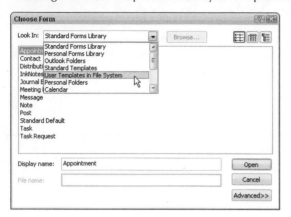

The template path defaults to the standard Office 2007/Windows Vista template location, C:\Users\Your Name\App Data\Roaming\Microsoft\Templates, but there is a Browse button that lets you select a template from another location. After selecting the template, you can open it with the Open button, and you will see your custom form at last (though its colors may have changed, because of changes in the Windows Vista and Office 2007 color palette).

Set a reference to the default local Contacts folder:

```
Set fld = nms.GetDefaultFolder(olFolderContacts)
```

Set a reference to the Folders collection of a folder called "Custom Contacts" under the top-level Personal Folders folder (via the previously set `flds` variable):

```
Set fld = flds("Custom Contacts")
```

Set a reference to a custom public folder:

```
Set flds = nms.Folders("Public Folders").Folders
Set fld = _
    flds("All Public Folders").Folders("Custom Folder")
```

Set a reference to the currently open folder, via the active Explorer:

```
Set exp = appOutlook.ActiveExplorer
Set fld = exp.CurrentFolder
```

Test whether the current folder is a Contacts folder:

```
If fld.DefaultItemType <> olContactItem Then
    MsgBox _
    "This folder is not a Contacts folder; canceling"
  GoTo ErrorHandlerExit
End If
```

Set a reference to the currently open item, via the active Inspector:

```
Set ins = appOutlook.ActiveInspector
Set itm = ins.CurrentItem
```

Test whether the open item is a mail message, and set a mail message variable to it if so:

```
If itm.Class = olMail Then
    Set msg = itm
End If
```

Set a reference to the contact whose name is "Helen Feddema":

```
Set fld = nms.GetDefaultFolder(olFolderContacts)
Set con = fld.Items("Helen Feddema")
```

Set a reference to a built-in Outlook item property:

```
strFullName = con.FullName
```

Set a reference to a custom Outlook item property of the Yes/No data type:

```
blnCustomer = con.UserProperties("Customer")
```

Standard `GetObject` line and error handler to default to `CreateObject` in case Outlook is not running:

```
Dim appOutlook As Outlook.Application

Set appOutlook = GetObject(, "Outlook.Application")
```

[Your code here]

```
ErrorHandlerExit:
    Exit Sub

ErrorHandler:
    'Outlook is not running; open Outlook with CreateObject
    If Err.Number = 429 Then
        Set appOutlook = CreateObject("Outlook.Application")
```

```
        Resume Next
    Else
        MsgBox "Error No: " & Err.Number _
            & "; Description: " & Err.Description
        Resume ErrorHandlerExit
    End If
```

Referencing Outlook Items in VBA Code

Microsoft has chosen to use the same word (for example, Note) to reference different item types (a mail message's message class and a Note item in the interface), and to give items confusingly different names in code than they have in the user interface (for example, a Journal item has a message class of "Activity"). Table 8.1 will help you find the right name or named constant for each situation.

TABLE 8.1

Referencing Outlook Items

Interface Name	Object Model Name	Message Class	OlObjectClass Constant	OlItemType Constant
Contact	ContactItem	IPM.Contact	olContact	olContactItem
Task	TaskItem	IPM.Task	olTask	olTaskItem
Mail Message	MailItem	IPM.Note	olMail	olMailItem
Appointment	AppointmentItem	IPM.Appointment	olAppointment	olAppointmentItem
Journal Entry	JournalItem	IPM.Activity	olJournal	olJournalItem
Note	NoteItem	IPM.StickyNote	olNote	olNoteItem

The message class can be used to create an item of a specific type, or to determine what type of object you are dealing with (for example, in the active Inspector). It can also be seen in the "Publish Form As" dialog box when publishing an Outlook item to a library or folder, as shown in Figure 8.20.

The message class of a custom form consists of the form name appended to the standard object's message class, with a separating period. The OlObjectClass named constants are used to determine what type of item you are dealing with, using the Class property of an object, whereas the OlItemType named constants are used for setting or determining the default item type of a folder, using a Folder's DefaultItemType property. See the sample procedures in the next sections for examples that use these constants.

FIGURE 8.20

The Outlook "Publish Form As" dialog box, showing the message class of a custom Outlook form.

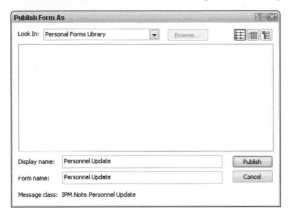

Working with Outlook Appointments

You may have calendar (appointment) data stored in an Access table, perhaps dating back to before Outlook became a part of Office. Because Outlook has a much richer interface for working with calendars than Access, I recommend exporting the Access calendar data to Outlook and working with it in Outlook calendars in the future.

To export data from an Access appointments table (such as the table from the sample Events database, called tblEvents) to Outlook appointments, use the function listed next (it can also be run from the mcrExportAppointments macro):

```
Public Function ExportAppointmentsToOutlook()

On Error GoTo ErrorHandler

    Dim fldCalendar As Outlook.Folder
    Dim appt As Outlook.AppointmentItem
    Dim strApptName As String
    Dim dteStartTime As Date
    Dim dteEndTime As Date
    Dim strStatus As String
    Dim lngStatus As Long

    Set appOutlook = GetObject(, "Outlook.Application")
    Set nms = appOutlook.GetNamespace("MAPI")
    Set fldCalendar = nms.GetDefaultFolder(olFolderCalendar)
```

```
Set dbs = CurrentDb
Set rst = dbs.OpenRecordset("tblEvents")

With rst
   Do While Not .EOF
```

Check that there is an appointment subject.

```
strApptName = Nz(![Title])
Debug.Print "Appointment name: " & strApptName
If strApptName = "" Then
   GoTo NextAppt
End If
```

Check for valid dates, and convert blank dates into 1/1/4501 (that is a blank date in Outlook).

```
If IsNull(![Start Time]) = True Then
   dteStartTime = #1/1/4501#
Else
   dteStartTime = Nz(![Start Time])
End If

 If IsNull(![End Time]) = True Then
   dteEndTime = #1/1/4501#
Else
   dteEndTime = Nz(![End Time])
End If
```

Create a new appointment item in the local Calendar folder.

```
Set appt = fldCalendar.Items.Add
appt.Subject = strApptName
appt.Start = dteStartTime
appt.End = dteEndTime
appt.Location = Nz(![Location])
appt.Body = Nz(![Description])
appt.Close (olSave)

NextAppt:
      .MoveNext
    Loop
  End With

  MsgBox "Appointments exported to Outlook"

ErrorHandlerExit:
  Exit Function

ErrorHandler:
```

Outlook is not running; open Outlook with CreateObject.

```
If Err.Number = 429 Then
    Set appOutlook = CreateObject("Outlook.Application")
    Resume Next
Else
    MsgBox "Error No: " & Err.Number _
        & "; Description: " & Err.Description
    Resume ErrorHandlerExit
End If

End Function
```

Figure 8.21 shows the exported appointments in the Outlook calendar.

FIGURE 8.21

Appointments in the Outlook calendar exported from Access.

To import appointments from your local Outlook calendar into an Access table (tblImportedCalendar), use the following function (it can also be run from the mcrImportCalendar macro):

```
Public Function ImportApptsFromOutlook()

On Error GoTo ErrorHandler

    Dim fldCalendar As Outlook.Folder
    Dim appt As Outlook.AppointmentItem
    Dim strApptName As String
    Dim dteStartTime As Date
    Dim dteEndTime As Date
    Dim strLocation As String
    Dim strSQL As String
    Dim strDescription As String

    Set appOutlook = GetObject(, "Outlook.Application")
    Set nms = appOutlook.GetNamespace("MAPI")
    Set fldCalendar = nms.GetDefaultFolder(olFolderCalendar)
```

Clear table of old data.

```
strSQL = "DELETE * FROM tblImportedCalendar"
DoCmd.SetWarnings False
DoCmd.RunSQL strSQL

Set dbs = CurrentDb
Set rst = dbs.OpenRecordset("tblImportedCalendar")
```

Iterate through the appointments in the local Calendar folder and import them to the Access table.

```
For Each itm In fldCalendar.Items
    If itm.Class = olAppointment Then
        Set appt = itm
            With appt
                strApptName = Nz(.Subject)
                dteStartTime = Nz(.Start)
                dteEndTime = Nz(.End)
                strLocation = Nz(.Location)
                strDescription = Nz(.Body)
            End With

            With rst
                rst.AddNew
                ![Subject] = strApptName

                If dteStartTime <> #1/1/4501# Then
                    ![Start Time] = dteStartTime
                End If

                If dteEndTime <> #1/1/4501# Then
                    ![End Time] = dteEndTime
                End If
                ![Location] = strLocation
                ![Description] = strDescription
                .Update
            End With
    End If
Next itm

rst.Close
DoCmd.OpenTable "tblImportedCalendar"

ErrorHandlerExit:
    Exit Function

ErrorHandler:
```

Outlook is not running; open Outlook with CreateObject.

```
If Err.Number = 429 Then
   Set appOutlook = CreateObject("Outlook.Application")
   Resume Next
Else
   MsgBox "Error No: " & Err.Number _
      & "; Description: " & Err.Description
   Resume ErrorHandlerExit
End If

End Function
```

Figure 8.22 shows the table of imported appointments, which is automatically opened at the end of the procedure.

FIGURE 8.22

A table of appointments imported from an Outlook calendar folder.

For a more realistic scenario, in which you want to create appointments based on data in an Access table of project data, use the CreateProjectAppts function (it can also be run from the mcrCreateProjectAppts macro). This function selects records in tblContactsWithProjects that have a last meeting date older than a month ago, and creates an Outlook appointment for a project meeting for the following Monday for each of those records, writing data from several fields in the Access record to the appointment item:

```
Public Function CreateProjectAppts()

On Error GoTo ErrorHandler

   Dim fldCalendar As Outlook.Folder
   Dim appt As Outlook.AppointmentItem
   Dim dteMonthAgo As Date
   Dim dteLastMeeting As Date
   Dim dteNextMonday As Date
   Dim strProject As String

   Set appOutlook = GetObject(, "Outlook.Application")
   Set nms = appOutlook.GetNamespace("MAPI")
```

```
Set fldCalendar = nms.GetDefaultFolder(olFolderCalendar)
Set dbs = CurrentDb
Set rst = dbs.OpenRecordset("tblContactsWithProjects")
dteMonthAgo = DateAdd("m", -1, Date)
dteNextMonday = NextMondayTime()

With rst
    Do While Not .EOF
```

Check whether the last meeting date is older than a month ago.

```
        dteLastMeeting = Nz(![LastMeetingDate])
        strProject = Nz(![CurrentProject])

        If dteLastMeeting < dteMonthAgo Then
```

Create a new appointment item in the local Calendar folder.

```
            Set appt = fldCalendar.Items.Add
            appt.Subject = strProject
            appt.Start = dteNextMonday
            appt.Duration = "60"
            appt.ReminderSet = True
            appt.Body = "Monthly project meeting"
            appt.Close (olSave)
        End If
        .MoveNext
        Loop
    End With

    MsgBox "Outlook project meeting appointments created "

ErrorHandlerExit:
    Exit Function

ErrorHandler:
```

Outlook is not running; open Outlook with CreateObject.

```
    If Err.Number = 429 Then
        Set appOutlook = CreateObject("Outlook.Application")
        Resume Next
    Else
        MsgBox "Error No: " & Err.Number _
            & "; Description: " & Err.Description
        Resume ErrorHandlerExit
    End If

End Function
```

Figure 8.23 shows one of the appointments created by the procedure.

A project meeting appointment created from data in an Access table.

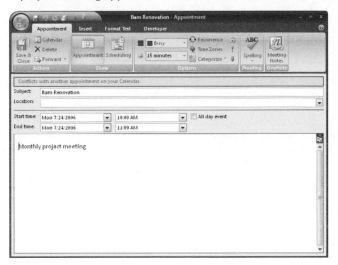

Working with Outlook Tasks

As with appointments, if you have an Access table of tasks created many Office versions ago, I recommend exporting the task data to Outlook, so it can be maintained in the Task List (in Outlook 2007, renamed the To Do List) for future use.

The table that I imported from the sample Tasks database (tblTasks) to Outlook tasks can be used as an example of how to export Access task data to Outlook. The following function does the export (it can also be run from the mcrExportTasksToOutlook macro):

```
Public Function ExportTasksToOutlook()

On Error GoTo ErrorHandler

    Dim fldTasks As Outlook.Folder
    Dim tsk As Outlook.TaskItem
    Dim strTaskName As String
    Dim dteStartDate As Date
    Dim dteDueDate As Date
    Dim strStatus As String
    Dim lngStatus As Long
```

```
Dim strPriority As String
Dim lngPriority As Long
Dim strDescription As String

Set appOutlook = GetObject(, "Outlook.Application")
Set nms = appOutlook.GetNamespace("MAPI")
Set fldTasks = nms.GetDefaultFolder(olFolderTasks)
Set dbs = CurrentDb
Set rst = dbs.OpenRecordset("tblTasks")

With rst
   Do While Not .EOF
```

Check that there is a task subject.

```
strTaskName = Nz(![Title])
Debug.Print "Task: " & strTaskName
If strTaskName = "" Then
   GoTo NextTask
End If
```

Check for valid dates, and convert blank dates into 1/1/4501 (that is a blank date in Outlook).

```
If IsNull(![Start Date]) = True Then
   dteStartDate = #1/1/4501#
Else
   dteStartDate = Nz(![Start Date])
End If

 If IsNull(![Due Date]) = True Then
   dteDueDate = #1/1/4501#
Else
   dteDueDate = Nz(![Due Date])
End If
```

Convert the text Status value to a number for Outlook.

```
strStatus = Nz(![Status])
lngStatus = Switch(strStatus = "Not started", _
   0, strStatus = "In progress", 1, _
   strStatus = "Completed", 2, _
   strStatus = "Waiting on someone else", 3, _
   strStatus = "Deferred", 4, _
   "", 0)
```

Convert the text Priority value to a number for Outlook.

```
strPriority = Nz(![Priority])
lngPriority = Switch(strPriority = "(1) High", _
    1, strPriority = "(2) Normal", 2, _
        strPriority = "(3) Low", 3, _
        "", 0)
strDescription = Nz(![Description])
```

Create a new task item in the selected Tasks folder.

```
Set tsk = fldTasks.Items.Add
tsk.Subject = strTaskName
tsk.StartDate = dteStartDate
tsk.DueDate = dteDueDate
tsk.Status = lngStatus
tsk.Body = strDescription
tsk.PercentComplete = Nz(![% Complete])
tsk.Close (olSave)

NextTask:
        .MoveNext
        Loop
    End With

    MsgBox "Tasks exported to Outlook"

ErrorHandlerExit:
    Exit Function

ErrorHandler:
```

Outlook is not running; open Outlook with CreateObject.

```
If Err.Number = 429 Then
    Set appOutlook = CreateObject("Outlook.Application")
    Resume Next
Else
    MsgBox "Error No: " & Err.Number _
        & "; Description: " & Err.Description
    Resume ErrorHandlerExit
End If

End Function
```

Figure 8.24 shows the exported tasks in the Tasks folder (in Outlook 2007, this folder is now called the To Do List).

Tasks in the Outlook To Do List exported from an Access table.

To import tasks from your local Outlook Tasks folder into an Access table (tblImportedTasks), use the following function (it can also be run from the mcrImportTasksFromOutlook macro):

```
Public Function ImportTasksFromOutlook
On Error GoTo ErrorHandler

    Dim fldTasks As Outlook.Folder
    Dim tsk As Outlook.TaskItem
    Dim strTaskName As String
    Dim dteStartDate As Date
    Dim dteDueDate As Date
    Dim strStatus As String
    Dim lngStatus As Long
    Dim strPriority As String
    Dim lngPriority As Long
    Dim strDescription As String
    Dim lngPercentComplete As Long
    Dim itm As Object
    Dim strSQL As String

    Set appOutlook = GetObject(, "Outlook.Application")
    Set nms = appOutlook.GetNamespace("MAPI")
    Set fldTasks = nms.GetDefaultFolder(olFolderTasks)
```

Clear table of old data.

```
    strSQL = "DELETE * FROM tblImportedTasks"
    DoCmd.SetWarnings False
    DoCmd.RunSQL strSQL

    Set dbs = CurrentDb
    Set rst = dbs.OpenRecordset("tblImportedTasks")
```

Iterate through tasks in the Tasks folder and import them to the Access table.

```
    For Each itm In fldTasks.Items
        If itm.Class = olTask Then
            Set tsk = itm
```

```
With tsk
    strTaskName = Nz(.Subject)
    dteStartDate = Nz(.StartDate)
    dteDueDate = Nz(.DueDate)
    lngStatus = Nz(.Status)
    lngPriority = Nz(.Importance)
    strDescription = Nz(.Body)
    lngPercentComplete = Nz(.PercentComplete)
End With

With rst
    rst.AddNew
    ![Subject] = strTaskName

    If dteStartDate <> #1/1/4501# Then
        ![Start Date] = dteStartDate
    End If

    If dteDueDate <> #1/1/4501# Then
        ![Due Date] = dteDueDate
    End If

    'Convert Priority number to text for Access
    strPriority = Switch(lngPriority = 1, _
        "(1) High", _
        lngPriority = 2, "(2) Normal", _
        lngPriority = 3, "(3) Low", _
        0, "")
    ![Priority] = strPriority
```

Convert the Status numeric value to text for Access

```
    strStatus = Switch(lngStatus = 0, _
        "Not started", _
        lngStatus = 1, "In progress", _
        lngStatus = 2, "Completed", _
        lngStatus = 3, _
        "Waiting on someone else", _
        lngStatus = 4, "Deferred", _
        0, "")
    ![Status] = strStatus

    If lngPercentComplete > 0 Then
        lngPercentComplete = _
            lngPercentComplete / 100
    End If

    ![PercentComplete] = lngPercentComplete
    ![Notes] = strDescription
```

```
                .Update
            End With
        End If
    Next itm

    rst.Close
    DoCmd.OpenTable "tblImportedTasks"

ErrorHandlerExit:
    Exit Function

ErrorHandler:
```

Outlook is not running; open Outlook with CreateObject.

```
    If Err.Number = 429 Then
        Set appOutlook = CreateObject("Outlook.Application")
        Resume Next
    Else
        MsgBox "Error No: " & Err.Number _
            & "; Description: " & Err.Description
        Resume ErrorHandlerExit
    End If

End Function
```

Figure 8.25 shows the table of imported tasks.

FIGURE 8.25

A table of tasks imported from Outlook.

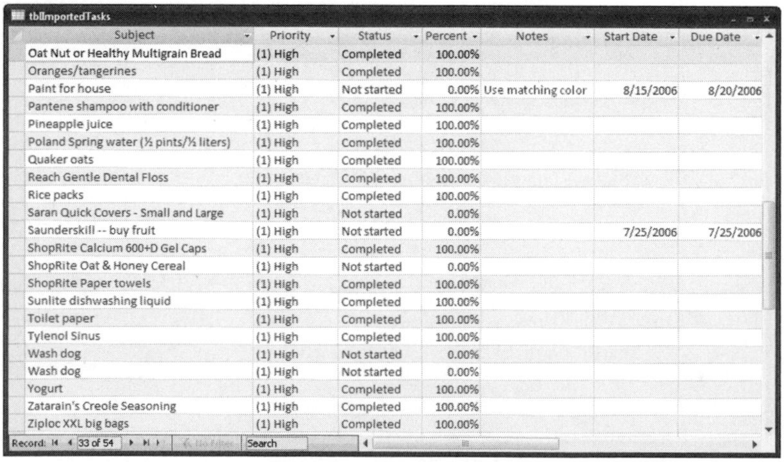
tblImportedTasks

Subject	Priority	Status	Percent	Notes	Start Date	Due Date
Oat Nut or Healthy Multigrain Bread	(1) High	Completed	100.00%			
Oranges/tangerines	(1) High	Completed	100.00%			
Paint for house	(1) High	Not started	0.00%	Use matching color	8/15/2006	8/20/2006
Pantene shampoo with conditioner	(1) High	Completed	100.00%			
Pineapple juice	(1) High	Completed	100.00%			
Poland Spring water (½ pints/½ liters)	(1) High	Completed	100.00%			
Quaker oats	(1) High	Completed	100.00%			
Reach Gentle Dental Floss	(1) High	Completed	100.00%			
Rice packs	(1) High	Completed	100.00%			
Saran Quick Covers - Small and Large	(1) High	Not started	0.00%			
Saunderskill -- buy fruit	(1) High	Not started	0.00%		7/25/2006	7/25/2006
ShopRite Calcium 600+D Gel Caps	(1) High	Completed	100.00%			
ShopRite Oat & Honey Cereal	(1) High	Not started	0.00%			
ShopRite Paper towels	(1) High	Completed	100.00%			
Sunlite dishwashing liquid	(1) High	Completed	100.00%			
Toilet paper	(1) High	Completed	100.00%			
Tylenol Sinus	(1) High	Completed	100.00%			
Wash dog	(1) High	Not started	0.00%			
Wash dog	(1) High	Not started	0.00%			
Yogurt	(1) High	Completed	100.00%			
Zatarain's Creole Seasoning	(1) High	Completed	100.00%			
Ziploc XXL big bags	(1) High	Completed	100.00%			

Record: 33 of 54 Search

For a more realistic scenario, in which you want to create tasks based on data in an Outlook table, see the CreateProjectTasks function (it can be run from the mcrCreateProjectTasks macro). This function creates an Outlook task for each record in tblContactsWithProjects that has not had its supplies replenished for a month or more, and writes data from several fields in the Access record to the task item:

```
Public Function CreateProjectTasks()

On Error GoTo ErrorHandler

    Dim fldTasks As Outlook.Folder
    Dim tsk As Outlook.TaskItem
    Dim dteMonthAgo As Date
    Dim dteReplenished As Date
    Dim dteNextMonday As Date
    Dim strProject As String

    Set appOutlook = GetObject(, "Outlook.Application")
    Set nms = appOutlook.GetNamespace("MAPI")
    Set fldTasks = nms.GetDefaultFolder(olFolderTasks)
    Set dbs = CurrentDb
    Set rst = dbs.OpenRecordset("tblContactsWithProjects")
    dteMonthAgo = DateAdd("m", -1, Date)
    dteNextMonday = NextMonday()

    With rst
        Do While Not .EOF
```

Check whether supplies were last replenished more than a month ago.

```
            dteReplenished = Nz(![SuppliesReplenished])
            strProject = Nz(![CurrentProject])

            If dteReplenished < dteMonthAgo Then
```

Create a new task in the local Tasks folder.

```
                Set tsk = fldTasks.Items.Add
                tsk.Subject = "Replenish supplies for " _
                    & strProject
                tsk.StartDate = dteNextMonday
                tsk.Status = 0
                tsk.Importance = 1
                tsk.Close (olSave)
            End If
            .MoveNext
            Loop
    End With

    MsgBox "Outlook project tasks created"
```

```
ErrorHandlerExit:
    Exit Function

ErrorHandler:
```

Outlook is not running; open Outlook with CreateObject.

```
    If Err.Number = 429 Then
        Set appOutlook = CreateObject("Outlook.Application")
        Resume Next
    Else
        MsgBox "Error No: " & Err.Number _
            & "; Description: " & Err.Description
        Resume ErrorHandlerExit
    End If

End Function
```

Figure 8.26 shows one of the tasks created by this procedure.

FIGURE 8.26

A task created from data in an Access table.

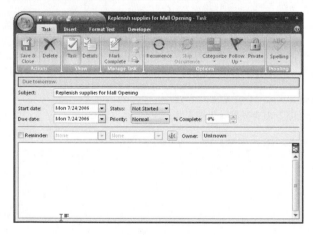

Working with Outlook Contacts

Outlook offers a convenient and attractive interface for working with contacts (though, as noted earlier in this chapter, it does not support linking companies to contacts or other one-to-many links). Most people keep Outlook open at all times, whereas they may only open an Access database as needed. Because of this, if you have a single table of Access contacts, you may wish to export the data to Outlook, so you can quickly open a contact item without having to first open an Access database.

CROSS-REF If you have a set of linked Access tables of contact data, and you want to keep the data in the tables synchronized with matching Outlook contact items, you need more than a simple export. See Chapter 11 for a discussion of two-way synchronizing between Access and Outlook contacts.

To export data from an Access flat-file contacts table (such as tblContactsToExport) to Outlook contacts in a custom Contacts folder called Contacts from Access, use the function listed as follows (it can also be run from the mcrExportFlatFileContactsToOutlook macro):

```
Public Function ExportFlatFileContactsToOutlook()

On Error GoTo ErrorHandler

    Set appOutlook = GetObject(, "Outlook.Application")

    Dim lngContactID As Long
    Dim lngContactCount As Long
    Dim fld As Outlook.Folder
    Dim fldContacts As Outlook.Folder
    Dim conNew As Outlook.ContactItem
    Dim conTest As Outlook.ContactItem
    Dim strFullName As String
    Dim strFirstName As String
    Dim strLastName As String
    Dim strBusinessPhone As String
    Dim strMobilePhone As String
    Dim strFaxNumber As String
    Dim strNotes As String
    Dim strJobTitle As String
    Dim strStreetAddress As String
    Dim strCity As String
    Dim strStateProv  As String
    Dim strPostalCode As String
    Dim strCountry As String
    Dim strCompanyName As String
    Dim strEMail As String
    Dim strSalutation As String

    Set appOutlook = GetObject(, "Outlook.Application")
    Set nms = appOutlook.GetNamespace("MAPI")
```

Use the following line to export to the default local Contacts folder:

```
    'Set fldContacts = nms.GetDefaultFolder(olFolderTasks)

    On Error Resume Next
```

Use the following lines to export to a custom Contacts folder, creating it if necessary. If setting a reference to the folder fails, the folder will be created.

```
        Set fld = nms.Folders("Personal Folders")
        Set fldContacts = fld.Folders("Contacts from Access")
        If fldContacts Is Nothing Then
            Set fldContacts = _
                fld.Folders.Add("Contacts from Access", _
                olFolderContacts)
        End If

    On Error GoTo ErrorHandler

        lngContactCount = 0
        Set dbs = CurrentDb
        Set rst = dbs.OpenRecordset("tblContactsToExport")

        With rst
            Do While Not .EOF
```

Check for required name information.

```
                strFullName = Nz(![FirstName]) & " " _
                    & Nz(![LastName])
                Debug.Print "Contact name: " & strFullName
                If strFullName = "" Then
                    GoTo NextContact
                End If
```

Check whether there already is an Outlook contact item for this person.

```
    On Error Resume Next

                Set conTest = fldContacts.Items(strFullName)
                If conTest.FullName <> strFullName Then
```

No matching contact found.

```
                    Debug.Print strFullName & " not found"
                ElseIf conTest.FullName = strFullName Then
                    Debug.Print strFullName & " found"
                    GoTo NextContact
                End If

    On Error GoTo ErrorHandler

                lngContactID = Nz(![ContactID])
                strCompanyName = Nz(![CompanyName])
                strFirstName = Nz(![FirstName])
                strLastName = Nz(![LastName])
                strSalutation = Nz(![Salutation])
                strEMail = Nz(![EmailName])
                strJobTitle = Nz(![JobTitle])
                strBusinessPhone = Nz(![WorkPhone]) _
```

```
                & IIf(Nz(![WorkExtension]) <> "", " x " _
                & ![WorkExtension], "")
            strMobilePhone = Nz(![MobilePhone])
            strFaxNumber = Nz(![FaxNumber])
            strNotes = Nz(![Notes])
            strStreetAddress = Nz(![StreetAddress])
            strCity = Nz(![City])
            strStateProv = Nz(![StateOrProvince])
            strPostalCode = Nz(![PostalCode])
            strCountry = Nz(![Country])
```

Create a new contact item in the selected Contacts folder.

```
            Set conNew = fldContacts.Items.Add
            With conNew
                .CustomerID = lngContactID
                .FirstName = strFirstName
                .LastName = strLastName
                .JobTitle = strJobTitle
                .BusinessAddressStreet = strStreetAddress
                .BusinessAddressCity = strCity
                .BusinessAddressState = strStateProv
                .BusinessAddressPostalCode = strPostalCode
                .BusinessAddressCountry = strCountry
                .CompanyName = strCompanyName
                .Email1Address = strEMail
                .BusinessTelephoneNumber = strBusinessPhone
                .BusinessFaxNumber = strFaxNumber
                .MobileTelephoneNumber = strMobilePhone
                .NickName = strSalutation
                .Body = strNotes
                .Close (olSave)
            End With
            lngContactCount = lngContactCount + 1
NextContact:
            .MoveNext
            Loop
    End With

    rst.Close

    If lngContactCount = 0 Then
        MsgBox "No unique contacts to export to Outlook"
    Else
        MsgBox lngContactCount & " contact(s) exported to Outlook"
    End If

ErrorHandlerExit:
    Exit Function

ErrorHandler:
```

Outlook is not running; open Outlook with CreateObject.

```
If Err.Number = 429 Then
    Set appOutlook = CreateObject("Outlook.Application")
    Resume Next
Else
    MsgBox "Error No: " & Err.Number _
        & "; Description: " & Err.Description
    Resume ErrorHandlerExit
End If

End Function
```

Figure 8.27 shows some of the contacts exported to the custom Contacts from Access folder.

FIGURE 8.27

Contacts in a custom Outlook folder exported from Access, in the new Business Card view.

To import contacts from your local Outlook Contacts folder into an Access table (tblImportedContacts), use the following function (it can also be run from the mcrImportContactsFromOutlook macro):

```
Public Function ImportContactsFromOutlook()

On Error GoTo ErrorHandler

    Dim lngContactCount As Long
    Dim fld As Outlook.Folder
    Dim fldContacts As Outlook.Folder
    Dim con As Outlook.ContactItem
    Dim strFullName As String
    Dim strFirstName As String
    Dim strLastName As String
    Dim strBusinessPhone As String
    Dim strHomePhone As String
    Dim strMobilePhone As String
    Dim strFaxNumber As String
    Dim strNotes As String
    Dim strJobTitle As String
    Dim strWorkAddress As String
    Dim strWorkCity As String
    Dim strWorkStateProv  As String
    Dim strWorkPostalCode As String
    Dim strWorkCountry As String
    Dim strHomeAddress As String
    Dim strHomeCity As String
    Dim strHomeStateProv  As String
    Dim strHomePostalCode As String
    Dim strHomeCountry As String
    Dim strCompanyName As String
    Dim strEMail As String
    Dim strSalutation As String
    Dim itm As Object
    Dim strSQL As String
    Dim strWebSite As String

    Set appOutlook = GetObject(, "Outlook.Application")
    Set nms = appOutlook.GetNamespace("MAPI")
```

Use the following line to import from the default local Contacts folder:

```
    'Set fldContacts = nms.GetDefaultFolder(olFolderTasks)

On Error Resume Next
```

Use the following lines to set a reference to a custom Contacts folder, creating it if necessary. If setting a reference to the folder fails, the folder will be created.

```
Set fld = nms.Folders("Personal Folders")
Set fldContacts = fld.Folders("Contacts to Export")
If fldContacts Is Nothing Then
   Set fldContacts = _
      fld.Folders.Add("Contacts to Export", _
      olFolderContacts)
End If

On Error GoTo ErrorHandler
```

Clear the table of old data.

```
strSQL = "DELETE * FROM tblImportedContacts"
DoCmd.SetWarnings False
DoCmd.RunSQL strSQL

lngContactCount = 0
Set dbs = CurrentDb
Set rst = dbs.OpenRecordset("tblImportedContacts")
```

Iterate through contacts in selected Contacts folder and import them to the Access table.

```
For Each itm In fldContacts.Items
   If itm.Class = olContact Then
      Set con = itm
         With con
            strFirstName = Nz(.FirstName)
            strLastName = Nz(.LastName)
            strJobTitle = Nz(.JobTitle)
            strWorkAddress = Nz(.BusinessAddressStreet)
            strWorkCity = Nz(.BusinessAddressCity)
            strWorkStateProv = Nz(.BusinessAddressState)
            strWorkPostalCode = _
               Nz(.BusinessAddressPostalCode)
            strWorkCountry = Nz(.BusinessAddressCountry)
            strHomeAddress = Nz(.HomeAddress)
            strHomeCity = Nz(.HomeAddressCity)
            strHomeStateProv = Nz(.HomeAddressState)
            strHomePostalCode = Nz(.HomeAddressPostalCode)
            strHomeCountry = Nz(.HomeAddressCountry)
            strCompanyName = Nz(.CompanyName)
            strEMail = Nz(.Email1Address)
            strBusinessPhone = _
               Nz(.BusinessTelephoneNumber)
            strFaxNumber = Nz(.BusinessFaxNumber)
            strMobilePhone = Nz(.MobileTelephoneNumber)
            strSalutation = Nz(.NickName)
```

```
                strWebSite = Nz(.WebPage)
                strNotes = Nz(.Body)
                .Close (olSave)
            End With

            With rst
                rst.AddNew
                ![CompanyName] = strCompanyName
                ![FirstName] = strFirstName
                ![LastName] = strLastName
                ![Salutation] = strSalutation
                ![EmailName] = strEMail
                ![JobTitle] = strJobTitle
                ![WorkPhone] = strBusinessPhone
                ![MobilePhone] = strMobilePhone
                ![FaxNumber] = strFaxNumber
                ![Notes] = strNotes
                ![WorkAddress] = strWorkAddress
                ![WorkCity] = strWorkCity
                ![WorkStateOrProvince] = strWorkStateProv
                ![WorkPostalCode] = strWorkPostalCode
                ![WorkCountry] = strWorkCountry
                ![HomeAddress] = strHomeAddress
                ![HomeCity] = strHomeCity
                ![HomeStateOrProvince] = strHomeStateProv
                ![HomePostalCode] = strHomePostalCode
                ![HomeCountry] = strHomeCountry
                ![WorkPhone] = strHomePhone
                ![WebSite] = strWebSite
                .Update
            End With
        lngContactCount = lngContactCount + 1
    End If
Next itm

rst.Close

If lngContactCount = 0 Then
    MsgBox "No contacts to import from Outlook"
Else
    MsgBox lngContactCount _
        & " contact(s) imported from Outlook"
End If
ErrorHandlerExit:
Exit Function

If Err.Number = 429 Then
    Set appOutlook = CreateObject("Outlook.Application")
    Resume Next
```

```
      Else
         MsgBox "Error No: " & Err.Number _
            & "; Description: " & Err.Description
         Resume ErrorHandlerExit
      End If

   End Function
```

FIGURE 8.28

A table of contact data imported from an Outlook folder.

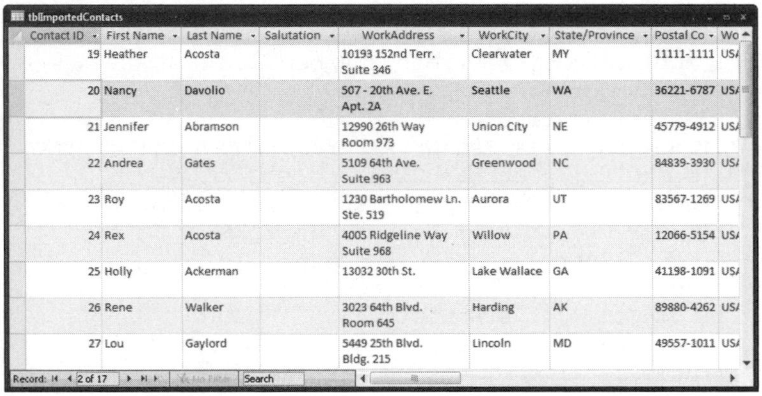

Contact ID	First Name	Last Name	Salutation	WorkAddress	WorkCity	State/Province	Postal Co	Wo
19	Heather	Acosta		10193 152nd Terr. Suite 346	Clearwater	MY	11111-1111	US/
20	Nancy	Davolio		507 - 20th Ave. E. Apt. 2A	Seattle	WA	36221-6787	US/
21	Jennifer	Abramson		12990 26th Way Room 973	Union City	NE	45779-4912	US/
22	Andrea	Gates		5109 64th Ave. Suite 963	Greenwood	NC	84839-3930	US/
23	Roy	Acosta		1230 Bartholomew Ln. Ste. 519	Aurora	UT	83567-1269	US/
24	Rex	Acosta		4005 Ridgeline Way Suite 968	Willow	PA	12066-5154	US/
25	Holly	Ackerman		13032 30th St.	Lake Wallace	GA	41198-1091	US/
26	Rene	Walker		3023 64th Blvd. Room 645	Harding	AK	89880-4262	US/
27	Lou	Gaylord		5449 25th Blvd. Bldg. 215	Lincoln	MD	49557-1011	US/

CROSS-REF When working with contacts, the ideal situation would be to maintain your most complete information in a set of linked Access tables, and synchronize them with Outlook contacts that would display most of the information in an easy-to-use interface. Chapter 11 covers synchronizing linked Access contact tables with a folder of Outlook contacts.

Summary

This chapter has described the components of the Outlook object model you need to understand in order to work with Outlook objects and has given you examples of exporting Access data to Outlook and importing Outlook data into Access (or linking to it), as well as creating new Outlook items based on data changes in Access tables. While there are both advantages and disadvantages to storing contacts in Access and Outlook, I recommend exporting tasks and appointments from Access tables to Outlook, so they can be managed in its superior interface. For contacts, the decision depends on which is more important to you: the convenience and attractive interface of Outlook contacts, or the more sophisticated Access relational database interface, allowing you to set up one-to-many links between companies and contacts, or contacts and phones or IDs.

Chapter 9

Working with Files and Folders

In the previous chapters I discussed creating Word documents, Excel worksheets, and various types of Outlook items using VBA Automation code. But these aren't the only types of documents you need to work with — sometimes you need to create a plain text document, or import data from one into an Access table. But, before you can work with these documents, you need to work with folders. This chapter covers writing code that works with Windows Explorer folders and text files, using several different methods.

As Access versions have progressed, the available tools for working with files or folders have advanced. In Access 1.0, the notoriously cryptic callback function was the only way to get a list of files to display in a combo box or listbox. By Windows 95, the CommonDialog control was a possibility, at least if you had the Developer edition of Office. But the CommonDialog control was plagued with version problems — if you put one version of it on a form, and sent the database to another person who had a different version of the control, the other person would just get the mysterious message "There is no object in this control" on opening the form with the CommonDialog control.

CROSS-REF See Chapter 8 for information on working with Outlook folders.

Another advance came with the Scripting Runtime library, which provided a FileSystemObject object (yes, that's two objects!) that is very useful for finding, working with, or creating files and folders in code. However, it doesn't offer a dialog-type interface for selecting files or folders.

The next advance came with Office XP, which introduced a new tool for working with files and folders. The FileDialog object (part of the Office

---

IN THIS CHAPTER

Creating Windows folders

Creating FolderPicker and FilePicker dialogs using the Office FileDialog object

Writing data to text files using the FileSystemObject, legacy VB statements, and ADO

Reading data from text files using the FileSystemObject, legacy VB statements, and ADO

Loading files into Attachment fields and saving attachments to files

---

object model) lets you pop up a dialog for selecting a file or a folder, with several dialog type options. This dialog lets users easily select a file or folder, whose name can then be used in code for further operations.

There is no longer any reason to use a `Callback` function or the `CommonDialog` control for working with files and folders, so this chapter covers using the `FileSystemObject` and the `FileDialog` object for working with files and folders, and components of the ADO object model and legacy VB statements for working with text files.

Working with Windows Explorer Folders

When you save documents (of any sort) to your computer's hard drive, you need to specify the folder (otherwise everything will end up either in your root Documents folder or the current folder, making it very hard to find specific documents). If you work with Word, Excel, or Outlook templates, you also need to specify a templates folder, so your code will look in the right place for your templates. You can get the default user templates folder from the Word File Options dialog, but again, you probably don't want to keep all your templates in the root Templates folder.

CROSS-REF See the Word Export.accdb sample database's main menu for command buttons with code for selecting the Documents and Templates paths.

To work with Windows folders, you have two options: the Office `FileDialog` object, or the `FileSystemObject`. These two methods are discussed in the following sections.

NOTE The sample database for this chapter is Files and Folders.accdb.

The Office FileDialog Object

To allow the maximum amount of user choice, combined with convenience, I like to put one or two folder selection command buttons on a database's main menu, for selecting folders that will be used throughout the database. In the sample database for this chapter, Files and Folders.accdb, for example, the main menu has a section with two sets of controls for selecting a folder; one has a command button that pops up a Folder Picker dialog for selecting the Input Documents folder (used for storing documents to be loaded into Attachment fields or textboxes on forms), and the other opens an Output Documents Folder Picker for selecting the folder where files saved from attachments are to be stored. After a folder is selected, its name is displayed in the textbox under the command button. Figure 9.1 shows a main menu with these options.

FIGURE 9.1

A main menu with a Backup button and button/textbox controls for selecting an Input Documents path and an Output Documents path for use in the database.

The Input Documents Path and Output Documents Path buttons run procedures that create a `FileDialog` object. `FileDialog` objects can be created as a File Picker, or a Folder Picker dialog; in this case the `msoFileDialogFolderPicker` named constant is used when creating the dialog, to make it a Folder Picker dialog:

```
Private Sub cmdInputDocsPath_Click()

On Error GoTo ErrorHandler
```

Create a FileDialog object as a Folder Picker dialog box.

```
Set fd = Application.FileDialog(msoFileDialogFolderPicker)
Set txt = Me![txtInputDocsPath]
strPath = GetInputDocsPath()

With fd
   .title = "Browse for folder where input documents " _
      & "are stored"
   .ButtonName = "Select"
   .InitialView = msoFileDialogViewDetails
   .InitialFileName = strPath
   If .Show = -1 Then
      txt.Value = CStr(fd.SelectedItems.Item(1))
```

```
        Else
            Debug.Print "User pressed Cancel"
        End If
    End With

On Error Resume Next

    DoCmd.RunCommand acCmdSaveRecord

ErrorHandlerExit:
    Exit Sub

ErrorHandler:
    MsgBox "Error No: " & Err.Number _
        & "; Description: " & Err.Description
    Resume ErrorHandlerExit

End Sub

Private Sub cmdOutputDocsPath_Click()

On Error GoTo ErrorHandler
```

Create a FileDialog object as a Folder Picker dialog box.

```
        Set fd = Application.FileDialog(msoFileDialogFolderPicker)
        Set txt = Me![txtOutputDocsPath]
        strPath = GetOutputDocsPath()

        With fd
            .title = "Browse for folder where saved documents " _
                & "should be stored"
            .ButtonName = "Select"
            .InitialView = msoFileDialogViewDetails
            .InitialFileName = strPath
            If .Show = -1 Then
                txt.Value = CStr(fd.SelectedItems.Item(1))
            Else
                Debug.Print "User pressed Cancel"
            End If
        End With

On Error Resume Next

    DoCmd.RunCommand acCmdSaveRecord

ErrorHandlerExit:
    Exit Sub
```

```
ErrorHandler:
   MsgBox "Error No: " & Err.Number _
       & "; Description: " & Err.Description
   Resume ErrorHandlerExit

End Sub
```

In the cmdInputDocsPath_Click event procedure, the GetInputDocsPath() function is used to get the saved Input Documents path value from tblInfo (if there is one); otherwise the default Documents folder is opened. The user can select another path, or accept the default path; the value selected from the dialog is saved to the txtInputDocsPath textbox on the form, which is bound to the InputDocsPath field in tblInfo. The cmdOutputDocsPath_Click event procedure stores the selected template path to txtOutputDocsPath, which is stored in the OutputDocsPath field in tblInfo.

NOTE I use a tblInfo table in most of my databases to store data that is needed throughout the database, such as path information. Although you can use global variables for this purpose, they won't persist from one session to another, and it isn't easy to examine their values, so I prefer to store these values in a table.

The custom Input and Output Documents paths stored in tblInfo are picked up wherever needed in the database, using the GetInputDocsPath() and GetOutputDocsPath() functions, listed next:

```
Public Function GetInputDocsPath() As String

On Error GoTo ErrorHandler

   Set dbs = CurrentDb
   Set rst = dbs.OpenRecordset("tblInfo")
   rst.MoveFirst
   strPath = Nz(rst![InputDocsPath])
```

Add a terminating backslash, if the path doesn't have one.

```
   If Len(strPath) > 1 And Right(strPath, 1) <> "\" Then
      GetInputDocsPath = strPath & "\"
   Else
      GetInputDocsPath = strPath
   End If
   rst.Close

ErrorHandlerExit:
   Exit Function

ErrorHandler:
   MsgBox "Error No: " & Err.Number & "; Description: " & _
      Err.Description
   Resume ErrorHandlerExit
```

```
End Function

Public Function GetOutputDocsPath() As String

On Error GoTo ErrorHandler

    Set dbs = CurrentDb
    Set rst = dbs.OpenRecordset("tblInfo")
    rst.MoveFirst
    strPath = Nz(rst![OutputDocsPath])
```

Add a terminating backslash, if the path doesn't have one.

```
    If Len(strPath) > 1 And Right(strPath, 1) <> "\" Then
        GetOutputDocsPath = strPath & "\"
    Else
        GetOutputDocsPath = strPath
    End If
    rst.Close

ErrorHandlerExit:
    Exit Function

ErrorHandler:
    MsgBox "Error No: " & Err.Number & "; Description: " & _
        Err.Description
    Resume ErrorHandlerExit

End Function
```

Figure 9.2 shows the Folder Picker dialog for selecting a custom Output Documents path.

To use the `FileDialog` object in your code, you need to set a reference to the Office object library; that reference is not set by default in a newly created Access 2007 database. Figure 9.3 shows the Office 12.0 reference being checked in the References dialog for the Files and Folders database.

FIGURE 9.2

Selecting a custom folder for storing documents in a database.

FIGURE 9.3

Setting a reference to the Office 12.0 object library.

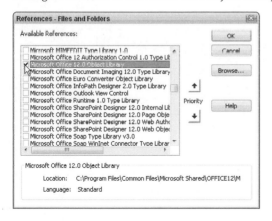

The `FileDialog` object has several useful methods and properties:

- `Filters.Add` — Lets you specify the filter(s) for displaying files, such as
  `fd.Filters.Add "Word documents", "*.doc"`

- `InitialFileName` — The default file name, for a File Picker dialog; the default path for a Folder Picker dialog

- `ButtonName` — The button caption (in case you want something other than "Select").

- `DialogType` — A selection of File Picker, Folder Picker, Open, or Save As dialog type (from the `MsoFileDialogType` enum, which can be viewed in the Object Browser).

- `InitialView` — Lets you set the view for the dialog (Details, Large Icons, Preview, and so on). Look at the `MsoFileDialogView` enum in the Object Browser for the full selection.

- `AllowMultiSelect` — If set to True, lets users select multiple files in the dialog (for File Picker dialogs only).

Figure 9.4 shows the `MsoFileDialogView` enum, with all the options for setting the view for the dialog.

FIGURE 9.4

Viewing the `MsoFileDialogView` enum in the Object Browser.

The FileSystemObject

The `FileSystemObject` library provides another way to work with Windows folders (and files). To use the components of the object library in a database, you need to set a reference, in this case to the Scripting Runtime library, as shown in Figure 9.5.

If you don't see the Microsoft Scripting Runtime selection in the References dialog, you can get this library by downloading Microsoft Windows Script 5.6 (or whatever is the current version), plus the Microsoft Windows Script 5.6 Documentation files from the Microsoft Windows Scripting Downloads page at `http://www.microsoft.com/downloads/details.aspx?familyid=01592C48-207D-4BE1-8A76-1C4099D7BBB9&displaylang=en`.

FIGURE 9.5

Setting a reference to the Scripting Runtime library.

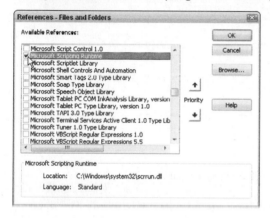

The Help file shown in Figure 9.6 (`script56.chm`) is a compiled HTML Help file. You'll find it very helpful, because it includes a Help book with full information on the components of the `FileSystemObject`, plus useful code samples.

FIGURE 9.6

The FileSystemObject Help file.

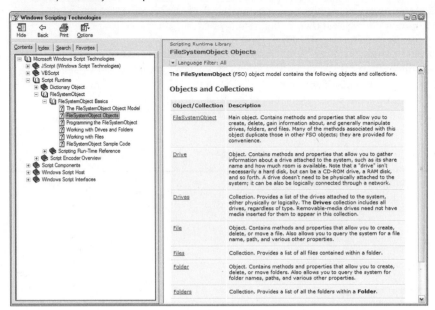

A Digression on Access Help

In my opinion, Access Help reached its highest point in Access 3.1, when it was provided in the form of a Windows Help file, every bit of which was written specifically for the current version of Access, and was available without an Internet connection. In successive versions of Access, Help moved to the HTML format, which introduced the possibility of retrieving Help topics that were not relevant to Access (say from the MSDN Library that came with VB 6.0), because properties, methods, controls, and other objects may occur in many different Microsoft applications, although they may not (usually don't) work exactly the same. If you are trying to determine which properties of a Tab control will work on an Access form, it isn't much help if the Help topic you find is for a Tab control on an Office UserForm or a VB form.

Access 2007 Help is even less useful; it searches all of Office online (at least, if you are connected to the Internet; otherwise, you won't get any help at all), using a shamefully ineffective search engine. I entered "Tab control" into the search box in the Access Help window and got the list of topics shown in the following figure. Not a single one of them is relevant. One might think that Access doesn't support Tab controls, but of course that is not the case.

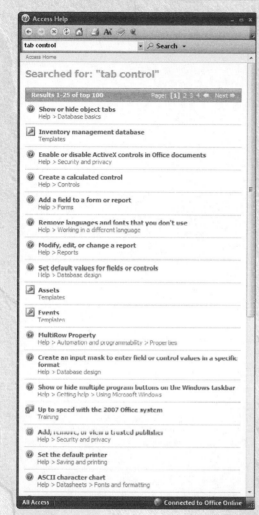

A list of inappropriate Help topics on searching for "Tab control."

There is a Table of Contents option in Access Help, but it is very sparse compared to the table of contents for Help in previous Access versions, and (curiously) it is quite different depending on whether or not you are connected to the Internet. Rather than giving full coverage of all the controls you can put on an Access form, the Controls heading (in the online version of the Table of Contents, and as shown in the following figure) has only four topics, covering only the most commonly used controls.

continued

continued

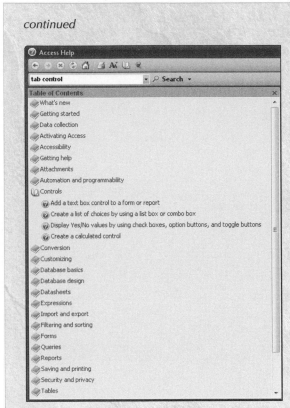

The Controls book in the Access Help Table of Contents.

The offline version of the Table of Contents has a VBA Reference section, with a section on controls, and it does point to a Help topic for the Tab control — but the topic is not available offline! And in any case, Search won't find it.

Does that mean there is no help available for the Tab control? Not at all. I entered "Tab control on Access forms" into Google and got a page of relevant topics, starting with a very useful tutorial on using the Access Tab control. It isn't specific to Access 2007, but that doesn't matter because Tab controls weren't changed in this version. Note that some of the hits are from the Microsoft web site, so Access Help can't even find appropriate help topics in Microsoft's own Support files! My conclusion: if you need help for Access 2007, try Google.

Using Google to get help for Access.

There is another option for help, at least when you are writing VBA code: As shown in the following figure, you can use the Object Browser (opened by the F2 key in the Visual Basic window) to view components of the Access object model and their attributes. In previous versions of Access, clicking the yellow question mark button would usually open an appropriate Help topic. However, this is no longer the case in Access 2007. Selecting the `TabControl` object in the Access library and clicking the Help button just opens the main Help window, where you can search ineffectually for help on the Tab control, just as I described previously.

continued

continued

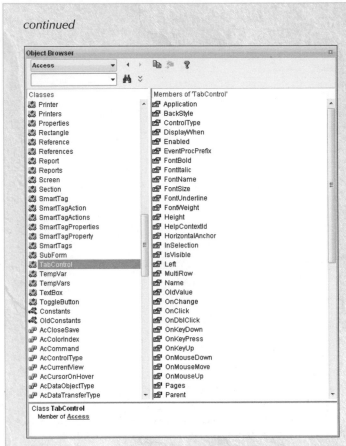

Selecting an Access object in the Object Browser.

In Access 2003, clicking the Help button for the Tab control in the Object Browser opened an appropriate Help topic.

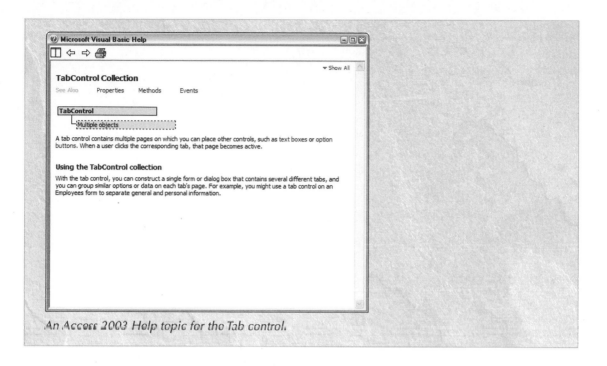

An Access 2003 Help topic for the Tab control.

Backing up Your Database

Everybody knows that data should be backed up frequently, and I like to make it as convenient as possible to back up a database. My standard database main menu features a Backup button, which calls the BackupDB procedure listed next. I created the Backup code and menu button in an earlier version of Access, when there was no way of backing up a database without closing it down.

Since that time, Microsoft has added a backup command that doesn't require closing down the database, though it's still not as convenient as my one-click backup. The Access 2007 backup command is available through the Manage button on the File menu (shown in Figure 9.7). Selecting the "Back Up Database" option opens the Save As dialog shown in Figure 9.8.

FIGURE 9.7

The Access 2007 Back Up Database selection.

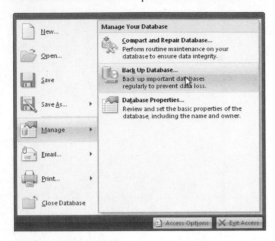

FIGURE 9.8

The built-in database save dialog.

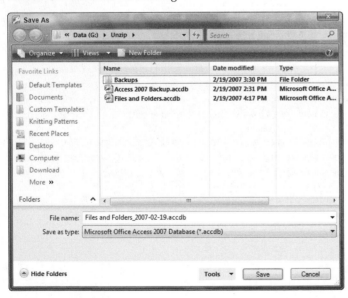

NOTE   If you are running the backup code in Windows Vista, you may be unable to back up databases in certain folders, because of Vista security restrictions. This is a Vista issue, not a problem with the database, as you can backup the database after moving it to another folder with lower security.

Though it is much easier to back up an Access database in Access 2007 than in previous versions, the new "Back Up Database" selection on the Manage menu defaults to saving the database copy in the same folder as the database itself. If you want to save your backups to another folder (which I prefer, to avoid confusion between databases and their backups), you have to browse for that folder. The BackupDB function in the following basBackup module saves backups to a folder called Backups under the database folder; you can modify the hard-coded path for saving backups as desired if you want to save your backups to another location. If you want to save backups to a Daily Backups folder on drive E, for example, you would replace the lines of code

```
strBackupPath = Application.CurrentProject.Path _
    & "\Backups\"
```

with

```
strBackupPath = "E:\Daily Backups\"
```

See Chapter 14 for a discussion of an add-in with user-selectable backup options, including selection of the backup folder from a Folder Picker dialog.

The Access 2007 Backup.accdb database contains the table, module, and macros that are used to do the database backups. These database objects can be imported into any Access 2007 database, and the BackupDB function can be run from the mcrBackup macro, or from a button on the main menu. The basBackup module is listed as follows:

```
Option Explicit
Option Compare Database

Private dbs As DAO.Database
Private fld As Scripting.Folder
Private fso As Scripting.FileSystemObject
Private intReturn As Integer
Private rst As DAO.Recordset
Private strBackupPath As String
Private strCurrentDB As String
Private strDayPrefix As String
Private strDBName As String
Private strDefault As String
Private strFinalSaveName As String
Private strPrompt As String
Private strSaveName As String
Private strTitle As String

Public Function BackupDB()
```

Requires a reference to the Microsoft Scripting Runtime library.

```
On Error GoTo ErrorHandler

    Set fso = CreateObject("Scripting.FileSystemObject")
    strCurrentDB = Application.CurrentProject.FullName
    Debug.Print "Current db: " & strCurrentDB
    strBackupPath = Application.CurrentProject.Path _
        & "\Backups\"
```

Attempt to set a reference to the backup folder.

```
    Set fld = fso.GetFolder(strBackupPath)
    strDayPrefix = Format(Date, "mm-dd-yyyy")
    strSaveName = Left(Application.CurrentProject.Name, _
        Len(Application.CurrentProject.Name) - 6) _
        & " " & SaveNo & ", " & strDayPrefix & ".accdb"
    strSaveName = strBackupPath & strSaveName
    Debug.Print "Backup save name: " & strSaveName
    strTitle = "Database backup"
    strPrompt = "Accept or edit name of database copy"
    strDefault = strSaveName
    strFinalSaveName = InputBox(prompt:=strPrompt, _
        title:=strTitle, Default:=strDefault)

    Set dbs = CurrentDb
    Set rst = dbs.OpenRecordset("tblBackupInfo")
    With rst
        .AddNew
        ![SaveDate] = Format(Date, "d-mmm-yyyy")
        ![SaveNumber] = SaveNo
        .Update
        .Close
    End With
    fso.CopyFile strCurrentDB, strFinalSaveName

ErrorHandlerExit:
    Exit Function

ErrorHandler:
    If Err.Number = 76 Then
```

If the backup folder was not found, create it.

```
        fso.CreateFolder strBackupPath
        Resume Next
    Else
```

```
          MsgBox "Error No: " & Err.Number _
              & "; Description: " & Err.Description
          Resume ErrorHandlerExit
      End If

  End Function

  Public Function SaveNo() As String

  On Error GoTo ErrorHandler

      Dim intDayNo As Integer
      Dim strNextNo As String
```

Create a unique save number for today.

```
      intDayNo = Nz(DMax("[SaveNumber]", "tblBackupInfo", _
          "[SaveDate] = Date()"))
      Debug.Print "Day no. " & intDayNo
      strNextNo = CStr(intDayNo + 1)
      Debug.Print "Next No. " & strNextNo
      SaveNo = strNextNo

  ErrorHandlerExit:
      Exit Function

  ErrorHandler:
      MsgBox "Error No: " & Err.Number _
          & "; Description: " & Err.Description
      Resume ErrorHandlerExit

  End Function
```

The SaveNo() function creates an incrementing number for the current backup by picking up the latest number stored for today's date from tblBackupInfo and adding 1 to it.

The BackupDB procedure backs up the current database, creating a save name from the database's name (picked up from the Name property of the CurrentProject property of the Application object), plus the SaveNo() value and today's date, formatted with dashes. (You can change the date format as desired, so long as you don't use slashes or other characters that are not permitted in file names.) The proposed save name is presented in an InputBox, where it can be edited as desired, such as adding info on specific changes made to the database; it is then saved to a folder called Backups under the current database folder.

The GetFolder method of the FileSystemObject is used to reference the Backups folder; if the folder is not found, the function's error handler creates the folder using the CreateFolder method. A record is added to tblBackupInfo with the date and the save number, and finally the

CopyFile method of the FileSystemObject is used to copy the current database to a backup with the final save name in the Backups folder.

The tblBackupInfo table stores dates and incrementing numbers for the backup names. The backups you make on a given day will have a number (starting with 1) and the date, so they don't overwrite each other, and you will know the order in which the backups were created. Figure 9.9 shows the InputBox presented by the BackupDB function; you can accept the proposed save name or edit it as desired.

FIGURE 9.9

Saving a database copy using the BackupDB function.

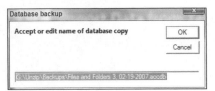

Working with Text Files

For purposes of working with text files in VBA code, there are three types of text files: comma-delimited, fixed-width (columnar), or free-form. Data from the first two types of text files can be imported or exported using the TransferText method in Access, and comma-delimited files can be processed with the TransferSpreadsheet method. If you just need to read data from (or write data to) a text file, but not import into a table, you can work with text files using the FileSystemObject, the legacy VB methods, or ADO.

 **CROSS-REF** Exporting to (and importing from) comma-delimited and fixed-width text files is covered in Chapter 10.

Writing Data to Text Files

If your code iterates through a recordset, doing (or not doing) some action for each record, a text file is a handy way to document which records have been processed, or perhaps just to document records that were skipped because of missing information. You can write informational data to a text file using three methods: the legacy VB statements (Open *FileName* For Input/Output As #*n*); components of the FileSystemObject object model (the TextStream object in particular); or components of the ADO object model (the Stream object in particular).

The sample Select Contacts for Email form (frmEMailMerge), shown in Figure 9.10, has a multi-select listbox for selecting contacts to receive an email, textboxes for entering the message subject and body, and an option group for selecting the method of creating a text file containing information about the skipped records.

FIGURE 9.10

A form with options to create a text file with information about skipped records using three different methods.

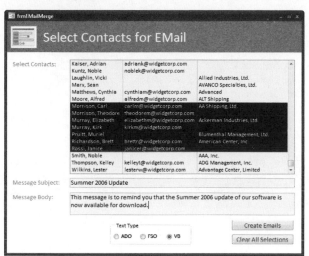

The complete `cmdCreateEMails_Click` event procedure is listed next; the code first checks that the message subject and body text have been entered on the form and sets a reference to the Outlook Application object, deletes the old text file, if it exists, then sets up a `Select Case` statement to work with text files differently, according to which option was selected in the Text Type option group:

```
Private Sub cmdCreateEMails_Click()

On Error GoTo ErrorHandler

    Dim appOutlook As Outlook.Application
    Dim fso As Scripting.FileSystemObject
    Dim msg As Outlook.MailItem
    Dim strBody As String
    Dim strEMailRecipient
    Dim strSubject As String
    Dim strTo As String
    Dim varItem As Variant
    Dim strTest As String
    Dim lngContactID As Long
    Dim strFullName As String
    Dim strText As String
    Dim strCompanyName As String
    Dim strDocsPath As String
    Dim strFile As String
```

```
Dim blnSomeSkipped As Boolean
Dim intTextType As Integer
Dim strTitle As String
Dim strPrompt As String
Dim txt As Scripting.TextStream
Dim tstr As ADODB.Stream

Set lst = Me![lstSelectContacts]
intTextType = Nz(Me![fraTextType].Value, 2)
strDocsPath = GetCustomDocsPath()
```

Check that at least one contact has been selected.

```
If lst.ItemsSelected.Count = 0 Then
   strTitle = "No contact selected"
   strPrompt = "Please select at least one contact"
   MsgBox prompt:=strPrompt, Buttons:=vbExclamation _
      + vbOKOnly, title:=strTitle
   lst.SetFocus
   GoTo ErrorHandlerExit
End If
```

Test for required message fields.

```
strSubject = Nz(Me![txtMessageSubject].Value)
If strSubject = "" Then
   strTitle = "No subject entered"
   strPrompt = "Please enter a subject"
   MsgBox prompt:=strPrompt, Buttons:=vbExclamation _
      + vbOKOnly, title:=strTitle
   Me![txtMessageSubject].SetFocus
   GoTo ErrorHandlerExit
End If

strBody = Nz(Me![txtMessageBody].Value)
If strBody = "" Then
   strTitle = "No message body entered"
   strPrompt = "Please enter the message body"
   MsgBox prompt:=strPrompt, Buttons:=vbExclamation _
      + vbOKOnly, title:=strTitle
   Me![txtMessageBody].SetFocus
   GoTo ErrorHandlerExit
End If
```

Checks passed; proceed to create a message using the selected text output method.

```
Set appOutlook = GetObject(, "Outlook.Application")
strFile = strDocsPath & "Skipped Records.txt"
Debug.Print "Text file: " & strFile

On Error Resume Next
```

284

Delete existing file, if there is one.

```
Kill strFile

On Error GoTo ErrorHandler

Select Case intTextType

    Case 1
```

ADO

```
Set tstr = New ADODB.Stream
tstr.Open
strText = "Information on progress creating " _
    & "Outlook mail messages"
tstr.WriteText Data:=strText, Options:=adWriteLine
tstr.WriteText Data:=vbCrLf & vbCrLf

blnSomeSkipped = False

For Each varItem In lst.ItemsSelected
```

Get the Contact ID and name for reference.

```
lngContactID = Nz(lst.Column(0, varItem))
Debug.Print "Contact ID: " & lngContactID
strFullName = Nz(lst.Column(1, varItem))
```

Check for email address.

```
strEMailRecipient = Nz(lst.Column(2, varItem))
strTest = strEMailRecipient
Debug.Print "Email address: " & strTest
If strTest = "" Then
    blnSomeSkipped = True
    strText = "Contact No. " & lngContactID _
        & " (" & strFullName _
        & ") skipped; no email address"
    tstr.WriteText Data:=vbCrLf
    tstr.WriteText Data:=strText, _
        Options:=adWriteLine
    GoTo NextContactADO
End If
```

Check for company name.

```
strCompanyName = Nz(lst.Column(3, varItem))
strTest = strCompanyName
Debug.Print "Company name: " & strTest
```

```
                    If strTest = "" Then
                        blnSomeSkipped = True
                        strText = "Contact No. " & lngContactID _
                            & " (" & strFullName _
                            & ") skipped; no company name"
                        tstr.WriteText Data:=vbCrLf
                        tstr.WriteText Data:=strText, _
                            Options:=adWriteLine
                        GoTo NextContactADO
                    End If
```

Has required info; create new mail message and send to contact.

```
                    Set msg = appOutlook.CreateItem(olMailItem)
                    With msg
                        .To = strEMailRecipient
                        .Subject = strSubject
                        .Body = strBody
                        .Send
                    End With

            NextContactADO:
                    Next varItem

                    If blnSomeSkipped = True Then
```

Write final line and save text file.

```
                        strText = "End of File"
                        tstr.WriteText Data:=vbCrLf
                        tstr.WriteText Data:=strText
                        tstr.SaveToFile FileName:=strFile, _
                            Options:=adSaveCreateNotExist
                    End If

            Case 2
```

FSO

```
                    Set fso = CreateObject("Scripting.FileSystemObject")
                    Set txt = fso.CreateTextFile(FileName:=strFile, _
                        overwrite:=True)
                    strText = "Information on progress creating " _
                        & "Outlook mail messages"
                    txt.WriteLine Text:=strText
                    txt.WriteBlankLines Lines:=2

                    blnSomeSkipped = False

                    For Each varItem In lst.ItemsSelected
```

Get Contact ID and name for reference.

```
lngContactID = Nz(lst.Column(0, varItem))
Debug.Print "Contact ID: " & lngContactID
strFullName = Nz(lst.Column(1, varItem))
```

Check for email address.

```
strEMailRecipient = Nz(lst.Column(2, varItem))
strTest = strEMailRecipient
Debug.Print "Email address: " & strTest
If strTest = "" Then
    blnSomeSkipped = True
    strText = "Contact No. " & lngContactID _
        & " (" & strFullName _
        & ") skipped; no email address"
    txt.WriteBlankLines Lines:=1
    txt.WriteLine Text:=strText
    GoTo NextContactFSO
End If
```

Check for company name.

```
strCompanyName = Nz(lst.Column(3, varItem))
strTest = strCompanyName
Debug.Print "Company name: " & strTest
If strTest = "" Then
    blnSomeSkipped = True
    strText = "Contact No. " & lngContactID _
        & " (" & strFullName _
        & ") skipped; no company name"
    txt.WriteBlankLines Lines:=1
    txt.WriteLine Text:=strText
    GoTo NextContactFSO
End If
```

Has required info; create new mail message and send to contact.

```
Set msg = appOutlook.CreateItem(olMailItem)
With msg
    .To = strEMailRecipient
    .Subject = strSubject
    .Body = strBody
    .Send
End With

NextContactFSO:
    Next varItem
```

Write final line.

```
        strText = "End of File"
        txt.WriteBlankLines Lines:=1
        txt.WriteLine Text:=strText

    Case 3
```

VB

Open text file for writing information about export progress.

```
        Open strFile For Output As #1
        strText = "Information on progress creating " _
           & "Outlook mail messages"
        Print #1, strText
        Print #1,
        Print #1,

        blnSomeSkipped = False

        For Each varItem In lst.ItemsSelected
```

Get Contact ID and name for reference.

```
        lngContactID = Nz(lst.Column(0, varItem))
        Debug.Print "Contact ID: " & lngContactID
        strFullName = Nz(lst.Column(1, varItem))
```

Check for email address.

```
        strEMailRecipient = Nz(lst.Column(2, varItem))
        strTest = strEMailRecipient
        Debug.Print "Email address: " & strTest
        If strTest = "" Then
           blnSomeSkipped = True
           strText = "Contact No. " & lngContactID _
              & " (" & strFullName _
              & ") skipped; no email address"
           Print #1,
           Print #1, strText
           GoTo NextContactVB
        End If
```

Check for company name.

```
        strCompanyName = Nz(lst.Column(3, varItem))
        strTest = strCompanyName
        Debug.Print "Company name: " & strTest
```

```
        If strTest = "" Then
           blnSomeSkipped = True
           strText = "Contact No. " & lngContactID _
              & " (" & strFullName _
              & ") skipped; no company name"
           Print #1,
           Print #1, strText
           GoTo NextContactVB
        End If
```

Has required info; create new mail message and send to contact.

```
        Set msg = appOutlook.CreateItem(olMailItem)
        With msg
           .To = strEMailRecipient
           .Subject = strSubject
           .Body = strBody
           .Send
        End With

   NextContactVB:
        Next varItem

        If blnSomeSkipped = True Then
```

Write final line and close text file.

```
        strText = "End of file"
        Print #1,
        Print #1, strText
        Close #1
     End If


   End Select
```

Open text file in Notepad.

```
   Shell "Notepad " & strFile

ErrorHandlerExit:
   Exit Sub

ErrorHandler:
```

Outlook is not running; open Outlook with CreateObject.

```
   If Err.Number = 429 Then
      Set appOutlook = CreateObject("Outlook.Application")
      Resume Next
   ElseIf Err.Number = 55 Then
```

File is already open; close it.

```
        Close #1
        Resume
    Else
        MsgBox "Error No: " & Err.Number _
            & "; Description: " & Err.Description
        Resume ErrorHandlerExit
    End If

    End Sub
```

Figure 9.11 shows a typical text file created by the cmdCreateEMails_Click event procedure code (the text file is the same regardless of the method used to create it).

FIGURE 9.11

A text file with information on skipped records.

Figure 9.12 shows one of the email messages created by the previous code.

As is so often the case with Access, you have a choice of several techniques to use when working with text files in VBA code. Any of the three methods discussed in the next sections can create a text file and write to it; which method you use depends on such factors as your familiarity with the technique, or the need for extra references in the database to support the code. I generally use the FileSystemObject method, partly because I usually have a reference set to the Scripting Runtime library for other purposes and partly because its syntax is the most intuitive. If your database has a reference to the ADO library, but not the Scripting Runtime library, you can use the ADO method to avoid the need for setting an extra reference; if you don't have a reference set to either the ADO or Scripting Runtime libraries, you can use the VB method to avoid setting an extra reference.

FIGURE 9.12

FIGURE 9.12

An email message created from code.

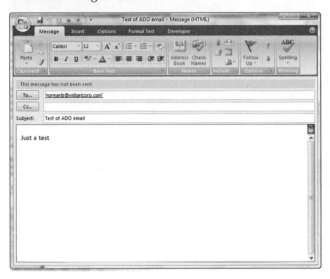

ADO

The ActiveX Data Objects (ADO) model isn't the best method for working with Access data, but it does offer some extra features that are very handy for working with text files, in particular the `Stream` object. The ADO case in the `cmdCreateEMails_Click` event procedure starts by setting a variable to a `Stream` object in the ADO object model (note that the object model prefix is ADODB), using the `New` keyword. The next line opens the new `Stream` object (you can't write to it unless it is open). A string of introductory text to be written to the file is saved to the `strText` variable and then written to a line in the stream using the `WriteText` method. To create two blank lines in the text file, `WriteText` is then used with two `vbCrLf` constants (representing a CR + LF, meaning carriage return plus linefeed — antique terminology dating back to the days of manual typewriters).

 **You need a reference to the ActiveX Data Objects object library to support this code.**

The code iterates through the ItemsSelected collection of the lstSelectContacts listbox, checking each record for required fields (Email and CompanyName). For each record that lacks data in one or both of the required fields (and thus won't get an email message), an `If . . . Then` statement writes a line containing information on which record has been skipped, and why, plus another blank line. At the end of the Case, a final line is written, and the stream is saved to a text file using the `SaveToFile` method with the `adSaveCreateNotExist` option, which creates the file if it does not exist.

FileSystemObject

The `FileSystemObject` object library provides an alternate approach to working with text files, using the `TextStream` object. The FSO case in the `cmdCreateEMails_Click` event procedure starts by creating a `FileSystemObject` variable and then creating a `TextStream` variable using the `CreateTextFile` method. A string of introductory text to be written to the file is saved to the `strText` variable and then written to a line in the text file using the `WriteLine` method. To create two blank lines in the text file, the `WriteBlankLines` method is then used with the `Lines` argument set to 2.

 You need a reference to the Microsoft Scripting Runtime object library to support this code.

The code iterates through the ItemsSelected collection of the lstSelectContacts listbox, checking each record for required fields (Email and CompanyName). For each record that lacks data in one or both of the required fields (and thus won't get an email message), an `If . . . Then` statement writes a line containing information on which record has been skipped, and why, plus another blank line. When all the items have been processed, a final line is written to the text file.

VB

The third case uses legacy VB statements from the earliest days of Access; no object model reference is needed. The `Open strFile For Output As #1` statement creates and opens the text file for output. A string of introductory text to be written to the file is saved to the `strText` variable and then written to a line in the text file using the rather unintuitive `Print #1` method. To create two blank lines in the text file, two `Print #1` lines with no argument are used.

The code iterates through the ItemsSelected collection of the lstSelectContacts listbox, checking each record for required fields (Email and CompanyName). For each record that lacks data in one or both of the required fields (and thus won't get an email message), an `If . . . Then` statement writes another blank line and a line containing information on which record has been skipped.

At the end of the case, a final line is written, and the file is closed using the `Close #1` statement. This does not delete the text file, just closes it.

Reading Data from Text Files

Just as you can write data to text files, you can use legacy VB statements, `FileSystemObject` code, or ADO code to read data from text files. The Import Data from Text File form (frmTextImport) has a command button for selecting a text file to import (Figure 9.13 shows the form, and Figure 9.14 shows the File Picker dialog opened by this button), and an option group with a choice of ADO, FSO (FileSystemObject), and VB-type text imports; the imported data is written to the large Imported Text textbox when you click the "Load Data From File" button. A "Clear Imported Data" button clears the Imported Text textbox so you can start over.

FIGURE 9.13

A form with a choice of loading data from a text file using three different methods.

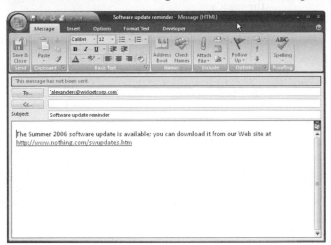

FIGURE 9.14

Selecting a text file for importing data.

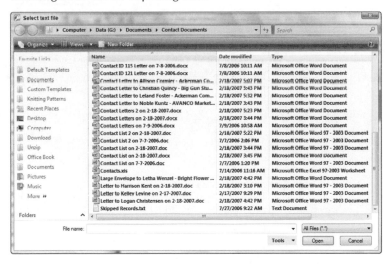

The `cmdLoadData_Click` event procedure that reads data from a text file is simpler than the code that writes data, because two of the three methods (in their own way) can import all the data from a text file without needing to process each line separately. The `cmdLoadData_Click` procedure starts by setting a reference to the textbox that holds the name of the selected text file, and checks that there is a file name in the box. If there is a file name, it is saved to a variable, and then a `Select Case` statement is set up to process the import separately depending on whether the user selects ADO, FSO, or VB in an option group:

```
Private Sub cmdLoadData_Click()

On Error GoTo ErrorHandler

    Dim fso As Scripting.FileSystemObject
    Dim strText As String
    Dim strFile As String
    Dim intTextType As Integer
    Dim strTitle As String
    Dim strPrompt As String
    Dim txt As Scripting.TextStream
    Dim stm As ADODB.Stream
    Dim txtData As Access.TextBox
    Dim strTextFile As String
    Dim strData As String
    Dim strLine As String

    Set txtData = Me![txtSelectedTextFile]
    strTextFile = Nz(txtData.Value)
    If strTextFile = "" Then
       strTitle = "No text file selected"
       strPrompt = "Please select a text file"
       MsgBox prompt:=strPrompt, Buttons:=vbExclamation _
          + vbOKOnly, title:=strTitle
       GoTo ErrorHandlerExit
    Else
       Debug.Print "Text file: " & strTextFile
    End If

    intTextType = Nz(Me![fraTextType].Value, 2)

    Select Case intTextType

       Case 1
```
ADO
```
          Set stm = New ADODB.Stream

          With stm
             .Charset = "ASCII"
```

```
                    .Open
                    .LoadFromFile strTextFile
                    .Position = 0
                    strData = .ReadText(adReadAll)
                End With
```

Close Stream object.

```
                stm.Close

            Case 2
```

FSO

```
                Set fso = CreateObject("Scripting.FileSystemObject")
                Set txt = fso.OpenTextFile(FileName:=strTextFile, _
                    IOMode:=ForReading)
```

Read all data from file.

```
                strData = txt.ReadAll
```

Close file.

```
                txt.Close

            Case 3
```

VB

Open text file for reading data.

```
                Open strTextFile For Input As #2
                Do While Not EOF(2)
```

Save data from a line in the text file to a variable.

```
                    Input #2, strLine
                    strData = strData & IIf(strData <> "", _
                        vbCrLf, "") & strLine
                Loop
```

Close file.

```
                Close #2

        End Select
```

Write data to text box on form.

```
Me![txtImportedText].Value = strData

ErrorHandlerExit:
   Exit Sub

ErrorHandler:
   MsgBox "Error No: " & Err.Number _
      & "; Description: " & Err.Description
   Resume ErrorHandlerExit

End Sub
```

The next sections describe the specific techniques used in the code for the ADO, FSO, and VB methods for loading data from a selected text file.

ADO

For the ADO option, a Stream variable is set, using the New keyword, the Stream object is opened, and the selected text file is loaded, using the LoadFromFile method. The ReadText method is used with the adReadAll named constant as its argument to read in all the text from the text file, and that data is then written to the strData variable. Finally, the Stream object is closed.

FSO

For the FSO (FileSystemObject) option, first a variable is set to the FileSystemObject, and then the text file is opened with the OpenTextFile method of the FileSystemObject, with the ForReading value for the IOMode argument. All of the data from the text file is read using the ReadAll method, and it is saved to the strData variable. Finally, the text file is closed.

VB

The last method, VB, uses the Open strTextFileForInput As #2 statement to open the file, and sets up a Do While . . . Loop structure to process all of the lines in the text file, saving data from each line to the strData variable, incrementing it line by line with a vbCrLf constant in between lines. When all the lines have been processed, the text file is closed.

Finally, however the data has been accumulated, the strData variable is written to the txtImportedText textbox, as shown in Figure 9.15.

FIGURE 9.15

A form with data loaded from a text file, using the FileSystemObject method.

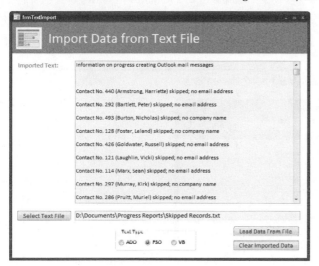

Working with Attachment Fields

NEW FEATURE The Attachment data type discussed in this section is new to Access 2007.

Previous versions of Access had an OLE Object field data type, which only supported certain types of objects and was quite cumbersome to use (not to mention causing terrible database bloat). By contrast, in Access 2007, it is quite easy to store files of any type in a field of the new Attachment data type, and the attachments are automatically compressed to save database space. The Contacts form, frmContactsWithAttachments (opened from the Browse Contacts button on the main menu) has such a field. If an attachment has already been added to the field, it shows as an icon (at least, if it is of a type recognized by Office); Figure 9.16 shows a record with a Word 2007 document attachment.

NOTE The attachment icons differ according to the Office version of the stored attachment file. A Word document's icon has a Word document with a W image over the upper-left corner; the style of the W differs for Word 97-2003 (.doc) or Word 2007 (.docx) documents. For a Word 2007 document, the W is similar to the one displayed in a Word 2007 document's taskbar icon; for Word 97-2003 documents, the W is the older style W that was used as the Word icon in Office 97. Other Office documents also have different icons depending on their version.

I discussed using the `FileSystemObject` (Scripting Runtime library) for working with folders in an earlier section of this chapter; you can also use the `FileSystemObject` to work with files in a folder, or create files. One possible use is to select a file from a folder to store in a new Attachment data type field in an Access table.

A form with an attachment field, showing a stored Word 2007 document.

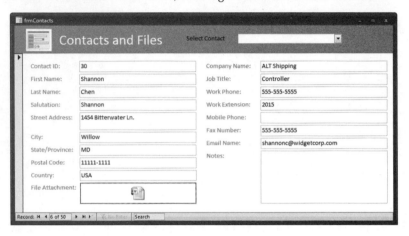

To add an attachment, just double-click the field; this opens the Attachments dialog (shown in Figure 9.17), where you can view existing attachments (multiple attachments can be stored in one Attachment field), or add a new one by clicking the Add button.

The Attachment dialog, showing a stored Word 2007 document.

The Add button in the Attachments dialog (shown in Figure 9.17) opens a Choose File dialog (shown in Figure 9.18) where you can select a file to store in the Attachment field.

FIGURE 9.18

Selecting a TIF file in the Choose File dialog.

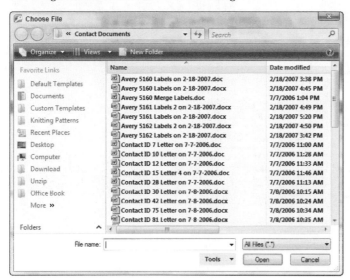

NOTE   If you store multiple files in an Attachment field, only the first file's icon will be displayed in the form control.

Though it is easy enough to store an attachment or two manually, if you have a folder full of attachments that need to be stored in hundreds of records, it is easier to use VBA code to store the attachments, or to extract attachments and save them to a folder. As an example, suppose you have a folder containing numerous Word documents and Excel worksheets (both in Office 2007 and earlier formats) related to contacts. Each document name starts with "Contact ID" and a number, which corresponds to the ContactID field in tblContacts in the sample database.

Loading Files into Attachment Fields

NEW FEATURE   The Recordset2 object (new to Access 2007) is used to work with fields of the Attachment type.

The `LoadAttachments` procedure listed next iterates through the documents in the folder selected by the Input Documents Path button on the main menu, and for any document that starts with "Contact ID" saves the document to the corresponding contact record's File field (this field is of the Attachment data type). An Attachment field can contain multiple attachments, and the collection of attachments is represented in VBA code as a separate recordset of attachments belonging to a record in a table. Using a `Recordset2` object (new to Access 2007) to work with the attachments lets you use the new `LoadFromFile` and `SaveToFile` methods to work with the attachments.

Figure 9.19 shows a folder with Contact ID documents of various types for loading as attachments.

FIGURE 9.19

A folder with some Contact ID documents, for creating attachments.

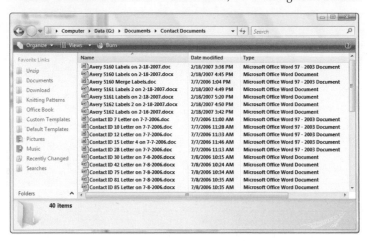

In the LoadAttachments function listed as follows, declaring the rstAttachments variable as a Recordset2 object (instead of a Recordset object) allows use of the new LoadFromFile and SaveToFile methods, which I use to load files into Attachment fields, or save files from Attachment fields:

```
Public Function LoadAttachments()

On Error GoTo ErrorHandler

    Dim intSpace As Integer
    Dim strTest As String
    Dim strSearch As String

    strDocsPath = GetInputDocsPath()
    Set fso = CreateObject("Scripting.FileSystemObject")
    Set fld = fso.GetFolder(strDocsPath)
    Set dbs = CurrentDb
    Set rstTable = dbs.OpenRecordset("tblContacts", dbOpenDynaset)

    For Each fil In fld.Files
        strFile = fil.Name
        Debug.Print "File name: " & strFile
        Debug.Print "File type: " & fil.Type
```

Check whether file name starts with 'Contact ID'

```
        If Left(strFile, 10) = "Contact ID" Then
```

Extract Contact ID from file name, using `Mid` and `InStr` functions to start at the beginning of the number and end before the space following the number, if there is one.

```
strTest = Mid(String:=strFile, Start:=12, Length:=3)
intSpace = InStr(strTest, " ")

If intSpace > 0 Then
   lngContactID = CLng(Mid(String:=strTest, _
      Start:=1, Length:=intSpace - 1))
Else
   lngContactID = CLng(strTest)
End If

strSearch = "[ContactID] = " & lngContactID
Debug.Print "Search string: " & strSearch
strFileAndPath = strDocsPath & strFile
```

Search for matching Contact ID in table.

```
rstTable.MoveFirst
rstTable.FindFirst strSearch
If rstTable.NoMatch = True Then
   strTitle = "Can't find contact"
   strPrompt = "Contact ID " & lngContactID _
      & " not found in table; can't add attachment"
   GoTo NextDoc
Else
   rstTable.Edit
```

Create recordset of attachments for this record, using the new Recordset2 type recordset.

```
Set rstAttachments = _
   rstTable.Fields("File").Value
```

Turn off the error handler to prevent errors if the code attempts to add the same file twice; in this case the Attachments recordset won't be updated.

```
On Error Resume Next

   With rstAttachments
      .AddNew
      .Fields("FileData").LoadFromFile _
         (strFileAndPath)
      .Update
      .Close
   End With
   rstTable.Update
   Debug.Print "Added " & strFileAndPath _
      & " as attachment to Contact ID " _
      & lngContactID; "'s record"
End If
```

```
          End If

    NextDoc:
        Next fil
```

Open the Contacts form to see the attachments that have been loaded.

```
        DoCmd.OpenForm FormName:="frmContacts"

    ErrorHandlerExit:
        Exit Function

    ErrorHandler:
        MsgBox "Error No: " & Err.Number _
            & "; Description: " & Err.Description

    End Function
```

Figure 9.20 shows the main menu of the sample database, Files and Folders.accdb, with the Load Attachments option selected; this selection calls the `LoadAttachments` function.

FIGURE 9.20

The main menu, with an Attachments button with two options, for loading or saving attachments.

Saving Attachments to Files

The `SaveAttachments` procedure performs the opposite function: working with a recordset based on tblContacts, it uses a `Recordset2` type recordset to iterate through the attachments collection of a record and saves each one to a file in the Output Documents folder selected on the main menu:

```
Public Function SaveAttachments()

On Error GoTo ErrorHandler

    Dim intSpace As Integer
    Dim strTest As String
    Dim strSearch As String

    strDocsPath = GetOutputDocsPath()
    Debug.Print "Output docs path: " & strDocsPath
    Set fso = CreateObject("Scripting.FileSystemObject")
    Set fld = fso.GetFolder(strDocsPath)
    Set dbs = CurrentDb
    Set rstTable = dbs.OpenRecordset("tblContacts")

    Do While Not rstTable.EOF
```

Create recordset of attachments for this record.

```
        Set rstAttachments = _
            rstTable.Fields("File").Value
        With rstAttachments
            Do While Not .EOF
                strFileAndPath = strDocsPath _
                    & .Fields("FileName")
```

Save this attachment to a file in the Output Docs folder.

```
                Debug.Print "Saving " & strFileAndPath _
                    & " to " & strDocsPath & " folder"
```

Turn off error handler to prevent errors if the file already exists in the folder.

```
On Error Resume Next

                .Fields("FileData").SaveToFile strFileAndPath
                .MoveNext
            Loop
            .Close
        End With
        rstTable.MoveNext
    Loop

    rstTable.Close
    strPrompt = "All new attachments saved to " _
        & strDocsPath & " folder"
    strTitle = "Done!"
    MsgBox strPrompt, vbOKOnly + vbInformation, strTitle
```

```
ErrorHandlerExit:
    Exit Function

ErrorHandler:
    MsgBox "Error No: " & Err.Number _
        & "; Description: " & Err.Description
    Resume ErrorHandlerExit

End Function
```

NEW FEATURE   In Access 2007, it is much easier to save a database to an older format, as well as saving a copy of the database in the current format (the long awaited "Database Save As"); the three choices are right on the Save As submenu of the Office menu, as shown in Figure 9-21.

FIGURE 9.21

Saving a database in Access 2002-2003 format.

Summary

In this chapter you learned how to use the Office `FileDialog` object to allow easy selection of a folder for loading or saving documents. In addition, you learned how to use a variety of techniques for creating text files, saving data to them, and loading data from them to Access tables, using ADO, the `FileSystemObject`, and legacy VB statements, and also how to save attachments from files to the new Attachment field (or extract attachments from such fields and save them as files), using VBA code. These techniques will allow you to work with text files in a variety of ways, to add extra functionality to your databases, over and above working with Office documents.

Chapter 10

Working with External Data

IN THIS CHAPTER

Importing and exporting comma-delimited and fixed-width text files

Importing and exporting dBASE, Paradox, and Lotus 1-2-3 files

Importing and exporting XML and HTML files

Emailing exported text files

In the previous chapter, you learned how to work with text files, using one old method and two new ones. For some types of text files, you can also use methods of the Access Application object for importing and exporting text files when working with data in VBA code. The TransferText method has been used to import data from (or export data to) comma-delimited or fixed-width files since the early days of Access, and it is still useful in Access 2007, when you are working with files in these formats. In Office XP, the TransferText method was updated to also export to and import from HTML files.

Typically, comma-delimited or fixed-width files are produced by mainframe computers, and you may need to import these files into your Access tables or export data from Access tables to comma-delimited or fixed-width files for import into mainframe applications. Additionally, you can use these formats to export data to or import data from other applications whose formats aren't directly supported by Access.

If you have data in Excel or Lotus spreadsheets, you can use the TransferSpreadsheet method to import data from them or export data to spreadsheets. And the TransferDatabase method can be used to transfer data between Access tables and legacy databases or spreadsheets.

These three methods don't have the power or flexibility of Automation code, which can iterate through the records in a table, perhaps using a filtered recordset, and write data from specific fields to a worksheet. But if you need to import all the data from a Lotus worksheet or a dBASE database, so you can work with it in Access, these methods come in handy.

These days, it is not likely that you would want to export Access data to a Lotus spreadsheet or a dBASE database, but there is still a need to export comma-delimited or fixed-width text files, so the `TransferText` method is also useful for exporting data from Access to text files.

Working with Text Files Using the TransferText Method

When you use the `TransferText` method in VBA code, you can supply a specification name. A specification for an import or export is created when you run the export or import manually. The process of creating a specification (and reusing it in the interface) has been streamlined in Access 2007; I cover the creation of an export specification in the next section. Specifications are handy when you need to set a number of custom options for an export or import, especially if you plan to re-run the export or import in the interface; however, they are not required.

Creating an Import or Export Specification

The process of creating an import specification for importing a fixed-width text file is described next; you create specifications for importing a comma-delimited text file, or exporting either of those file types, in a similar manner, with different options depending on the file type. You might want to use an import specification, for example, if you receive a text file of comma-delimited data downloaded from a mainframe every week, and you need to import the weekly data into an Access table.

1. First, click the Text File button on the External Data menu, as shown in Figure 10.1.

FIGURE 10.1

Starting an import of a text file.

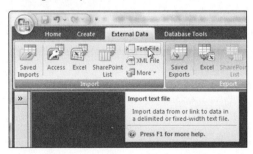

2. Next, in the Get External Data - Text File dialog box (shown in Figure 10.2), use the Browse button to select the text file to import (Jobs 02-Jul-2006.txt in the example).

FIGURE 10.2

Selecting a text file to import.

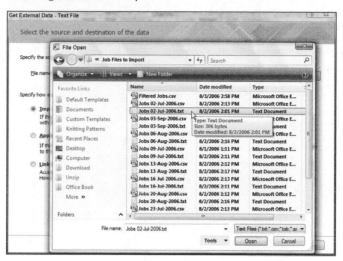

3. After selecting the file, clicking OK on the Get External Data - Text File dialog box opens the Import Text Wizard (Figure 10.3), with a selection of Delimited or Fixed Width; generally Access pre-selects the correct option.

FIGURE 10.3

The Import Text Wizard dialog box.

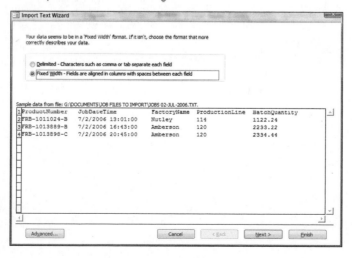

4. Clicking Next brings up a screen where you can adjust the column widths, as shown in Figure 10.4.

FIGURE 10.4

Adjusting columns in a fixed-width file.

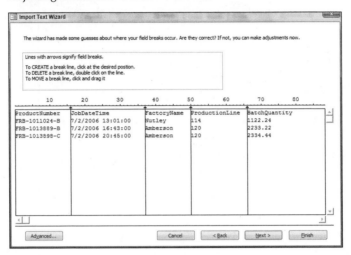

5. The next screen, shown in Figure 10.5, lets you specify field names if they are lacking in the text file (this is often the case with files exported from mainframes). The figure shows the first field (originally named ProductNumber, and given a default field name of Field1 by the wizard) being renamed with its original name. You can also change the data type of the field, if necessary; for example, making a Text field containing numeric data a Long Integer or Currency field, or a Text field containing date/time data a Date/Time field.

6. The screen in Figure 10.6 lets you add, select, or not specify a primary key; in this case, because the data will be appended to a table that has an AutoNumber field, the "No primary key" option is correct.

7. You will next see a screen that lets you enter the name of the target Access table.

FIGURE 10.5

Specifying field names for an imported text file.

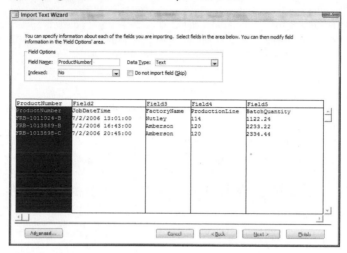

FIGURE 10.6

Primary key choices for an imported text file.

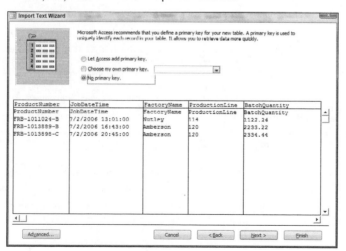

You have now supplied all the information needed to set up the specification; the next steps, where you save the specification, are new to Access 2007.

NEW FEATURE Clicking the Finish button opens a new Save Import Steps screen (shown in Figure 10.7). If you check the "Save import steps" checkbox, more controls appear on the dialog, where you can enter the name and description of the saved import specification, and even create an Outlook task to run it automatically at a specified interval.

FIGURE 10.7

Saving an import specification.

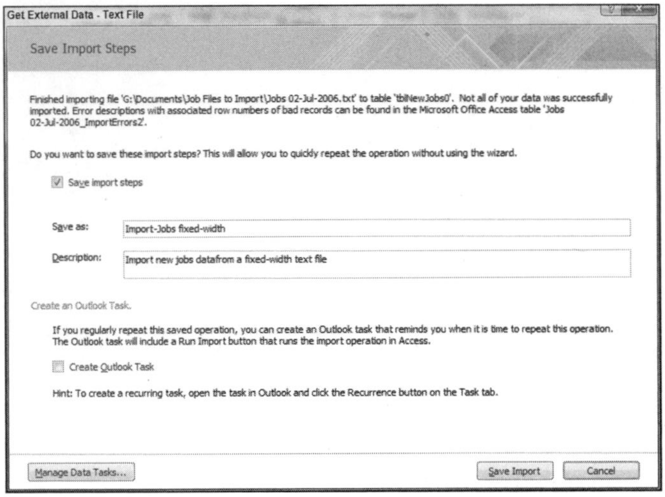

Clicking the Save Import button saves the import specification. This allows you to select the saved specification and run it in the future from the Saved Imports button on the External Data tab of the Ribbon (shown in Figure 10.1), which saves a lot of time compared with going through all the steps of the wizard each time you want to do the import.

CAUTION Unfortunately, Access 2007 VBA code doesn't recognize saved specifications. This feature worked for several previous versions, but at present it is broken, so we must wait for a patch or service pack to fix it. For now, only code that avoids using specifications will work. (You can import from, or export to, a comma-delimited file without a specification, but not a fixed-width file.)

The Manage Data Tasks screen is shown in Figure 10.8. It has two tabs, one for saved imports and the other for saved exports. On each tab, you can select a saved specification to run.

FIGURE 10.8

The Manage Data Tasks dialog, where you can select a saved import or export specification.

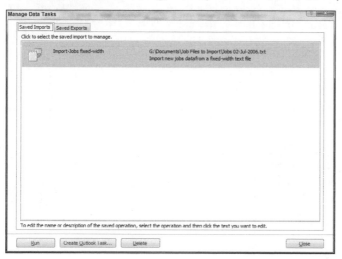

NOTE Sometimes the wizard doesn't recognize that the first line of a text file contains the field names. In that case, you need to give the fields appropriate names, and then delete the first row, with the field names as data, after the import is finished (you will probably get some Type Conversion errors in the Import Errors table for that line). Figure 10.9 shows the table of imported jobs data, and the Import Errors table with errors on the first row containing the field names.

FIGURE 10.9

A table of imported text data, with field names in the first data row, and an Import Errors table.

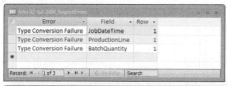

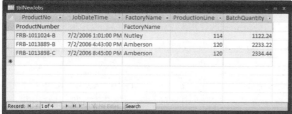

Importing and Exporting Text File Data in VBA Code

The main menu of the sample application, External Data.accdb (shown in Figure 10.10), has buttons for opening various forms that import and export data in a variety of file formats. Writing VBA code to do the imports and exports gives you one-click convenience, particularly useful if you have to do an import or export task frequently, for example importing weekly Jobs data downloaded from a mainframe computer or emailed as a fixed-width or comma-delimited text file.

The main menu of the External Data sample database.

Importing Text Data

The following steps illustrate how to import data from a text file into an Access table, using VBA code running from controls on an Access form (frmImportTextData, illustrated in Figure 10.11):

1. Selecting the "Import Data from Text Files" option and clicking the button to its left opens the Import Job Data from Text File (frmImportTextData) form, as shown in Figure 10.11.

   If a text file was previously selected, its name is displayed in the textbox to the right of the "Source Text File" button.

2. You can use the selected file (if one is listed), or you can select another by clicking the "Source Text File" button, which opens a File Picker dialog box. The File Picker dialog box is filtered to display either comma-delimited (.csv) or fixed-width (.txt) files, according to the option selected in the Import Text Type option group. In Figure 10.12, I've selected a comma-delimited text file for import.

FIGURE 10.11

The Import Job Data from Text File form, as initially opened.

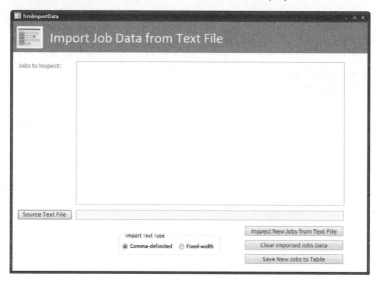

FIGURE 10.12

Selecting a comma-delimited text file for import.

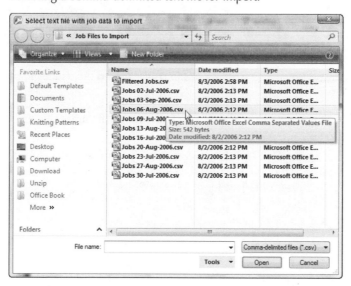

3. After selecting a text file, click the "Inspect New Jobs from Text File" button to import data from the text file to a temporary table, tblNewJobs.

The code running from this button sets the table as the source object of the Jobs to Inspect subform, so you can see the new records before actually appending them to the tblJobs table, as shown in Figure 10.13.

FIGURE 10.13

The new jobs imported from a comma-delimited text file.

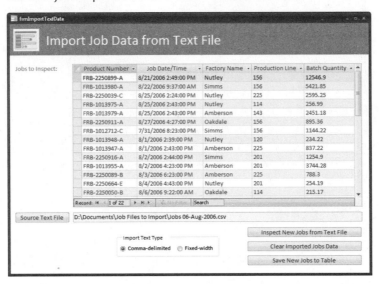

4. After inspecting the new data, you can either discard the data or import it into the tblJobs table.

- Clicking the "Clear Imported Jobs Data" button discards the data (it is not added to tblJobs).
- Clicking the "Save New Jobs to Table" button runs an append query that adds the new Jobs data to tblJobs. The code does some data type conversion (as shown in Figure 10.14), because all the fields in the text file are text fields.

FIGURE 10.14

An append query that does some data type conversion before appending the newly imported jobs to the main tblJobs table.

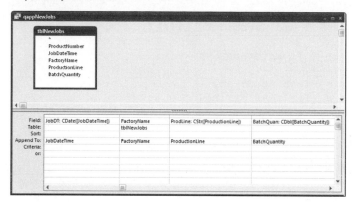

If you clicked the "Save New Jobs to Table" button, the new records that were displayed on the form were added to tblJobs.

The relevant procedures from the form code module are listed next. The "Clear Imported Jobs" command button's event procedure clears the datasheet, calls the SaveTextFile Sub procedure, and clears the previously selected file name from the textbox:

```
Private Sub cmdClearData_Click()

On Error Resume Next

    Me![subNewJobs].SourceObject = ""
    Call SaveTextFile("")
    Me![txtSelectedTextFile].Value = ""

End Sub
```

NOTE Importing data from fixed-width text files has become much more difficult in Access 2007 than in previous versions of Access. Specifications now store the file name internally, and thus you must create a separate specification for each text file you want to create. This means that the flexible method I use, where you can select the file to import, will not work. I recommend sticking to comma-delimited file imports, if possible.

The "Inspect New Jobs from Text File" command button's event procedure first checks that a text file has been selected and then sets variables with the name of the target table for importing and the import type. Next, a `Select Case` statement handles the two types of import (comma-delimited and fixed-width) separately, using the `TransferText` statement with different arguments:

```
Private Sub cmdInspectJobs_Click()

On Error GoTo ErrorHandler

    Dim strText As String
    Dim strTitle As String
    Dim strPrompt As String
    Dim txtData As Access.TextBox
    Dim strTextFile As String
    Dim strTable As String
    Dim strSpec As String

    Set txtData = Me![txtSelectedTextFile]
    strTextFile = Nz(txtData.Value)
    If strTextFile = "" Then
        strTitle = "No text file selected"
        strPrompt = "Please select a text file"
        MsgBox prompt:=strPrompt, Buttons:=vbExclamation _
            + vbOKOnly, title:=strTitle
        GoTo ErrorHandlerExit
    Else
        Debug.Print "Text file: " & strTextFile
    End If

    strTable = "tblNewJobs"
    intTextType = Nz(Me![fraTextType].Value, 1)

    Select Case intTextType

Case 1
```

Comma-delimited:

```
        DoCmd.TransferText transfertype:=acImportDelim, _
            TableName:=strTable, _
            FileName:=strTextFile, _
            hasfieldnames:=True

    Case 2
```

Fixed-width

```
    strSpec = "Import-Jobs 13-Aug-2006"
            'New style syntax
```

```
Application.CurrentProject.ImportExportSpecifications(strSpec).
Execute

        'Old style syntax causes error
        'DoCmd.TransferText transfertype:=acImportFixed, _
            specificationname:=strSpec, _
            TableName:=strTable, _
            FileName:=strTextFile, _
            hasfieldnames:=True

    End Select
```

Assign table as the subform's source object.

```
        Me![subNewJobs].SourceObject = "fsubNewJobs"

    ErrorHandlerExit:
        Exit Sub

    ErrorHandler:
        MsgBox "Error No: " & Err.Number _
            & "; Description: " & Err.Description
        Resume ErrorHandlerExit

    End Sub
```

The "Save New Jobs to Table" command button's event procedure runs an append query that adds the selected jobs to tblNewJobs:

```
    Private Sub cmdSaveJobs_Click()

    On Error GoTo ErrorHandler

        DoCmd.SetWarnings False
        DoCmd.OpenQuery "qappNewJobs"
        strTitle = "Jobs imported"
        strPrompt = "New jobs imported into tblJobs from " _
            & GetTextFile()
        MsgBox strPrompt, vbInformation + vbOKOnly, strTitle

    ErrorHandlerExit:
        Exit Sub

    ErrorHandler:
        MsgBox "Error No: " & Err.Number _
            & "; Description: " & Err.Description
        Resume ErrorHandlerExit

    End Sub
```

The "Source Text File" command button's event procedure opens a File Picker dialog for selecting a text file for importing, filtering for either text or comma-delimited files depending on the option selected on the form:

```
Private Sub cmdSourceTextFile_Click()

On Error GoTo ErrorHandler

    Dim fd As Office.FileDialog
    Dim txt As Access.TextBox
    Dim strPath As String
    Dim strFilter As String
```

Create a `FileDialog` object as a File Picker dialog box.

```
    Set fd = Application.FileDialog(msoFileDialogFilePicker)
    Set txt = Me![txtSelectedTextFile]
```

Set the initial path to the custom Input Documents path.

```
    strPath = GetInputDocsPath()
    intTextType = Nz(Me![fraTextType].Value, 1)

    With fd
        .title = "Select text file with job data to import"
        .ButtonName = "Select"
        .Filters.Clear
        If intTextType = 1 Then
            .Filters.Add "Comma-delimited files", "*.csv"
        ElseIf intTextType = 2 Then
            .Filters.Add "Fixed-width files", "*.txt"
        End If
        .InitialView = msoFileDialogViewDetails
        .InitialFileName = strPath
        If .Show = -1 Then
            strTextFile = CStr(fd.SelectedItems.Item(1))
        Else
            Debug.Print "User pressed Cancel"
        End If
    End With

    txt.Value = strTextFile
```

Save the value to tblInfo; the form can't be bound to that table because the main menu is bound to it, and thus it is locked.

```
    SaveTextFile (strTextFile)
    Me![txtSelectedTextFile].Value = strTextFile

ErrorHandlerExit:
    Exit Sub
```

```
ErrorHandler:
   MsgBox "Error No: " & Err.Number _
      & "; Description: " & Err.Description
   Resume ErrorHandlerExit

End Sub
```

The "Import Text Type" option group's event procedure first checks that the selected text file is the right type, and clears it if not, then sets up a `Select Case` statement to process comma-delimited and text files differently, calling the `SaveTextFile` Sub:

```
Private Sub fraTextType_AfterUpdate()

On Error GoTo ErrorHandler

   Dim strExt As String
```

Check that the selected text file is the right type, and clear the file selection if not.

```
   intTextType = Nz(Me![fraTextType].Value, 1)
   strTextFile = GetTextFile()

   If Len(strTextFile) > 4 Then
      strExt = Right(strTextFile, 3)
   End If

   Select Case intTextType

      Case 1
```

Comma-delimited

```
      If strExt = "txt" Then
         SaveTextFile ("")
         Me![txtSelectedTextFile].Value = ""
      End If

      Case 2
```

Fixed-width

```
      If strExt = "csv" Then
         SaveTextFile ("")
         Me![txtSelectedTextFile].Value = ""
      End If

      Case 3
         If strExt <> "csv" And strExt <> "txt" Then
            SaveTextFile ("")
            Me![txtSelectedTextFile].Value = ""
         End If
```

```
        End Select

    ErrorHandlerExit:
        Exit Sub

    ErrorHandler:
        MsgBox "Error No: " & Err.Number _
            & "; Description: " & Err.Description
        Resume ErrorHandlerExit

    End Sub
```

Exporting Text Data

When exporting data to text files (say, for import into a mainframe computer program, or another application that can import data from comma-delimited or fixed-width text files), often you need to filter the data, usually by date. The Export Job Data to Text File (frmExportTextData) form has two textboxes bound to Date fields that you can use to select dates for a date range used to filter the records to be exported to a text file.

NEW FEATURE Controls bound to Date fields on an Access 2007 form have a long-awaited feature shown in Figure 10.15: a pop-up calendar to make it easy to select a date.

FIGURE 10.15

The Export Job Data to Text File form, with a pop-up date selector.

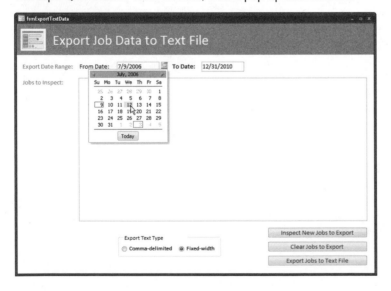

1. To open the "Export Job Data to Text File form (frmExportTextData), select the "Export Data to Text Files" option on the main menu and click the button to its left. This form lets you export a range of records filtered by date to either a comma-delimited or fixed-width text file.

2. After you select the From Date and To Date, either by typing them in or using the date selector pop-up, click the "Inspect New Jobs to Export" button to show the jobs in the selected date range in the Jobs to Inspect (fsubNewJobs) subform, as shown in Figure 10.16.

3. If you don't want to go ahead with the export, use the "Clear Jobs to Export" button to clear the selected jobs.

4. To proceed with the export, use the "Export Jobs to Text File" button to run code using the `TransferText` method to export the selected date range of jobs to a text file of the type selected in the "Export Text Type" option group. Figure 10.17 shows an exported comma-delimited file opened in Excel (which is the default application for .csv files).

FIGURE 10.16

Inspecting jobs in a given date range to export to a text file.

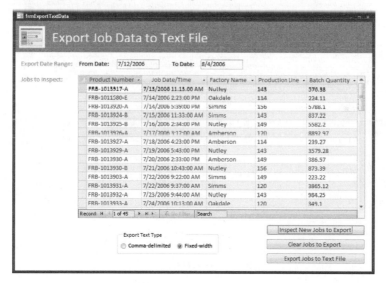

FIGURE 10.17

An exported comma-delimited text file opened in Excel.

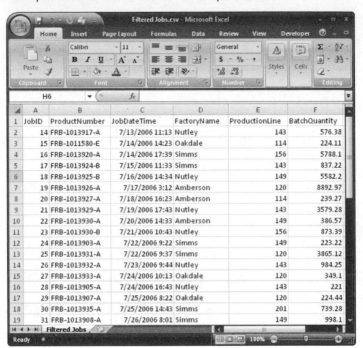

The new method of dealing with specs works well with fixed-width exports, at least so long as you always want to export to the save file name, as I do in the sample code.

The relevant procedures from the form module are listed next. The "Clear Jobs to Export" button's event procedure clears the datasheet subform of jobs:

```
Private Sub cmdClearData_Click()

On Error Resume Next

    Me![subFilteredJobs].SourceObject = ""

End Sub
```

The "Export Jobs to Text File" button's event procedure sets up a Select Case statement to export the selected jobs, using the TransferText statement with different arguments:

```
Private Sub cmdExportJobs_Click()

On Error GoTo ErrorHandler

    Dim intTextType As Integer
    Dim strQuery As String
    Dim strTextFile As String
    Dim strTitle As String
    Dim strPrompt As String

    intTextType = Nz(Me![fraTextType].Value, 1)
    strQuery = "qryFilteredJobs"

    Select Case intTextType

        Case 1
```

Comma-delimited

```
            strTextFile = GetOutputDocsPath() _
                &"Filtered Jobs.csv"
            DoCmd.TransferText transfertype:=acExportDelim, _
                TableName:=strQuery, _
                FileName:=strTextFile, _
                hasfieldnames:=True

        Case 2
```

Fixed-width

```
            strTextFile = GetOutputDocsPath() _
                &"Filtered Jobs.txt"
    strSpec = "Export@@hyFilteredJobs"
            strTextFile = GetOutputDocsPath() & "Filtered Jobs.txt"
            'New style syntax

Application.CurrentProject.ImportExportSpecifications(strSpec).Ex
ecute

            'Old style syntax causes error
            'DoCmd.TransferText transfertype:=acExportFixed, _
                TableName:=strQuery, _
                FileName:=strTextFile, _
                hasfieldnames:=True

    End Select
```

```
        strTitle = "Exported jobs"
        strPrompt = "Exported filtered jobs to " & strTextFile
        MsgBox strPrompt, vbInformation + vbOKOnly, strTitle

ErrorHandlerExit:
    Exit Sub

ErrorHandler:
    MsgBox "Error No: " & Err.Number _
        & "; Description: " & Err.Description
    Resume ErrorHandlerExit

End Sub
```

The "Inspect New Jobs to Export" button's event procedure sets the form datasheet's source object to the subform bound to qryFilteredJobs, to display the selected jobs:

```
Private Sub cmdInspectNewJobs_Click()

On Error Resume Next

    Me![subFilteredJobs].SourceObject = "fsubFilteredJobs"

End Sub
```

Working with Legacy Database and Spreadsheet Files

Since the earliest days of Access (when dBASE and Paradox were major forces in the database world, and Lotus 1-2-3 was the leading spreadsheet application) Access could import from or export to these formats. Some people are still using these programs, or at least have old files created by them in past years, so you still might need to import data from a dBASE, Paradox, or Lotus file or (though it's much less likely) export to one of those formats. Access still supports importing from these legacy formats, and you can also export to them, both in the interface and in VBA code.

Importing Database Files

The form for importing data from legacy application files is similar to the form for importing from text files; it differs in offering a selection of three legacy application types: dBASE, Paradox, and Lotus. The following steps describe importing Jobs data from a dBASE file:

1. To open the Import Job Data from Application File (frmImportAppData) form, select the "Import Data from App Files" option on the main menu and click the button to its left (see Figure 10.10). The Job Data from Application File form is shown in its initial state in Figure 10.18.

A form for importing data from legacy database and spreadsheet application files.

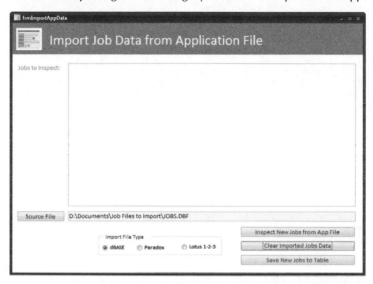

2. Click the Source File button to select a file of the type selected in the "Import File Type" option group from a File Picker dialog, as shown in Figure 10.19.

3. As with text files, click the "Inspect New Jobs from App File" button to import data from the selected file to a temporary table. The code sets that table as the source object of the Jobs to Inspect subform, so you can see the new records before appending them to the tblJobs table, as shown in Figure 10.20.

FIGURE 10.19

Selecting a dBASE file to import.

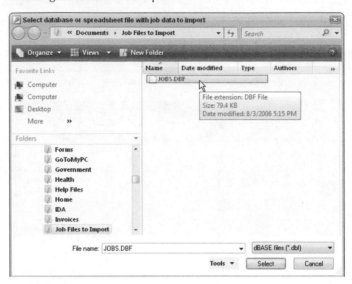

FIGURE 10.20

Inspecting new job data imported from a dBASE IV database file.

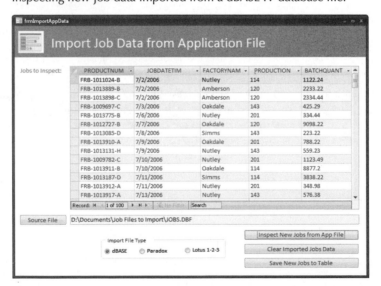

NOTE When importing from (or exporting to) dBASE or Paradox formats using the **TransferDatabase** method, the **DatabaseName** argument takes the path, not the database name; the database name is set with the **Source** argument. The path must be set without a final backslash, or else it will cause an error.

4. Use the "Clear Imported Jobs Data" button to clear the imported data without adding it to tblJobs.

5. Use the "Save New Jobs to Table" button to append the imported jobs data to tblJobs. Importing a Paradox file is quite similar; only the database type argument is different. Figure 10.21 shows new jobs data imported from a Paradox 4 database.

FIGURE 10.21

Inspecting data imported from a Paradox database.

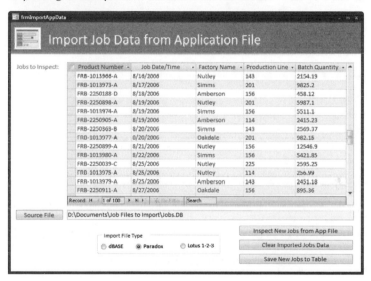

Curiously, there isn't an enum of named constants for the values used to set the **DatabaseType** argument of the **TransferDatabase** method; you have to type in the values. Table 10.1 lists the values you need to use for different versions of dBASE and Paradox.

TABLE 10.1

DatabaseType Argument Values for dBASE and Paradox

Database Version	DatabaseType Value
dBASE III	dBASE III
dBASE IV	dBASE IV
dBASE 5	dBASE 5.0
Paradox 3.x	Paradox 3.X
Paradox 4.x	Paradox 4.X
Paradox 5.x	Paradox 5.X
Paradox 7.x	Paradox 7.X

Now that the data is in an Access table, you can proceed to work with it as needed.

Importing Spreadsheet Files

If you have old Lotus 1-2-3 spreadsheet files, you can import data from them into Access tables using the `TransferSpreadsheet` method, which works much like the `TransferText` method, importing all the data from a worksheet. Unlike database files, you can use named argument values from the `AcSpreadSheetType` enum for spreadsheets of various versions; these values are listed in Table 10.2.

TABLE 10.2

SpreadsheetType Named Constants for Lotus 1-2-3

Lotus Version	SpreadsheetType Named Constants
Lotus WK1	acSpreadsheetTypeLotusWK1
Lotus WK3	acSpreadsheetTypeLotusWK3
Lotus WK4	acSpreadsheetTypeLotusWK4
Lotus WJ2	acSpreadsheetTypeLotusWJ2

When you inspect new job data imported from a Lotus spreadsheet (as shown in Figure 10.22), the Job Date/Time field looks strange, because the field is created as a Number field. However, when you click the Save Jobs to Table button, the CDate() function in the qappNewJobs append query converts the numeric date value into the correct format before appending the data to tblJobs. This type of tweaking of imported data is often required, to ensure that the data arriving in the target Access table is the correct data type.

Numeric values in the Job Date/Time field for data imported from a Lotus 1-2-3 spreadsheet.

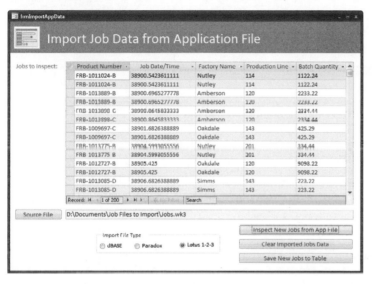

The relevant procedures from the Import Job Data from Application File form module are listed next. The "Clear Imported Jobs Data" button's event procedure clears the datasheet of records, calls the SaveAppFile Sub, clears the textbox of the file name, and deletes the temporary tables of new jobs:

```
Private Sub cmdClearData_Click()

On Error Resume Next

    Me![subNewJobs].SourceObject = ""
    Call SaveAppFile("")
    Me![txtSelectedAppFile].Value = ""
```

Delete new jobs tables

```
        DoCmd.DeleteObject acTable, "tblNewJobs"
        DoCmd.DeleteObject acTable, "tblNewJobsDB"

    End Sub
```

The "Inspect New Jobs from App File" button's event procedure first checks that an application file has been selected, parses out the file path and file name for use in different arguments of the TransferDatabase statement, then sets up a Select Case statement to do the import differently for the three application types:

```
    Private Sub cmdInspectJobs_Click()

    On Error GoTo ErrorHandler

        Dim strText As String
        Dim strTitle As String
        Dim strPrompt As String
        Dim txtData As Access.TextBox
        Dim strAppFile As String
        Dim strTable As String
        Dim strSpec As String
        Dim strDBPath As String
        Dim strDBName As String
        Dim strAppFileAndPath As String

        Set txtData = Me![txtSelectedAppFile]

        strAppFileAndPath = Nz(txtData.Value)
        If strAppFileAndPath = "" Then
            strTitle = "No application file selected"
            strPrompt = "Please select an application file"
            MsgBox prompt:=strPrompt, Buttons:=vbExclamation _
                + vbOKOnly, title:=strTitle
            GoTo ErrorHandlerExit
        Else
```

Parse out file path and file name.

```
        strDBPath = SplitDBPath(strAppFileAndPath)
```

Trim off last backslash.

```
        Debug.Print "DB path length: " & Len(strDBPath)
        strDBPath = Left(strDBPath, Len(strDBPath) - 1)
        strDBName = SplitDBName(strAppFileAndPath)
    End If
```

```
intFileType = Nz(Me![fraFileType].Value, 1)

Select Case intFileType

    Case 1
```

dBASE

```
        strTable = "tblNewJobsDB"
        Debug.Print "DB Path: " & strDBPath
        Debug.Print "DB Name: " & strDBName
        DoCmd.TransferDatabase transfertype:=acImport, _
            databasetype:="dBASE IV", _
            databasename:=strDBPath, _
            objecttype:=acTable, _
            Source:=strDBName, _
            Destination:=strTable, _
            structureonly:=False
```

Assign the appropriate form as the subform's source object.

```
        Me![subNewJobs].SourceObject = "fsubNewJobsDB"

    Case 2
```

Paradox

```
        strTable = "tblNewJobs"
        DoCmd.TransferDatabase transfertype:=acImport, _
            databasetype:="Paradox 4.X", _
            databasename:=strDBPath, _
            objecttype:=acTable, _
            Source:=strDBName, _
            Destination:=strTable, _
            structureonly:=False
```

Assign the appropriate form as the subform's source object.

```
        Me![subNewJobs].SourceObject = "fsubNewJobs"

    Case 3
```

Lotus 1-2-3

```
        strTable = "tblNewJobs"
        DoCmd.TransferSpreadsheet transfertype:=acImport, _
            spreadsheettype:=acSpreadsheetTypeLotusWK3, _
            TableName:=strTable, _
            FileName:=strAppFileAndPath, _
            hasfieldnames:=True
```

Assign the appropriate form as the subform's source object.

```
        Me![subNewJobs].SourceObject = "fsubNewJobs"

    End Select

ErrorHandlerExit:
    Exit Sub

ErrorHandler:
    MsgBox "Error No: " & Err.Number _
        & "; Description: " & Err.Description
    Resume ErrorHandlerExit

End Sub
```

The "Save New Jobs to Table" button's event procedure sets up a `Select Case` statement to run one of three append queries to append the new Jobs data to the tblJobs table:

```
Private Sub cmdSaveJobs_Click()

On Error GoTo ErrorHandler

    DoCmd.SetWarnings False

    intFileType = Nz(Me![fraFileType].Value, 1)

    Select Case intFileType

        Case 1
```
dBASE
```
            DoCmd.OpenQuery "qappNewJobsDB"

        Case 2
```
Paradox
```
            DoCmd.OpenQuery "qappNewJobsPdox"

        Case 3
```
Lotus 1-2-3
```
            DoCmd.OpenQuery "qappNewJobsLotus"

    End Select
```

```
      strTitle = "Jobs imported"
      strPrompt = "New jobs imported into tblJobs from " _
         & GetAppFile()
      MsgBox strPrompt, vbInformation + vbOKOnly, strTitle

ErrorHandlerExit:
   Exit Sub

ErrorHandler:
   MsgBox "Error No: " & Err.Number _
      & "; Description: " & Err.Description
   Resume ErrorHandlerExit

End Sub
```

The Source File button's event procedure opens a File Picker dialog for selecting an application file for importing, filtering for dBASE, Paradox, or Lotus files depending on the option selected on the form.

```
   Private Sub cmdSourceFile_Click()

On Error GoTo ErrorHandler

      Dim fd As Office.FileDialog
      Dim txt As Access.TextBox
      Dim strPath As String
      Dim strFilter As String
```

Create a FileDialog object as a File Picker dialog box.

```
      Set fd = Application.FileDialog(msoFileDialogFilePicker)
      Set txt = Me![txtSelectedAppFile]
```

Set the initial path to the custom Input Documents path

```
      strPath = GetInputDocsPath()
      intFileType = Nz(Me![fraFileType].Value, 1)

      With fd
         .title = "Select database or spreadsheet file with " _
            & "job data to import"
         .ButtonName = "Select"
         .Filters.Clear

      Select Case intFileType

         Case 1
            .Filters.Add "dBASE files", "*.dbf"
```

```
            Case 2
            .Filters.Add "Paradox files", "*.db"

            Case 3
            .Filters.Add "Lotus 1-2-3 files", "*.wk3"

        End Select

        .InitialView = msoFileDialogViewDetails
        .InitialFileName = strPath
        If .Show = -1 Then
            strAppFile = CStr(fd.SelectedItems.Item(1))
        Else
            Debug.Print "User pressed Cancel"
        End If
    End With

    txt.Value = strAppFile
```

Save the value to tblInfo.

```
        SaveAppFile (strAppFile)

ErrorHandlerExit:
    Exit Sub

ErrorHandler:
    MsgBox "Error No: " & Err.Number _
        & "; Description: " & Err.Description
    Resume ErrorHandlerExit

End Sub
```

The "Import File Type" option group's `After_Update` procedure first checks that the selected application file is the right type, and clears it if not, then sets up a `Select Case` statement to process the three types of application files differently, calling the `SaveTextFile` Sub:

```
Private Sub fraFileType_AfterUpdate()

On Error GoTo ErrorHandler

    Dim strExt As String
```

Check that selected application file is the right type, and clear the file selection if not.

```
        intFileType = Nz(Me![fraFileType].Value, 1)

        If Len(GetTextFile()) > 4 Then
            strExt = Right(strAppFile, 3)
        End If
```

```
        Select Case intFileType

            Case 1

dBASE

                If strExt <> "dbf" Then
                    SaveAppFile ("")
                    Me![txtSelectedAppFile].Value = ""
                End If

            Case 2

Paradox

                If strExt <> ".db" Then
                    SaveAppFile ("")
                    Me![txtSelectedAppFile].Value = ""
                End If

            Case 3

Lotus 1-2-3

                If strExt <> "wk3" Then
                    SaveAppFile ("")
                    Me![txtSelectedAppFile].Value = ""
                End If

        End Select

        Me![subNewJobs].SourceObject = ""

    ErrorHandlerExit:
        Exit Sub

    ErrorHandler:
        MsgBox "Error No: " & Err.Number _
            & "; Description: " & Err.Description
        Resume ErrorHandlerExit

    End Sub
```

After importing data from the legacy application file, it is now in an Access table, where you can work with it in the future.

Exporting Database and Spreadsheet Files

These days, it isn't very likely that you would need to export data from Access to a dBASE, Paradox, or Lotus file (and in any case, as discussed in the "Exporting Text Files" section, you can export to a comma-delimited text file that can be imported into those applications). However, Access still offers the option of doing exports to these legacy applications, as discussed in this section.

If you select the "Export Data to App Files" option on the main menu and click the button to its left, the Export Job Data to Application File form (frmExportAppData) opens. This form (much like the Export Job Data to Text File form) lets you export a range of records filtered by date to a dBASE, Paradox, or Lotus 1-2-3 file. Figure 10.23 shows filtered data ready to export to a dBASE file.

Filtered records for export to a dBASE file.

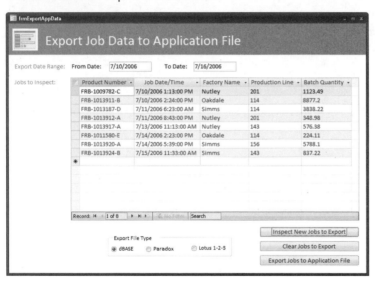

The "Clear Jobs to Export" button clears the selected records, and the "Export Jobs to Application File" button does the export to a file of the selected format; this procedure is listed next. Similar to the other export procedures, this procedure sets up a `Select Case` statement to do the export differently according to the selected application type; the `TransferDatabase` statement with various arguments:

```
Private Sub cmdExportJobs_Click()

On Error GoTo ErrorHandler

    Dim intFileType As Integer
    Dim strQuery As String
```

```
Dim strAppFile As String
Dim strTitle As String
Dim strPrompt As String
Dim strOutputPath As String
Dim strDBName As String

intFileType = Nz(Me![fraFileType].Value, 1)
strQuery = "qryFilteredJobs"
strOutputPath = GetOutputDocsPath()
```

Trim off last backslash.

```
strOutputPath = Left(strOutputPath, _
    Len(strOutputPath) - 1)

Select Case intFileType

    Case 1
```

dBASE

```
        strDBName = "Jobs.dbf"
        strAppFile = strOutputPath & "\" & strDBName
        DoCmd.TransferDatabase transfertype:=acExport, _
            databasetype:="dBASE IV", _
            databasename:=strOutputPath, _
            objecttype:=acTable, _
            Source:=strQuery, _
            Destination:=strDBName, _
            structureonly:=False

    Case 2
```

Paradox

```
        strDBName = "Jobs.db"
        strAppFile = strOutputPath & "\" & strDBName
        DoCmd.TransferDatabase transfertype:=acExport, _
            databasetype:="Paradox 5.X", _
            databasename:=strOutputPath, _
            objecttype:=acTable, _
            Source:=strQuery, _
            Destination:=strDBName, _
            structureonly:=False

    Case 3
```

337

Lotus 1-2-3

```
        strAppFile = strOutputPath & "\Jobs.wk1"
        DoCmd.TransferSpreadsheet transfertype:=acExport, _
            spreadsheettype:=acSpreadsheetTypeLotusWK1, _
            TableName:=strQuery, _
            FileName:=strAppFile, _
            hasfieldnames:=True

    End Select

    strTitle = "Exported jobs"
    strPrompt = "Exported filtered jobs to " & strAppFile
    MsgBox strPrompt, vbInformation + vbOKOnly, strTitle

ErrorHandlerExit:
    Exit Sub

ErrorHandler:
    MsgBox "Error No: " & Err.Number _
        & "; Description: " & Err.Description
    Resume ErrorHandlerExit

End Sub
```

Working with XML and HTML Files

Sometimes Microsoft introduces a new technology long before it has any real-world use. The XML and HTML file formats, though very useful for developing web sites, to date lack utility as vehicles for exporting or importing Access data. XML in particular appears to be a new technology (not that new; it was introduced in Office XP) that as of yet doesn't have much use for Access data import and export, though perhaps it will in the future. As far as I can see, any Access-related data exchange tasks that you can do with XML or HTML can be done better by other methods, such as the comma-delimited or worksheet formats.

That said, you may need to export an Access table or query to HTML format for posting on a web site; XML files, though perhaps promising for future use, are at present minimally useful for importing or exporting Access data.

Importing HTML and XML Files

If you do need to import data into Access from an HTML or XML file (or just want to experiment with these options) you can use the Import HTML or XML Job Data form (frmImportHTMLXMLData), which opens if you select the Import HTML or XML Data option on the main menu and click the button to its left (see Figure 10.11).

Clicking the "Inspect New Jobs from HTML File" button displays the imported records in the subform, as shown in Figure 10.24.

FIGURE 10.24

Inspecting data imported from an HTML file.

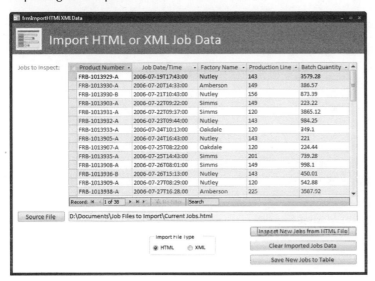

If you select the XML option, data from the XML file is displayed in the subform, as shown in Figure 10.25.

FIGURE 10.25

Inspecting data imported from an XML file.

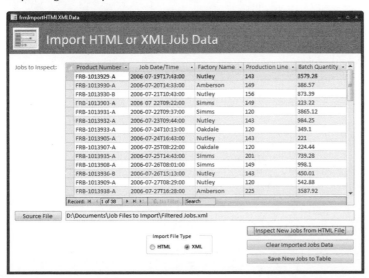

NOTE When you import data from an XML file, there is no option for specifying the name of the Access table; it will have the same name as the original data source, possibly with an appended number.

The code for the "Inspect New Jobs From HTML File" button is listed below:

```
Private Sub cmdInspectJobs_Click()

On Error GoTo ErrorHandler

    Dim strText As String
    Dim strTitle As String
    Dim strPrompt As String
    Dim txtData As Access.TextBox
    Dim strAppFile As String
    Dim strTable As String
    Dim strSpec As String
    Dim strHTMLXMLFileAndPath As String
    Dim strHTMLXMLFile As String
    Dim strHTMLXMLPath As String

    Set txtData = Me![txtSelectedAppFile]

    strTable = "tblNewJobs"
    strHTMLXMLFileAndPath = Nz(txtData.Value)
    If strHTMLXMLFileAndPath = "" Then
        strTitle = "No application file selected"
        strPrompt = "Please select an application file"
        MsgBox prompt:=strPrompt, Buttons:=vbExclamation _
            + vbOKOnly, Title:=strTitle
        GoTo ErrorHandlerExit
    Else
Parse out the file name; it is needed later in the procedure.
        strHTMLXMLFile = SplitDBName(strHTMLXMLFileAndPath)

Trim off the file extension.
        strHTMLXMLFile = Mid(strHTMLXMLFile, 1, InStr(1,
strHTMLXMLFile, ".") @@hy 1)
        Debug.Print "Trimmed file name: " & strHTMLXMLFile
    End If

    intFileType = Nz(Me![fraFileType].Value, 1)

    Select Case intFileType
```

```
        Case 1
HTML
            DoCmd.TransferText transfertype:=acImportHTML, _
                TableName:=strTable, _
                FileName:=strHTMLXMLFileAndPath, _
                hasfieldnames:=True

Assign the appropriate form as the subform's source object.
            Me![subNewJobs].SourceObject = "fsubNewJobs"

        Case 2
XML
            ImportXML DataSource:=strHTMLXMLFileAndPath, _
                importoptions:=acStructureAndData
            DoCmd.SetWarnings False

There is no argument for specifying the name of the table that is
created when an XML file is imported; it comes in as the name
stored in the XML file (usually the XML file name), possibly with
a number added on.
            DoCmd.Rename newname:=strTable, objecttype:=acTable, _
                oldname:=strHTMLXMLFile

Assign the appropriate form as the subform's source object.
            Me![subNewJobs].SourceObject = "fsubNewJobs"

    End Select

ErrorHandlerExit:
    Exit Sub

ErrorHandler:
    MsgBox "Error No: " & Err.Number _
        & "; Description: " & Err.Description
    Resume ErrorHandlerExit

End Sub
```

Exporting HTML and XML Files

If you want to experiment with exporting Access data to HTML or XML files, try the Export Job Data to HTML or XML File form. If you select the "Export HTML or XML Data" option on the main menu (see Figure 10.10) and click the button to its left, the Export Job Data to HTML or

XML File (frmExportHTMLXMLData) form will open (as shown in Figure 10.26). The form has From Date and To Date textboxes for specifying a date range; clicking the "Inspect New Jobs to Export" button loads the subform with the records from the selected date range.

FIGURE 10.26

Inspecting the filtered job records to export to an HTML or XML file.

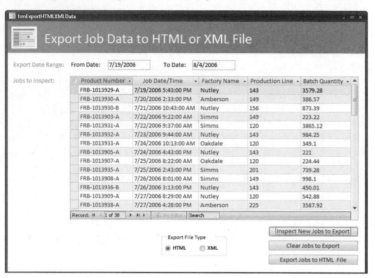

Clicking the "Export Jobs to HTML File" button (or "Export Jobs to XML File"; the caption changes with the selection in the "Export File Type" option group) starts the export. The HTML export is done with the `TransferText` method with the `acExportHTML` value for the `TransferType` argument; the XML export is done with the `ExportXML` method of the Access `Application` object.

Figure 10.27 shows an exported HTML file opened in Internet Explorer 7. Unfortunately, it is completely unformatted and thus probably won't be very useful.

FIGURE 10.27

An exported HTML file opened in Internet Explorer.

The code for clearing old data and inspecting the jobs to export is similar to the code for other export types; only the event procedure for the "Export Jobs to HTML/XML File" button is listed as follows; it uses a `Select Case` statement to export the data to either an HTML file (using the `TransferText` method) or an XML file, using the `ExportXML` method of the Access Application object:

```
Private Sub cmdExportJobs_Click()

On Error GoTo ErrorHandler

    Dim intFileType As Integer
    Dim strQuery As String
    Dim strTitle As String
    Dim strPrompt As String
    Dim strOutputPath As String
    Dim strFileName As String
    Dim strFileNameAndPath As String

    intFileType = Nz(Me![fraFileType].Value, 1)
    strQuery = "qryFilteredJobs"
```

```
        strOutputPath = GetOutputDocsPath()

    Select Case intFileType

        Case 1
```

HTML

```
            strFileName = "Jobs.htm"
            strFileNameAndPath = strOutputPath & strFileName
            DoCmd.TransferText transfertype:=acExportHTML, _
                TableName:=strQuery, _
                FileName:=strFileNameAndPath, _
                hasfieldnames:=True

        Case 2
```

XML

```
            strFileName = "Jobs.xml"
            strFileNameAndPath = strOutputPath & strFileName
            ExportXML objecttype:=acExportQuery, _
                DataSource:=strQuery, _
                datatarget:=strFileNameAndPath

    End Select

    strTitle = "Exported jobs"
    strPrompt = "Exported filtered jobs to " & strFileNameAndPath
    MsgBox strPrompt, vbInformation + vbOKOnly, strTitle

ErrorHandlerExit:
    Exit Sub

ErrorHandler:
    MsgBox "Error No: " & Err.Number _
        & "; Description: " & Err.Description
    Resume ErrorHandlerExit

End Sub
```

If you open an XML file in IE 7, running on Windows Vista, you'll see a yellow bar with a security warning. If you click the bar you can select to allow blocked content, as shown in Figure 10.28.

FIGURE 10.28

A security warning when opening an XML file in Windows Vista.

If you select to allow blocked content, you'll get another security warning, shown in Figure 10.29.

Finally, the XML file displays (see Figure 10.30), but as source code, not a properly formatted document, so it (like the HTML file) is not very useful.

FIGURE 10.29

Another Vista security warning.

FIGURE 10.30

An XML file opened in Internet Explorer.

You can also open an XML file in Excel. After selecting it, you get an Open XML dialog with three options, as shown in Figure 10.31. To see what the formatted XML data looks like, select the "As an XML table" option.

FIGURE 10.31

Three options for opening an XML file in Excel.

If you accept the default option of "As an XML table," you'll get the message shown in Figure 10.32.

Creating an XML schema when opening an XML file in Excel.

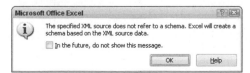

After accepting this message, the XML file finally opens in Excel, as shown in 10.33, with an extra column called "generated" indicating the time the file was created.

An XML file opened in Excel.

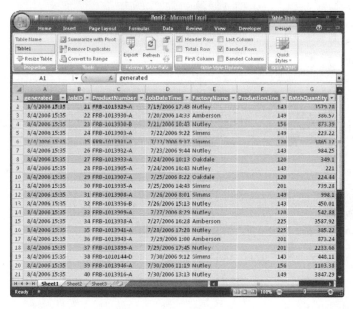

> **NOTE** If you want to export data from Access to Excel, I recommend using the worksheet or comma-delimited format instead of XML; they are much easier to work with, and support older versions of Excel that can't open XML files.

> **NOTE** You can also use the Save method of an ADO recordset with the `adPersistXML` named constant as the value of its `PersistFormat` argument, to produce an XML file, but a file produced using this method also opens as source code.

Emailing Exported Text Files

Once you have created text files from your Access data, you might want to email them to others who need to review the data. Clicking the "Send Job Lists to Contacts" button opens a form (shown in Figure 10-34) where you can select multiple contacts, and a job file (either .csv or .txt) to send as an attachment to the selected contacts. The figure also shows three email messages with the selected job file attachment.

FIGURE 10.34

A form for selecting contacts and a job file to email to them, with three email messages created from the form.

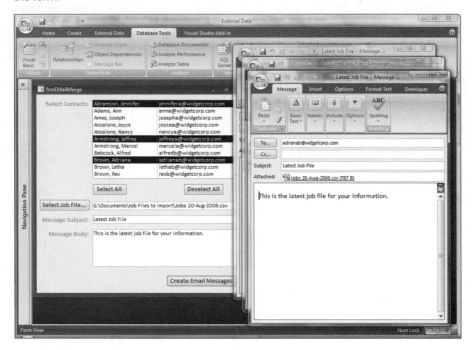

The cmdMergetoEMailMulti_Click event procedure is listed below:

```
Private Sub cmdMergetoEMailMulti_Click()

On Error GoTo ErrorHandler

    Dim strJobFile As String

    Set lst = Me![lstSelectContacts]
```

Check that at least one contact has been selected.

```
If lst.ItemsSelected.Count = 0 Then
   MsgBox "Please select at least one contact"
   lst.SetFocus
   GoTo ErrorHandlerExit
End If
```

Test for required fields.

```
strSubject = Me![txtSubject].Value
If strSubject = "" Then
   MsgBox "Please enter a subject"
   Me![txtSubject].SetFocus
   GoTo ErrorHandlerExit
End If

strBody = Me![txtBody].Value
If strBody = "" Then
   MsgBox "Please enter a message body"
   Me![txtBody].SetFocus
   GoTo ErrorHandlerExit
End If

For Each varItem In lst.ItemsSelected
```

Check for email address.

```
strEMailRecipient = Nz(lst.Column(1, varItem))
Debug.Print "EMail address: " & strEMailRecipient
If strEMailRecipient = "" Then
   GoTo NextContact
End If

strJobFile = Nz(Me![txtJobFile])
```

Create a new mail message with the job file attachment and send to contact.

```
Set appOutlook = GetObject(, "Outlook.Application")
Set msg = appOutlook.CreateItem(olMailItem)
With msg
   .To = strEMailRecipient
   .Subject = strSubject
   .Body = strBody
   If strJobFile <> "" Then
      .Attachments.Add strJobFile
   End If
   .Display
End With
```

```
NextContact:
   Next varItem
ErrorHandlerExit:
   Set appOutlook = Nothing
   Exit Sub
ErrorHandler:
```

Outlook is not running; open Outlook with CreateObject.

```
If Err.Number = 429 Then
   Set appOutlook = CreateObject("Outlook.Application")
   Resume Next
Else
   MsgBox "Error No: " & Err.Number _
      & "; Description: " & Err.Description
   Resume ErrorHandlerExit
End If

End Sub
```

> **NOTE**   You may have contacts that have only an email address, or a phrase like "Tech. Support" entered as the last name, or contacts with just a first name, or a whole name entered into the LastName field, or sets of contacts who work for the same company, where the company name is entered differently on different contact records. Importing from such contacts can cause problems, such as creating multiple Company records with variations of a company name.
>
> I am planning to upgrade the Synchronizing Contacts database to deal with various types of problem data, and to add some new features; look for an updated version of the database on my Web site, http://www.helenfeddema.com.

Summary

This chapter dealt with exporting to, and importing from, a variety of file formats, ranging from the oldest formats to those so new that they are scarcely useful yet. Text files, both comma-delimited and fixed-width (columnar), have been used for data export and import since the earliest days of computers, and they are still very useful, especially the comma-delimited file format. Files exported to this format can be imported by a great many applications, which makes it very useful for exporting data that is to be imported by an application not directly supported as an Access export type. The reverse is also true: many applications can export their data to a fixed-width or comma-delimited file, from which they can be imported into Access tables.

If you have data in ancient dBASE, Paradox, or Lotus files, Access offers options for importing from these files, so you can get your old data into Access tables. Although it isn't likely to be required these days, you can also export data from Access tables to these legacy formats.

And finally, the new HTML and XML formats are supported — but not very well. These import and export types still have little utility for importing data into Access tables, either because they simply don't work or because they aren't really relevant. Hopefully, these file formats will be better supported for Access import and export in future versions of Office.

Chapter 11

Synchronizing Access and Outlook Contacts

For a long time — really, since Office 97, when Outlook was introduced — I have wanted to write VBA code to synchronize Access contacts with Outlook contacts. My Access contacts are stored in a set of linked tables, with companies linked to contacts and contacts linked to addresses, phone numbers, and IDs of various sorts, which allows maximum flexibility for entering data and at the same time avoids having to enter the same data in multiple records. Outlook, on the other hand, has a very attractive and convenient interface for entering contact data, but unfortunately stores all contact data in a flat-file MAPI database, with a limited number of fields for addresses, phone numbers, and IDs.

Though it isn't difficult to write code to simply import data from Outlook to an Access table, or export data from an Access table to Outlook contacts, if the Access contacts are a set of linked tables, as they should be, the task is much more difficult — but not impossible. Live linking is out of the question, because of the difference in structure between a folder of Outlook contacts and a set of linked Access tables, but the contacts can be compared, and data copied from an Outlook contact to an Access contact (or vice versa), using an intermediary flat-file table filled with data from the linked Access tables. This chapter describes the technique I use to first denormalize Access data for comparison with Outlook contacts and then renormalize the updated data in order to write it back to the linked Access tables.

CROSS-REF See the "Working with Outlook Contacts" section in Chapter 8 for information on exchanging data between a single Access contacts table and Outlook contacts.

IN THIS CHAPTER

Updating Outlook contacts from Access, and vice versa

Copying attachments from Outlook to Access, and vice versa

Creating a Denormalized Table from a Set of Linked Tables

There are situations where you need to create a single table filled with data from a set of linked Access tables (denormalize the tables). One such situation is the preparation of a data file for import by a mainframe, or a legacy database or spreadsheet application; another is for use in Access VBA code or by a query.

> **NOTE** The process of creating a single flat-file table from data in a set of linked tables is called *denormalizing*; the reverse process — writing data from a flat-file table back to a set of linked tables — is called *renormalizing*.

If you encounter a "Query too complex" message when trying to run a deeply nested query based on multiple tables (this is less of a problem now than with previous versions of Access, but still might happen with extremely complex queries), you can run a make-table query to create a flat-file table based on some of the linked queries and use that table as part of the final query, to reduce its complexity. The techniques I use in this chapter to prepare a single table of Access data for comparison with Outlook contacts can be modified for use anywhere you need to produce a single flat-file table of data from linked Access tables.

> **NOTE** The sample database for this chapter is Synchronizing Contacts.accdb.

In Access, my contact-related data is stored in a set of linked tables, as shown in the Relationships diagram (Figure 11.1).

The tables are normalized, which means that they are designed so that data of a particular type is stored in only one table, and only the linking ID fields have matching values. The tblCompanyInfo table is linked one-to-many with two tables: tblCompanyIDsPhones and tblContactInfo, because a company can have multiple phone numbers and IDs, and also multiple contacts. tblContactInfo is also linked one-to-many with two tables: tblContactIDsPhones, containing phone numbers and IDs for contacts, and tblContactAddresses, containing addresses.

FIGURE 11.1

The Relationships diagram for the Synchronizing Contacts database.

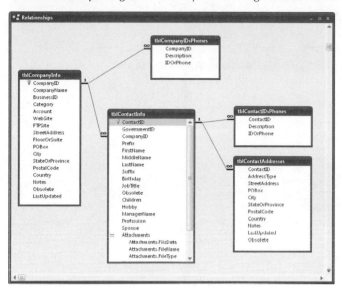

Because Outlook only supports a fixed number of addresses and emails (three of each), and a larger (17) but still fixed number of phone numbers, for purposes of synchronizing contact data between Outlook and Access, only the matching addresses, emails, and phone numbers will be synchronized. Practically, this is not likely to leave much data unsynchronized, except in the case of phone numbers.

TIP For best results when synchronizing data, when entering a phone number or ID in one of the subforms on frmContactInfo, select one of the default selections for addresses, emails, and phone numbers from the drop-down list; they are the only selections that will be synchronized with Outlook contact items.

Figure 11.2 shows a phone number being selected on the Contact Information (frmContactInfo) form.

FIGURE 11.2

Selecting a default phone number type on the Contact Information form.

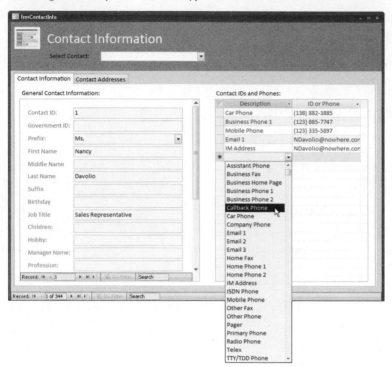

Of course, you will sometimes need to enter phone numbers that aren't on this list of default phone number choices (such as the Coffee Harvest Line number shown in Figure 11.4); you can enter a custom phone or ID description manually as needed, but these phone numbers and IDs won't be synchronized with Outlook.

Figure 11.3 shows the Contact Addresses tab of the Contact Information form; unless you need to enter data for very wealthy people who have more than three addresses, the standard three choices should be enough.

FIGURE 11.3

Selecting an address type for a new contact address.

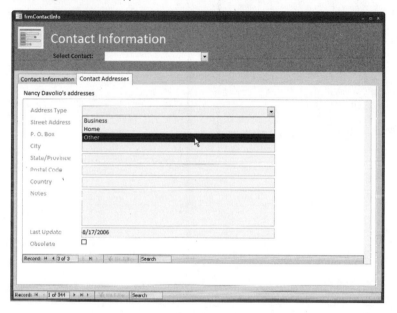

The Company and Contact Information (frmCompanyInfo) form displays company and contact information so you can easily match up contacts with their companies. Figure 11.4 shows the Company Info tab of this form, with a Company IDs and Phones subform.

FIGURE 11.4

The Company Info tab of the Company and Contact Information form.

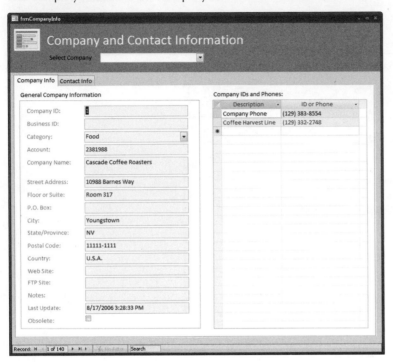

Figure 11.5 shows the Contact Info tab, with a Contact IDs and Phones subform.

FIGURE 11.5

The Contact Info tab of the Company and Contact Information form.

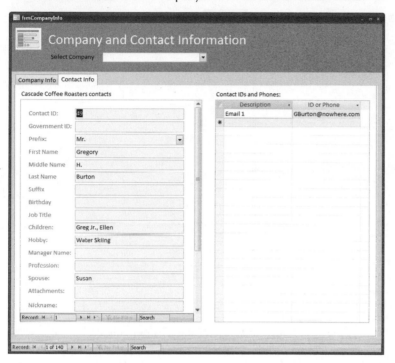

The sample database's main menu (shown in Figure 11.6) has a command button for selecting the Attachments folder path; its event procedure uses the same technique as for similar command buttons in earlier chapters, opening an Office Folder Picker dialog to let you select a folder. In this chapter the selected folder is used to temporarily store files for use as attachments when copying attachments from an Access table record to an Outlook contact or vice versa.

FIGURE 11.6

The main menu of the Synchronizing Contacts database.

The code for the Attachments Folder Path button (listed next) starts by popping up a Folder Picker dialog for selecting the folder where files to be used as attachments are stored. The selected path is saved to the textbox under the command button:

```
Private Sub cmdAttachmentsFolderPath_Click()

On Error GoTo ErrorHandler
```

Create a FileDialog object as a Folder Picker dialog box.

```
Set fd = Application.FileDialog(msoFileDialogFolderPicker)
Set txt = Me![txtOutputDocsPath]
strPath = GetOutputDocsPath()

With fd
   .Title = "Browse for folder where attachments " _
      & "should be stored"
   .ButtonName = "Select"
   .InitialView = msoFileDialogViewDetails
   .InitialFileName = strPath
```

```
        If .Show = -1 Then
            txt.Value = CStr(fd.SelectedItems.Item(1))
        Else
            Debug.Print "User pressed Cancel"
        End If
    End With

On Error Resume Next

    DoCmd.RunCommand acCmdSaveRecord

ErrorHandlerExit:
    Exit Sub

ErrorHandler:
    MsgBox "Error No: " & Err.Number _
        & "; Description: " & Err.Description
    Resume ErrorHandlerExit

End Sub
```

Comparing Outlook and Access Contacts

The Select Form combo box on the main menu (Figure 11.7) lets you select three forms, two of which compare Access and Outlook data. One of the data comparison forms is sorted by Contact ID and the other by contact name (sorting by name is useful for matching Access and Outlook contacts when the Outlook contact lacks a value in the CustomerID property).

NOTE   Outlook contact items have a number of very useful built-in ID fields, which for some inexplicable reason are not displayed on the standard Contact item. The CustomerID field is the one I use to link Outlook contacts to Access records in tblContactInfo (using the key field ContactID). The GovernmentIDNumber field (corresponding to GovernmentID in tblContactInfo) can be used to store a Social Security Number (for the United States) or the equivalent government ID number for other countries. There is also another field useful for storing a company ID: OrganizationalIDNumber, corresponding to CompanyID in tblCompanyInfo.

TIP   To test synchronizing Contacts data, make a new Contacts folder and copy some (or all) of your contacts to it from your regular Contacts folder; that way, you can experiment with making various changes without messing up your real contact data.

FIGURE 11.7

Selecting a form for comparing Access and Outlook contacts.

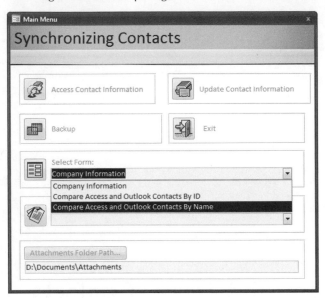

When you select one of these forms to open, a message box, shown in Figure 11.8, pops up.

FIGURE 11.8

A question on opening a comparison form.

You will get several other messages as the tables of Access and Outlook data are created, including an Outlook Select Folder dialog for selecting the Outlook Contacts folder to use when synchronizing the Access and Outlook contacts. This dialog is shown in Figure 11.9.

FIGURE 11.9

An Outlook Select Folder dialog for selecting the Contacts folder for synchronizing.

Re-creating the Flat-file Tables of Access and Outlook Data

If you have recently entered new contact data or modified existing contact records, either in Access or Outlook, click Yes to refresh the data in the tables that will be compared. Clicking Yes calls two procedures that clear tblOutlookContacts and tblAccessContacts and fill them with up-to-date data. The ImportOutlookContacts procedure (listed next) is simpler: it copies data from all the contact items in the selected folder to records in tblOutlookContacts:

```
Public Function ImportOutlookContacts()
'Called from cmdForms_Click on fmnuMain

On Error GoTo ErrorHandler

    Set appOutlook = GetObject(, "Outlook.Application")

    Dim fldContacts As Outlook.Folder
    Dim con As Outlook.ContactItem
    Dim strSQL As String
    Dim strTable As String

    Set appOutlook = GetObject(, "Outlook.Application")
    Set nms = appOutlook.GetNamespace("MAPI")
```

Set a variable to the Contacts folder to use when synchronizing:

Use the following lines to import from the default local Contacts folder.

```
    'Set fldContacts = nms.GetDefaultFolder(olFolderContacts)
    'GoTo ImportData
```

Use the following section of code to allow selection of a custom Contacts folder from the Folder Picker dialog.

```
SelectContactFolder:
    Set fldContacts = nms.PickFolder
    If fldContacts Is Nothing Then
        strTitle = "Select Folder"
        strPrompt = "Please select a Contacts folder"
        MsgBox strPrompt, vbExclamation + vbOKOnly, strTitle
        GoTo SelectContactFolder
    End If

    Debug.Print "Default item type: " & _
        fldContacts.DefaultItemType
    If fldContacts.DefaultItemType <> olContactItem Then
        MsgBox strPrompt, vbExclamation + vbOKOnly, strTitle
        GoTo SelectContactFolder
    End If

    Debug.Print fldContacts.Items.Count & " items in " _
        & fldContacts.Name & " folder"
```

Clear the table of Outlook contact data of old records:

```
ImportData:
    strTable = "tblOutlookContacts"
    strSQL = "DELETE * FROM " & strTable
    DoCmd.SetWarnings False
    DoCmd.RunSQL strSQL

    Set dbs = CurrentDb
    Set rstTarget = dbs.OpenRecordset(strTable)
```

Iterate through contacts in the selected Contacts folder and import them to the Access table, setting each field in the target table with the value of a field in the current contact item:

```
For Each itm In fldContacts.Items
    If itm.Class = olContact Then
        Set con = itm
        rstTarget.AddNew
        With con
            rstTarget![CustomerID] = Nz(.CustomerID)
            rstTarget![Title] = Nz(.Title)
            rstTarget![FirstName] = Nz(.FirstName)
            rstTarget![MiddleName] = Nz(.MiddleName)
            rstTarget![LastName] = Nz(.LastName)
            rstTarget![Suffix] = Nz(.Suffix)
            rstTarget![Nickname] = Nz(.Nickname)
            rstTarget![CompanyName] = Nz(.CompanyName)
            rstTarget![Department] = Nz(.Department)
            rstTarget![JobTitle] = Nz(.JobTitle)
```

```
rstTarget![BusinessAddressStreet] = _
    Nz(.BusinessAddressStreet)
rstTarget![BusinessAddressPostOfficeBox] = _
    Nz(.BusinessAddressPostOfficeBox)
rstTarget![BusinessAddressCity] = _
    Nz(.BusinessAddressCity)
rstTarget![BusinessAddressState] = _
    Nz(.BusinessAddressState)
rstTarget![BusinessAddressPostalCode] = _
    Nz(.BusinessAddressPostalCode)
rstTarget![BusinessAddressCountry] = _
    Nz(.BusinessAddressCountry)
rstTarget![BusinessHomePage] = _
    Nz(.BusinessHomePage)
rstTarget![FTPSite] = Nz(.FTPSite)
rstTarget![HomeAddressStreet] = _
    Nz(.HomeAddressStreet)
rstTarget![HomeAddressPostOfficeBox] = _
    Nz(.HomeAddressPostOfficeBox)
rstTarget![HomeAddressCity] = _
    Nz(.HomeAddressCity)
rstTarget![HomeAddressState] = _
    Nz(.HomeAddressState)
rstTarget![HomeAddressPostalCode] = _
    Nz(.HomeAddressPostalCode)
rstTarget![HomeAddressCountry] = _
    Nz(.HomeAddressCountry)
rstTarget![OtherAddressStreet] = _
    Nz(.OtherAddressStreet)
rstTarget![OtherAddressPostOfficeBox] = _
    Nz(.OtherAddressPostOfficeBox)
rstTarget![OtherAddressCity] = _
    Nz(.OtherAddressCity)
rstTarget![OtherAddressState] = _
    Nz(.OtherAddressState)
rstTarget![OtherAddressPostalCode] = _
    Nz(.OtherAddressPostalCode)
rstTarget![OtherAddressCountry] = _
    Nz(.OtherAddressCountry)
rstTarget![AssistantTelephoneNumber] = _
    Nz(.AssistantTelephoneNumber)
rstTarget![BusinessFaxNumber] = _
    Nz(.BusinessFaxNumber)
rstTarget![BusinessTelephoneNumber] = _
    Nz(.BusinessTelephoneNumber)
rstTarget![Business2TelephoneNumber] = _
    Nz(.Business2TelephoneNumber)
rstTarget![CallbackTelephoneNumber] = _
    Nz(.CallbackTelephoneNumber)
rstTarget![CarTelephoneNumber] = _
    Nz(.CarTelephoneNumber)
```

```
rstTarget![CompanyMainTelephoneNumber] = _
    Nz(.CompanyMainTelephoneNumber)
rstTarget![HomeFaxNumber] = _
    Nz(.HomeFaxNumber)
rstTarget![HomeTelephoneNumber] = _
    Nz(.HomeTelephoneNumber)
rstTarget![Home2TelephoneNumber] = _
    Nz(.Home2TelephoneNumber)
rstTarget![ISDNNumber] = Nz(.ISDNNumber)
rstTarget![MobileTelephoneNumber] = _
    Nz(.MobileTelephoneNumber)
rstTarget![OtherFaxNumber] = _
    Nz(.OtherFaxNumber)
rstTarget![OtherTelephoneNumber] = _
    Nz(.OtherTelephoneNumber)
rstTarget![PagerNumber] = Nz(.PagerNumber)
rstTarget![PrimaryTelephoneNumber] = _
    Nz(.PrimaryTelephoneNumber)
rstTarget![RadioTelephoneNumber] = _
    Nz(.RadioTelephoneNumber)
rstTarget![TTYTDDTelephoneNumber] = _
    Nz(.TTYTDDTelephoneNumber)
rstTarget![TelexNumber] = Nz(.TelexNumber)
rstTarget![Account] = Nz(.Account)
rstTarget![AssistantName] = Nz(.AssistantName)
```

Use special handling for a date field (a blank date in Outlook is actually a date of 1/1/4501):

```
If .Birthday <> #1/1/4501# Then
    rstTarget![Birthday] = .Birthday
End If
If .Anniversary <> #1/1/4501# Then
    rstTarget![Anniversary] = .Anniversary
End If
If .LastModificationTime <> #1/1/4501# Then
    rstTarget![LastUpdated] = _
        .LastModificationTime
End If

rstTarget![Categories] = Nz(.Categories)
rstTarget![Children] = Nz(.Children)
rstTarget![PersonalHomePage] = _
    Nz(.PersonalHomePage)
rstTarget![Email1Address] = Nz(.Email1Address)
rstTarget![Email1DisplayName] = _
    Nz(.Email1DisplayName)
rstTarget![Email2Address] = Nz(.Email2Address)
rstTarget![Email2DisplayName] = _
    Nz(.Email2DisplayName)
rstTarget![Email3Address] = Nz(.Email3Address)
rstTarget![Email3DisplayName] = _
```

```
            Nz(.Email3DisplayName)
        rstTarget![GovernmentIDNumber] = _
            Nz(.GovernmentIDNumber)
        rstTarget![Hobby] = Nz(.Hobby)
        rstTarget![ManagerName] = Nz(.ManagerName)
        rstTarget![OrganizationalIDNumber] = _
            Nz(.OrganizationalIDNumber)
        rstTarget![Profession] = Nz(.Profession)
        rstTarget![Spouse] = Nz(.Spouse)
        rstTarget![WebPage] = Nz(.WebPage)
        rstTarget![IMAddress] = Nz(.IMAddress)
```

Use special handling for attachments, calling another procedure:

```
        If .Attachments.Count > 0 Then
            Set rstTargetAttachments = _
                rstTarget![Attachments].Value
            Call CopyOutlookAttsToAccess(con, _
                rstTargetAttachments)
        End If

        rstTarget.Update
        .Close (olSave)
      End With
    End If
  Next itm

  rstTarget.Close

  strTitle = "Outlook table created"
  strPrompt = "Table of Outlook contact data ("
    & strTable _
    & ") created and filled with data from the " _
    & fldContacts.Name & " folder"
  MsgBox strPrompt, vbInformation + vbOKOnly, strTitle

ErrorHandlerExit:
  Exit Function

ErrorHandler:
  'Outlook is not running; open Outlook with CreateObject
  If Err.Number = 429 Then
    Set appOutlook = CreateObject("Outlook.Application")
    Resume Next
  Else
    MsgBox "Error No: " & Err.Number _
        & "; Description: " & Err.Description
    Resume ErrorHandlerExit
  End If

End Function
```

> **TIP**   If you always synchronize your Access contacts to the same Outlook folder, you can comment out the `SelectContactFolder` code segment and insert a hard-coded folder path instead; if you want to use the default local Contacts folder, just remove the apostrophe on the line `'Set fldContacts = nms.GetDefaultFolder(olFolderContacts)`, and either comment out or delete the `SelectContactFolder` code segment.

The other procedure, `CreateDenormalizedContactsTable`, is considerably more complex, because it has to take data from five linked tables, creating one record per contact and updating its fields from different tables:

```
Public Function CreateDenormalizedContactsTable()
'Called from cmdForms_Click on fmnuMain

On Error GoTo ErrorHandler

    Dim lngTargetID As Long
    Dim strQueryContacts As String
    Dim strQueryContactIDs As String
    Dim strQueryCompanyIDs As String
    Dim strQueryContactAddresses As String
    Dim strTargetCustomerID As String

    Set dbs = CurrentDb
    strQueryContacts = "qryAccessContacts"
    strQueryContactIDs = "qryContactIDsPhones"
    strQueryCompanyIDs = "qryCompanyIDsPhones"
    strQueryContactAddresses = "qryContactAddresses"
```

Clear tables of old data.

```
    DoCmd.SetWarnings False
    strTable = "tblAccessContacts"
    strSQL = "DELETE * FROM " & strTable
    DoCmd.RunSQL strSQL
```

The rstTarget recordset is based on tblAccessContacts; this is the table to be filled with denormalized data. rstSource represents the first table of linked Access data, tblContactInfo. Information from this table is written to matching fields in the target table, with special handling for attachments (see the section on attachments for more information on this topic):

```
    Set rstSource = dbs.OpenRecordset(strQueryContacts, _
        dbOpenDynaset)
    Set rstTarget = dbs.OpenRecordset(strTable, _
        dbOpenDynaset)

    Do While Not rstSource.EOF
```

Create one record in the target table per contact, and write company and contact data to it; also create one record in the match table per contact, for use in comparing contacts:

```
rstTarget.AddNew
rstTarget![CustomerID] = Nz(rstSource!CustomerID)
strTargetCustomerID = rstTarget![CustomerID]
rstTarget![CompanyName] = _
   Nz(rstSource!CompanyName)
rstTarget![Account] = Nz(rstSource!Account)
rstTarget![Categories] = Nz(rstSource!Categories)
rstTarget![OrganizationalIDNumber] = _
   Nz(rstSource!OrganizationalIDNumber)
rstTarget![WebPage] = Nz(rstSource!WebPage)
rstTarget![FTPSite] = Nz(rstSource!FTPSite)
rstTarget![Title] = Nz(rstSource!Title)
rstTarget![FirstName] = Nz(rstSource!FirstName)
rstTarget![MiddleName] = Nz(rstSource!MiddleName)
rstTarget![LastName] = Nz(rstSource!LastName)
rstTarget![Suffix] = Nz(rstSource!Suffix)
rstTarget![Nickname] = Nz(rstSource!Nickname)
rstTarget![Department] = Nz(rstSource!Department)
rstTarget![JobTitle] = Nz(rstSource!JobTitle)
rstTarget![AssistantName] = Nz(rstSource!AssistantName)
rstTarget![Birthday] = Nz(rstSource!Birthday)
rstTarget![Anniversary] = Nz(rstSource!Anniversary)
rstTarget![Children] = Nz(rstSource!Children)
rstTarget![GovernmentIDNumber] = _
   Nz(rstSource!GovernmentIDNumber)
rstTarget![Hobby] = Nz(rstSource!Hobby)
rstTarget![ManagerName] = Nz(rstSource!ManagerName)
rstTarget![Profession] = Nz(rstSource!Profession)
rstTarget![Spouse] = Nz(rstSource!Spouse)
```

Use special handling for attachments, calling another procedure:

```
Set rstSourceAttachments = _
   rstSource![Attachments].Value
If rstSourceAttachments.RecordCount > 0 Then
   Set rstTargetAttachments = _
      rstTarget![Attachments].Value
   Call CopyAccessAttsToAccess(rstSourceAttachments, _
      rstTargetAttachments)
Else
   rstSourceAttachments.Close
End If

rstTarget![LastUpdated] = Nz(rstSource!LastUpdated)
rstTarget.Update
rstSource.MoveNext
Loop

rstSource.Close
```

The next source object is `qryContactIDsPhones` (see Figure 11.10). It has only two fields, so to match the many phone and ID fields in the target table I created a query with many calculated fields, one for each phone or ID field in tblAccessContacts.

FIGURE 11.10

A calculated field that converts a phone number in tblContactIDsPhones into a value to be written to tblAccessContacts.

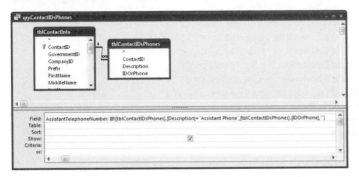

Each calculated field returns a value for a phone number or ID matching one of the standard Outlook Phone and ID selections; a portion of the code that works with this query is listed below:

```
Set rstSource = dbs.OpenRecordset(strQueryContactIDs, _
    dbOpenDynaset)

Do While Not rstSource.EOF
```

Search for target record and update Contact ID and phone fields:

```
strTargetCustomerID = rstSource![CustomerID]
strSearch = "[CustomerID] = " & Chr$(39) _
    & strTargetCustomerID & Chr$(39)
```

Uncomment the following line to inspect the search string in the Immediate window.

```
'Debug.Print "Search string: " & strSearch
rstTarget.FindFirst strSearch
If rstTarget.NoMatch = False Then
    GoTo NextSourceRecord1
End If
rstTarget.Edit
rstTarget![AssistantTelephoneNumber] = _
    Nz(rstSource!AssistantTelephoneNumber)
```

```
rstTarget![BusinessFaxNumber] = _
    Nz(rstSource!BusinessFaxNumber)
rstTarget![BusinessTelephoneNumber] = _
    Nz(rstSource!BusinessTelephoneNumber)
rstTarget![Business2TelephoneNumber] = _
    Nz(rstSource!Business2TelephoneNumber)
rstTarget![CallbackTelephoneNumber] = _
    Nz(rstSource!CallbackTelephoneNumber)
rstTarget![CarTelephoneNumber] = _
    Nz(rstSource!CarTelephoneNumber)
rstTarget![HomeFaxNumber] = _
    Nz(rstSource!HomeFaxNumber)
rstTarget![HomeTelephoneNumber] = _
    Nz(rstSource!HomeTelephoneNumber)
rstTarget![Home2TelephoneNumber] = _
    Nz(rstSource!Home2TelephoneNumber)
rstTarget![ISDNNumber] = Nz(rstSource!ISDNNumber)
rstTarget![MobileTelephoneNumber] = _
    Nz(rstSource!MobileTelephoneNumber)
rstTarget![OtherFaxNumber] = _
    Nz(rstSource!OtherFaxNumber)
rstTarget![OtherTelephoneNumber] = _
    Nz(rstSource!OtherTelephoneNumber)
rstTarget![PagerNumber] = Nz(rstSource!PagerNumber)
rstTarget![PrimaryTelephoneNumber] = _
    Nz(rstSource!PrimaryTelephoneNumber)
rstTarget![RadioTelephoneNumber] = _
    Nz(rstSource!RadioTelephoneNumber)
rstTarget![TTYTDDTelephoneNumber] = _
    Nz(rstSource!TTYTDDTelephoneNumber)
rstTarget![TelexNumber] = Nz(rstSource!TelexNumber)
rstTarget![Email1Address] = _
    Nz(rstSource!Email1Address)
rstTarget![Email1DisplayName] = _
    Nz(rstSource!Email1DisplayName)
rstTarget![Email2Address] = _
    Nz(rstSource!Email2Address)
rstTarget![Email2DisplayName] = _
    Nz(rstSource!Email2DisplayName)
rstTarget![Email3Address] = _
    Nz(rstSource!Email3Address)
rstTarget![Email3DisplayName] = _
    Nz(rstSource!Email3DisplayName)
rstTarget![IMAddress] = Nz(rstSource!IMAddress)
rstTarget![PersonalHomePage] = _
    Nz(rstSource!PersonalHomePage)
rstTarget.Update
```

```
NextSourceRecord1:
     rstSource.MoveNext
  Loop

  rstSource.Close
```

Company phones and IDs are handled similarly; only one possible value (Company Phone) is synchronized, because that is the only one that matches a field in Outlook:

```
  Set rstSource = dbs.OpenRecordset(strQueryCompanyIDs, _
     dbOpenDynaset)

  Do While Not rstSource.EOF
```

Search for target record and update Company Phone field.

```
     strTargetCustomerID = rstSource![CustomerID]
     strSearch = "[CustomerID] = " & Chr$(39) _
        & strTargetCustomerID & Chr$(39)
     'Debug.Print "Search string: " & strSearch
     rstTarget.FindFirst strSearch
     rstTarget.Edit
     rstTarget![CompanyMainTelephoneNumber] = _
        Nz(rstSource!CompanyMainTelephoneNumber)
     rstTarget.Update

NextSourceRecord2:
     rstSource.MoveNext
  Loop

  rstSource.Close
```

Finally, contact addresses are processed, using a query that converts each address field to the appropriate Business, Home, or Other address field in the target table. Figure 11.11 shows one of the calculated fields in this query.

FIGURE 11.11

A calculated query field that converts StreetAddress to BusinessAddressStreet.

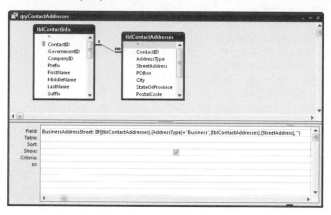

The rstSource recordset is then selected, based on a query that selects contact addresses; the code looks for a matching target record, and if it is found, it is updated with information from the recordset:

```
Set rstSource = _
    dbs.OpenRecordset(strQueryContactAddresses, _
        dbOpenDynaset)

Do While Not rstSource.EOF
    strTargetCustomerID = rstSource![CustomerID]
    strSearch = "[CustomerID] = " & Chr$(39) _
        & strTargetCustomerID & Chr$(39)
    'Debug.Print "Search string: " & strSearch
    rstTarget.FindFirst strSearch
    rstTarget.Edit
    rstTarget![BusinessAddressStreet] = _
        Nz(rstSource!BusinessAddressStreet)
    rstTarget![BusinessAddressPostOfficeBox] = _
        Nz(rstSource!BusinessAddressPostOfficeBox)
    rstTarget![BusinessAddressCity] = _
        Nz(rstSource!BusinessAddressCity)
    rstTarget![BusinessAddressState] = _
        Nz(rstSource!BusinessAddressState)
    rstTarget![BusinessAddressPostalCode] = _
        Nz(rstSource!BusinessAddressPostalCode)
    rstTarget![BusinessAddressCountry] = _
        Nz(rstSource!BusinessAddressCountry)
```

371

```
        rstTarget![HomeAddressStreet] = _
            Nz(rstSource!HomeAddressStreet)
        rstTarget![HomeAddressPostOfficeBox] = _
            Nz(rstSource!HomeAddressPostOfficeBox)
        rstTarget![HomeAddressCity] = _
            Nz(rstSource!HomeAddressCity)
        rstTarget![HomeAddressState] = _
            Nz(rstSource!HomeAddressState)
        rstTarget![HomeAddressPostalCode] = _
            Nz(rstSource!HomeAddressPostalCode)
        rstTarget![HomeAddressCountry] = _
            Nz(rstSource!HomeAddressCountry)
        rstTarget![OtherAddressStreet] = _
            Nz(rstSource!OtherAddressStreet)
        rstTarget![OtherAddressPostOfficeBox] = _
            Nz(rstSource!OtherAddressPostOfficeBox)
        rstTarget![OtherAddressCity] = _
            Nz(rstSource!OtherAddressCity)
        rstTarget![OtherAddressState] = _
            Nz(rstSource!OtherAddressState)
        rstTarget![OtherAddressPostalCode] = _
            Nz(rstSource!OtherAddressPostalCode)
        rstTarget![OtherAddressCountry] = _
            Nz(rstSource!OtherAddressCountry)
        rstTarget.Update

NextSourceRecord3:
        rstSource.MoveNext
    Loop

    strTitle = "Access table created"
    strPrompt = "Denormalized table of Access data (" _
        & strTable & ") created"
    MsgBox strPrompt, vbInformation + vbOKOnly, _
        strTitle

ErrorHandlerExit:
    rstSource.Close
    rstTarget.Close

    Exit Function

ErrorHandler:
    MsgBox "Error No: " & Err.Number _
        & "; Description: " & Err.Description
    Resume ErrorHandlerExit

End Function
```

The two tables (tblOutlookContacts and tblAccessContacts) have matching fields; they are displayed in subforms on the two forms used for comparing Access and Outlook contact data. Figure 11.12 shows the form that compares contacts by Contact ID (frmCompareContactsByID), with data from an Access contact on the left and the matching Outlook contact (if there is one) on the right.

FIGURE 11.12

A form that compares Outlook and Access contacts by ContactID.

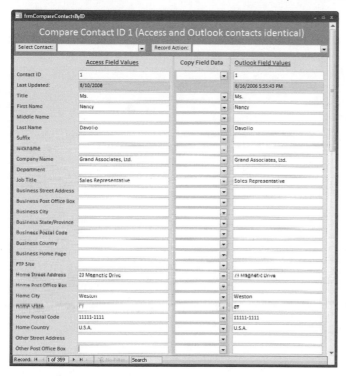

Figure 11.13 shows the form that compares contacts by name.

FIGURE 11.13

A form that compares Outlook and Access contacts by name.

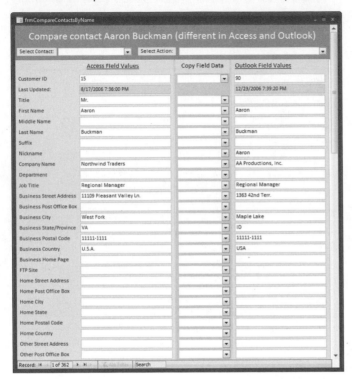

Copying Contact Data from Access to Outlook (or Vice Versa)

The Select Contact combo box at the top left lets you select a contact, sorted by Contact ID. Figure 11.14 shows the combo box with its list dropped down.

The Select Action combo box on the right side of the header of the form shown in Figure 11.11 offers a different set of choices, depending on whether the Outlook and Access contacts are identical, different, or one is missing, as shown in Table 11.1.

FIGURE 11.14

Selecting a contact by Contact ID.

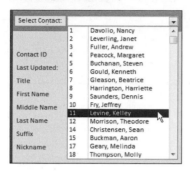

TABLE 11.1

Contact Match Status and Actions to Select

Contact Status	Available Actions
Outlook and Access contacts are identical	Go to next contact record Mark contact for deletion Copy all Access contacts to Outlook Copy all Outlook contacts to Access
Outlook and Access contacts are different	Modify Access contact to match Outlook contact Modify Outlook contact to match Access contact Go to next contact record Mark contact for deletion Copy all Access contacts to Outlook Copy all Outlook contacts to Access
No Outlook contact	Create new Outlook contact to match Access contact Go to next contact record Mark contact for deletion Copy all Access contacts to Outlook Copy all Outlook contacts to Access
No Access contact	Create new Access contact to match Outlook contact Go to next contact record Mark contact for deletion Copy all Access contacts to Outlook Copy all Outlook contacts to Access

To copy data in one field, rather than updating an entire contact record, select either "Access to Outlook" or "Outlook to Access" in the combo box in the center Copy Field Data section of the form, as shown in Figure 11.15, where the value "Vice President" in the Access contact record is being replaced by "Senior Vice President" from the Outlook record. You can also type in new data, or edit existing data, as needed, before copying the record.

FIGURE 11.15

Copying a single field's data from Outlook to Access.

If you want to completely remove a contact, select "Mark Record for Deletion" and it will be deleted when the contacts are updated. When you have finished copying, editing, and marking records for deletion, the "Update Contact Information" button on the main menu offers you a choice of updating the Access contacts first, and then the Outlook contacts. All data (including attachments, if any) from tblOutlookContacts will be copied back to the contacts in the selected Contacts folder, creating new contacts as needed. The procedure that updates the Outlook contacts is listed here:

```
Public Sub UpdateAllOutlookContacts()
'Called from cmdUpdateContactInfo_Click() on fmnuMain

On Error GoTo ErrorHandler

    Set appOutlook = GetObject(, "Outlook.Application")
    Set nms = appOutlook.GetNamespace("MAPI")
    strTable = "tblOutlookContacts"
    Set dbs = CurrentDb
    Set rstSource = _
        dbs.OpenRecordset(strTable, dbOpenDynaset)
```

You can use the following lines to export to the default local Contacts folder, or a hard-coded folder of your choice. To use the default Contacts folder, just remove the apostrophe at the beginning of the next line (this is called *uncommenting* a line of code, because the apostrophe in front of the line turns it into a comment); to use a hard-coded custom folder, enter its name.

```
'Set fldContacts = nms.GetDefaultFolder(olFolderContacts)
'GoTo UpdateContacts
```

Use the following section of code to allow selection of a custom Contacts folder from the Folder Picker dialog:

```
SelectContactFolder:
On Error Resume Next
    Set fldContacts = nms.PickFolder
    If fldContacts Is Nothing Then
        strTitle = "Select Folder"
        strPrompt = "Please select a Contacts folder"
        MsgBox strPrompt, vbExclamation + vbOKOnly, strTitle
        GoTo SelectContactFolder
    End If

    Debug.Print "Default item type: " _
        & fldContacts.DefaultItemType
    If fldContacts.DefaultItemType <> olContactItem Then
        MsgBox strPrompt, vbExclamation + vbOKOnly, _
            strTitle
        GoTo SelectContactFolder
    End If

UpdateContacts:
    Do While Not rstSource.EOF
```

Search for each contact in selected Contacts folder in case it already exists, and set a reference to it, searching first by CustomerID and then by first name and last name. (Outlook contacts may lack a value in the CustomerID property):

```
strCustomerID = Nz(rstSource![CustomerID])
strSearch = "[CustomerID] = " & Chr$(39) _
    & strCustomerID & Chr$(39)
Debug.Print "Search string: " & strSearch
blnDelete = rstSource![Delete]
```

Search by CustomerID.

```
Set con = fldContacts.Items.Find(strSearch)
If TypeName(con) = "Nothing" Then
    Debug.Print "Customer ID " & strCustomerID _
        & " not found in " & fldContacts.Name & " folder"
    strFirstName = Nz(rstSource![FirstName])
    strLastName = Nz(rstSource![LastName])
    strSearch = "[FirstName] = " & Chr$(39) _
```

```
                            & strFirstName & Chr$(39) _
                         & " And [LastName] = " & Chr$(39) _
                            & strLastName & Chr$(39)
                   'Debug.Print "Search string: " & strSearch
```

Search by name.

```
                   Set con = fldContacts.Items.Find(strSearch)
                   If TypeName(con) = "Nothing" Then
                      Debug.Print "Contact name " & strFirstName _
                         & " " & strLastName & " not found in " _
                         & fldContacts.Name & " folder"
```

Create new contact item.

```
                   Debug.Print "Creating new contact item with " _
                      & "CustomerID " & strCustomerID
                      If blnDelete = False Then
                         Set con = fldContacts.Items.Add
                      Else
                         GoTo NextSourceRecord
                      End If
                   Else
                      Debug.Print "Found contact name " _
                         & strFirstName _
                         & " " & strLastName
                      If blnDelete = True Then
                         con.Delete
                         GoTo NextSourceRecord
                      End If
                   End If
                Else
                   Debug.Print "Found Customer ID " _
                      & strCustomerID
                   If blnDelete = True Then
                      con.Delete
                      GoTo NextSourceRecord
                   End If
                End If
             End If
```

Update contact item with values from controls on the Outlook subform:

```
          On Error GoTo ErrorHandler

             con.CustomerID = Nz(rstSource![CustomerID])
             con.Title = Nz(rstSource![Title])
             con.FirstName = Nz(rstSource![FirstName])
             con.MiddleName = Nz(rstSource![MiddleName])
             con.LastName = Nz(rstSource![LastName])
             con.Suffix = Nz(rstSource![Suffix])
             con.Nickname = Nz(rstSource![Nickname])
```

```
con.CompanyName = Nz(rstSource![CompanyName])
con.Department = Nz(rstSource![Department])
con.JobTitle = Nz(rstSource![JobTitle])
con.BusinessAddressStreet = _
   Nz(rstSource![BusinessAddressStreet])
con.BusinessAddressPostOfficeBox = _
   Nz(rstSource![BusinessAddressPostOfficeBox])
con.BusinessAddressCity = _
   Nz(rstSource![BusinessAddressCity])
con.BusinessAddressState = _
   Nz(rstSource![BusinessAddressState])
con.BusinessAddressPostalCode = _
   Nz(rstSource![BusinessAddressPostalCode])
con.BusinessAddressCountry = _
   Nz(rstSource![BusinessAddressCountry])
con.BusinessHomePage = _
   Nz(rstSource![BusinessHomePage])
con.FTPSite = Nz(rstSource![FTPSite])
con.HomeAddressStreet = _
   Nz(rstSource![HomeAddressStreet])
con.HomeAddressPostOfficeBox = _
   Nz(rstSource![HomeAddressPostOfficeBox])
con.HomeAddressCity = _
   Nz(rstSource![HomeAddressCity])
con.HomeAddressState = _
   Nz(rstSource![HomeAddressState])
con.HomeAddressPostalCode = _
   Nz(rstSource![HomeAddressPostalCode])
con.HomeAddressCountry = _
   Nz(rstSource![HomeAddressCountry])
con.OtherAddressStreet = _
   Nz(rstSource![OtherAddressStreet])
con.OtherAddressPostOfficeBox = _
   Nz(rstSource![OtherAddressPostOfficeBox])
con.OtherAddressCity = _
   Nz(rstSource![OtherAddressCity])
con.OtherAddressState = _
   Nz(rstSource![OtherAddressState])
con.OtherAddressPostalCode = _
   Nz(rstSource![OtherAddressPostalCode])
con.OtherAddressCountry = _
   Nz(rstSource![OtherAddressCountry])
con.AssistantTelephoneNumber = _
   Nz(rstSource![AssistantTelephoneNumber])
con.BusinessFaxNumber = _
   Nz(rstSource![BusinessFaxNumber])
con.BusinessTelephoneNumber = _
   Nz(rstSource![BusinessTelephoneNumber])
con.Business2TelephoneNumber = _
   Nz(rstSource![Business2TelephoneNumber])
```

```
con.CallbackTelephoneNumber = _
    Nz(rstSource![CallbackTelephoneNumber])
con.CarTelephoneNumber = _
    Nz(rstSource![CarTelephoneNumber])
con.CompanyMainTelephoneNumber = _
    Nz(rstSource![CompanyMainTelephoneNumber])
con.HomeFaxNumber = Nz(rstSource![HomeFaxNumber])
con.HomeTelephoneNumber = _
    Nz(rstSource![HomeTelephoneNumber])
con.Home2TelephoneNumber = _
    Nz(rstSource![Home2TelephoneNumber])
con.ISDNNumber = Nz(rstSource![ISDNNumber])
con.MobileTelephoneNumber = _
    Nz(rstSource![MobileTelephoneNumber])
con.OtherFaxNumber = Nz(rstSource![OtherFaxNumber])
con.OtherTelephoneNumber = _
    Nz(rstSource![OtherTelephoneNumber])
con.PagerNumber = Nz(rstSource![PagerNumber])
con.PrimaryTelephoneNumber = _
    Nz(rstSource![PrimaryTelephoneNumber])
con.RadioTelephoneNumber = _
    Nz(rstSource![RadioTelephoneNumber])
con.TTYTDDTelephoneNumber = _
    Nz(rstSource![TTYTDDTelephoneNumber])
con.TelexNumber = Nz(rstSource![TelexNumber])
con.Account = Nz(rstSource![Account])
con.AssistantName = Nz(rstSource![AssistantName])
con.Categories = Nz(rstSource![Categories])
con.Children = Nz(rstSource![Children])
con.PersonalHomePage = _
    Nz(rstSource![PersonalHomePage])
con.Email1Address = Nz(rstSource![Email1Address])
con.Email1DisplayName = _
    Nz(rstSource![Email1DisplayName])
con.Email2Address = Nz(rstSource![Email2Address])
con.Email2DisplayName = _
    Nz(rstSource![Email2DisplayName])
con.Email3Address = Nz(rstSource![Email3Address])
con.Email3DisplayName = _
    Nz(rstSource![Email3DisplayName])
con.GovernmentIDNumber = _
    Nz(rstSource![GovernmentIDNumber])
con.Hobby = Nz(rstSource![Hobby])
con.ManagerName = Nz(rstSource![ManagerName])
con.OrganizationalIDNumber = _
    Nz(rstSource![OrganizationalIDNumber])
con.Profession = Nz(rstSource![Profession])
con.Spouse = Nz(rstSource![Spouse])
con.WebPage = Nz(rstSource![WebPage])
con.IMAddress = Nz(rstSource![IMAddress])
```

Use special date handling (a blank date in Outlook is actually a date of 1/1/4501):

```
If Nz(rstSource![Birthday]) <> "" Then
    con.Birthday = Nz(rstSource![Birthday])
Else
    con.Birthday = #1/1/4501#
End If
If Nz(rstSource![Anniversary]) <> "" Then
    con.Anniversary = Nz(rstSource![Anniversary])
Else
    con.Anniversary = #1/1/4501#
End If
```

Use special handling for attachments, calling another procedure:

```
Set rstSourceAttachments = _
    rstSource![Attachments].Value
If rstSourceAttachments.RecordCount > 0 Then
    Call CopyAccessAttsToOutlook(con, _
        rstSourceAttachments)
Else
    rstSourceAttachments.Close
End If

con.Close (olSave)

strFirstName = ""
strLastName = ""
strCustomerID = ""

NextSourceRecord:
    rstSource.MoveNext
    Loop

    strTitle = "Outlook contacts updated"
    strPrompt = "All Outlook contacts in the " _
        & fldContacts.Name & " folder updated"
    MsgBox strPrompt, vbInformation + vbOKOnly, _
        strTitle

ErrorHandlerExit:
    Exit Sub

ErrorHandler:
    'Outlook is not running; open Outlook with CreateObject
    If Err.Number = 429 Then
        Set appOutlook = CreateObject("Outlook.Application")
        Resume Next
    Else
        MsgBox "Error No: " & Err.Number _
```

```
                & "; Description: " & Err.Description
          Resume ErrorHandlerExit
      End If


      End Sub
```

The UpdateAllAccessContacts procedure has the more complex task of copying updated contact data from tblAccessContacts back to the linked contact tables. This procedure does the reverse of
the CreateDenormalizedContactsTable procedure; using tblAccessContacts as a data source,
it updates the linked contact data in tblCompanyInfo, tblContactInfo, tblCompanyIDsPhones,
tblContactAddresses, and tblContactIDsAndPhones, creating new records as needed:

```
      Public Sub UpdateAllAccessContacts()
      'Called from cmdUpdateContactInfo_Click() on fmnuMain

      On Error GoTo ErrorHandler

          Dim lngContactID As Long
          Dim lngCompanyID As Long
          Dim strSourceTable As String
          Dim strTarget As String
          Dim strAddressType As String
          Dim strDescription As String

          Set dbs = CurrentDb
          strSourceTable = "tblAccessContacts"

          Set rstSource = dbs.OpenRecordset(strSourceTable, _
            dbOpenDynaset)

      UpdateCompanyInfo:
          Do While Not rstSource.EOF
             Debug.Print "Processing Target ID: " _
                & rstSource![TargetID]
```

Search for matching Company record in target table, and update it if found; otherwise, create new
company record, and write company data to it.

```
             strTarget = "tblCompanyInfo"
             Set rstTarget = dbs.OpenRecordset(strTarget, _
               dbOpenDynaset)
             blnDelete = rstSource![Delete]
             If blnDelete = True Then
```

To avoid problems with deleting records in a table on the "one" side of a one-to-many relationship,
before updating the tables, the procedure runs three delete queries to delete records linked to contacts marked for deletion:

```
On Error Resume Next
        DoCmd.SetWarnings False
        DoCmd.OpenQuery "qdelContactIDs"
        DoCmd.OpenQuery "qdelContactAddresses"
        DoCmd.OpenQuery "qdelContacts"
        GoTo NextSourceRecord
    End If
```

Next, records in tblCompanyInfo are updated as needed:

```
On Error GoTo ErrorHandler
        lngCompanyID = Nz(rstSource![OrganizationalIDNumber])
        strSearch = "[CompanyID] = " & lngCompanyID
        Debug.Print "Search string: " & strSearch
        rstTarget.FindFirst strSearch
        If rstTarget.NoMatch = True Then
```

Create new company record in target table.

```
        rstTarget.AddNew
    Else
        rstTarget.Edit
    End If
    rstTarget![CompanyName] = _
        Nz(rstSource!CompanyName)
    rstTarget![Account] = Nz(rstSource!Account)
    rstTarget![Category] = Nz(rstSource!Categories)
    rstTarget![WebSite] = Nz(rstSource!WebPage)
    rstTarget![FTPSite] = Nz(rstSource!FTPSite)
    rstTarget![LastUpdated] = Now
    rstTarget.Update
    rstTarget.Close
```

Next, records in tblContactInfo are updated as needed:

```
UpdateContactInfo:
```

Search for matching contact record in target table, and update it if found; otherwise, create a new contact record, and write contact data to it:

```
        strTarget = "tblContactInfo"
        Set rstTarget = dbs.OpenRecordset(strTarget, _
            dbOpenDynaset)
        strCustomerID = rstSource![CustomerID]
        lngContactID = CLng(strCustomerID)
        strSearch = "[ContactID] = " & lngContactID
        Debug.Print "Search string: " & strSearch
        rstTarget.FindFirst strSearch
        If rstTarget.NoMatch = True Then
```

Create a new contact record in the target table.

```
            rstTarget.AddNew
            rstTarget![CustomerID] = strCustomerID
            rstTarget![ContactID] = CLng(strCustomerID)
        Else
            rstTarget.Edit
        End If

        rstTarget![Prefix] = Nz(rstSource!Title)
        rstTarget![FirstName] = Nz(rstSource!FirstName)
        rstTarget![MiddleName] = Nz(rstSource!MiddleName)
        rstTarget![LastName] = Nz(rstSource!LastName)
        rstTarget![Suffix] = Nz(rstSource!Suffix)
        rstTarget![Nickname] = Nz(rstSource!Nickname)
        rstTarget![Department] = Nz(rstSource!Department)
        rstTarget![JobTitle] = Nz(rstSource!JobTitle)
        rstTarget![AssistantName] = _
            Nz(rstSource!AssistantName)
        rstTarget![Birthday] = Nz(rstSource!Birthday)
        rstTarget![Anniversary] = Nz(rstSource!Anniversary)
        rstTarget![Children] = Nz(rstSource!Children)
        rstTarget![GovernmentID] = _
            Nz(rstSource!GovernmentIDNumber)
        rstTarget![Hobby] = Nz(rstSource!Hobby)
        rstTarget![ManagerName] = _
            Nz(rstSource!ManagerName)
        rstTarget![Profession] = Nz(rstSource!Profession)
        rstTarget![Spouse] = Nz(rstSource!Spouse)
        rstTarget![LastUpdated] = Now
```

Special handling for attachments.

```
        Set rstSourceAttachments = _
            rstSource![Attachments].Value
        If rstSourceAttachments.RecordCount > 0 Then
            Set rstTargetAttachments = _
                rstTarget![Attachments].Value
            Call CopyAccessAttsToAccess(rstSourceAttachments, _
                rstTargetAttachments)
        Else
            rstSourceAttachments.Close
        End If

        rstTarget.Update
        rstTarget.Close

UpdateContactAddresses:
```

To update data in tblContactAddresses, if there is data in any of the Business address fields, the strAddressType variable is set to Business, and the code searches for matching records in tblContactAddresses. If none are found, a new address record is created; if a record is found, its fields are updated from the appropriate fields in tblAccessContacts. The Home and Other address fields are handled similarly:

```
strTarget = "tblContactAddresses"
Set rstTarget = dbs.OpenRecordset(strTarget, _
    dbOpenDynaset)
```

Update Business address info.

```
If Nz(rstSource!BusinessAddressStreet) <> "" Or _
    Nz(rstSource!BusinessAddressPostOfficeBox) <> "" _
    Or Nz(rstSource!BusinessAddressCity) <> "" _
    Or Nz(rstSource!BusinessAddressState) <> "" _
    Or Nz(rstSource!BusinessAddressPostalCode) <> "" _
    Or Nz(rstSource!BusinessAddressCountry) <> "" Then
    strAddressType = "Business"
    strSearch = "[ContactID] = " & lngContactID _
        & " And [AddressType] = " & Chr$(39) _
        & strAddressType & Chr$(39)
    Debug.Print "Search string: " & strSearch
    rstTarget.FindFirst strSearch
    If rstTarget.NoMatch = True Then
```

Create a new contact address record in the target table.

```
        rstTarget.AddNew
        rstTarget![ContactID] = lngContactID
        rstTarget![AddressType] = strAddressType
    Else
        rstTarget.Edit
    End If

     rstTarget![StreetAddress] = _
        Nz(rstSource!BusinessAddressStreet)
    rstTarget![POBox] = _
        Nz(rstSource!BusinessAddressPostOfficeBox)
    rstTarget![City] = _
        Nz(rstSource!BusinessAddressCity)
    rstTarget![StateOrProvince] = _
        Nz(rstSource!BusinessAddressState)
    rstTarget![PostalCode] = _
        Nz(rstSource!BusinessAddressPostalCode)
    rstTarget![Country] = _
        Nz(rstSource!BusinessAddressCountry)
    rstTarget.Update
End If
```

Update Home address info.

```
If Nz(rstSource!HomeAddressStreet) <> "" _
   Or Nz(rstSource!HomeAddressPostOfficeBox) <> "" _
   Or Nz(rstSource!HomeAddressCity) <> "" _
   Or Nz(rstSource!HomeAddressState) <> "" _
   Or Nz(rstSource!HomeAddressPostalCode) <> "" _
   Or Nz(rstSource!HomeAddressCountry) <> "" Then
   strAddressType = "Home"
 strSearch = "[ContactID] = " & lngContactID _
   & " And [AddressType] = " & Chr$(39) _
   & strAddressType & Chr$(39)
 Debug.Print "Search string: " & strSearch
 rstTarget.FindFirst strSearch
 If rstTarget.NoMatch = True Then
```

Create a new contact address record in the target table.

```
   rstTarget.AddNew
   rstTarget![ContactID] = lngContactID
   rstTarget![AddressType] = strAddressType
 Else
   rstTarget.Edit
 End If

 rstTarget![StreetAddress] = _
   Nz(rstSource!HomeAddressStreet)
 rstTarget![POBox] = _
   Nz(rstSource!HomeAddressPostOfficeBox)
 rstTarget![City] = _
   Nz(rstSource!HomeAddressCity)
 rstTarget![StateOrProvince] = _
   Nz(rstSource!HomeAddressState)
 rstTarget![PostalCode] = _
   Nz(rstSource!HomeAddressPostalCode)
 rstTarget![Country] = _
   Nz(rstSource!HomeAddressCountry)
 rstTarget.Update
 End If
```

Update Other address info.

```
If Nz(rstSource!OtherAddressStreet) <> "" _
   Or Nz(rstSource!OtherAddressPostOfficeBox) <> "" _
   Or Nz(rstSource!OtherAddressCity) <> "" _
   Or Nz(rstSource!OtherAddressState) <> "" _
   Or Nz(rstSource!OtherAddressPostalCode) <> "" _
   Or Nz(rstSource!OtherAddressCountry) <> "" Then
   strAddressType = "Other"
```

```
strSearch = "[ContactID] = " & lngContactID _
    & " And [AddressType] = " & Chr$(39) _
    & strAddressType & Chr$(39)
Debug.Print "Search string: " & strSearch
rstTarget.FindFirst strSearch
If rstTarget.NoMatch = True Then
```

Create a new contact address record in the target table.

```
    rstTarget.AddNew
    rstTarget![ContactID] = lngContactID
    rstTarget![AddressType] = strAddressType
Else
    rstTarget.Edit
End If

rstTarget![StreetAddress] = _
    Nz(rstSource!OtherAddressStreet)
rstTarget![POBox] = _
    Nz(rstSource!OtherAddressPostOfficeBox)
rstTarget![City] = _
    Nz(rstSource!OtherAddressCity)
rstTarget![StateOrProvince] = _
    Nz(rstSource!OtherAddressState)
rstTarget![PostalCode] = _
    Nz(rstSource!OtherAddressPostalCode)
rstTarget![Country] = _
    Nz(rstSource!OtherAddressCountry)
rstTarget.Update
End If

rstTarget.Close

UpdateCompanyPhone:
```

If there is a value in the Company Phone record in the source database, it is written to a record in
the target table (this is the only company phone number or ID that can be matched with Outlook,
so it is the only one that is synchronized). If none is found, a new record is created and updated
with the Company Phone number:

```
strTarget = "tblCompanyIDsPhones"
Set rstTarget = dbs.OpenRecordset(strTarget, _
    dbOpenDynaset)
strDescription = "Company Phone"
strSearch = "[CompanyID] = " & lngCompanyID _
    & " And [Description] = " & Chr$(39) _
    & strDescription & Chr$(39)
Debug.Print "Search string: " & strSearch
rstTarget.FindFirst strSearch
If rstTarget.NoMatch = True Then
```

Create a new company phone record in the target table.

```
        rstTarget.AddNew
        rstTarget![CompanyID] = lngCompanyID
        rstTarget![Description] = "Company Phone"
Else
        rstTarget.Edit
End If

rstTarget![IDOrPhone] = _
        Nz(rstSource!CompanyMainTelephoneNumber)
rstTarget.Update
rstTarget.Close
```

The Contact IDs and Phones in tblContactIDsPhones are updated in a similar manner: First the code searches for a value in one of these fields, and if it is found, the `strDescription` variable is set with the phone or ID description, and a record is sought using ContactID and strDescription. If a record is found, it is updated; otherwise a new record is created in tblContactIDsAndPhones and the phone number or ID is written to it:

```
    UpdateContactIDs:
```

Search for a matching Contact ID record in the target table, and update it if found; otherwise, create a new record, and write Contact ID data to it.

```
        strTarget = "tblContactIDsPhones"
        Set rstTarget = dbs.OpenRecordset(strTarget, _
            dbOpenDynaset)

        If Nz(rstSource![AssistantTelephoneNumber]) <> "" Then
            strDescription = "Assistant Phone"
            strSearch = "[ContactID] = " & lngContactID _
                & " And [Description] = " & Chr$(39) & _
                    strDescription & Chr$(39)
            Debug.Print "Search string: " & strSearch
            rstTarget.FindFirst strSearch
            If rstTarget.NoMatch = True Then
```

Create a new contact ID record in the target table.

```
            rstTarget.AddNew
            rstTarget![ContactID] = lngContactID
            rstTarget![Description] = strDescription
        Else
            rstTarget.Edit
        End If
        rstTarget![IDOrPhone] = _
            Nz(rstSource![AssistantTelephoneNumber])
        rstTarget.Update
End If
```

```
If Nz(rstSource![BusinessFaxNumber]) <> "" Then
    strDescription = "Business Fax"
    strSearch = "[ContactID] = " & lngContactID _
        & " And [Description] = " & Chr$(39) _
        & strDescription & Chr$(39)
    Debug.Print "Search string: " & strSearch
    rstTarget.FindFirst strSearch
    If rstTarget.NoMatch = True Then
```

Create a new contact ID record in the target table.

```
        rstTarget.AddNew
        rstTarget![ContactID] = lngContactID
        rstTarget![Description] = strDescription
    Else
        rstTarget.Edit
    End If

    rstTarget![IDOrPhone] = _
        Nz(rstSource![BusinessFaxNumber])
    rstTarget.Update
End If
```

[I am not listing a great number of similar code segments, each of which updates a different phone number or ID.]

```
If Nz(rstSource![PersonalHomePage]) <> "" Then
    strDescription = "Web Page"
    strSearch = "[ContactID] = " & lngContactID _
        & " And [Description] = " & Chr$(39) _
        & strDescription & Chr$(39)
    Debug.Print "Search string: " & strSearch
    rstTarget.FindFirst strSearch
    If rstTarget.NoMatch = True Then
```

Create a new contact ID record in the target table.

```
        rstTarget.AddNew
        rstTarget![ContactID] = lngContactID
        rstTarget![Description] = strDescription
    Else
        rstTarget.Edit
    End If

    rstTarget![IDOrPhone] = _
        Nz(rstSource![PersonalHomePage])
    rstTarget.Update
End If

NextSourceRecord:
    rstSource.MoveNext
```

389

```
        Loop

        rstTarget.Close

        strTitle = "Access tables updated"
        strPrompt = "Linked Access tables of contact data " _
        & "updated from form"
        MsgBox strPrompt, vbInformation + vbOKOnly, strTitle

ErrorHandlerExit:
    On Error Resume Next
        rstSource.Close
        rstTarget.Close
    Exit Sub

ErrorHandler:
    MsgBox "Error No: " & Err.Number _
        & "; Description: " & Err.Description
    Resume ErrorHandlerExit

End Sub
```

In case you want to copy all the Access contacts to Outlook, or vice versa, there are two selections on the Select Action combo box's list that will let you do this. The "Copy All Access Contacts to Outlook" selection runs the CopyAccessContactsToOutlook procedure, which first puts up a confirmation message to ensure that the user wants to wipe out the existing Outlook contacts, and replace them with contacts copied from Access. If the user clicks Yes, the procedure first calls the CreateDenormalizedContactsTable procedure to write data to tblAccessContacts, and then runs code that is similar to the code in the UpdateAllOutlookContacts procedure, except that it skips the searching and just creates all new Outlook contact items.

Similarly, the "Copy All Outlook Contacts to Access" selection runs the CopyAllOutlook ContactsToAccess procedure, which asks for confirmation, then runs the ImportOutlook Contacts procedure to write data from Outlook contacts to tblOutlookContacts, then runs code that is similar to the code in the UpdateAllAccessContacts procedure, except that it doesn't search for matching records, just creates new Access records for all the Outlook contact records.

NOTE When copying all Outlook contacts to Access, you will end up with Access and Outlook contacts whose CustomerID values don't match. This is because the ContactID field in tblContactInfo is an AutoNumber field, so it can't be set to a specific value. There are two ways to deal with this discrepancy: Use the Compare by Name form if you don't care whether the Customer ID is the same in Access and Outlook; or select the "Copy All Access Contacts to Outlook" selection to save the Access ContactID AutoNumber value back to the matching Outlook records.

Working with Attachments

Outlook has had attachments for many versions now; Access 2007 introduced the Attachment data type for Access tables. In Outlook, attachments are a collection belonging to various item types, primarily mail messages; Access 2007 attachments are a recordset belonging to a field of the Attachment data type. Because both an Outlook contact item and an Access table may have attachments, I needed to be able to handle copying attachments from an Outlook contact item to an Access table and vice versa.

NEW FEATURE The Attachment field data type is new to Access 2007.

When you add a field of the Attachment data type to an Access 2007 table, it has three subfields, which you can see in the Relationships diagram (see Figure 11.1). The attachment itself is stored in the FileData subfield; its file name and path in the FileName subfield, and the file type in the FileType subfield. Generally, you only need to work with the FileData and FileName subfields when copying Access attachments.

The situation with Outlook attachments is simpler: you just save the attachment file name and path to the Attachments collection of an item, using the Add method of that collection.

Most likely, you will have some attachments, either in your Outlook contacts, or in Access contact records, so my synchronizing code needs to handle attachments. To copy attachments from one place to another, you need to save them to files in a folder; the folder used for this purpose is selected using the Attachments Folder Path button on the main menu, which runs an event procedure that pops up a Folder Picker dialog. The procedures listed next are called from the longer procedures that do the copying of data between the two Access compare tables, as seen on the two contact comparison forms, or between Access and Outlook:

```
Public Sub CopyAccessAttsToOutlook(con As _
   Outlook.ContactItem, rstSourceAttachments As _
   DAO.Recordset2)
'Called from UpdateAllOutlookContacts

On Error GoTo ErrorHandler

   Set fso = CreateObject("Scripting.FileSystemObject")

   With rstSourceAttachments
      Do While Not .EOF
         strDocsPath = GetOutputDocsPath
```

Need to extract the file name from the FileName field, using the SplitFileName function, because it sometimes contains the path (sometimes multiple times) as well as the file name.

```
               strFile = _
```

```
SplitFileName(rstSourceAttachments.Fields("FileName"))
               Debug.Print "File name: " & strFile
               strFileAndPath = strDocsPath & strFile
               Debug.Print "File and path: " & strFileAndPath
```

```
       On Error Resume Next
```

Check whether this file already exists in the folder, and save it to the folder if not.

```
               Set fil = fso.GetFile(strFileAndPath)
               If fil Is Nothing Then
```

Save this attachment to a file in the Output Docs folder.

```
                  .Fields("FileData").SaveToFile strFileAndPath
                  Debug.Print "Saving " & strFileAndPath _
                     & " to " & strDocsPath & " folder"
               End If
```

Add this attachment to the Attachments collection of the Outlook contact item.

```
               Debug.Print "Adding attachment " & strFileAndPath _
                  & " to " & con.FullName & " contact"
               con.Save
               con.Attachments.Add Source:=strFileAndPath, _
                  Type:=olByValue
               con.Close (olSave)
               Kill strFileAndPath
               .MoveNext
            Loop
```

```
         rstSourceAttachments.Close
      End With
```

```
   ErrorHandlerExit:
      Exit Sub
```

```
   ErrorHandler:
      MsgBox "Error No: " & Err.Number _
         & "; Description: " & Err.Description
      Resume ErrorHandlerExit
```

```
   End Sub
```

```
   Public Sub CopyOutlookAttsToAccess(con _
      As Outlook.ContactItem, rstTargetAttachments As _
      DAO.Recordset2)
```

```
'Called from NewAccessContactAndID and
'ImportOutlookContacts

On Error GoTo ErrorHandler

    Set fso = CreateObject("Scripting.FileSystemObject")

    For Each att In con.Attachments

Extract the file name from the Attachment FileName property.
        strFile = att.FileName
        strDocsPath = GetOutputDocsPath
        strFileAndPath = strDocsPath & strFile
        Debug.Print "File and path: " & strFileAndPath

On Error Resume Next
```

Check whether this file already exists in the folder, and save it to the folder if not

```
        Set fil = fso.GetFile(strFileAndPath)
        If fil Is Nothing Then
```

Save this attachment to a file in the Output Docs folder.

```
            att.SaveAsFile strFileAndPath
        End If

On Error GoTo ErrorHandler
```

Load this attachment to the Attachments field of the target table.

```
        With rstTargetAttachments
            .AddNew
            .Fields("FileData").LoadFromFile _
                (strFileAndPath)
            .Update
        End With
        Kill strFileAndPath
    Next att

ErrorHandlerExit:
    Exit Sub

ErrorHandler:
    MsgBox "Error No: " & Err.Number _
        & "; Description: " & Err.Description
    Resume ErrorHandlerExit

End Sub
```

```
Public Sub CopyAccessAttsToAccess(rstSourceAttachments _
    As DAO.Recordset2, rstTargetAttachments _
    As DAO.Recordset2)
'Called from CreateDenormalizedContactsTable,
'UpdateAllAccessContacts, UpdateOutlookContactID,
'UpdateAccessContactID, UpdateOutlookContactName,
'UpdateAccessContactName, UpdateAllAccessContacts,
'UpdateOutlookContactID, cboAttachments_Click on
'fsubCopyFieldData

On Error GoTo ErrorHandler

    Set fso = CreateObject("Scripting.FileSystemObject")

    Do While Not rstSourceAttachments.EOF
```

Need to extract the file name from the FileName field, using the SplitFileName function, because it sometimes contains the path (sometimes multiple times) as well as the file name.

```
        strFile = _

SplitFileName(rstSourceAttachments.Fields("FileName"))
        Debug.Print "File name: " & strFile
        strFileAndPath = strDocsPath & strFile
        Debug.Print "File and path: " & strFileAndPath

On Error Resume Next
```

Check whether this file already exists in the folder, and save it to the folder if not.

```
        Set fil = fso.GetFile(strFileAndPath)
        If fil Is Nothing Then
```

Save this attachment to a file in the Output Docs folder.

```
            rstSourceAttachments.Fields("FileData").SaveToFile _
                strFileAndPath
            Debug.Print "Saving " & strFileAndPath
        End If
```

Load this attachment to the Attachments field of the target table.

```
        rstTargetAttachments.AddNew
        rstTargetAttachments.Fields("FileData").LoadFromFile _
            (strFileAndPath)
        rstTargetAttachments.Update
        Kill strFileAndPath
        rstSourceAttachments.MoveNext
```

```
        Loop

        rstSourceAttachments.Close
        rstTargetAttachments.Close

ErrorHandlerExit:
    Exit Sub

ErrorHandler:
    If Err.Number = 3839 Then
        'File already exists; delete it
        Kill strFileAndPath
        Resume
    Else
        MsgBox "Error No: " & Err.Number _
            & "; Description: " & Err.Description
        Resume ErrorHandlerExit
    End If

End Sub

Function SplitFileName(strFileAndPath) As String

On Error GoTo ErrorHandler

    Dim strFullPath() As String
    Dim intUBound As Integer
```

Extract the file name from the variable with the file and path.

```
        strFullPath = Split(strFileAndPath, "\", -1, vbTextCompare)
        intUBound = UBound(strFullPath)
        strFile = strFullPath(intUBound)
        SplitFileName = strFile

ErrorHandlerExit:
    Exit Function

ErrorHandler:
    MsgBox "Error No: " & Err.Number & "; Description: " &
Err.Description
    Resume ErrorHandlerExit

End Function
```

Figure 11.16 shows an Outlook contact with an attachment created from an Access contact record.

FIGURE 11.16

An Outlook contact with an attachment created from an Access contact record.

Summary

The synchronizing techniques in this chapter will allow you to maintain your contact data in a set of linked Access tables, adding any number of custom phone numbers and IDs as needed, and synchronize your Access data to Outlook contacts, so you can work with the standard properties of contacts in the convenient Outlook contact interface, and work with any additional custom fields you need in Access, without having to manually enter (and update) the same contact data in Access and Outlook.

In addition, you can use the denormalizing and renormalizing techniques used to work with contacts for any situation that requires converting a set of linked Access tables to a single flat-file table, or the reverse — something that is likely to arise when exchanging data with legacy programs or mainframe databases.

Chapter 12

Going Beyond the Basics

Earlier chapters in this book described how to work with Word, Excel, and Outlook, using VBA code to create Word documents, Excel worksheets, and Outlook items and fill them with data from Access. This chapter describes some more advanced techniques for working with other Office components, such as those you might need in a database with shipping and ordering information.

Creating Fancy Word Shipping Labels

In Chapter 6 you learned how to create basic mailing labels, with name and address information pulled from a table or query, using either the TypeText method or mail merge. A name and address is all you need to print a set of labels for a monthly mailing to a list of club members, or to a list of people who receive a regularly scheduled product shipment. But in the real world, often there are much more complex requirements for printing labels. Before shipping a product, you might also need to check the inventory for a product, the date the product is required, and the availability of shipping supplies, vehicles, and personnel to do the shipping.

> **NOTE** The sample database for this chapter is Northwind Plus.accdb.

You might also need to print more information on your shipping labels in addition to the address, such as the Order No., Product No., Product Name, Category, the case number in a sequence of cases, or other such data. To print labels with extra information, or to make decisions on whether a set of labels should be printed, you need more elaborate VBA code.

IN THIS CHAPTER

Creating Word shipping labels with information about shipments

Creating Excel PivotCharts filled with Access data

Emailing Access reports of shipping and reordering information

The sample Northwind Plus database contains tables from the Northwind.mdb database, with several extra fields in some tables, queries (used in the next section), and three new forms — two main forms (one for selecting records for shipping and one for reordering depleted inventory) plus a supplementary form for editing product amounts.

NOTE   When opening Northwind Plus in Vista, you may get the security alert shown in Figure 12.1. To temporarily enable the database's code, click the "Enable Content" button and select the "Enable this content" option in the dialog. To prevent this security alert from appearing every time you open the database, sign the VBA code with a digital signature, as described in the sidebar.

FIGURE 12.1

A Vista security alert when opening a database with unsigned VBA code.

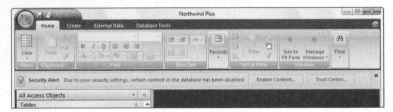

Creating a Digital Signature for Signing Your Access VBA Code

1. On the Windows Vista Start menu, select All Programs.

2. Select the Microsoft Office folder.

3. Select the Microsoft Office Tools folder.

4. Select the Digital Certificate for VBA projects item:

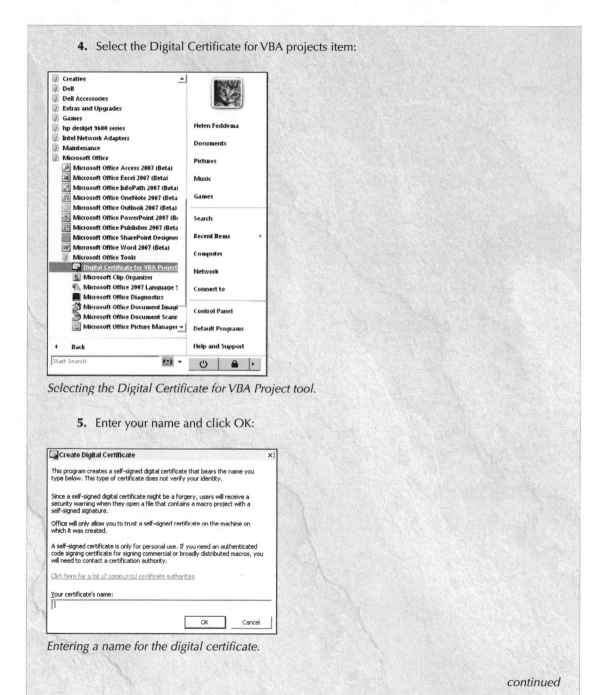

Selecting the Digital Certificate for VBA Project tool.

5. Enter your name and click OK:

Entering a name for the digital certificate.

continued

continued

6. You should get a success message:

Success message after creating a digital certificate.

7. Click the Office button, select the Publish command, and then the Package and Sign command.

8. Select the certificate to use on the Select Certificate dialog:

9. Click Create to save the package file to a location of your choice:

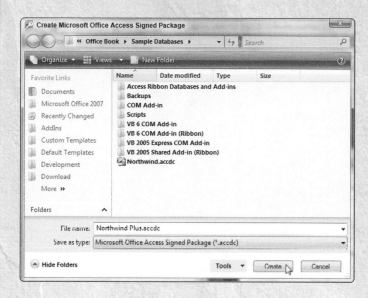

10. If this is the first time you have used this certificate, the Microsoft Office Access Security Notice dialog opens:

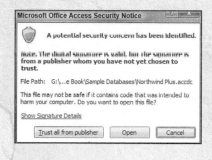

continued

continued

11. You can click the Show Signature Details to view the available information about the selected certificate:

12. After clicking the "Trust all from publisher" button on the Microsoft Office Access Security Notice dialog, you can work on the database.

13. In future, if you open the package file, you will get a dialog offering to extract the database:

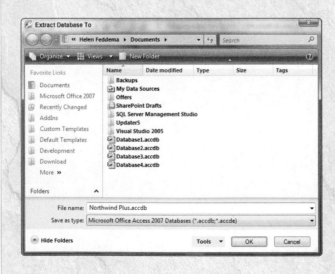

14. On clicking OK, the extracted database opens as a normal Access 2007 database.

Figure 12.2 shows the main menu of the Northwind Plus sample database, with buttons for opening the two main forms, and buttons to select the Documents and Templates folders. The folder selection buttons function like the similar controls in several other chapters, using a Folder Picker dialog created by the Office FileDialog object.

FIGURE 12.2

The main menu of the Northwind Plus sample database.

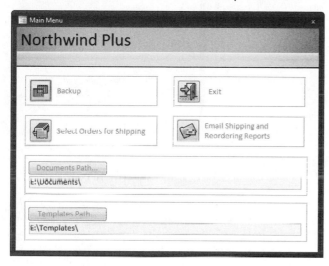

> **NOTE** I could have determined which orders were ready to ship just by examining the available inventory and the date the order is required, but in the real world these are not the only factors to consider — if there aren't enough people to do the shipping, or all the trucks are out on the road, you can't ship the product, even if there is enough inventory.

Figure 12.3 shows the order selection form.

FIGURE 12.3

The form used for inspecting orders and marking them for shipment.

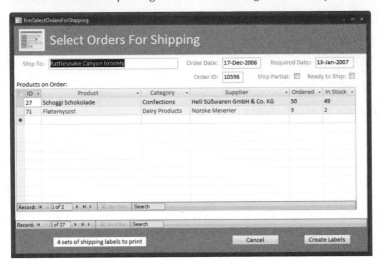

The Select Orders for Shipping form (frmSelectOrdersForShipping) is a main form with a datasheet subform. It is used to inspect orders that are in the correct time range for shipping and mark them for shipping now. The main form displays fields from the orders, and the datasheet subform lists the products on the selected order. On the main form, the "Ship Partial" checkbox is checked if a partial order can be shipped, in case there is enough inventory to ship at least one product on the order. The "Ready to Ship" checkbox indicates that the order is ready to ship, taking into account factors over and above the available inventory.

To print shipping labels with extra information, I made a query (qryNorthwindShippingLabels), based on qryNorthwindAll (a query that includes all the linked Northwind data tables), containing all the information to print on the labels. Apart from the shipping name and address, the query also includes the following fields:

- OrderDate
- RequiredDate (with a criterion of `>Date()) And <DateAdd("d",30,Date())` to just include orders required from tomorrow to less than 30 days in the future
- DateShipped
- Supplier (an alias for CompanyName in tblSuppliers)
- ProductID
- ProductName
- OrderID
- NoCases (an alias for Quantity)

- CategoryName
- ReadyToShip, a Boolean field with a criterion of True to select orders that are ready to ship

The cmdCreateLabels event procedure is listed here, with explanation of how it processes the sets of labels to print:

```
Private Sub cmdCreateLabels_Click()

On Error GoTo ErrorHandler

    Dim appWord As Word.Application
    Dim blnShipPartial As Boolean
    Dim dbs As DAO.Database
    Dim doc As Word.Document
    Dim fil As Scripting.File
    Dim fso As New Scripting.FileSystemObject
    Dim lngCaseNo As Long
    Dim lngNoCases As Long
    Dim lngCasesInStock As Long
    Dim lngCount As Long
    Dim lngSet As Long
    Dim lngNoSets As Long
    Dim lngOrderID As Long
    Dim lngSetNo As Long
    Dim lngSubtract As Long
    Dim rstOrder As DAO.Recordset
    Dim rstShip As DAO.Recordset
    Dim strCategory As String
    Dim strDocsPath As String
    Dim strOrderDate As String
    Dim lngProductID As Long
    Dim strProductName As String
    Dim strPrompt As String
    Dim strQueryShip As String
    Dim strQueryOrder As String
    Dim strSaveName As String
    Dim strSaveNameAndPath As String
    Dim strShipAddress As String
    Dim strShipCityStatePC As String
    Dim strShipCountry As String
    Dim strShipDate As String
    Dim strShipName As String
    Dim strSQL As String
    Dim strSupplier As String
    Dim strTemplate As String
    Dim strTemplateNameAndPath As String
    Dim strTemplatePath As String
    Dim strTitle As String
    Dim varValue As Variant
```

Set the Word Application variable:

```
Set appWord = GetObject(, "Word.Application")
appWord.Visible = True
```

Get User Templates and Documents paths from the user's selections on the main menu, using two functions that pick up the saved paths from tblInfo:

```
strTemplatePath = GetTemplatesPath
Debug.Print "Template path: " & strTemplatePath
strDocsPath = GetDocumentsPath
Debug.Print "Documents folder: " & strDocsPath
strTemplate = "Avery 5164 Shipping Labels.dotx"
strTemplateNameAndPath = strTemplatePath & strTemplate
Debug.Print "Template name and path: " _
    & strTemplateNameAndPath


On Error Resume Next
```

Look for the template in the templates folder, by attempting to set a FileSystemObject File variable to it:

```
Set fil = fso.GetFile(strTemplateNameAndPath)
If fil Is Nothing Then
    strPrompt = "Can't find " & strTemplate & " in " _
        & strTemplatePath & "; canceling"
    MsgBox strPrompt, vbCritical + vbOKOnly
    GoTo ErrorHandlerExit
End If


On Error GoTo ErrorHandler
```

Calculate the number of sets of labels to print:

```
lngSelected = Nz(DCount("*", _
    "qrySelectedNorthwindShippingLabels"))
    Me![lblSetsToPrint].Caption = lngSelected _
        & " sets of shipping labels to print"
```

Exit with a message if no orders have been selected:

```
If lngSelected = 0 Then
    strTitle = "Can't print labels"
    strPrompt = "No orders selected; please mark some " _
        & "orders for shipping"
    MsgBox strPrompt, vbExclamation + vbOKOnly, strTitle
    GoTo ErrorHandlerExit
End If
```

Set up a recordset (rstShip) based on the `qrySelectedNorthwindShippingLabels` query, which has one record for each product on a selected order:

```
Set dbs = CurrentDb
strQueryShip = "qrySelectedNorthwindShippingLabels"
Set rstShip = dbs.OpenRecordset(strQueryShip)
```

Get the number of records for use in updating the progress meter:

```
rstShip.MoveLast
rstShip.MoveFirst
lngNoSets = rstShip.RecordCount
```

Start the progress meter in the status bar, using the SysCmd object:

```
strPrompt = "Creating " & lngNoSets _
    & " sets of shipping labels"
Application.SysCmd acSysCmdInitMeter, strPrompt, _
    lngNoSets
```

Set up a loop for processing the sets of labels for the orders:

```
For lngSet = 1 To lngNoSets
    lngOrderID = rstShip![OrderID]
    blnShipPartial = rstShip![ShipPartial]
```

Create a filtered recordset (rstOrder) for this order only, with records corresponding to the products on the order:

```
strQueryOrder = "qryOrder"
Set dbs = CurrentDb
strSQL = "SELECT * FROM " & strQueryShip & " WHERE " _
    & "[OrderID] = " & lngOrderID & ";"
Debug.Print "SQL for " & strQueryOrder & ": " & strSQL
lngCount = CreateAndTestQuery(strQueryOrder, strSQL)
Debug.Print "No. of records found: " & lngCount

Set rstOrder = dbs.OpenRecordset(strQueryOrder)
```

Set up a loop to process each product on this order, checking whether there is enough inventory to ship the product on this order:

```
Do While Not rstOrder.EOF
    lngProductID = rstOrder![ProductID]
    strProductName = rstOrder![ProductName]
    lngNoCases = rstOrder![NoCases]
    lngCasesInStock = rstOrder![CasesInStock]
    If lngNoCases > lngCasesInStock Then
        If blnShipPartial = False Then
```

For orders with ShipPartial unchecked, can't ship the order because one product has inadequate inventory:

```
strTitle = "Inadequate inventory"
strPrompt = "Only " & lngCasesInStock _
    & " cases in inventory; can't fill Order ID " _
    & lngOrderID & " for " & strProductName
MsgBox strPrompt, vbExclamation, strTitle
GoTo NextOrder
ElseIf blnShipPartial = True Then
```

For orders with ShipPartial checked, can't ship this product on the order:

```
strTitle = "Inadequate inventory"
strPrompt = "Only " & lngCasesInStock _
    & " cases in inventory; can't fill " _
    & strProductName & " item on " _
    & "Order ID " & lngOrderID
MsgBox strPrompt, vbExclamation, strTitle
```

Figure 12.4 shows a typical "Inadequate inventory" message when there isn't enough inventory to fill a product line item on an order with ShipPartial checked.

FIGURE 12.4

A message indicating that there is inadequate inventory to ship a product item on an order.

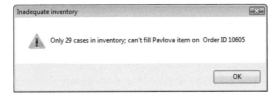

Check the next product on the order:

```
            GoTo NextProduct
        End If
    Else
```

There is enough inventory to ship this product; create a new labels document for this set of labels from the template:

```
Set doc = _
    appWord.Documents.Add(Template:= _
        strTemplateNameAndPath, _
    documenttype:=wdNewBlankDocument, _
    Visible:=True)
doc.Activate
```

Set variables with information to print on all the labels for this order:

```
strCategory = rstOrder![CategoryName]
strOrderDate = CStr(rstOrder![OrderDate])
strShipName = rstOrder![ShipName]
strShipAddress = rstOrder![ShipAddress]
strShipCityStatePC = rstOrder![ShipCityStatePC]
strShipCountry = rstOrder![ShipCountry]
strSupplier = rstOrder![Supplier]
strShipDate = Format(Date, "dd-mmm-yyyy")
```

Set up a loop to print a set of labels for this order, one label per case shipped:

```
For lngCaseNo = 1 To lngNoCases
    With appWord.Selection
```

Put data into one label (one cell in the Word document):

```
.TypeText Text:="FROM:" & vbTab
.MoveLeft Unit:=wdCharacter, Count:=1
.MoveLeft Unit:=wdWord, Count:=2, _
    Extend:=wdExtend
.Font.Bold = True
.EndKey Unit:=wdLine
.Font.Bold = False
.TypeText Text:="Northwind Traders"
.TypeParagraph
```

Indent the left margin to match the tab setting, so the address will line up with the name.

> **NOTE** Instead of looking up Word methods, properties, and other object model components in the Object Browser, you can capture the syntax for a Word action by recording a macro in Word, then copying and pasting the VBA code into your Access VBA procedure. Just insert your Word application variable where needed and trim the arguments you don't need to prepare the code for use in Access.

```
.ParagraphFormat.TabIndent (1)
.TypeText Text:="2839 El Presidio St."
.TypeParagraph
.TypeText Text:="Nowhere, WA 92838"
.TypeParagraph
```

Return to the normal left margin before printing "TO:":

```
.ParagraphFormat.LeftIndent = 8
.TypeParagraph
.Font.Bold = True
.TypeText Text:="TO:" & vbTab
.MoveLeft Unit:=wdCharacter, Count:=1
.MoveLeft Unit:=wdCharacter, Count:=3, _
    Extend:=wdExtend
```

```
            .EndKey Unit:=wdLine
            .Font.Bold = False
            .TypeText strShipName
            .TypeParagraph
```

Indent the left margin to match the tab setting, so the address will line up with the name:

```
            .ParagraphFormat.TabIndent (1)
            .TypeText strShipAddress
            .TypeParagraph
            .TypeText strShipCityStatePC
            .TypeParagraph
            .TypeText strShipCountry
            .TypeParagraph
```

Return to the normal left margin before printing the extra information:

```
            .ParagraphFormat.LeftIndent = 8
            .TypeParagraph
            .Font.Size = 10
            .Font.Bold = True
            .TypeText "Order ID:" & vbTab _
                & CStr(lngOrderID)
            .TypeParagraph
            .TypeText "Category:" & vbTab _
                & strCategory
            .TypeParagraph
            .TypeText "Product: " & vbTab & "ID " _
                & lngProductID & " (" _
                & strProductName & ")"
            .TypeParagraph
            .TypeText "Supplier:" & vbTab _
                & strSupplier
            .TypeParagraph
            .TypeText "Ship date:" & vbTab _
                & strShipDate
            .TypeParagraph
            .Font.Size = 12
            .Font.Bold = False
            .TypeParagraph
            .TypeText vbTab & "Case " _
                & lngCaseNo & " of " & lngNoCases
            .MoveRight Unit:=wdCell
        End With
    Next lngCaseNo
```

Save the Word labels document for this set of labels:

```
    strSaveName = "Shipping Labels for Order ID " _
        & lngOrderID & " (" & strProductName _
        & ") shipped on " & strShipDate & ".doc"
```

```
        strSaveNameAndPath = strDocsPath & strSaveName
        Debug.Print "Save name: " & strSaveName
```

```
    On Error Resume Next
```

Check for the existence of a file with this name, and delete it if found:

```
        Set fil = fso.GetFile(strSaveNameAndPath)
        If Not fil Is Nothing Then
            Kill strSaveNameAndPath
        End If
```

```
    On Error GoTo ErrorHandler
        doc.SaveAs FileName:=strSaveNameAndPath
```

Update the progress meter:

```
        Application.SysCmd acSysCmdUpdateMeter, lngSet
```

Update the ReadyToShip field in tblOrders to False:

```
        DoCmd.SetWarnings False
        strSQL = "UPDATE tblOrders SET "
            & "tblOrders.ReadyToShip = False " _
            & "WHERE OrderID = " & lngOrderID
        Debug.Print "SQL string: " & strSQL
        DoCmd.RunSQL strSQL
```

Subtract the amount of product shipped from the in stock amount in tblProducts:

```
        lngSubtract = lngCasesInStock - lngNoCases
        strSQL = "UPDATE tblProducts SET "
            & "tblProducts.UnitsInStock = " _
            & lngSubtract & " WHERE ProductID = " _
            & lngProductID
        Debug.Print "SQL string: " & strSQL
        DoCmd.RunSQL strSQL
```

In tblOrderDetails, set QuantityShipped to QuantityOrdered, and DateShipped to today's date:

```
        strSQL = "UPDATE tblOrderDetails SET " _
            & "tblOrderDetails.QuantityShipped = " _
            & "[QuantityOrdered], " _
            & "tblOrderDetails.DateShipped = Date() " _
            & "WHERE tblOrderDetails.OrderID = " _
            & lngOrderID _
            & " And tblOrderDetails.ProductID = " _
            & lngProductID & ";"
        Debug.Print "SQL string: " & strSQL
        DoCmd.RunSQL strSQL
```

```
strTitle = "Set of labels created"
strPrompt = _
    "A set of shipping labels created " _
    & "for Order ID " & lngOrderID _
    & ", Product ID " & lngProductID _
    & " (" & strProductName & ")"
MsgBox strPrompt, vbInformation, strTitle
```

Figure 12.5 shows the success message for the last set of labels, with the progress meter at full in the Access window status bar.

A message indicating that a set of labels has been created for an order.

```
        End If

NextProduct:
    rstOrder.MoveNext
    Loop

NextOrder:
    rstShip.MoveNext
```

Recalculate the number of sets of labels to print:

```
        lngSelected = Nz(DCount("*", _
            "qrySelectedNorthwindShippingLabels"))
        Me![lblSetsToPrint].Caption = lngSelected _
            & " sets of shipping labels to print"
    Next lngSet

    DoCmd.Close acForm, Me.Name

Finished:
    strTitle = "Finished!"
    strPrompt = _
        "One set of shipping labels created for each " _
```

```
            & "order shipped on " _
            & Format(Date, "dd-mmm-yyyy")
      MsgBox strPrompt, vbInformation, strTitle

   ErrorHandlerExit:
```

Figure 12.6 shows the "Finished!" message after all the sets of labels have been created.

The success message after all labels have been printed.

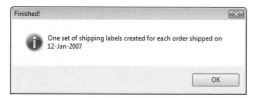

Clear the progress meter:

```
      Application.SysCmd acSysCmdClearStatus

      Exit Sub

   ErrorHandler:
      If Err = 429 Then
```

Word is not running; open Word with `CreateObject`:

```
         Set appWord = CreateObject("Word.Application")
         Resume Next
      Else
         MsgBox "Error No: " & Err.Number & "; Description: " _
            & Err.Description
         Resume ErrorHandlerExit
      End If

      End Sub
```

The `GetDocumentsPath` function that retrieves the Documents path from tblInfo is listed next; the `GetTemplatesPath` function is similar:

```
   Public Function GetDocumentsPath() As String

   On Error GoTo ErrorHandler

      Set dbs = CurrentDb
      Set rst = dbs.OpenRecordset("tblInfo")
```

413

```
        rst.MoveFirst
        GetDocumentsPath = rst![DocumentsPath] & "\"
        rst.Close

   ErrorHandlerExit:
        Exit Function

   ErrorHandler:
        MsgBox "Error No: " & Err.Number & "; Description: " & _
            Err.Description
        Resume ErrorHandlerExit

   End Function
```

Figure 12.7 shows a page of shipping labels.

FIGURE 12.7

A set of Word shipping labels filled with data from Access.

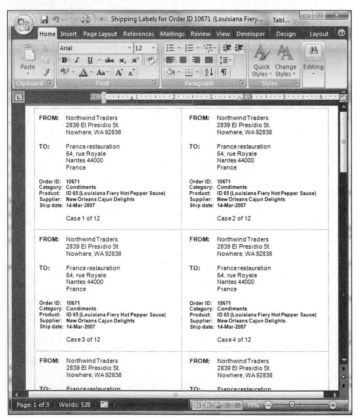

Every development project has unique requirements; when using Access to create mailing labels (or any other type of Word documents), you have the freedom to create tables and forms that exactly meet your needs, storing all (and only) the information you need to select and print the data you need on Word documents. The code used to create the shipping labels described in this section includes several techniques that are useful for producing Word documents of various types, such as creating filtered recordsets for working with detail records, calculating "x of y" numbers when working with sets of records, displaying a progress meter in the status bar, and updating tables from code.

Creating Excel PivotCharts from Access Queries

You can create great interactive charts and tables using Access's own tools (PivotCharts and PivotTables), as noted in Chapter 1. However, there is a drawback to using Access PivotCharts and PivotTables — they are only interactive while working in Access. If you save a PivotChart or PivotTable as a PDF (if you have installed the Save as PDF utility) or Snapshot file, and send it to someone else, it is just an image, not an interactive chart or table. If you need to put Access data into an interactive chart or table for others to work with (even if they don't have Access installed), you can use a different approach: Export the Access data to an Excel worksheet, and then create an Excel PivotChart or PivotTable that users can manipulate as they wish.

 When you create an Excel PivotChart, it is automatically created with a linked PivotTable.

The first step in creating an Excel PivotChart is to create an Access query with the data to be charted. Excel PivotCharts are not exactly the same as Access PivotCharts; in particular, they lack the date grouping feature that automatically creates a variety of date sorts from a Date field (Year, Month, Quarter, Week). If you want to analyze data in an Excel PivotChart by month, quarter, or year, you need to do the breakdown in an Access query, before exporting the data to Excel, or create the date groups manually in Excel by using the Group command.

In Office 2007, you can create an Excel PivotChart manually, following these steps:

1. Create an Access query with the data to be charted; `qryQuarterlySalesByCategory` has only three fields: OrderQuarter, Category, and Price. The OrderQuarter field extracts the year and quarter from the OrderDate field, using this expression:

    ```
    OrderQuarter: Year([OrderDate]) & " Q" &
    DatePart("q",[OrderDate])
    ```

2. Export this query to Excel using the Excel command in the Export group of the External Data tab of the Ribbon, as shown in Figure 12.8.

FIGURE 12.8

Exporting a query to Excel using a Ribbon command.

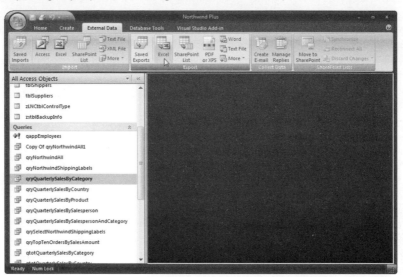

3. On the Export dialog, edit the worksheet name as desired, and browse for an alternate location if you don't want to store the worksheet in the default Documents folder (in Figure 12.9, I edited the worksheet name and left the folder at the default setting).

FIGURE 12.9

Editing the worksheet save name in the Export dialog.

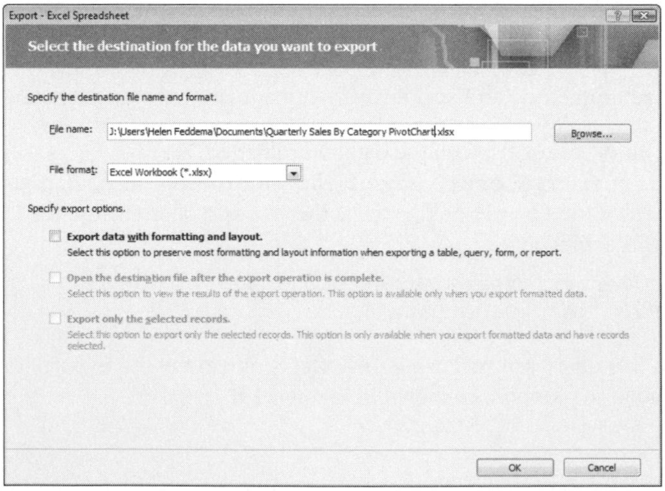

4. Open the newly created worksheet in Excel.

5. Click anywhere in the data range, select the Insert tab of the Ribbon, and select PivotChart from the drop-down in the Tables group, as shown in Figure 12.10.

FIGURE 12.10

Creating a PivotChart from data in an Excel worksheet.

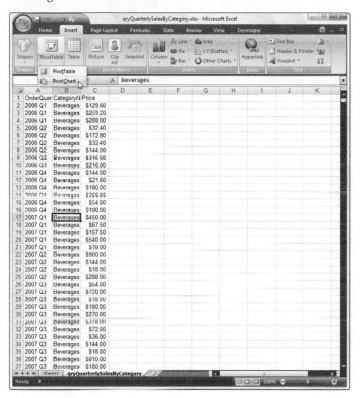

6. The Create PivotTable with PivotChart dialog opens, as shown in Figure 12.11, with the range preselected; just click OK to create the PivotChart in another worksheet in the same workbook.

FIGURE 12.11

The Create PivotTable with PivotChart dialog.

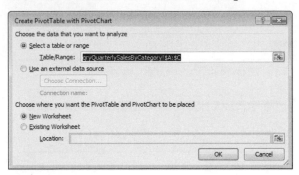

7. The new, blank PivotChart appears, as shown in Figure 12.12.

FIGURE 12.12

A newly created Excel PivotChart.

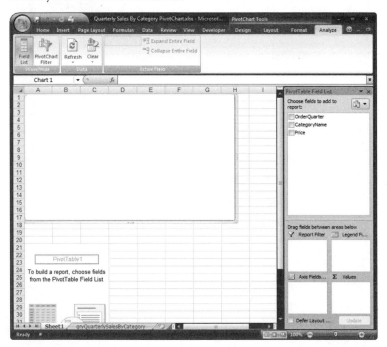

8. The layout of a PivotChart is different in Excel than in Access (a discrepancy Microsoft should clear up, but that is another matter). The fields from the query are listed in the PivotTable Field List in the panel on the right of the worksheet; I dragged OrderQuarter to the Axis Fields drop zone, CategoryName to the Legend Fields drop zone, and Price to the Values drop zone (Excel automatically makes it a Sum of Price). Figure 12.13 shows the plainly formatted PivotChart at this point.

FIGURE 12.13

An Excel PivotChart with fields assigned to drop zones.

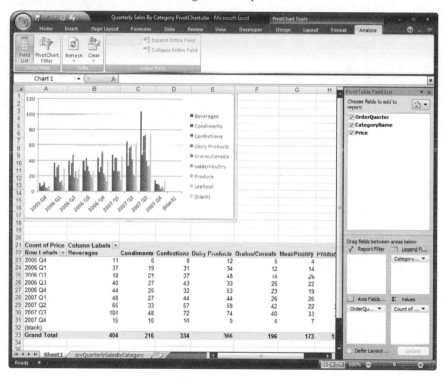

9. To format the left axis number, right-click any category value in the PivotChart and select "Format Axis" from the context menu, as shown in Figure 12.14.

FIGURE 12.14

Formatting axis number.

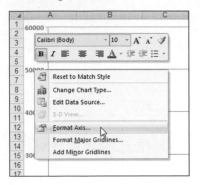

10.   The Format Axis dialog opens; I formatted the left axis number for U.S. Currency by selecting Number for the Axis Option, Currency for the Category, 0 decimal places, and $ English (U.S.) for the Symbol, as shown in Figure 12.15.

FIGURE 12.15

Formatting the left axis for U.S. Currency.

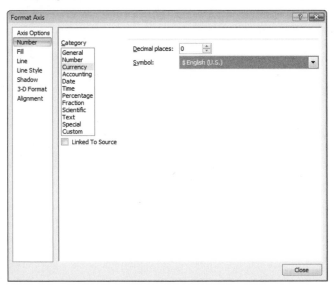

> **NOTE** When the PivotChart (or one of its components) is selected, you should see special
> PivotChart commands in the Design and Layout groups of the Ribbon; if you don't see
> them, click the PivotChart to give it the focus.

11. To give the chart a title (generally a good idea), I selected Layout 1 in the Chart
    Layouts group on the Design tab of the Ribbon (in PivotChart Tools mode), as shown in
    Figure 12.16.

FIGURE 12.16

The PivotChart Tools.

12. This selection adds a Chart Title control to the chart; right-click it and select Edit Text to
    edit the chart name as desired; I made it "Quarterly Sales by Category."

13. The final step is to select a chart style. The default style (contrasting color bars) is gener-
    ally fine, but there are lots more choices available. To select a different chart style, drop
    down the More button at the lower-right corner of the Chart Styles group, as shown in
    Figure 12.17.

FIGURE 12.17

Opening the palette of chart styles.

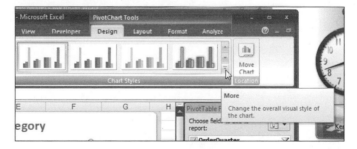

14. A palette of 54 styles opens as shown in Figure 12.18.
15. The formatted PivotChart is shown in Figure 12.19.

FIGURE 12.18

Selecting a chart style from the palette.

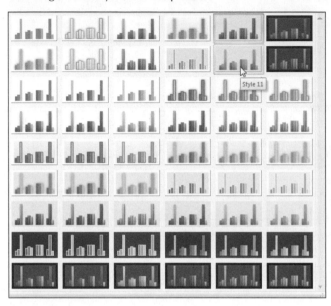

FIGURE 12.19

A PivotChart with contrasting color bars and a light background.

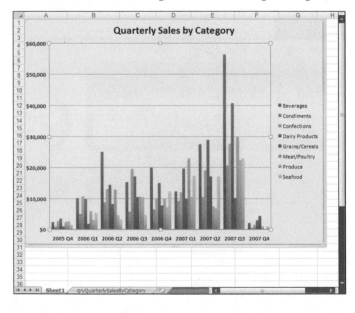

16. For a computer presentation, a dark background may be preferable; Figure 12.20 shows the PivotChart with a dark background style selected.

FIGURE 12.20

A PivotChart with contrasting color bars and a dark background.

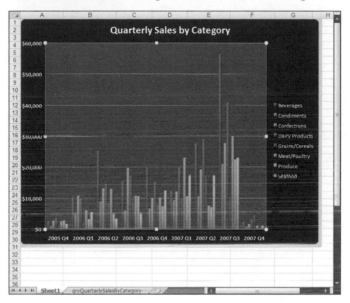

NOTE   The four styles you most recently selected appear in the top row of the Chart Styles group, so they are always available for one-click selection.

NEW FEATURE   Excel 2007 has a new feature: Chart templates. However, these templates only work with standard charts, not PivotCharts, so unfortunately they are no use when creating PivotCharts.

The bar charts produced in this section are only a small selection of the PivotChart types you can produce in Excel, based on Access data. The six most popular chart types are shown in the Charts group of the Insert tab on the Ribbon, shown in Figure 12.21.

FIGURE 12.21

The six most popular Excel chart types.

To see all the available chart types, click the Other Charts command, then the All Chart Types command at the bottom of the drop-down chart palette, as shown in Figure 12.22.

Selecting the All Charts command to see all the Excel chart types.

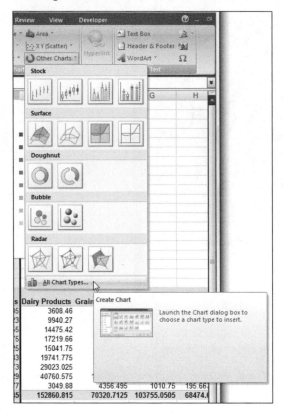

The Create Chart dialog opened by the All Charts command is shown in Figure 12.23.

FIGURE 12.23

The Create Chart dialog.

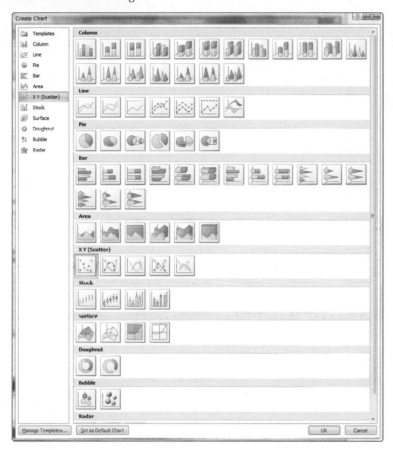

Though most chart types are available in both Access and Excel, there are some differences: The Polar chart type is only available in Access, and the Surface chart type is only available in Excel. Figure 12.24 shows the Access chart types on the left, and the Excel chart types on the right, to make it easier to identify the chart type you want to use.

FIGURE 12.24

Access and Excel chart types.

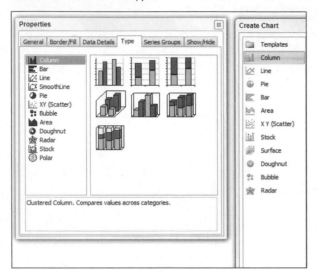

Emailing Shipping and Reordering Reports

After you ship out orders, using the shipping labels described in an earlier section, you might need to produce reports detailing the amounts of different products that were shipped and the amounts that need to be ordered to replenish stock, and then email these reports to various persons. The Shipping Reports and Reordering form, shown in Figure 12.25, lets you see the inventory for all products where the amount in stock plus the amount on order is at or under the reorder level for that product. The ReorderAmount field (initially set to zero for all products) indicates the number of cases you want to reorder.

Since this form only has data if at least one product is below the inventory reorder level, when you click the "Email Shipping and Reordering Reports" button on the main menu, if there is enough inventory for all products, you will get the message shown in Figure 12.26.

A form for replenishing inventory.

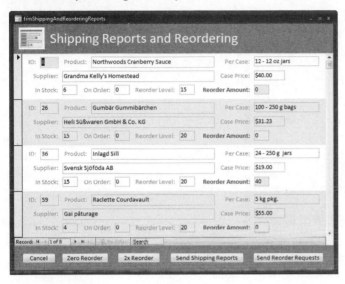

A message when all products have enough inventory.

If you click the Yes button on this dialog, the Edit Amounts form will open, as shown in Figure 12.27, where you can edit product amounts as needed.

FIGURE 12.27

A form for editing product amounts.

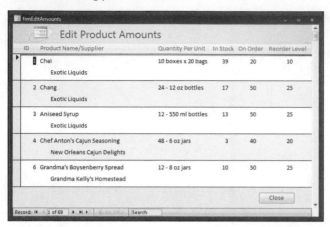

On the Shipping Reports and Reordering form, the "2x Reorder" button sets the Reorder Amount to twice the Reorder Level for all records; the "Zero Reorder" button sets the Reorder Amount to zero for all records. You can also manually edit the Reorder Amount for any product as desired. After setting the Reorder Amount as desired for all records, click the "Send Shipping Reports" button to save the Shipping report (rptShipping) as a PDF file, update field values in tblProducts as needed, and create a new email message with the report file attached to it, ready to email to the appropriate address (if the report is always sent to the same person or department, the email address could be hard-coded). Figure 12.28 shows the shipping report.

NEW FEATURE Although saving to the PDF format didn't make it to the release version of Access 2007, Microsoft has provided a downloadable utility that adds PDF support to Access. This utility can be downloaded from http://www.microsoft.com/downloads/details.aspx?familyid= F1FC413C-6D89-4F15-991B-63B07BA5F2E5&displaylang=en (or search the Microsoft Downloads page for "Save to PDF"). Once you have downloaded and installed it, you will see a new "Save to PDF" selection on the Save As submenu of the File menu, as shown in Figure 12.29, and you can use the `acFormatPDF` named constant as the value of the `outputfile` argument of the `OutputTo` method to create a PDF file, as in the code sample below.

FIGURE 12.28

A shipping report listing the products shipped today.

FIGURE 12.29

The new PDF selection for saving a database object.

FIGURE 12.30

An email message with an attached PDF file created from an Access report.

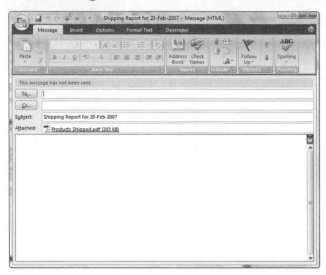

Clicking the "Send Reorder Requests" button works similarly; it creates a PDF file from the Products to Reorder report and emails it as an attachment. Figure 12.31 shows the Products to Reorder report.

FIGURE 12.31

The Products to Reorder report.

The cmdReorderInventory event procedure is listed here:

```
Private Sub cmdReorderInventory_Click()
```

This error handler skips to the CreateSnapshot section if there is an error on the line that outputs the file to the PDF format.

```
On Error GoTo CreateSnapshot

    strCurrentPath = Application.CurrentProject.Path
    strReport = "rptProductsToReorder"
```

First try to export the Products to Reorder report to PDF (this will only work if you have installed the Save to PDF utility)

```
    strReportFile = strCurrentPath & "\Products To Reorder.pdf"
    Debug.Print "Report and path: " & strReportFile
    DoCmd.OutputTo objecttype:=acOutputReport, _
        objectname:=strReport, _
        outputformat:=acFormatPDF, _
        outputfile:=strReportFile
```

If the PDF file was created successfully, go to the CreateEmail section, skipping the CreateSnapshot section of code.

```
    GoTo CreateEmail

On Error GoTo ErrorHandler

CreateSnapshot:
```

Export the report to snapshot format.

```
    strReportFile = strCurrentPath & "\Products To Reorder.snp"
    Debug.Print "Report and path: " & strReportFile
    DoCmd.OutputTo objecttype:=acOutputReport, _
        objectname:=strReport, _
        outputformat:=acFormatSNP, _
        outputfile:=strReportFile

CreateEmail:
```

Create an Outlook email message, fill in its subject, and attach the PDF or snapshot file to the message:

```
    Set appOutlook = GetObject(, "Outlook.Application")
    Set msg = appOutlook.CreateItem(olMailItem)
    msg.Attachments.Add strReportFile
    msg.Subject = "Products to reorder for " _
        & Format(Date, "dd-mmm-yyyy")
    msg.Save
```

Ask for confirmation to set all ReorderAmount values to zero, and add the amount ordered to UnitsOnOrder:

```
strTitle = "Confirmation"
strPrompt = "Clear reorder and on order amounts?"
intReturn = MsgBox(strPrompt, vbQuestion + vbYesNo, _
    strTitle)
If intReturn = vbYes Then
    DoCmd.SetWarnings False
    strSQL = "UPDATE qryProductsToReorder SET " _
        & "qryProductsToReorder.UnitsOnOrder = " _
        & "[UnitsOnOrder]+[ReorderAmount], " _
        & "qryProductsToReorder.ReorderAmount = 0;"
    Debug.Print "SQL string: " & strSQL
    DoCmd.RunSQL strSQL
End If
```

Display the Outlook email message with the PDF or snapshot attachment:

```
msg.Display
DoCmd.Close acForm, Me.Name

ErrorHandlerExit:
    Exit Sub

ErrorHandler:
    MsgBox "Error No: " & Err.Number _
        & "; Description: " & Err.Description
    Resume ErrorHandlerExit

End Sub
```

Summary

The techniques described in this chapter should give you more ideas about how you can use Word, Excel, and Outlook to expand the functionality of Access databases, using VBA code to examine data and make decisions about what data should be exported, and to format the Office documents filled with Access data.

Part III

Adding More Functionality to Office

Chapter 13

Creating COM Add-ins with Visual Basic 6

O
ffice 2000 introduced COM add-ins as a new development tool, an alternative to creating VBA add-ins for Access, Excel, Outlook, and Word. A COM add-in is created as a Dynamic Link Library (DLL) that is registered to work with Office applications. COM add-ins (at least theoretically) can be written to work with multiple Office programs, though realistically, because of the differences in functionality between Access, Word, Outlook, and Excel, only very simple COM add-ins of the "Hello, World!" type can actually be designed to work across multiple Office applications.

If you bought the Developer Edition of Office 2000 (or later, Office XP) you could create COM add-ins in the Access Visual Basic window, using its support for opening and editing VBA projects, although it wasn't easy because of the lack of debugging support. There was no Developer Edition of Office 2003, and there is none for Office 2007, so that option is no longer viable, unless you still have the Developer Edition of Office 2000 or Office XP installed.

CROSS-REF Visual Studio Tools for Office lets you create Visual Studio add-ins for some Office components, but unfortunately, even the latest edition, the one that supports Office 2007, still lacks support for creating Access add-ins. See Chapter 16 for a discussion of creating Visual Studio add-ins for working with the Access 2007 Ribbon.

However, that doesn't mean you can't create COM add-ins for Office 2007. Visual Basic was last updated in 1998 (v. 6.0), but it is still quite useful, and is fully supported by Microsoft, unlike most other Microsoft applications of that vintage. If you have been working with VB 6 for years, you don't have to put aside your hard-won expertise and start learning Visual Studio 2005; you can create COM add-ins that will work in Office 2007 using VB 6. (If you do want to learn how to create add-ins with Visual Studio 2005, see Chapter 16.)

In earlier versions of Access, COM add-ins placed buttons on the menu or toolbar you specified, using the CommandBars collection. In Access 2007, COM add-ins place buttons in the Toolbar Commands group of the Add-Ins tab of the Ribbon, for backwards compatibility with the old CommandBars collection.

In addition to COM add-ins and Access add-ins, Access 2007 also offers a brand-new option: using the XML programming language to add controls to the Ribbon, powered by code written in VBA. This technique is covered in Chapter 15.

Creating a COM Add-in Using Visual Basic 6.0

When you create a COM add-in, instead of creating a library database with a USysRegInfo table (as you would for an Access add-in), you create a VB project, with a special Designer module, a standard module, and (optionally) a form. When creating a COM add-in using VB 6, you can save time by using a COM add-in project template. The one I use was created for use in the Developer Edition of Office 2000, but with some minor modifications, it works fine in VB as well.

Using the COM Add-in Template

To make the COM add-in template available as one of the selections when creating a new VB project, copy the COM Add-in template files to the Projects folder under the VB Templates folder (usually C:\Program Files\Microsoft Visual Studio\VB98\Template\Projects), as shown in Figure 13.1.

When you next open VB, you will see a COM Add-In selection as one of the available project template choices, as shown in Figure 13.2.

Once you've selected the COM Add-In template and have clicked OK, a new project is created based on the template, including a form, a module, and a designer. These objects are located in the Project Explorer (on the right side of the VB window), as shown in Figure 13.3.

FIGURE 13.1

Copying the COM Add-In project files into the VB Projects folder.

FIGURE 13.2

The COM Add-In project template selection in VB 6.

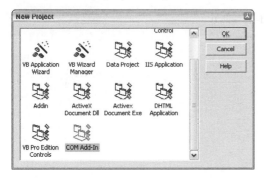

A new VB project created from the COM Add-in project template.

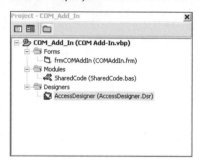

To set a reference in a VB 6 project, drop-down the Project menu and select References, as shown in Figure 13.4.

Opening the VB 6 References dialog.

NOTE   For best functioning, a COM add-in designed to run in Access should have a reference set to the Access and (if needed) DAO object libraries, as shown in Figure 13.5. If you create your own COM add-in from scratch, you will probably need to set one or both of these references; I have set them in the sample VB template project, so they are already checked in projects made from this template.

FIGURE 13.5

References set to the Access and DAO object libraries in the VB References dialog.

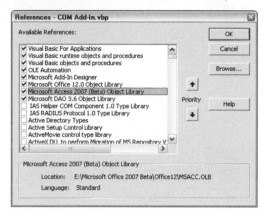

You can now modify the form (if you need a form in your add-in), and the code in the standard module and designer, to create a custom COM add-in for use in Access:

1. First open the designer and fill in the basic information about the add-in on its General tab (the Advanced tab rarely needs to be modified from its default settings).

2. Enter the add-in's display name and description in the "Addin Display Name" and "Addin Description" boxes, then select the Office application (Access in this case) from the Application drop-down list (see Figure 13.6). The currently running Office version is automatically selected in the Application Version box.

3. Finally, select the add-in's load behavior from the "Initial Load Behavior" drop-down — Startup is the appropriate choice if you want the add-in to always be available in any Access database (which is the usual case).

The SharedCode module (as its name suggests) contains code that applies to the entire add-in, such as an error handler and the standard code that creates and removes the add-in's toolbar buttons or menu items (for the rare case where a multi-application COM add-in puts a command on the same menu or toolbar in each Office application).

The code in the Designer (which I named AccessDesigner to indicate that it is an Access Designer) contains code specific to Access. (If you are creating a multi-application add-in, you need to create one Designer for each Office application that your add-in supports). Some of the standard code in the Designer works with the frmCOMAddIn form; if your add-in doesn't need to display a form, you can delete or comment out any code that references this form, but it is a good idea to leave all the procedures in the module, in case you might need them later on.

Figure 13.6

Entering the COM add-in's identifying information and other options in the Designer dialog.

The Designer code includes the procedures that implement the add-in's functionality; they require little (if any) modification from those that would run in an Access add-in.

Creating the LNC Control Renaming COM Add-in

The procedures that do the renaming of form and report controls in the LNC Control Renaming COM add-in are basically the same as the LNC Rename Access add-in, which was covered in detail in my earlier book *Expert One-on-One Microsoft Access Application Development*; this chapter concentrates on the differences needed to make the code work in a COM add-in.

CROSS-REF For more details on the LNC Rename add-in, see my book *Expert One-on-One Microsoft Access Application Development* (ISBN: 0764559044).

The SharedCode Module

Starting with a project created from the COM add-in project template, in the SharedCode module, I removed the standard declarations (the only declarations I need are the ones in the AccessDesigner module), and I also removed the standard `AddToCommandBar` and `DeleteFromCommandBar` functions. Because I needed to create (and remove) two command bar buttons, intended specifically for the Access Form Design and Report Design toolbars, I placed those procedures in the Access Designer.

I added the `StripChars` function to this module; it is called throughout the add-in to remove various characters and spaces from control names during renaming, so as prevent problems when the controls are referenced in code. I modified the standard template `AddInErr` procedure slightly; it creates a message box string that is called from error handlers in the add-in. The SharedCode module that contains these procedures is listed next:

```
Option Explicit

Public Function StripChars(strText _
    As String) As String
```
Strips a variety of non-alphanumeric characters from a text string.
```
On Error GoTo ErrorHandler

    Dim strTestString As String
    Dim strTestChar As String
    Dim lngFound As Long
    Dim i As Integer
    Dim strStripChars As String

    strStripChars = " `~!@#$%^&*()-_=+[{]};:',<.>/?" _
        & Chr$(34) & Chr$(13) & Chr$(10)
    strTestString = strText

    i = 1
    Do While i <= Len(strTestString)
```
Find a strippable character.
```
        strTestChar = Mid$(strTestString, i, 1)
        lngFound = InStr(strStripChars, strTestChar)
        If lngFound > 0 Then
          strTestString = Left(strTestString, i - 1) _
            & Mid(strTestString, i + 1)
        Else
          i = i + 1
        End If
    Loop

    StripChars = strTestString

ErrorHandlerExit:
    Exit Function

ErrorHandler:
    AddInErr Err
    Resume ErrorHandlerExit

End Function
```

```
Public Sub AddInErr(errX As ErrObject)

Displays message box with error information

    Dim strMsg As String

    strMsg = _
        "An error occurred in the " & App.Title _
        & vbCrLf & "Error #:" & errX.Number _
        & vbCrLf & "Description: " & errX.Description
    MsgBox strMsg, , "Error!"

End Sub
```

The AccessDesigner Module

The COM add-in needs several entries in the Declarations section of the AccessDesigner module. To open the designer module, open the Designers folder in the project tree, right-click the AccessDesigner item, and select View Code from the context menu, as shown in Figure 13.7.

Opening the AccessDesigner code module.

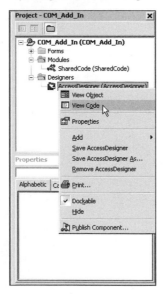

The standard designer code needs some modifications to enable it to work with add-in events that fire when the add-in is loaded or unloaded, or when the host application (Access in this case) starts or shuts down. These events are implemented via the IDTExtensibility2 library, using the Implements line at the beginning of the module.

The procedures starting with `Private Sub IDTExtensibility2` are the events supported by this library. You need to have all five event procedures in the Designer module, even though your add-in may not use all of them. The ones I don't need have only a comment line:

```
'No code needed, but must have the event stub
```

COM add-ins generally put one or more buttons or commands on a toolbar or menu in the host application; each one requires a `WithEvents` statement in the Declarations section of the Designer module, to support code on the Click event of the button or command. My LNC Control Renaming code has two such events, to support two toolbar buttons.

The remainder of the Declarations section contains groups of public and private variables for use in various add-in procedures. The procedures in this module have the functionality described next:

- The `OnConnection` event procedure sets the command bar button variables, and uses the `CreateFormCommandBarButton` and `CreateReportCommandBarButton` functions to create the buttons on the Form Design (or Report Design) Access toolbars (in older versions of Access), or in the Toolbar Commands group on the backward compatibility Add-Ins tab of the Ribbon (in Access 2007 running on Windows XP).

- The `OnDisconnection` event procedure runs a function that removes the two command bar buttons when the add-in is disconnected by unloading the add-in from the COM Add-Ins dialog (they are not removed when Access is closed).

- The two Click event procedures run the `LNCRenameFormControls` and `LNCRenameReportControls` functions, which respectively rename form and report controls.

> **NOTE** An Access 2000–2003 command bar button has its `OnAction` property set to the name of a macro (a Sub procedure with no arguments) that is run when the button is clicked; the syntax is different for buttons placed on command bars from a COM add-in. Instead, the `OnAction` property is set to the ProgId of the COM add-in, and the button's Click event is handled by the Click event procedure in the Designer module.

- The `CreateFormCommandBarButton` creates the Access toolbar button that renames controls on open forms. The function first sets the `pappAccess` variable to the Access.Application object, then sets a reference to the Form Design toolbar (where the button will be placed), looking for an existing button on this toolbar, using its Tag property, and creating it if it does not already exist.

- The `CreateReportCommandBarButton` procedure does a similar job for the Report Design toolbar button that renames report controls.

- The `RemoveAddInCommandBarButton` function (called by the `OnDisconnection` event procedure) removes the add-in's command buttons.

- The `LNCRenameFormControls` and `LNCRenameReportControls` functions are basically similar to the code in the Access LNC Rename add-in, so I will not discuss them in detail. The main difference is that the COM add-in functions rename controls on the open forms (or reports) only; the Rename Form Controls and Rename Report Controls menu add-ins rename controls on all forms or reports, whether or not they are open.

The AccessDesigner code is listed next, with the specific modifications needed to implement the add-in's functionality, using the event procedures supported by the IDTExtensibility2 library to create command bar buttons, and assign procedures to them. The module also contains the procedures used to do control renaming:

```
Implements IDTExtensibility2

Private WithEvents frmcbb As Office.CommandBarButton
Private WithEvents rptcbb As Office.CommandBarButton
```

Global variable to store reference to host application (Access)

```
Public pappAccess As Access.Application
```

Regular variables for creating toolbar buttons

```
Private cbrMenu As Office.CommandBar
Private cbbAddIn As Office.CommandBarButton
```

Public variables for handling renaming

```
Public pctl As Access.Control
Public pdbs As DAO.Database
Public pfrm As Access.Form
Public pintRenameFail As Integer
Public pintReturn As Integer
Public plngControlType As Long
Public prpt As Access.Report
Public prst As DAO.Recordset
Public pstrMessage As String
Public pstrNewCtlName As String
Public pstrOldCtlName As String
Public pstrSQL As String
Public pstrSourceObject As String
```

Private variables for handling renaming

```
Private i As Integer
Private blnTag As Boolean
Private intTag As Integer
Private strPrefix As String
Private blnUnbound As Boolean
Private strControlSource As String
Private strCaption As String
Private strObjectName As String
Private strCtlName As String
```

Constants for characters surrounding ProgID

```
Const PROG_ID_START As String = "!<"
Const PROG_ID_END As String = ">"


Private Sub IDTExtensibility2_OnAddInsUpdate(custom() _
    As Variant)

On Error GoTo ErrorHandler

    'No code needed, but must have the event stub

ErrorHandlerExit:
    Exit Sub

ErrorHandler:
    AddInErr Err
    Resume ErrorHandlerExit

End Sub


Private Sub IDTExtensibility2_OnBeginShutdown(custom() _
    As Variant)

On Error GoTo ErrorHandler

    'No code needed, but must have the event stub

ErrorHandlerExit:
    Exit Sub

ErrorHandler:
    AddInErr Err
    Resume ErrorHandlerExit

End Sub

Private Sub IDTExtensibility2_OnConnection(ByVal _
    Application As Object, ByVal ConnectMode _
    As AddInDesignerObjects.ext_ConnectMode, _
    ByVal AddInInst As Object, custom() As Variant)
```

Calls shared code to create a new command bar button to rename controls on a form or report.

```
On Error GoTo ErrorHandler

    Set frmcbb = CreateFormCommandBarButton(Application, _
        ConnectMode, AddInInst)
    Set rptcbb = CreateReportCommandBarButton(Application, _
        ConnectMode, AddInInst)

ErrorHandlerExit:
    Exit Sub

ErrorHandler:
    AddInErr Err
    Resume ErrorHandlerExit

End Sub


Private Sub IDTExtensibility2_OnDisconnection(ByVal _
    RemoveMode As AddInDesignerObjects.ext_DisconnectMode, _
    custom() As Variant)

On Error GoTo ErrorHandler
```

Call common procedure to disconnect add-in.

```
    RemoveAddInCommandBarButton RemoveMode

ErrorHandlerExit:
    Exit Sub

ErrorHandler:
    AddInErr Err
    Resume ErrorHandlerExit

End Sub


Private Sub IDTExtensibility2_OnStartupComplete(custom() _
    As Variant)

On Error GoTo ErrorHandler

    'No code needed, but must have the event stub

ErrorHandlerExit:
    Exit Sub
```

```
ErrorHandler:
   AddInErr Err
   Resume ErrorHandlerExit

End Sub


Private Sub frmcbb_Click(ByVal ctl As _
   Office.CommandBarButton, CancelDefault As Boolean)

On Error Resume Next

   Call LNCRenameFormControls

End Sub


Private Sub rptcbb_Click(ByVal ctl As _
   Office.CommandBarButton, CancelDefault As Boolean)

On Error Resume Next

   Call LNCRenameReportControls

End Sub

Public Function CreateFormCommandBarButton(ByVal _
   Application As Object, ByVal ConnectMode _
   As AddInDesignerObjects.ext_ConnectMode, _
   ByVal AddInInst As Object) As Office.CommandBarButton

On Error GoTo ErrorHandler
```

Store a reference to the Application object in a public variable so other procedures in the add-in can use it.

```
   Set pappAccess = Application
```

Return a reference to the command bar..

```
   Set cbrMenu = pappAccess.CommandBars("Form Design")
```

Add a button to call the add-in from the command bar, if it doesn't already exist.

Look for the button on the command bar.

```
   Set cbbAddIn = _
      cbrMenu.FindControl(Tag:="Rename Form Controls")

On Error Resume Next
   If cbbAddIn Is Nothing Then
```

Add the new button.

```
Set cbbAddIn = _
    cbrMenu.Controls.Add(Type:=msoControlButton, _
        Parameter:="Rename Form Controls")
```

Set the button's Caption, Tag, Style, and OnAction properties.

```
With cbbAddIn
    .Caption = "Rename &Form Controls"
    .Tag = "Rename Form Controls"
    .Style = msoButtonCaption
```

Run the main add-in function.

```
    .OnAction = PROG_ID_START & AddInInst.ProgId _
        & PROG_ID_END
End With
End If

On Error GoTo ErrorHandler
```

Return a reference to the new command bar button.

```
Set CreateFormCommandBarButton = cbbAddIn

ErrorHandlerExit:
    Exit Function

ErrorHandler:
    AddInErr Err
    Resume ErrorHandlerExit

End Function

Public Function CreateReportCommandBarButton(ByVal _
    Application As Object, ByVal ConnectMode As _
    AddInDesignerObjects.ext_ConnectMode, _
    ByVal AddInInst As Object) As Office.CommandBarButton

On Error GoTo ErrorHandler
```

Store a reference to the Application object in a public variable so other procedures in the add-in can use it.

```
Set pappAccess = Application
```

Return a reference to the command bar..

```
Set cbrMenu = pappAccess.CommandBars("Report Design")
```

Add a button to call the add-in from the command bar, if it doesn't already exist.

Look for the button on the command bar.

```
Set cbbAddIn = _
    cbrMenu.FindControl(Tag:="Rename Report Controls")
If cbbAddIn Is Nothing Then
```

Add the new button.

```
Set cbbAddIn = _
    cbrMenu.Controls.Add(Type:=msoControlButton, _
        Parameter:="Rename Report Controls")
```

Set the button's Caption, Tag, Style, and OnAction properties.

```
With cbbAddIn
    .Caption = "Rename &Report Controls"
    .Tag = "Rename Report Controls"
    .Style = msoButtonCaption
```

Run the main add-in function.

```
    .OnAction = PROG_ID_START & AddInInst.ProgId _
        & PROG_ID_END
End With
End If
```

Return a reference to the new commandbar button.

```
Set CreateReportCommandBarButton = cbbAddIn

ErrorHandlerExit:
    Exit Function

ErrorHandler:
    AddInErr Err
    Resume ErrorHandlerExit

End Function


Function RemoveAddInCommandBarButton(ByVal _
    RemoveMode As AddInDesignerObjects.ext_DisconnectMode)
```

This procedure removes the command bar buttons for the add-in if the user disconnected it.

```
On Error Resume Next
```

If the user unloaded the add-in, remove the button. Otherwise, the add-in is being unloaded because the application is closing; in that case, leave button as is.

```
If RemoveMode = ext_dm_UserClosed Then
```

Delete the custom command bar buttons.

```
        With pappAccess.CommandBars("Form Design")
            .Controls("Rename Form Controls").Delete
        End With

        With pappAccess.CommandBars("Report Design")
            .Controls("Rename Report Controls").Delete
        End With
    End If

ErrorHandlerExit:
    Exit Function

ErrorHandler:
    AddInErr Err
    Resume ErrorHandlerExit

End Function


    Public Function LNCRenameFormControls() As Variant
```

Renames all the controls on open forms.

```
On Error Resume Next
```

Generate table of control types to use in renaming controls (if it does not already exist).

```
    CreateCTTable
```

```
On Error GoTo ErrorHandler
```

Determine whether any forms are open, and exit if not.

```
    If pappAccess.Forms.Count = 0 Then
        MsgBox "No forms are open; exiting"
        GoTo ErrorHandlerExit
    End If
```

Determine whether original the control names should be stored in the Tag property.

```
pstrMessage = _
    "When processing form controls, should the original " _
    & "control name be saved to the control's Tag " _
    & "property?"
intTag = MsgBox(pstrMessage, vbYesNo + vbQuestion + _
    vbDefaultButton2, "Control Name Backup")

If intTag = vbYes Then
    blnTag = True
Else
    blnTag = False
End If
```

Process the open forms.

```
For Each pfrm In pappAccess.Forms

    For Each pctl In pfrm.Controls
        strCtlName = pctl.Name
        plngControlType = pctl.ControlType
        blnUnbound = False

        Select Case plngControlType
```

Controls with control source

```
        Case acTextBox
            strPrefix = "txt"
            i = ControlCS(pctl, strPrefix, blnTag)

        Case acComboBox
            strPrefix = "cbo"
            i = ControlCS(pctl, strPrefix, blnTag)

        Case acCheckBox
            strPrefix = "chk"
            strControlSource = pctl.ControlSource
            If blnUnbound = False Then
                i = ControlCS(pctl, strPrefix, blnTag)
            Else
                i = ControlNA(pctl, strPrefix, blnTag)
            End If

        Case acBoundObjectFrame
            strPrefix = "frb"
            i = ControlCS(pctl, strPrefix, blnTag)
```

```
Case acListBox
   strPrefix = "lst"
   i = ControlCS(pctl, strPrefix, blnTag)

Case acOptionGroup
   strPrefix = "fra"
   i = ControlCS(pctl, strPrefix, blnTag)

Case acOptionButton
   strPrefix = "opt"
   strControlSource = pctl.ControlSource
   If blnUnbound = False Then
      i = ControlCS(pctl, strPrefix, blnTag)
   Else
      i = ControlNA(pctl, strPrefix, blnTag)
   End If
```

Controls with caption only

```
Case acToggleButton
   strPrefix = "tgl"
   i = ControlCA(pctl, strPrefix, blnTag)

Case acLabel
   strPrefix = "lbl"
   i = ControlCA(pctl, strPrefix, blnTag)

Case acCommandButton
   strPrefix = "cmd"
   i = ControlCA(pctl, strPrefix, blnTag)
```

Controls with source object only

```
Case acSubform
   strPrefix = "sub"
   i = ControlSO(pctl, strPrefix, blnTag)
```

Controls with none of the above

```
Case acObjectFrame
   strPrefix = "fru"
   i = ControlNA(pctl, strPrefix, blnTag)

Case acImage
   strPrefix = "img"
   i = ControlNA(pctl, strPrefix, blnTag)

Case acTabCtl
   strPrefix = "tab"
   i = ControlNA(pctl, strPrefix, blnTag)
```

```
            Case acLine
                strPrefix = "lin"
                i = ControlNA(pctl, strPrefix, blnTag)

            Case acPage
                strPrefix = "pge"
                i = ControlNA(pctl, strPrefix, blnTag)

            Case acPageBreak
                strPrefix = "brk"
                i = ControlNA(pctl, strPrefix, blnTag)

            Case acRectangle
                strPrefix = "shp"
                i = ControlNA(pctl, strPrefix, blnTag)

        End Select
    Next pctl
Next pfrm

Call MsgBox("All form controls renamed!", _
    vbOKOnly, "Done")

ErrorHandlerExit:
    Exit Function

ErrorHandler:
```

If an option button or checkbox is unbound, set blnUnbound to True so the code uses the NA function instead of CS.

```
If Err.Number = 2455 Then
    blnUnbound = True
    Resume Next
Else
    AddInErr Err
    Resume ErrorHandlerExit
End If

End Function
```

[I am omitting the LNCRenameReportControls function from this listing, because it is substantially similar to the LNCRenameFormControls function.]

The following procedures rename form and report controls of various types. Controls are grouped depending on whether or not they are bound, and other relevant properties. Each group of controls (ControlCS, ControlCA, and so forth) needs different code to create an appropriate name for the control. The bound controls, for example, create a name using the name of the bound field; labels create a name using caption text, and so forth:

```
Public Function ControlCS(ctl As Access.Control, _
    strPrefix As String, blnTag As Boolean) As Integer
```

Does group renaming of all controls with control sources on a form or report.

```
On Error GoTo ErrorHandler

Dim strControlSource As String

strControlSource = Nz(ctl.ControlSource)
pstrOldCtlName = ctl.ControlName
```

Check whether control already is correctly named and also special case for controls whose original name starts with "Option" or "Frame" (same first three letters as prefix).

```
If Left(pstrOldCtlName, 3) = strPrefix And _
    Left(pstrOldCtlName, 6) <> "Option" And _
    Left(pstrOldCtlName, 3) = strPrefix And _
    Left(pstrOldCtlName, 5) <> "Frame" Then
    GoTo ErrorHandlerExit
```

If the control source is not empty, use it.

```
ElseIf strControlSource <> "" Then
    pstrNewCtlName = strPrefix & _
        StripChars(strControlSource)
Else
```

Otherwise, use the original control name.

```
    pstrNewCtlName = strPrefix & _
        StripChars(pstrOldCtlName)
End If
```

Fix name of "Page x of y" textbox controls on Database Wizard reports.

```
If pstrNewCtlName = "txtPagePageofPages" Then
    pstrNewCtlName = "txtPages"
End If
```

Show the user

- the original control name
- the control type
- control source
- proposed new name

and ask if the new name is acceptable.

```
pintRenameFail = True
Do While pintRenameFail
   pintRenameFail = False
   pintReturn = MsgBox( _
     "Rename " & _
       DLookup("[ControlTypeName]", _
       "zLNCtblControlType", _
       "[ControlType] = " & ctl.ControlType) _
       & " control currently named " _
       & pstrOldCtlName & vbCrLf & _
       "(control source: " & strControlSource & ") " _
       & "to" & vbCrLf & pstrNewCtlName & "?", _
     vbYesNo + vbQuestion + vbDefaultButton1, _
     "Rename control")
```

If the user clicks the Yes button, rename the control.

```
If pintReturn = vbYes Then
   If blnTag = True Then
       ctl.Tag = ctl.ControlName
   End If
   ctl.ControlName = pstrNewCtlName
```

Otherwise, pop up an input box to edit the name.

```
ElseIf pintReturn = vbNo Then
   pstrNewCtlName = _
       InputBox("Modify new control name", _
       "Rename control", pstrNewCtlName)
       ctl.ControlName = pstrNewCtlName
   End If
Loop

ErrorHandlerExit:
   Exit Function

ErrorHandler:
```

If the proposed control name is already in use, return to the renaming dialog.

```
pintRenameFail = True
If Err.Number = 2104 Then
   MsgBox "There is another control named " & _
       pstrNewCtlName & "; please try again", , _
       "Control Name Used"
   pstrNewCtlName = pstrNewCtlName & "1"
```

```
        Else
            AddInErr Err
            Resume ErrorHandlerExit
        End If

        Resume Next

    End Function


    Public Function ControlCA(ctl As Access.Control, _
        strPrefix As String, blnTag As Boolean) As Integer
```

Does group renaming of all controls with captions on a form or report.

```
        On Error GoTo ErrorHandler

        Dim strCaption As String

        pstrOldCtlName = ctl.ControlName
        strCaption = ctl.Caption

        If Left(pstrOldCtlName, 3) = strPrefix Then
            Exit Function
        ElseIf strCaption <> "" Then
            If Left(strCaption, 3) = "frm" Then
                pstrNewCtlName = strPrefix & _
                    Mid(StripChars(strCaption), 4)
            ElseIf Left(strCaption, 4) = "fsub" Then
                pstrNewCtlName = strPrefix & _
                    Mid(StripChars(strCaption), 5)
            Else
                pstrNewCtlName = strPrefix & _
                    StripChars(strCaption)
            End If
        ElseIf strCaption = "" Then
            If Left(pstrOldCtlName, 3) = "frm" Then
                pstrNewCtlName = strPrefix & _
                    Mid(StripChars(pstrOldCtlName), 4)
            ElseIf Left(pstrOldCtlName, 4) = "fsub" Then
                pstrNewCtlName = strPrefix & _
                    Mid(StripChars(pstrOldCtlName), 5)
            Else
                pstrNewCtlName = strPrefix & _
                    StripChars(pstrOldCtlName)
            End If
        End If

        If Right(pstrNewCtlName, 12) = "SubformLabel" Then
            pstrNewCtlName = Left(pstrNewCtlName, _
                Len(pstrNewCtlName) - 12)
```

```
      ElseIf Right(pstrNewCtlName, 5) = "Label" Then
         pstrNewCtlName = Left(pstrNewCtlName, _
            Len(pstrNewCtlName) - 5)
      End If

      pintRenameFail = True
      Do While pintRenameFail
         pintRenameFail = False
         pintReturn = MsgBox("Rename " _
            & DLookup("[ControlTypeName]", _
            "zLNCtblControlType", "[ControlType] = " _
            & ctl.ControlType) _
            & " control currently named " & pstrOldCtlName _
            & vbCrLf & "(caption: " & strCaption & ") to" _
            & vbCrLf & pstrNewCtlName & "?", vbYesNo + _
            vbQuestion + vbDefaultButton1, "Rename control")
         If pintReturn = vbYes Then
            If blnTag = True Then ctl.Tag = ctl.ControlName
            ctl.ControlName = pstrNewCtlName
         ElseIf pintReturn = vbNo Then
            pstrNewCtlName = _
               InputBox("Modify new control name", _
               "Rename control", pstrNewCtlName)
            ctl.ControlName = pstrNewCtlName
         End If
      Loop

ErrorHandlerExit:
   Exit Function

ErrorHandler:
```

If the proposed control name is already in use, return to the renaming dialog.

```
      pintRenameFail = True
      If Err.Number = 2104 Then
         MsgBox "There is another control named " & _
            pstrNewCtlName & "; please try again", , _
            "Control Name Used"
         pstrNewCtlName = pstrNewCtlName & "1"
      Else
         AddInErr Err
         Resume ErrorHandlerExit
      End If

      Resume Next

End Function


Public Function ControlSO(ctl As Access.Control, _
   strPrefix As String, blnTag As Boolean) As Integer
```

Does group renaming of all controls with source objects on a form or report.

```
'Called from RenameFormControls and RenameReportControls
'in this module

On Error GoTo ErrorHandler

    pstrOldCtlName = ctl.ControlName
    pstrSourceObject = Nz(ctl.SourceObject)

    If Left(pstrOldCtlName, 3) = strPrefix Then
        Exit Function
    ElseIf pstrSourceObject <> "" Then
        If Left(pstrSourceObject, 3) = "frm" Then
            pstrNewCtlName = strPrefix & _
                Mid(StripChars(pstrSourceObject), 4)
        ElseIf Left(pstrSourceObject, 4) = "fsub" Then
            pstrNewCtlName = strPrefix & _
                Mid(StripChars(pstrSourceObject), 5)
        Else
            pstrNewCtlName = strPrefix & _
                StripChars(pstrSourceObject)
        End If
    ElseIf pstrSourceObject = "" Then
        If Left(pstrOldCtlName, 3) = "frm" Then
            pstrNewCtlName = strPrefix & _
                Mid(StripChars(pstrOldCtlName), 4)
        ElseIf Left(pstrOldCtlName, 4) = "fsub" Then
            pstrNewCtlName = strPrefix & _
                Mid(StripChars(pstrOldCtlName), 5)
        Else
            pstrNewCtlName = strPrefix & _
                StripChars(pstrOldCtlName)
        End If
    Else
        pstrNewCtlName = strPrefix & _
            StripChars(pstrOldCtlName)
    End If

    If Right(pstrNewCtlName, 7) = "Subform" Then
        pstrNewCtlName = Left(pstrNewCtlName, _
            Len(pstrNewCtlName) - 7)
    End If

    pintRenameFail = True
    Do While pintRenameFail
        pintRenameFail = False
        pintReturn = MsgBox("Rename " _
            & DLookup("[ControlTypeName]", _
            "zLNCtblControlType", "[ControlType] = " _
```

```
                    & ctl.ControlType) _
                    & " control currently named " & pstrOldCtlName _
                    & vbCrLf & "(source object: " & pstrSourceObject _
                    & ") to" & vbCrLf & pstrNewCtlName & "?", vbYesNo _
                    + vbQuestion + vbDefaultButton1, "Rename control")
              If pintReturn = vbYes Then
                 If blnTag = True Then ctl.Tag = ctl.ControlName
                 ctl.ControlName = pstrNewCtlName
              ElseIf pintReturn = vbNo Then
                 pstrNewCtlName = _
                    InputBox("Modify new control name", _
                    "Rename control", pstrNewCtlName)
                 ctl.ControlName = pstrNewCtlName
              End If
        Loop

   ErrorHandlerExit:
        Exit Function

   ErrorHandler:
```

If the proposed control name is already in use, return to the renaming dialog.

```
        pintRenameFail = True
        If Err.Number = 2104 Then
           MsgBox "There is another control named " & _
              pstrNewCtlName & "; please try again", , _
              "Control Name Used"
           pstrNewCtlName = pstrNewCtlName & "1"
        Else
           AddInErr Err
           Resume ErrorHandlerExit
        End If
        Resume ErrorHandlerExit

   End Function


   Public Function ControlNA(ctl As Access.Control, _
        strPrefix As String, blnTag As Boolean) As Integer
```

Does group renaming of all controls not fitting the other categories on a form or report.

```
        'Called from RenameFormControls and RenameReportControls
        'in this module

        On Error GoTo ErrorHandler

        pstrOldCtlName = ctl.ControlName
```

Special case for lines whose default name is "Line" or "Option" (same first three letters as the standard prefix).

```
If Left(pstrOldCtlName, 3) = strPrefix And _
   Left(pstrOldCtlName, 6) <> "Option" And _
   Left(pstrOldCtlName, 4) <> "Line" Then
   Exit Function
Else
   pstrNewCtlName = strPrefix _
      & StripChars(pstrOldCtlName)
End If

pintRenameFail = True
Do While pintRenameFail
   pintRenameFail = False
   pintReturn = MsgBox("Rename " & _
      DLookup("[ControlTypeName]", _
      "zLNCtblControlType", "[ControlType] = " _
      & ctl.ControlType) & " control currently named " _
      & pstrOldCtlName & " to" & vbCrLf _
      & pstrNewCtlName & "?", vbYesNo + vbQuestion _
      + vbDefaultButton1, _
      "Rename control")
   If pintReturn = vbYes Then
      If blnTag = True Then ctl.Tag = ctl.ControlName
      ctl.ControlName = pstrNewCtlName
   ElseIf pintReturn = vbNo Then
      pstrNewCtlName = _
         InputBox("Modify new control name", _
         "Rename control", pstrNewCtlName)
      ctl.ControlName = pstrNewCtlName
   End If
Loop

ErrorHandlerExit:
   Exit Function

ErrorHandler:
```

If the proposed control name is already in use, return to the renaming dialog.

```
pintRenameFail = True
If Err.Number = 2104 Then
   MsgBox "There is another control named " & _
      pstrNewCtlName & "; please try again", , _
      "Control Name Used"
   pstrNewCtlName = pstrNewCtlName & "1"
Else
   AddInErr Err
```

```
        End If
        Resume ErrorHandlerExit

End Function


Public Function CreateCTTable()
'Called from LNCRenameFormControls and
'LNCRenameReportControls function
'in this module

    Dim strCTTable As String

    strCTTable = "zLNCtblControlType"
```

Delete the old table, if there is one.

```
        Set pdbs = CurrentDb
        strCTTable = "zLNCtblControlType"
        On Error Resume Next
        pdbs.TableDefs.Delete strCTTable

    On Error GoTo ErrorHandler
```

Generate the table of control types to use in renaming controls. If there is a "table not found" error, exit function.

```
        pstrSQL = "CREATE TABLE " & strCTTable & _
            "(ControlType LONG, ControlTypeName TEXT (50));"
        DoCmd.RunSQL pstrSQL
```

Append data to the table of control types.

```
        Set pdbs = CurrentDb
        Set prst = pdbs.OpenRecordset(strCTTable, dbOpenTable)
        With prst
            .AddNew
            !ControlType = 100
            !ControlTypeName = "Label"
            .Update
            .AddNew
            !ControlType = 101
            !ControlTypeName = "Rectangle"
            .Update
            .AddNew
            !ControlType = 102
            !ControlTypeName = "Line"
            .Update
            .AddNew
```

```
            !ControlType = 103
            !ControlTypeName = "Image"
            .Update
            .AddNew
            !ControlType = 104
            !ControlTypeName = "Command Button"
            .Update
            .AddNew
            !ControlType = 105
            !ControlTypeName = "Option Button"
            .Update
            .AddNew
            !ControlType = 106
            !ControlTypeName = "Check Box"
            .Update
            .AddNew
            !ControlType = 107
            !ControlTypeName = "Option Group"
            .Update
            .AddNew
            !ControlType = 108
            !ControlTypeName = "Bound Object Frame"
            .Update
            .AddNew
            !ControlType = 109
            !ControlTypeName = "Text Box"
            .Update
            .AddNew
            !ControlType = 110
            !ControlTypeName = "List Box"
            .Update
            .AddNew
            !ControlType = 111
            !ControlTypeName = "Combo Box"
            .Update
            .AddNew
            !ControlType = 112
            !ControlTypeName = "Subform/Subreport"
            .Update
            .AddNew
            !ControlType = 114
            !ControlTypeName = "Object Frame"
            .Update
            .AddNew
            !ControlType = 118
            !ControlTypeName = "Page Break"
            .Update
            .AddNew
```

```
            !ControlType = 122
            !ControlTypeName = "Toggle Button"
            .Update
            .AddNew
            !ControlType = 123
            !ControlTypeName = "Tab Control"
            .Update
            .AddNew
            !ControlType = 124
            !ControlTypeName = "Page"
            .Update
            .Close
        End With

    ErrorHandlerExit:
        Exit Function

    ErrorHandler:
        If Err.Number = 3010 Then
```

Control types table already exists.

```
            Exit Function
        Else
            AddInErr Err
            Resume ErrorHandlerExit
        End If

    End Function
```

Creating the DLL

After modifying the code in the SharedCode and AccessDesigner modules as needed, save the project with a meaningful name (I named the sample COM add-in "LNC Control Renaming"). The project name will also be used as the name of the DLL file when you make that file. The final step is creating the add-in's DLL by selecting File, Make Project Name.dll (with the actual project name replacing the "Project Name"). If there are any syntax errors in the project, you will get an error message at this point, and you can correct the errors and try again, until the DLL is successfully created.

TIP   To rename a VB project, select the project (the top line in the Project Explorer) and modify its name property in the properties sheet. To modify a Designer's name, open it, then select it and modify its name in the properties sheet. The name you give a VB project is the one that will be used by default when creating a DLL.

Installing a COM Add-in

If you copy the DLL file created by a COM add-in to the default Add-ins folder (usually C:\Documents and Settings*User Name*\Application Data\Microsoft\AddIns), its button(s) should automatically appear in the Toolbar Commands group of the Add-Ins tab of the Ribbon (as shown in Figure 13.8); at least if you are running Windows XP.

A COM add-in button on the Add-Ins tab of the Ribbon in Access 2007.

If you don't see your COM add-in's button(s) in an Access database after copying the DLL file to the Add-ins folder, you can install the add-in from the COM Add-Ins dialog, which can be opened from the Add-ins page of the Access Options dialog. To install a COM add-in manually, do the following:

1. For Windows Vista only, run Access as an administrator by right-clicking the MSACCESS.EXE file in the Office 12 subfolder under the Microsoft Office folder, and selecting "Run as administrator" from its right-click context menu.

2. In an Access database, click the Office button, then click the Access Options button at the lower right, as shown in Figure 13.9.

Opening the Access Options dialog.

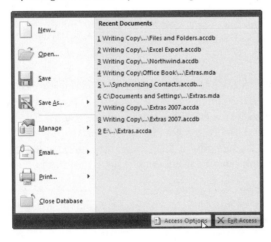

3. Select the Add-ins page on the Access Options dialog to see your installed add-ins (you'll see both Access and COM add-ins listed there, plus one or more add-ins that are installed with Office). If your add-in is listed in the "Inactive Application Add-Ins" group, you will need to install it in the COM Add-ins dialog.

4. To install or uninstall COM add-ins, select COM Add-ins in the drop-down list at the bottom of the screen, as shown in Figure 13.10.

The Add-ins page of the Access Options dialog.

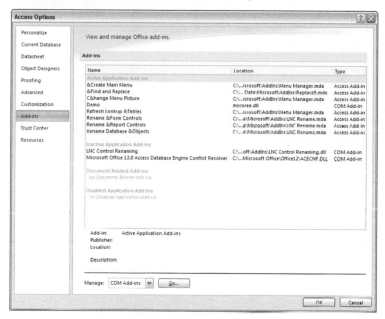

5. On clicking OK, you will see the old COM Add-Ins dialog, the same as in Access 2003, as shown in Figure 13.11.

The COM Add-Ins dialog box.

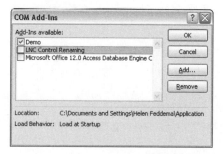

6. The name displayed in the "Add-Ins available" list is the one entered as the add-in's name in the Designer, but curiously, the description entered into the Designer's Description field does not appear on this dialog.

7. If your COM add-in doesn't appear in the list of available add-ins, click the Add button to browse for it; after locating it, click OK in the Add Add-In dialog, as shown in Figure 13.12.

FIGURE 13.12

Browsing for a COM Add-in DLL file.

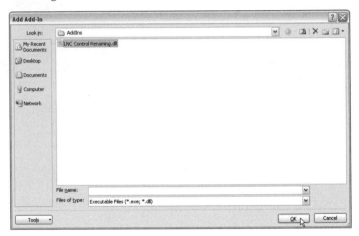

8. The COM add-in should now appear in the COM Add-Ins dialog. You can check its checkbox (if needed) and close the dialog; its button(s) should then appear on the Add-Ins tab of the Ribbon, in the appropriate context; for example, a button intended to display on the Form Design toolbar (like the one shown in Figure 13.6) will appear when you have a form open in design view.

NOTE   In Access 2000 through 2003, COM add-in buttons appeared on the designated toolbar or menu; in the case of this add-in, that would be the form or report design toolbar. In Access 2007, all the buttons appear directly on the Toolbar Commands group on the Add-Ins tab. If you are running Windows Vista, you won't see the Add-Ins tab unless you run Access as an administrator, as described in Step 1 above.

You can clear the add-in's checkbox to temporarily unload it, or you can select it and click Remove to uninstall it completely.

Troubleshooting a COM Add-in

If you copy the LNC Renaming.dll file to another computer, install the add-in, and find that you get an error message when running it from its button, open the LNC Renaming.vpb file in VB 6 and make the DLL again; this should fix the problem.

To reopen a COM add-in for editing, double-click the .vbp (VB project) file. You need to have any supporting files (.bas, .dsr, and .frm) in the same folder as the .vpb file, because they are all part of the project.

If your COM add-in isn't behaving as you expect, first unload it (from the COM Add-ins menu), then close Access and reopen a database to see if it now works. This can fix problems that may occur when an old version of the COM add-in code is being run instead of the current version.

WARNING If you have a database open with the COM add-in loaded, you will get a "Permission denied" message when trying to make the DLL, because the DLL is being used. Close any open databases and try again, and you should be able to save the modified DLL.

Next, check for duplicates of the DLL file (perhaps backup copies) that might be running instead of the current version of the DLL. In my experience, even DLLs not located in the AddIns folder may be run, so it's best to have only one DLL on your computer for any given add-in (the latest version). Backup copies can be transferred to another computer, to a disc, or zipped, to prevent confusion.

If you find that code referencing Access objects isn't running (with no error message, or an inappropriate error message, such as "No Forms Open" when you have forms open), you may need to add a specific Access application reference to your code. Specifically, whereas COM add-in code in an Access Designer using just Forms to reference the Access Forms collection, or Reports to reference the Reports collection of a database, ran fine in earlier versions of Office, in Office 2007 the Access application variable pappAccess must be used, so the current syntax needs to be pappAccess.Forms instead of just Forms.

If you change the name of a toolbar button created by a COM add-in, you may see the old button on the toolbar, instead of (or in addition to) the new one. To remove the old button, add a line of code to the RemoveAddInCommandBarButton function to remove the button, using the button's old name instead of "Old Control Name":

```
.Controls("Old Control Name").Delete
```

Create a new DLL, open an Access database to load the add-in, then unload the add-in from the COM Add-Ins dialog to run the code with the extra line once. Close Access, reopen the VB project, delete the line, and re-create the DLL. That should get rid of the old button.

Using a COM Add-in

Using a COM add-in is easy: just click the button it placed on the Add-Ins tab of the Ribbon, as shown in Figure 13.8. To rename controls on any open Access forms, for example, open a form in design view, and click the Rename Form Controls button on the Add-Ins tab. You will first get a message asking if you want to save the original control names to their Tag property, as shown in Figure 13.13.

FIGURE 13.13

A COM add-in question.

Saving the original control name to the Tag property can occasionally be useful, especially when you are renaming controls in a database created by someone else, and you may need to know the original control name in order to fix a reference later on. However, the default choice is No, because mostly there is no need to save the original control name.

After selecting a choice, the code then proceeds to cycle through the open forms and, for each form, cycle through its controls. For any control that doesn't have the appropriate control prefix, a new name is created, and presented for approval in a message box, as shown in Figure 13.14.

FIGURE 13.14

A proposed new control name.

Generally, the new name can be accepted as is; occasionally (for example, for labels with very lengthy captions, or controls with expressions), the new name needs to be edited, which is done by clicking No and then editing the control name in an InputBox.

Even in Access 2007, when you create a new bound form using the Form button in the Create tab of the Ribbon, all bound controls will have the same names as their fields, which can lead to circular reference errors when running code. Thus, it is a good idea to run the Rename Form Controls (or Rename Report Controls) command immediately after creating a bound form or report, before writing any code that references its fields or controls.

Comparing COM Add-ins with Access Add-ins

In previous versions of Office, COM add-ins had an advantage compared to Access add-ins: you could place a button on any menu or toolbar, whereas Access menu add-ins only appeared on the Add-ins menu. Although VB 6 COM add-ins do work in Access 2007, they have lost this advantage over Access add-ins, because all commands created by a COM add-in now appear in the Toolbar Commands group of the Add-Ins tab of the Ribbon, not in the appropriate group or tab of the Ribbon.

CROSS-REF   You can add groups, buttons, and menu selections to the Ribbon using XML; this technique is discussed in Chapter 15.

Compared to COM add-ins, Access add-ins have several extra features: you can create not only menu add-ins, but also wizards of various types, and builders; this lets you add functionality to different locations in an Access database. In Access 2000 through 2003, you could create wizards that would appear as extra choices on the New Form dialog, though in Access 2007 this must now be done using XML to modify the Ribbon. However, property builders that run from various properties still work fine in Access 2007 (at least if you are running Windows XP), so my LNC Rename add-in can be run from the Name property of a control to rename an individual control; this functionality can't be duplicated in a COM add-in.

Summary

In this chapter you learned how to create a VB 6 COM add-in that works with Access 2007, placing buttons in the Toolbar Commands group of the Add-Ins tab of the Ribbon. If you have a VB 6 add-in created in a previous version of Office, you can modify it slightly so that it will work in Access 2007, reusing your code. If, on the other hand, you want to learn a new programming language so you can put groups and buttons on specific tabs of the Ribbon, see the next two chapters for working with Ribbon XML and Visual Studio 2005 add-ins.

Chapter 14

Creating Access Add-ins

M ost of the sample databases for earlier chapters included objects
from the Access 2007 Backup database, used to make incremen-
tally numbered database backups. In order to use this feature in a
database, you need to import several objects from Access 2007 Backup.accdb
into the current database, and set a reference to the Microsoft Scripting
Runtime library, which is a nuisance. It would be much more convenient to
just have backup available in all your Access databases, say from a menu
command.

An Access add-in will do just that, encapsulating a set of database objects and
code into a single package that is available to all Access databases. In this
chapter I use as an example an Access add-in (Extras 2007.accda, that includes
an enhanced version of the Backup code (from basBackup in Access 2007
Backup.accdb), with some enhancements: a setup form for specifying the
backup folder; and a set of objects and code that let you print out lists of
tables or queries, and their fields, excluding those with user-specified
prefixes — very handy for when you need to know which fields are in which
tables during database development, or for documenting the database structure.

> **NOTE** The sample database for this chapter is Extras 2007.accda.

> **CAUTION** If you are attempting to install an add-in in Access 2007
> running on Windows Vista, you may get the security warning
> shown in Figure 14-1. This is probably because you are not running Access
> as an administrator. To run Access as an administrator, right-click the
> MSACCESS.EXE file in the Office 12 subfolder under the Microsoft Office
> folder, and select "Run as administrator," then open an Access database and
> install the add-in. This is not a problem when installing add-ins for Access 2007
> running on Windows XP.

IN THIS CHAPTER

Creating Access menu add-ins

Creating Access wizards

Creating Access property builders

Special considerations and troubleshooting for Access add-ins

FIGURE 14.1

A security warning when attempting to install an Access add-in for Access 2007 running on Windows Vista.

Add-In Manager

You do not have sufficient security permission to install this Add-In. Contact your system administrator for assistance.

OK

The Purpose of Access Add-ins

An Access add-in is a library database (an Access database with the extension .mda for Access 97–2003, or .accda for Access 2007) containing the objects and modules needed to support the add-in's functionality, and a special system table called UsysRegInfo with the Registry key information needed to install the add-in. Add-ins are typically stored in the default Microsoft AddIns folder (C:\Documents and Settings*User Name*\Application Data\Microsoft\AddIns), which was also the default Access add-ins folder for Access 2003). In Access 2007 the default folder for Microsoft's own add-ins is the ACCWIZ folder under the Office folder (on my system, this is E:\Microsoft Office 2007 Beta\Office12\ACCWIZ). However, it is a good idea to keep your own add-ins in the main AddIns folder (C:\Documents and Settings*User Name*\Application Data\Microsoft\AddIns for Windows XP or C:\Users\ *User Name* \AppData\Roaming\Microsoft\AddIns for Windows Vista) rather than mixed in with the ones installed by Office.

An add-in is installed using the Access Add-ins Manager (opened from the Add-Ins menu on the Database Tools tab of the Ribbon), and once an add-in has been installed, it can be used in any Access database.

NOTE Access add-ins created in earlier versions of Access (as .mda library databases) will generally run in Access 2007 running on Windows XP, at least if they don't have conflicts with the new interface. For example, my LNC Rename.mda add-in, which renames database objects and controls according to the Leszynski Naming Convention, works fine in Access 2007, although it doesn't process controls bound to fields of the new Attachment data type. An older add-in that creates custom menu bars, however, will definitely have problems, because the new Ribbon replaces the old command bars interface. In Windows Vista, security features currently prevent add-ins that create Wizards or Property Builders from running (this problem is scheduled to be fixed in an upcoming Service Patch).

Add-in Types

There are three types of Access add-ins, with several subtypes, as listed in Table 14.1.

All these types of add-ins are stored as wizards in the Registry. Sometimes you will see a Builder or Menu add-in referred to as a wizard, but I will reserve the term wizard for the add-ins that are invoked when a new object is created, as listed in the Wizard column of Table 14.1.

TABLE 14.1

Types of Access Add-ins

Wizard	Builder	Menu Add-in
Called when a new table, query, form, report, or control is created	Lets you set properties in design view	Not context-specific, called from the Add-ins menu
Subtypes		
Table Wizards	Property Builders	
Query Wizards	Expression Builders	
Form Wizards		
Report Wizards		
Control Wizards		

Creating a Library Database

This section walks you through creating a library database. To do this, start by creating a new Access database in the database format of your choice. You can create and save a database directly in the older .mda library database format, but for the new .accda format, you need to first create the database as an .accdb database, then change its extension to .accda later, in an Explorer pane, ignoring the dire warning that the file might become unusable.

Next, you need to create the USysRegInfo table to hold the crucial Registry information. As a shortcut, you can import this table from another library database (either .mda or .accda format), if you have one available; you may have to first make system tables visible, as described in this section. I recommend importing this table, because it will save you time in entering some very cryptic information, though of course you have to add (or modify) rows in the table with specific data for your add-in.

The USysRegInfo table is a system table, so you won't see it (or be able to edit its contents) unless you check the "Show System Objects" checkbox. In previous versions of Access, this checkbox was located on the View page of the Options dialog; in Access 2007 it is on the Navigation Options dialog, which can be opened in the following manner:

1. Click the Office button in the upper-left corner of the Access window.

2. Next, click the Access Options button on the Office menu, as shown in Figure 14.2.

FIGURE 14.2

The Access 2007 Office menu.

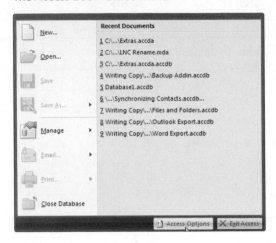

3. On the Access Options dialog, select the Current Database section, as shown in Figure 14.3.

FIGURE 14.3

The Current Database section of the Access Options dialog box.

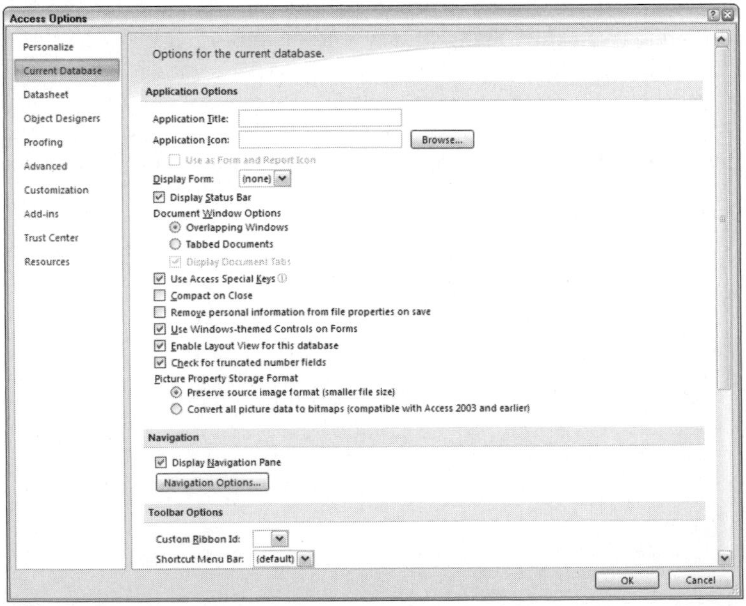

4. Click the Navigation Options button to open the Navigation Options dialog, where finally you can check the "Show System Objects" checkbox, as shown in Figure 14.4.

Checking the "Show System Objects" checkbox on the Navigation Options dialog.

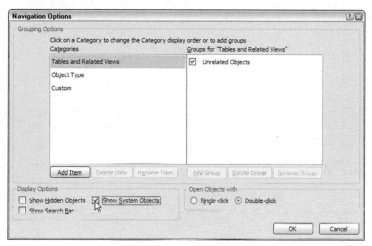

5. Click OK to close the Navigation Options dialog, and again to close the Access Options dialog.

In the Tables section of the Navigation Pane, you will now see a number of system tables, starting with the prefix MSys, and displayed in a dimmed font (Figure 14.5). If you imported the USysRegInfo table from another database, you will see it there too, although curiously, it is not dimmed.

You don't have to do anything special to make the USysRegInfo table a system table; a table with this name is automatically categorized as a system table. If you are creating the table from scratch, refer to Table 14.2 for a listing of the necessary fields and their data types.

FIGURE 14.5

System tables in the Navigation Pane.

TABLE 14.2

The USysRegInfo Table Fields

Field	Data Type	Usage
Subkey	Text	The name of the Registry subkey where a specific Registry setting is stored; can be either HKEY_CURRENT_ACCESS_PROFILE or HKEY_LOCAL_MACHINE. For Access add-ins, the HKEY_CURRENT_ACCESS_PROFILE is preferable, because it automatically uses the Registry section for the running version of Access, allowing the same add-in to work in multiple Access versions.
Type	Number	The type of entry to create; can be key (0), string (1), or DWORD (4)
ValName	Text	The name of the Registry value
Value	Text	The value of the Registry value

NOTE If you create the USysRegInfo table from scratch, you will get an error when entering the name "Value" for the last field (as shown in Figure 14.6). This is because Microsoft has violated its own rules by giving a field a name that is a reserved word (in this case, a property name). However, you can save the field, and it does work. Don't change the field name, because each field in this table must have a specific name to work correctly.

FIGURE 14.6

An error when creating the Value field in the UsysRegInfo table.

If you copy the USysRegInfo table from another add-in, it has a default value of `GenUniqueID()` for the Type field, and also has some useful information in the Description column telling you the value needed for each field data type, as shown in Figure 14.7.

FIGURE 14.7

An imported USysRegInfo table with Description information.

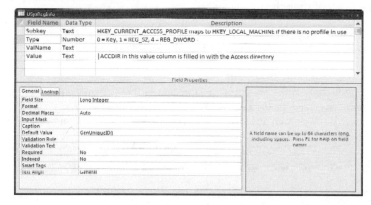

Each type of add-in requires a set of records in the USysRegInfo table, as described in the following sections. The Extras 2007 add-in that is the sample add-in for this chapter is a set of menu add-ins, which will be described in detail; for the other add-in types I will reference two add-ins that I created in earlier versions of Access.

NOTE You might think that add-ins would be found on the Add-Ins tab of the Ribbon in Access 2007 (this tab may not be visible if you are running Windows Vista). But this is not the case. Your Access add-ins are located on the Add-ins menu of the Database Tools tab. The Add-Ins tab has a set of menus like those in previous versions of Access, except that they don't work. The purpose of these non-functional menus is to display commands placed on the Access 2003 (or earlier) menus by add-ins working with the CommandBars collection. This is a very awkward method of implementing backwards compatibility; if you have such an add-in, you will probably want to redo it to place commands on various tabs of the Ribbon, as described in Chapter 15.

Menu Add-ins

A menu add-in needs three rows in the USysRegInfo table, each with an appropriate value in the Type field, and some with values in the ValName or Value field as well, as described in detail next:

- In the first row of the add-in, the Subkey field (which is the same for all the add-in's rows) has the Registry key information, referencing the Menu Add-Ins section under the HKEY_CURRENT_ACCESS_PROFILE key (which references the currently running version of Access), and ending with the command name to display on the Add-Ins menu, with an ampersand if desired to make a hot key. The Type field has a value of 0, indicating the start of a new add-in. The ValName and Value fields are blank.

- In the second row of the add-in, the Type field has a value of 1, the ValName field has the value "Library," and the Value field has the location and name of the library database, using the |ACCDIR\ placeholder to point to the AddIns folder (in earlier versions of Access, this was the Access folder itself, which explains the name).

- In the add-in's third row, the Type field has a value of 1, the ValName field has the value "Expression," and the Value field has the name of function to run (preceded by an equals sign, and followed by a pair of parentheses).

In Table 14.3, which lists the three rows for the "Back up Database" command on the AddIns menu, the italicized text is the information specific to this add-in; the other information is common to all menu add-ins.

> **TIP** When creating a UsysRegInfo table for an Access 2007 add-in that is to be run in Windows Vista, you need to change the capitalization of "Menu Add-ins" to Menu Add-Ins" (capitalizing the I); if you leave it lowercased as for previous versions of Office and Windows, you will not be able to install the add-in.

TABLE 14.3

USysRegInfo Rows Needed for a Menu Add-in

Subkey	Type	ValName	Value
HKEY_CURRENT_ACCESS_PROFILE\Menu Add-Ins\ *&Back up Database*	0		
HKEY_CURRENT_ACCESS_PROFILE\Menu Add-Ins\ *&Back up Database*	1	Library	|ACCDIR*Extras 2007.accda*
HKEY_CURRENT_ACCESS_PROFILE\Menu Add-Ins\ *&Back up Database*	1	Expression	*=BackupFrontEnd()*

> **TIP** If you make copies of your add-in library database from time to time while working on it (always a good idea), don't save the copies in the AddIns folder, because otherwise they will show up as extra selections in the Add-In Manager dialog, and it may not be clear which is the latest version of the add-in when installing it, or which version is running when you use the add-in.

Wizards

My Design Schemes add-in (which finally can be retired because of the superior formatting features of Access 2007) contains several Form Wizard add-ins.

Form Wizard add-ins need four rows in the USysRegInfo table, as described in the following list (the syntax is similar for Report wizards):

- In the first row of the add-in, the Subkey field (which is the same for all the add-in's rows) has the Registry key information, referencing the Form Wizards section under the HKEY_CURRENT_ACCESS_PROFILE key (which references the currently running version of Access), and ending with the command name to display on the Add-Ins menu, with an ampersand if desired to make a hot key. The Type field has a value of 0, indicating the start of a new add-in. The ValName and Value fields are blank.

- In the add-in's second row, the Type field has a value of 1, the ValName field has the value "Description", and the Value field has text to display on the initial wizard screen — in the case of the Custom Form Wizard, that is the New Form dialog.

- In the add-in's third row, the Type field has a value of 1, the ValName field has the value "Library", and the Value field has the location and name of the library database, using the |ACCDIR\ placeholder to point to the AddIns folder.

- In the add-in's fourth row, the Type field has a value of 1, the ValName field has the value "Function", and the Value field has the name of the function to run (without an equals sign).

Table 14.4 lists the USysRegInfo rows for the Custom Form Wizard command on the AddIns menu from the Design Schemes add-in.

TABLE 14.4

USysRegInfo Rows Needed for a Form Wizard Add-in

Subkey	Type	ValName	Value
HKEY_CURRENT_ACCESS_PROFILE\Wizards\ Form Wizards\Custom Form Wizard	0		
HKEY_CURRENT_ACCESS_PROFILE\Wizards\ Form Wizards\Custom Form Wizard	1	Description	Select a form type and color scheme for form background colors and control properties
HKEY_CURRENT_ACCESS_PROFILE\Wizards\ Form Wizards\Custom Form Wizard	1	Library	|ACCDIR\Design Schemes.mda
HKEY_CURRENT_ACCESS_PROFILE\Wizards\ Form Wizards\Custom Form Wizard	1	Function	StartDSWizard

 In a menu add-in, the function called from the add-in is preceded by an equals sign; in a wizard add-in, there is no equals sign.

Property Builders

My LNC Rename add-in (originally created in Access 97 and updated for Access 2000) is still useful in Access 2007 running on Windows XP, because Microsoft has not yet implemented automatic object and control naming according to a naming convention. This add-in lets you automatically rename database objects and form and report controls according to the Leszynski Naming Convention. It includes several menu add-ins and two property builders, which run from the Name property of a control (for renaming a single control) or the Detail section of a form or report (for renaming all controls in a form or report).

CROSS-REF   For more details on the LNC Rename add-in, see my book *Expert One-on-One Microsoft Access Application Development* (ISBN: 0764559044).

Property builders require five rows in the USysRegInfo table, as described in the following list:

- In the first row of the add-in, the Subkey field (which is the same for all the add-in's rows) has the Registry key information, referencing the Property Wizards section under the HKEY_CURRENT_ACCESS_PROFILE key (which references the currently running version of Access), and ending with the command name to display on the Add-Ins menu, with an ampersand if desired to make a hot key. The Type field has a value of 0, indicating the start of a new add-in. The ValName and Value fields are blank.

- In the add-in's second row, the Type field has a value of 1, the ValName field has the value "Description", and the Value field has text to display on the Builder dialog—in the case of the LNCBuilder property wizard, that is the Choose Builder dialog opened from the Name property of a control's properties sheet.

- In the add-in's third row, the Type field has a value of 4, the ValName field has the value "Can Edit", and the Value field has a value of 1, indicating that the wizard can be called for an existing object.

- In the add-in's fourth row, the Type field has a value of 1, the ValName field has the value "Library", and the Value field has the location and name of the library database, using the |ACCDIR\ placeholder to point to the AddIns folder.

- In the add-in's fifth row, the Type field has a value of 1, the ValName field has the value "Function", and the Value field has the name of the function to run (without an equals sign).

Table 14.5 lists the USysRegInfo rows for the property wizard for renaming a single control from the LNC Rename add-in.

TABLE 14.5

USysRegInfo Rows Needed for a Property Builder

Subkey	Type	ValName	Value
HKEY_CURRENT_ACCESS_PROFILE\Wizards\ Property Wizards\Name*LNC Builder*	0		
HKEY_CURRENT_ACCESS_PROFILE\Wizards\ Property Wizards\Name*LNC Builder*	1	Description	*LNC Rename Current Control*
HKEY_CURRENT_ACCESS_PROFILE\Wizards\ Property Wizards\Name*LNC Builder*	4	Can Edit	1
HKEY_CURRENT_ACCESS_PROFILE\Wizards\ Property Wizards\Name*LNC Builder*	1	Library	|ACCDIR*LNC Rename.mda*
HKEY_CURRENT_ACCESS_PROFILE\Wizards\ Property Wizards\Name*LNC Builder*	1	Function	*LNCBuilder*

 Strictly speaking, a library database contains add-ins (usually several), but usually the entire library database is referred to as an add-in.

Things You Need to Know When Writing Add-ins

There are several things to keep in mind when you attempt to write your own add-ins. Some are pitfalls that can prevent the add-in from functioning, and others are recommendations for good add-in design.

Special Requirements for Add-in Code

■ When you run an add-in, the code is running from another database (the add-in library database), and you need to take this into account when referencing database objects in your code. If you want to use an object in the library database, use CodeDb to set a reference to that database; if you want to reference an object in the calling database, use CurrentDb (both CodeDb and CurrentDb are used in the Extras 2007 add-in code).

■ Only functions can be run from the Registry; all the procedures referenced in the USysRegInfo table must be functions, even a procedure that would normally be a Sub (because it doesn't return a value). However, other procedures used in the add-in library database (the ones that are not run directly from the Registry, and are not referenced in the USysRegInto table) can be subs.

- An add-in can display forms, usually as unbound dialogs. Typically, all add-ins except menu add-ins use one or more forms (and menu add-ins can use forms too). The Extras 2007 add-in has a setup form where users can enter information that will be used by various procedures in the add-in.

- You can reference tables in the add-in library database using the CodeDb syntax, which lets you store add-in data in tables if needed. This is useful when you want to store information that will be used for all databases running the add-in, for example the lists of table and query prefixes for excluding tables and queries from listing, in the Extras 2007 add-in.

- Replace macros and queries with code run from public functions, so they can be run directly from the library's module(s).

- Bound forms run from an add-in have as their record source tables in the code database, not the calling database. If the form needs to display data from the calling database, it must be copied to a table in the code database after being filled with data from the calling database, as I do in the Extras 2007 add-in for backup options, and table and query fields.

- The DDL CreateTable statement creates a table in the current database; if you need to create a table in the code database, you have to use the more complex TableDef method in DAO, specifying CodeDb as the database in which to create the table.

- An add-in intended to work in both Access 2007 and earlier versions of Access may need to process both .mdb and .accdb extensions, or deal with the new Attachment data type.

- When the CopyObject method is run from an add-in, the code looks for the source object (the SourceObjectName argument) first in the library database, and then in the current database. This may require you to create a copy of a table, say with "Blank" at the end of its name, in order to copy a fresh, blank table to the calling database, overwriting a filled table, as I do in the Extras 2007 add-in code. Otherwise, you will end up copying the filled table from the calling database back to itself.

- When run from a library database, the RunSQL method of the DoCmd object works on tables in the calling database, and the OpenQuery method works on tables in the code database.

Tips on Add-in Construction

When creating Wizard-type add-ins, you can make then more user-friendly by modeling their appearance after the built-in Access add-ins. Access 2007 has many new interface features, but the wizards look much the same as in earlier versions (Access 97–2003), though there may be some cosmetic differences if you are running Office 2007 over Windows Vista. To make your Wizard forms look like the familiar Access wizards and builders, use the settings listed here:

- Set forms' AutoCenter property to Yes.
- Turn record selectors off.
- Set scroll bars to Neither.

- Turn navigation buttons off.
- If your wizard has several forms, make sure that controls used on more than one form in a series of wizard screens appear in the same place on each form.
- Make all the wizard forms dialog boxes by setting their Modal property to Yes, PopUp to Yes, and BorderStyle to Dialog, so the user can't move to the next box until the current one has been filled in.
- Copy wizard images from the Access wizards, save them as image files, and place them on your wizard forms.

The Extras Add-in Code

The code that implements the add-in's functionality for creating backup copies of the database or its back end, and for listing table and query fields, is listed in the next section.

Extras Options

The fdlgExtrasOptions form module contains the code behind the Extras Options dialog, where you can set up your preferences for the backup save folder, or the prefixes to exclude when listing fields:

```
Option Compare Database
Option Explicit

Private dbsCalling As DAO.Database
Private fd As Office.FileDialog
Private intChoice As Integer
Private prps As DAO.Properties
Private prp As DAO.Property
Private strBackupChoice As Integer
Private strBackupPath As String
Private strCallingDb As String
Private strPropName As String
Private strTable As String
Private tdfs As DAO.TableDefs
Private tdf As DAO.TableDef
Private txt As Access.TextBox
Private varPropValue As Variant


Private Sub cmdCancel_Click()

On Error Resume Next

    DoCmd.Close acForm, Me.Name, acSaveNo

End Sub
```

```
Private Sub cmdCustomBackupPath_Click()

On Error GoTo ErrorHandler

    Dim strSelectedPath As String
```

Create a FileDialog object as a Folder Picker dialog box.

```
    Set fd = Application.FileDialog(msoFileDialogFolderPicker)
    Set txt = Me![txtBackupPath]

    With fd
        .title = _
          "Browse for folder where backups should be stored"
        .ButtonName = "Select"
        .InitialView = msoFileDialogViewDetails
        .InitialFileName = strBackupPath
        If .Show = -1 Then
            strSelectedPath = CStr(fd.SelectedItems.Item(1))
            txt.Value = strSelectedPath
            Set dbsCalling = CurrentDb
            strPropName = "BackupPath"
            Call SetProperty(strName:=strPropName, _
                lngType:=dbText, varValue:=strSelectedPath)
        Else
            Debug.Print "User pressed Cancel"
        End If
    End With

ErrorHandlerExit:
    Exit Sub

ErrorHandler:
    MsgBox "Error No: " & err.Number _
        & "; Description: " & err.Description
    Resume ErrorHandlerExit

End Sub

Private Sub cmdSave_Click()

On Error Resume Next

    DoCmd.Close acForm, Me.Name

End Sub

Private Sub Form_Load()
```

```
On Error Resume Next

    DoCmd.RunCommand acCmdSizeToFitForm

On Error GoTo ErrorHandler

    intChoice = Nz(Me![BackupChoice], 2)

    Select Case intChoice

        Case 1
            Me![cmdCustomBackupPath].Enabled = False

        Case 2
            Me![cmdCustomBackupPath].Enabled = False

        Case 3
            Me![cmdCustomBackupPath].Enabled = True

    End Select

ErrorHandlerExit:
    Exit Sub

ErrorHandler:
    MsgBox "Error No: " & err.Number _
        & "; Description: " & err.Description
    Resume ErrorHandlerExit

End Sub

Private Sub fraBackupOptions_AfterUpdate()

On Error GoTo ErrorHandler

    intChoice = Nz(Me![fraBackupOptions].Valuc, 2)
    strBackupChoice = CStr(intChoice)
    strBackupPath = Nz(Me![BackupPath])

    Select Case intChoice

        Case 1
            Me![cmdCustomBackupPath].Enabled = False

        Case 2
            Me![cmdCustomBackupPath].Enabled = False

        Case 3
            Me![cmdCustomBackupPath].Enabled = True

    End Select
```

Save the user's choice to a database property in the calling database.

```
Set dbsCalling = CurrentDb
strPropName = "BackupChoice"
Call SetProperty(strName:=strPropName, _
    lngType:=dbText, varValue:=strBackupChoice)

ErrorHandlerExit:
   Exit Sub

ErrorHandler:
   MsgBox "Error No: " & err.Number _
      & "; Description: " & err.Description
   Resume ErrorHandlerExit

End Sub
```

basExtras Module

The basExtras standard module contains functions that are called from the USysRegInfo table:

```
Public Function ExtrasOptions()
'Called from USysRegInfo (menu add-in)

On Error GoTo ErrorHandler

   Dim strBackEndSyntaxChoice As String
   Dim strBackEndSyntax As String
   Dim strBackEndPathChoice As String
   Dim strBackEndPath As String
   Dim strDefault As String
```

Get info from database properties in the calling database, and write them to zstblBackupChoices in the code database for use as form's record source:

```
Set dbsCalling = CurrentDb
strPropName = "BackupChoice"
strDefault = "2"
strBackupChoice = GetProperty(strPropName, strDefault)
Debug.Print "Backup choice: " & strBackupChoice

strPropName = "BackupPath"
strDefault = ""
strBackupPath = GetProperty(strPropName, strDefault)
Debug.Print "Backup path: " & strBackupPath

strTable = "zstblBackupChoice"
Set dbsCode = CodeDb
Set rst = dbsCode.OpenRecordset(strTable)
```

```
        rst.MoveFirst
        rst.Edit
        rst![BackupChoice] = strBackupChoice
        rst![BackupPath] = strBackupPath
        rst.Update
        rst.Close


    On Error Resume Next
```

Copy the zstblBackupInfo table to the calling database, if needed:

```
        strCallingDb = CurrentDb.Name
        strTable = "zstblBackupInfo"
        Set tdfsCalling = dbsCalling.TableDefs
        Set tdfCalling = tdfsCalling(strTable)
        If tdfCalling Is Nothing Then
            Debug.Print strTable & " not found; about to copy it"
            DoCmd.CopyObject destinationdatabase:=strCallingDb, _
                newname:=strTable, _
                sourceobjectType:=acTable, _
                sourceobjectname:=strTable
            Debug.Print "Copied " & strTable
        End If
```

Open the dialog form for selecting options:

```
        strForm = "fdlgSetExtrasOptions"
        DoCmd.OpenForm FormName:=strForm, _
            view:=acNormal, _
            windowmode:=acDialog


    ErrorHandlerExit:
        Exit Function

    ErrorHandler:
        MsgBox "Error No: " & err.Number _
            & "; Description: " & err.Description
        Resume ErrorHandlerExit


    End Function

    Public Function CopyListObjects()
    'Called from listTableFields() and ListQueryFields()

    On Error Resume Next

        Dim ctr As DAO.Container
        Dim doc As DAO.Document
```

Copy various objects to the calling database, if they don't already exist. These objects are needed to support the add-in's functionality:

```
Set dbsCalling = CurrentDb
strCallingDb = CurrentDb.Name
Set tdfsCalling = dbsCalling.TableDefs
strTable = "zstblAccessDataTypes"
Set tdfCalling = tdfsCalling(strTable)
DoCmd.SetWarnings False
If tdfCalling Is Nothing Then
    Debug.Print strTable & " not found; about to copy it"
    DoCmd.CopyObject destinationdatabase:=strCallingDb, _
        newname:=strTable, _
        sourceobjectType:=acTable, _
        sourceobjectname:=strTable
End If

Set ctr = dbsCalling.Containers("Reports")
strReport = "zsrptTableAndFieldNames"
Set doc = ctr.Documents(strReport)
If doc Is Nothing Then
    DoCmd.CopyObject destinationdatabase:=strCallingDb, _
        newname:=strReport, _
        sourceobjectType:=acReport, _
        sourceobjectname:=strReport
End If

strReport = "zsrptQueryAndFieldNames"
Set doc = ctr.Documents(strReport)
If doc Is Nothing Then
    DoCmd.CopyObject destinationdatabase:=strCallingDb, _
        newname:=strReport, _
        sourceobjectType:=acReport, _
        sourceobjectname:=strReport
End If

ErrorHandlerExit:
    Exit Function

ErrorHandler:
    MsgBox "Error No: " & err.Number _
        & "; Description: " & err.Description
    Resume ErrorHandlerExit

End Function
```

Back up Database

The BackupFrontEnd function is called from the USysRegInfo table to back up the current database to the path selected in the Extra Options dialog:

```
Public Function BackupFrontEnd()
'Called from USysRegInfo

On Error GoTo ErrorHandler

    Set dbsCalling = CurrentDb
    Set tdfsCalling = dbsCalling.TableDefs
    Set fso = CreateObject("Scripting.FileSystemObject")
    strCurrentDB = Application.CurrentProject.Name
    Debug.Print "Current db: " & strCurrentDB
    intExtPosition = InStr(strCurrentDB, ".")
    strExtension = Mid(strCurrentDB, intExtPosition)
    intExtLength = Len(strExtension)
```

Create the backup path string depending on the user's choice, with a default of 2 ("Backups folder under the database folder") in case the user has not made a choice:

```
    strPropName = "BackupChoice"
    strBackupChoice = GetProperty(strPropName, "2")
    Debug.Print "Backup choice: " & strBackupChoice
    strPropName = "BackupPath"
    strPath = GetProperty(strPropName, "")
    Debug.Print "Custom backup path: " & strPath

    Select Case strBackupChoice

        Case "1"
```

Same folder as database

```
            strBackupPath = _
                Application.CurrentProject.Path & "\"

        Case "2"
```

Backups folder under database folder

```
            strBackupPath = _
                Application.CurrentProject.Path & "\Backups\"

        Case "3"
```

Custom folder

```
            strBackupPath = strPath & "\"

      End Select

      Debug.Print "Backup path: " & strBackupPath
```

Check whether the path is valid.

```
   On Error Resume Next

      Set sfld = fso.GetFolder(strBackupPath)
      If sfld Is Nothing Then
         If strBackupChoice = "3" Then
            strTitle = "Invalid path"
            strPrompt = strBackupPath _
               & " is an invalid path; please select " _
               & "another custom path"
            MsgBox strPrompt, vbOKOnly + vbExclamation, strTitle
            GoTo ErrorHandlerExit
         ElseIf strBackupChoice = "2" Then
```

Create folder.

```
            Set sfld = fso.CreateFolder(strBackupPath)
         End If
      End If
```

If setup has not been done, copy zstblBackupInfo to the calling database:

```
      strCallingDb = CurrentDb.Name
      strTable = "zstblBackupInfo"
      Set tdfCalling = dbsCalling.TableDefs(strTable)

      If tdfCalling Is Nothing Then
         Debug.Print strTable & " not found; about to copy it"
         DoCmd.CopyObject destinationdatabase:=strCallingDb, _
            newname:=strTable, _
            sourceobjectType:=acTable, _
            sourceobjectname:=strTable
         Debug.Print "Copied " & strTable
      End If
```

Create a proposed save name for the backup database file:

```
      strDayPrefix = Format(Date, "mm-dd-yyyy")
      strSaveName = Left(strCurrentDB, _
         Len(strCurrentDB) - intExtLength) & " Copy " & SaveNo _
         & ", " & strDayPrefix & strExtension
```

490

```
strProposedSaveName = strBackupPath & strSaveName
Debug.Print "Backup save name: " & strProposedSaveName
strTitle = "Database backup"
strPrompt = "Save database to " & strProposedSaveName _
    & "?"
strSaveName = Nz(InputBox(prompt:=strPrompt, _
    title:=strTitle, Default:=strProposedSaveName))
```

Deal with user canceling out of the InputBox.

```
If strSaveName = "" Then
    GoTo ErrorHandlerExit
End If

Set rst = dbsCalling.OpenRecordset("zstblBackupInfo")
With rst
    .AddNew
    ![SaveDate] = Format(Date, "d-mmm-yyyy")
    ![SaveNumber] = SaveNo
    .Update
    .Close
End With

fso.CopyFile Source:=CurrentDb.Name, _
    destination:=strSaveName

ErrorHandlerExit:
    Exit Function

ErrorHandler:
    MsgBox "Error No: " & err.Number & "; Description: " & _
        err.Description
    Resume ErrorHandlerExit

End Function
```

Back up Back End Database

The BackupBackEnd function is called from the USysRegInfo table to back up the current database's back end (if there is one) to the path selected in the Extra Options dialog:

```
Public Function BackupBackEnd()
'Called from USysRegInfo

On Error GoTo ErrorHandler

    Dim strBackEndDBNameAndPath As String
    Dim strBackEndDBName As String
    Dim strBackEndDBPath As String
    Dim strFilePath As String
```

```
Dim strFullDBName As String
Dim strFileName As String
Dim strFullPath() As String
Dim strDBName As String
Dim intUBound As Integer
Dim strConnect As String

Set dbsCalling = CurrentDb
Set tdfsCalling = dbsCalling.TableDefs
Set fso = CreateObject("Scripting.FileSystemObject")
strCurrentDB = Application.CurrentProject.Name
Debug.Print "Current db: " & strCurrentDB
strDayPrefix = Format(Date, "mm-dd-yyyy")
intExtPosition = InStr(strCurrentDB, ".")
strExtension = Mid(strCurrentDB, intExtPosition)
intExtLength = Len(strExtension)
strExcludeTable = "zstblTablePrefixes"
```

Create backup path string depending on user choice.

```
strPropName = "BackupChoice"
strBackupChoice = GetProperty(strPropName, "2")
Debug.Print "Backup choice: " & strBackupChoice
strPropName = "BackupPath"
strPath = GetProperty(strPropName, "")
Debug.Print "Custom backup path: " & strPath
```

Check whether there are any linked tables, and exit if not.

```
strBackEndDBNameAndPath = ""

On Error Resume Next
```

Get back end database name from Connect property of a table.

```
For Each tdfCalling In tdfsCalling
   strTable = tdfCalling.Name
   Debug.Print "Table name: " & strTable
   strConnect = Nz(tdfCalling.Connect)
   Debug.Print "Connect property: " & strConnect
   If strConnect <> "" Then
      strBackEndDBNameAndPath = Mid(strConnect, _
         InStr(strConnect, "=") + 1)
      Debug.Print "Back end db name and path: " _
         & strBackEndDBNameAndPath
      GoTo ContinueBackup
   End If

Next tdfCalling

On Error GoTo ErrorHandler
```

No linked tables found.

```
strTitle = "No back end"
strPrompt = "There are no linked tables in this database; " _
    & "please use the Back up Database command instead"
MsgBox strPrompt, vbExclamation + vbOKOnly, strTitle
GoTo ErrorHandlerExit
```

```
ContinueBackup:
```

Extract back end name and path from Connect property string.

```
strFullPath = Split(strBackEndDBNameAndPath, "\", -1, _
    vbTextCompare)
intUBound = UBound(strFullPath)
strBackEndDBName = strFullPath(intUBound)
strBackEndDBPath = Mid(strBackEndDBNameAndPath, 1, _
    Len(strBackEndDBNameAndPath) - Len(strBackEndDBName))
Debug.Print "Database name: " & strBackEndDBName
Debug.Print "Database path: " & strBackEndDBPath
```

```
On Error Resume Next
```

Check whether back end path is valid.

```
Set sfld = fso.GetFolder(strBackEndDBPath)
If sfld Is Nothing Then
    strTitle = "Invalid path"
    strPrompt = strBackEndDBPath _
        & " is an invalid path; please re-link tables and try
again"
    MsgBox strPrompt, vbOKOnly + vbExclamation, strTitle
    GoTo ErrorHandlerExit
End If
```

If setup has not been done, copy zstblBackupInfo to calling database.

```
strCallingDb = CurrentDb.Name
strTable = "zstblBackupInfo"
Set tdfCalling = dbsCalling.TableDefs(strTable)

If tdfCalling Is Nothing Then
    Debug.Print strTable & " not found; about to copy it"
    DoCmd.CopyObject destinationdatabase:=strCallingDb, _
        newname:=strTable, _
        sourceobjectType:=acTable, _
        sourceobjectname:=strTable
    Debug.Print "Copied " & strTable
End If
```

```
        Select Case strBackupChoice

            Case "1"
```

Same folder as back end database

```
                strBackupPath = strBackEndDBPath

            Case "2"
```

Backups folder under back end database folder

```
                strBackupPath = strBackEndDBPath & "Backups\"

            Case "3"
```

Custom folder

```
                strBackupPath = strPath

        End Select

        Debug.Print "Backup path: " & strBackupPath

    On Error Resume Next
```

Recheck whether selected path is valid.

```
        Set sfld = fso.GetFolder(strBackupPath)
        If sfld Is Nothing Then
            If strBackupChoice = "3" Then
                strTitle = "Invalid path"
                strPrompt = strBackupPath _
                  & " is an invalid path; please select another custom
    path"
                MsgBox strPrompt, vbOKOnly + vbExclamation, strTitle
                GoTo ErrorHandlerExit
            ElseIf strBackupChoice = "2" Then
```

Create folder.

```
                Set sfld = fso.CreateFolder(strBackupPath)
            End If
        End If

    On Error GoTo ErrorHandler
```

Create proposed save name for backup.

```
        strDayPrefix = Format(Date, "mm-dd-yyyy")
        strSaveName = Left(strBackEndDBName, _
```

```
            Len(strBackEndDBName) - intExtLength) _
            & " Copy " & BackEndSaveNo _
            & ", " & strDayPrefix & strExtension
        strProposedSaveName = strBackupPath & strSaveName
        Debug.Print "Backup save name: " & strProposedSaveName
        strTitle = "Database backup"
        strPrompt = "Save back end database to " _
            & strProposedSaveName & "?"
        strSaveName = Nz(InputBox(prompt:=strPrompt, _
            title:=strTitle, Default:=strProposedSaveName))
```

Deal with user canceling out of the InputBox.

```
        If strSaveName = "" Then
            GoTo ErrorHandlerExit
        End If

        Set rst = dbsCalling.OpenRecordset("zstblBackupInfo")
        With rst
            .AddNew
            ![BackEndSaveDate] = Format(Date, "d-mmm-yyyy")
            ![BackEndSaveNumber] = BackEndSaveNo
            .Update
            .Close
        End With

        fso.CopyFile Source:=strBackEndDBNameAndPath, _
            destination:=strSaveName

ErrorHandlerExit:
    Exit Function

ErrorHandler:
    MsgBox "Error No: " & Err.Number _
        & "; Description: " & Err.Description
    Resume ErrorHandlerExit

End Function
```

List Query Fields

The ListQueryFields function (called from the USysRegInfo table) lists the fields in all the select queries in the database, using the QueryDefs collection of the DAO object model:

```
        Public Function ListQueryFields()
        'Called from USysRegInfo

        On Error Resume Next

            Call CopyListObjects
```

```
Set dbsCode = CodeDb
Set dbsCalling = CurrentDb
```

Delete old table in code database (if there is one).

```
strTable = "zstblQueryAndFieldNames"
Set tdfsCode = dbsCode.TableDefs
Set tdfCode = tdfsCode(strTable)
If Not tdfCode Is Nothing Then
    tdfsCode.Delete (strTable)
End If
```

Delete old table in calling database (if there is one).

```
Set tdfsCalling = dbsCalling.TableDefs
Set tdfCalling = tdfsCalling(strTable)
If Not tdfCalling Is Nothing Then
    tdfsCalling.Delete (strTable)
End If
```

Create a new, blank table in the code database to fill with data:

```
DoCmd.CopyObject destinationdatabase:=strCodeDB, _
    newname:=strTable, _
    sourceobjectType:=acTable, _
    sourceobjectname:=strTable & "Blank"
```

Fill the table in the code database with table and field names from the calling database:

```
Set rst = dbsCode.OpenRecordset(strTable, dbOpenTable)
strExcludeTable = "zstblQueryPrefixes"

For Each qdf In dbsCalling.QueryDefs
    strQuery = qdf.Name
    Debug.Print "Query name: " & strQuery
    If ExcludePrefix(strQuery, strExcludeTable) = _
       False Then
       Set flds = qdf.Fields
       For Each fld In flds
          strFieldName = fld.Name
          With rst
             .AddNew
             !QueryName = strQuery
             !FieldName = strFieldName
             !DataType = fld.Type
             !Required = fld.Required
             .Update
          End With
       Next fld
    End If
```

```
        Next qdf

        rst.Close
```

Copy the filled table to the calling database so it will be available for printing in the calling database:

```
        strTable = "zstblQueryAndFieldNames"
        Set tdfCode = dbsCode.TableDefs(strTable)
        DoCmd.CopyObject destinationdatabase:=strCallingDb, _
            newname:=strTable, _
            sourceobjectType:=acTable, _
            sourceobjectname:=strTable

        DoCmd.OpenTable strTable

        strTitle = "Table filled"
        strPrompt = "Print report now?"
        intReturn = MsgBox(strPrompt, vbQuestion + vbYesNo, _
            strTitle)
        If intReturn = vbYes Then
            strReport = "zsrptQueryAndFieldNames"
            DoCmd.OpenReport strReport
        End If

ErrorHandlerExit:
    Exit Function

ErrorHandler:
    MsgBox "Error No: " & err.Number _
        & "; Description: " & err.Description
    Resume ErrorHandlerExit

End Function
```

List Table Fields

The `ListTableFields` function (called from the USysRegInfo table) lists the fields in all the tables in the database, using the TableDefs collection of the DAO object model:

```
        Public Function ListTableFields()
        'Called from USysRegInfo

        On Error Resume Next

            Call CopyListObjects
            Set dbsCode = CodeDb
            Set dbsCalling = CurrentDb
```

Delete the old table in code database (if there is one):

```
strTable = "zstblTableAndFieldNames"
Set tdfsCode = dbsCode.TableDefs
Set tdfCode = tdfsCode(strTable)
If Not tdfCode Is Nothing Then
    tdfsCode.Delete (strTable)
End If
```

Delete the old table in the calling database (if there is one):

```
Set tdfsCalling = dbsCalling.TableDefs
Set tdfCalling = tdfsCalling(strTable)
If Not tdfCalling Is Nothing Then
    tdfsCalling.Delete (strTable)
End If
```

Create a new, blank table in the code database to fill with data:

```
DoCmd.CopyObject destinationdatabase:=strCodeDB, _
    newname:=strTable, _
    sourceobjectType:=acTable, _
    sourceobjectname:=strTable & "Blank"
```

Fill the table in the code database with table and field names from the calling database:

```
Set rst = dbsCode.OpenRecordset(strTable, dbOpenTable)
strExcludeTable = "zstblTablePrefixes"

For Each tdfCalling In dbsCalling.TableDefs
    strTable = tdfCalling.Name
    If ExcludePrefix(strTable, strExcludeTable) = _
        False Then
        Set flds = tdfCalling.Fields
        For Each fld In flds
            strFieldName = fld.Name
            With rst
                .AddNew
                !TableName = strTable
                !FieldName = strFieldName
                !DataType = fld.Type
                !ValidationRule = fld.ValidationRule
                !Required = fld.Required
                .Update
            End With
        Next fld
    End If
Next tdfCalling

rst.Close
```

Copy the filled table to the calling database so it will be available for printing in the calling database:

```
strTable = "zstblTableAndFieldNames"
Set tdfCode = dbsCode.TableDefs(strTable)
DoCmd.CopyObject destinationdatabase:=strCallingDb, _
    newname:=strTable, _
    sourceobjectType:=acTable, _
    sourceobjectname:=strTable

DoCmd.OpenTable strTable

strTitle = "Table filled"
strPrompt = "Print report now?"
intReturn = MsgBox(strPrompt, vbQuestion + vbYesNo, _
    strTitle)
If intReturn = vbYes Then
    strReport = "zsrptTableAndFieldNames"
    DoCmd.OpenReport strReport
End If

ErrorHandlerExit:
    Exit Function

ErrorHandler:
    MsgBox "Error No: " & err.Number _
        & "; Description: " & err.Description
    Resume ErrorHandlerExit

End Function
```

Other Procedures

The SetProperty and GetProperty functions are called from various procedures in the add-in to save values to custom database properties, or retrieve values from them:

```
Public Sub SetProperty(strName As String, lngType As Long, _
    varValue As Variant)
'Called from various procedures

On Error GoTo ErrorHandler
```

Attempt to set the specified property:

```
Set dbsCalling = CurrentDb
Set prps = dbsCalling.Properties
prps(strName) = varValue

ErrorHandlerExit:
    Exit Sub
```

```
ErrorHandler:
    If err.Number = 3270 Then
```

The property was not found; create it:

```
        Set prp = dbsCalling.CreateProperty(Name:=strName, _
            Type:=lngType, Value:=varValue)
        dbsCalling.Properties.Append prp
        Resume Next
    Else
        MsgBox "Error No: " & err.Number _
            & "; Description: " & err.Description
        Resume ErrorHandlerExit
    End If

End Sub

Public Function GetProperty(strName As String, _
    strDefault As String) As Variant
'Called from various procedures

On Error GoTo ErrorHandler
```

Attempt to get the value of the specified property:

```
        Set dbsCalling = CurrentDb
        GetProperty = dbsCalling.Properties(strName).Value

ErrorHandlerExit:
    Exit Function

ErrorHandler:
    If err.Number = 3270 Then
```

The property was not found; use default value:

```
        GetProperty = strDefault
        Resume Next
    Else
        MsgBox "Error No: " & err.Number _
            & "; Description: " & err.Description
        Resume ErrorHandlerExit
    End If

End Function
```

The SaveNo and BackEndSaveNo functions create an incremented number for the database (or back-end database) copies:

```
Public Function SaveNo() As String
'Called from BackupFrontEnd()

On Error GoTo ErrorHandler
```

Create a unique incrementing save number for today:

```
intDayNo = Nz(DMax("[SaveNumber]", "zstblBackupInfo", _
    "[SaveDate] = Date()"))
Debug.Print "Day no. " & intDayNo
strNextNo = CStr(intDayNo + 1)
Debug.Print "Next No. " & strNextNo
SaveNo = strNextNo

ErrorHandlerExit:
    Exit Function

ErrorHandler:
    MsgBox "Error No: " & err.Number & "; Description: " & _
        err.Description
    Resume ErrorHandlerExit

End Function

Public Function BackEndSaveNo() As String
'Called from BackupBackEnd()

On Error GoTo ErrorHandler
```

Create a unique save number for today:

```
intDayNo = Nz(DMax("[BackEndSaveNumber]", _
    "zstblBackupInfo", _
    "[BackEndSaveDate] = Date()"))
Debug.Print "Back end Day no. " & intDayNo
strNextNo = CStr(intDayNo + 1)
Debug.Print "Back end Next No. " & strNextNo
BackEndSaveNo = strNextNo

ErrorHandlerExit:
    Exit Function

ErrorHandler:
    MsgBox "Error No: " & err.Number & "; Description: " & _
        err.Description
    Resume ErrorHandlerExit

End Function
```

Finalizing the Add-in

After getting your functions, forms, and other objects to work correctly, the final step is to enter identifying information into specific properties of the library database's properties sheet, to give users information about the add-in when it is listed in the Add-In Manager dialog. The information about an add-in that appears in the Add-In Manager dialog comes from the Summary page of the add-in database's properties sheet. To open the properties sheet for the add-in, select File, Manage, Database Properties, as shown in Figure 14.8.

FIGURE 14.8
_____

Opening the database properties sheet.

Once opened, the properties sheet looks like the one in Access 2003 (shown in Figure 14.9).

The text you enter in the library database's properties sheet is used as follows:

- The Title field's value is displayed as the add-in's name in the list of available add-ins.

- The value of the Company field (not the Author field, as you might expect) appears as the add-in author's name under the list of available add-ins.

- The Comments field's value appears as the add-in's description at the bottom of the Add-In Manager dialog.

FIGURE 14.9

Entering the add-in's identification information in the properties sheet.

Troubleshooting Add-ins

If you need to step through add-in code to determine what is causing a problem, you have two options. One is to place a Stop statement in the add-in code, which will stop the code at that point when it is executing, so you can step through the code from that point. To do this, you must first close any open database, then open the add-in library database and add the Stop statement, save and close the add-in, then open a database and run the add-in that has the Stop statement in its code. Later, you will need to remove the Stop statement from the add-in code in a similar fashion.

The other (and quicker) alternative is to set a reference to the library database, so you can open its code modules and place breakpoints, and even modify the code temporarily, to test various alternatives. To set a reference to an Access add-in library database, complete the following steps:

> **TIP** If you plan to set a reference to a library database so you can step through its code easily (as described next), give its Visual Basic project a meaningful name, so it will say "Extras" (or whatever) instead of "Project1" in the References dialog. To name the VB project, open the Visual Basic window, select the project row (the top row) in the Project Explorer, and rename it in the Name property of the properties sheet, as shown in Figure 14.10.

FIGURE 14.10

Renaming an add-in's project.

1. Open a module in any Access database, and select Tools, References to open the References dialog, as shown in Figure 14.11.

FIGURE 14.11

The References dialog in Access 2007.

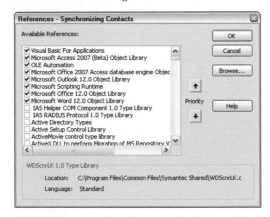

2. Click the Browse button to browse for the add-in library database, and select Add-ins (*.mda) in the Files of Type drop-down list, if you are setting a reference to an Access 2003 or earlier (.mda) library database, or All Files (*.*) to set a reference to an Access 2007 (.accda) library database (see Figure 14.12).

FIGURE 14.12

Setting a reference to an Access 2002-2003 library database.

3. Click Open to set the reference; the project name of the add-in now appears checked in the References dialog, as shown in Figure 14.13.

FIGURE 14.13

A reference to an add-in library database.

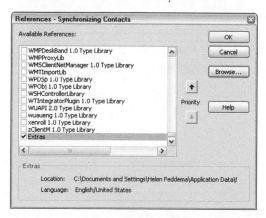

4. Now you can see the add-in project in the Project Explorer, and open its module(s) and work with them much like modules in the current database, as shown in Figure 14.14.

FIGURE 14.14

Opening an add-in module in the Visual Basic window of a database.

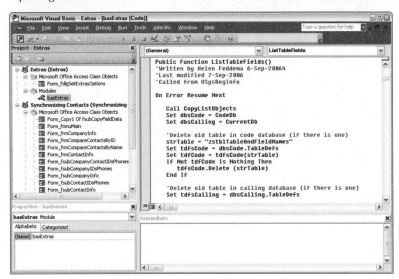

> **CAUTION** Though you can edit code in a library database after setting a reference to it, and run the code to test whether the modifications fix a problem, the changes aren't saved to the library database, so save any modified code to a text file, which you can then copy and paste into the library database when you next open it directly.

Interpreting Add-in Error Messages

You may get this error message (Figure 14.15) when running (or attempting to run) an add-in in Access 2007.

FIGURE 14.15

An error message when running an add-in.

Sometimes this error occurs when you have made changes to the add-in, but Access is still running the old code. In case this is the cause of the problem, try uninstalling the add-in from the Add-In Manager dialog, then reinstall it. In some cases, this will fix the problem. If you still get the error message after reinstalling the add-in, it may be because you created a sub instead of a function for use in the USysRegInfo table (only functions can be called from the Registry), or you changed the name of the function to be called, so the one in the Registry can't be found. Check that the function entries in the USysRegInfo table match the function names in the library database (and that the called procedures are functions, not subs).

If a form in your add-in doesn't appear when the function that should open it is run, without any error message, this may be because the form's record source is missing. You won't get an error; the form just doesn't open. Check that the form's record source exists, and is located in the code database, not the calling database. In some cases it may be necessary to fill a table in the calling database, and then copy it back to the code database to use as a form's record source, as I do in the Extras add-in.

If you get a "This feature is not installed" error message when trying to run the add-in, it might result from any number of errors in the add-in's code. First, check for problems in the following areas:

- Incorrect syntax in an add-in function (for example, the wrong number or type of arguments).
- Mismatch between the function name in the USysRegInfo table and the code module.
- The add-in's name was changed, but the reference to it in the USysRegInfo table still has the old name.
- General syntax errors in the add-in code.
- The add-in code has not been compiled.

Then, complete the following steps:

1. First uninstall the database and close Access.
2. Open the library database, fix any errors, and compile the add-in database.
3. Repeat as needed until the add-in runs without errors.

Installing an Add-in

An add-in only needs to be installed once in any Access database; after it is installed, it is available to all Access databases. To install the Extras 2007 add-in, first copy the library database to your AddIns folder. In Access 2007 running on Windows XP, the AddIns folder is in the same place as in Office 2003, C:\Documents and Settings*User Name*\Application Data\Microsoft\AddIns; if you are running Windows Vista, the AddIns folder is in J:\Users\Helen Feddema\AppData\Roaming\Microsoft\AddIns.

If you are attempting to install an add-in in Access 2007 running on Windows Vista, you may get a security warning. In that case, try running Access as an administrator, by right-clicking the MSACCESS.EXE file in the Office 12 subfolder under the Microsoft Office folder, and selecting the "Run as administrator" selection. Now, you should be able to install the add-in.

Another Vista requirement: In the USysRegInfo table, change the capitalization of "Menu Add-ins" (to "Menu Add-Ins", with a capital I). According to Microsoft, this case sensitivity will be addressed in an upcoming service patch, but you need to make the change to enable menu add-ins to work in Vista right now.

If you prefer to keep your own add-ins in a custom folder, you can add another folder to the list of trusted locations by selecting File, Access Options, and then selecting the Trust Center page of the Access Options dialog, as shown in Figure 14.16.

 See the "Getting Your Add-ins to Work in Vista" sidebar in Chapter 15 for more information about the specific requirements for installing add-ins in Windows Vista.

FIGURE 14.16

The Trust Center page of the Access Options dialog box.

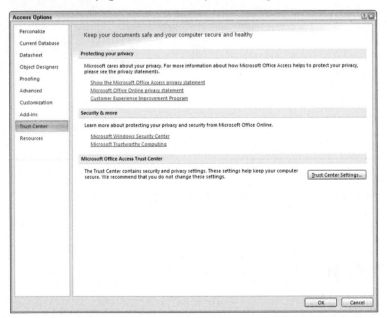

Click the Trust Center Settings button and select the Trusted Locations page. Next, use the "Add new location" button to add the folder where you want to store your add-ins, as shown in Figure 14.17.

Next, open any Access database, and select the Database Tools tab of the Ribbon, click the Add-Ins drop-down in the Database Tools group, and select Add-In Manager (see Figure 14.18).

FIGURE 14.17

Adding a folder to the Trusted Locations group.

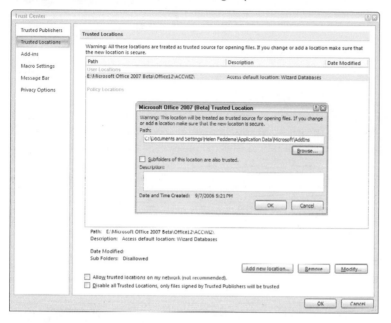

FIGURE 14.18

Opening the Add-In Manager in Access 2007.

Once you have opened the Add-In Manager, it looks just like the familiar dialog from earlier versions of Access, listing the add-ins that are found in the AddIns folder, and letting you install or uninstall them. To install the Extras 2007 add-in, select it and click the Install button, as shown in Figure 14.19.

Installing the Extras 2007 add-in.

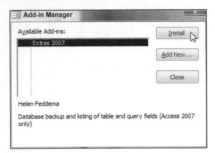

After clicking Install, an x appears to the left of the installed add-in, and when you close the Add-In Manager, several new selections appear on the Add-Ins menu, as shown in Figure 14.20.

Add-ins from the Extras 2007.accda library database on the Add-Ins menu.

NOTE The three menu add-ins starting with "Rename" at the bottom of the list are from my LNC Rename add-in.

Using the Extras 2007 Add-in

After installing the Extras 2007.accda add-in, you can run its three menu add-ins from the Add-Ins menu, which is found in the Database Tools group on the Database Tools Ribbon.

TIP If you are creating an add-in that can be used in several versions of Access (it doesn't need any special new features of Access 2007, and doesn't create menus or toolbars that will only work in older versions), create the add-in in an older format, so it can run in both the older version(s) and Access 2007. The LNC Rename.mda add-in will run in any version of Access from Access 2000 through Access 2007, at least if you are running on Windows XP.

Signing Add-in Code with a Digital Signature — Not!

You may be used to signing code in Access 2003 (or earlier) databases with a digital signature (see the "Creating a Digital Signature for Signing Your Access VBA Code" Sidebar in Chapter 12 for details on how to create your personal digital signature). It might seem like a good idea to sign an Access 2007 add-in's code with a digital signature—but if you try it, you will run into roadblocks. After creating a personal digital signature, if you try to select the signature from Tools, Digital Signature in the add-in's module window, you will get a lengthy and puzzling message (see the figure below). Note that the .accda format is not mentioned.

You can follow the instructions for an .accdb database, and select File, Publish, Package and Sign from the library database, select the digital signature, and create a signed package (it will have the .accdc extension). But if you attempt to install the .accdc file as an add-in, you will get an "Unrecognized database format" error message, and you can't install the signed package file. Thus (at the present time, at least) there is no way to digitally sign an Access 2007 add-in library database.

Extras Options

This selection opens a setup dialog (shown in Figure 14.21) with an option group for selecting the folder for storing database backups, and two subforms listing the table and query prefixes for tables and queries you would like to omit when using the List Query Fields or List Table Fields add-ins. These tables are pre-filled with system prefixes, dashes and underscores, and "Copy Of" (the latter is the prefix used in Access 2007 object copies).

If you select the Custom Path option, a command button is enabled that opens a Folder Picker dialog where you can select a custom backup folder. The backup choice is stored separately for each database, using database properties; the prefixes, however, are stored in the code database, so they are the same for all databases.

You don't need to open the Extras setup dialog to use the other menu add-ins; if you haven't made any selections, the code uses the default backup choice of option 2 (Backups folder under database folder), and the standard prefixes.

FIGURE 14.21

The Extras 2007 add-ins Setup dialog.

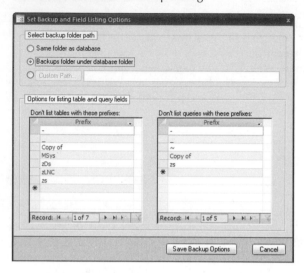

Back up Database

This option makes a backup of the current database (either a standalone database or a front-end database), presenting the proposed name of the database copy in an InputBox, so you can edit it if desired, for example to add specific information about a milestone achieved. The InputBox is shown in Figure 14.22.

Back up Back End Database

This option makes a backup of the current database's back end database, if there is one, and puts up an informative message if the database doesn't contain any linked tables. The InputBox is similar to that for the Back up Database menu add-in.

FIGURE 14.22

A proposed name for a backup copy of the Northwind sample database.

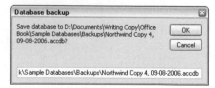

List Query Fields

This command fills a table with the names of select queries (omitting those whose prefixes are on the Exclude list), and their field names, and offers to print a report based on that table. The table is shown in Figure 14.23.

 Only select queries will be listed. Although queries of other types (action queries) are listed by name in the QueryDefs collection, they have no fields to list.

FIGURE 14.23

A table filled with query names and fields.

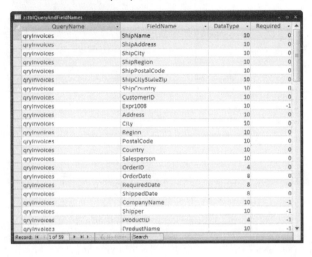

Note the Expr1008 field name, indicating that the same field is included in the query twice. The fields in the table are listed in the order that they occur in the query in design view; the report based on this table gives an alphabetical listing, as shown in Figure 14.24.

The table and report are stored in the calling database, and thus they can be opened later without re-running the menu add-in.

FIGURE 14.24

The Query and Field Names report.

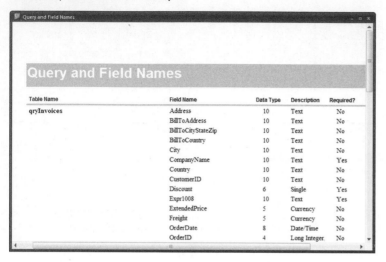

List Table Fields

This add-in works the same as the List Query Fields add-in, except that it lists tables and their fields instead of queries and their fields.

Access add-ins, once you have learned the special techniques needed to create them, are a great way of enhancing your Access databases with extra functionality, even supporting multiple versions of Access.

Summary

This chapter dealt with creating Access add-ins in the Access 2007 (.accda) library database format (you can use the same techniques to create add-ins in the older .mda format for use with databases created in previous Access database formats as well as Access 2007). Access add-ins let you encapsulate a set of database objects (primarily code and forms), for use in any Access database, as a way of adding extra functionality to a database without the need to manually import objects into any database where you need the functionality.

The next chapter covers using Ribbon XML to work with the Access ribbon, in Access add-ins as well as other types of add-ins.

Chapter 15

Customizing the Ribbon with XML in Access Databases and Add-ins

A s a power user or developer, you may be used to manually customizing the Access toolbars and menus, removing controls you don't need, moving others to more convenient locations, and in general reorganizing the toolbars and menus just as you prefer, and you may have written functions to run from custom toolbar buttons or menu commands. If you expect to continue these practices in Access 2007, you're in for a shock.

The new Office 2007 Ribbon is a major interface change for Access (as well as the other Office applications), and it requires a major change in programming techniques for customizing the Access interface. Instead of working with the CommandBars collection to create menus and toolbars, or add commands to the standard ones, you customize the Ribbon with XML code stored in a table, working with tabs and groups instead of menus and toolbars (although the Ribbon does include one menu — the Office menu — and one toolbar — the Quick Access Toolbar).

For other Office applications, such as Word and Excel, Ribbon customization requires creating and loading a separate XML document, but in Access, you have a much more convenient option: just create a table containing the XML code for creating the Ribbon, load it automatically by closing and reopening the database, and then select the Ribbon you want to use from the Access Options screen. After one more closing and reopening of the database, your Ribbon customizations will appear.

Sources of Information on Customizing the Ribbon

The MSDN document "Customizing the Office (2007) Ribbon User Interface for Developers" (Parts 1 through 3) is a very useful reference when creating Ribbon XML for Access (and other Office applications).

The list of Control IDs (Access Ribbon Controls.xls) is invaluable for working with the Ribbon; it lists the control, group, and tab names you need to use when creating Ribbon XML code. You can download this worksheet from `http://www.microsoft.com/downloads/details.aspx?family id=4329d9e9-4d11-46a5-898d-23e4f331e9ae&displaylang=en` on the Microsoft web site.

Several blogs are also valuable resources for information on working with the Ribbon in VBA or VB code: In Erik Rucker's blog, see the July 13, 2006 posting on Customizing the New Access UI for information on customizing the Access Ribbon. The blogs maintained by Jensen Harris and Patrick Schmid have lots of valuable information on Ribbon customization (Jensen Harris is the program manager in charge of the Office UI team, and Patrick Schmid is an MVP). The Third of Five blog is also useful. See the Office Developer Center web site for the latest list of Office-related blogs. However, note that this worksheet was last updated in November 2006, and some of the names have changed since then, so it is not entirely accurate, especially for group and tab names.

Here are links to the resources mentioned in the previous paragraph:

- Customizing the Office (2007) Ribbon User Interface for Developers, Parts 1 through 3:
    - `http://msdn2.microsoft.com/en-us/library/ms406046.` `aspx#OfficeCustomizingRibbonUIforDevelopers_AppLevel`
    - `http://msdn2.microsoft.com/en-us/library/aa338199.aspx`
    - `http://msdn2.microsoft.com/en-us/library/aa722523.aspx`
- Office 2007 Developer Center: `http://msdn2.microsoft.com/en-us/office/` `aa905358.aspx`
- Ribbon Extensibility in Access 2007: `http://msdn2.microsoft.com/en-us/` `library/bb187398.aspx`
- Transitioning Your Existing Access Applications to Access 2007: `http://msdn2.` `microsoft.com/en-us/library/bb203849.aspx`
- Erik Rucker's blog: `http://blogs.msdn.com/access`
- Jensen Harris' blog: `http://blogs.msdn.com/jensenh/default.aspx`
- Patrick Schmid's blog: `http://pschmid.net/blog/2006/10/09/58`
- Third of Five Blog: `http://blogs.msdn.com/thirdoffive/`

Useful Tools for Creating and Editing XML Code

Though you can create XML code in any text editor — even Notepad — it is a lot easier to create and edit XML code in a specialized editor. Several XML editors are available free of charge, or as part of another application; they are described in the following sections.

XML Notepad 2007

One such tool is XML Notepad 2007, available as a free download from the Downloads page of the Microsoft web site, at the following link.

```
http://www.microsoft.com/downloads/details.aspx?FamilyID=72d6aa49
-787d-4118-ba5f-4f30fe913628&DisplayLang=en
```

Figure 15.1 shows the TreeView tab of the XML Notepad editor, with the List Fields XML code. This view shows each attribute on a separate line of the tree in the left pane, with its value displayed in the right pane.

CAUTION   The XML Notepad 2007 utility was updated towards the end of the beta of Office 2007/Windows Vista, and it worked well at that time. Unfortunately, in the release version of Vista, it has a curious problem: it will only run minimized or maximized, not restored. Hopefully this glitch will clear up with a patch some time soon. Until that time, when you run this utility, it will appear minimized; right-click its taskbar icon and select Maximize to open it full-screen.

FIGURE 15.1

The Tree View tab of the XML Notepad 2007 editor.

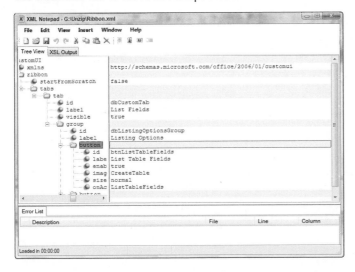

The XSL Output tab of this editor shows the code in an indented layout, as shown in Figure 15.2.

VB 2005 XML Editor

If you have a recent edition of VB .NET, Visual Basic, or Visual Studio (2005 and up), you can use the XML editor that is a component of these programs. If you have the Express Edition of Visual Basic 2005, SQL Server 2005, or Visual Web Developer 2005 (free downloads from the Visual Studio page of the Microsoft web site found here: `http://msdn.microsoft.com/vstudio/express/vb/download/`), these editions of VB and SQL Server also contain XML editors. See Figure 15.4 later in this chapter for a view of XML code in this editor.

FIGURE 15.2

The XSL Output tab of the XML Notepad 2007 editor.

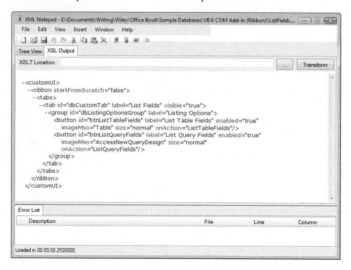

Office 2007 Custom UI Editor

From `http://openxmldeveloper.org/archive/2006/05/26/CustomUIeditor.aspx` you can download the Custom UI Editor Tool, for use in writing XML code to customize the Office 2007 Ribbon.

I installed this utility, attempted to open a saved XML file in it (one that opened fine in the VB 2005 Express XML editor and XML Notepad 2007), and got a message that the file contains corrupted data. However, I was able to copy XML code to the clipboard and paste it into the editor window. The Custom UI Editor (see Figure 15.3) is not as useful for editing XML Ribbon code as either the VB 2005 XML Editor or XML Notepad 2007, so I would recommend using one of those editors instead.

If you have Visual Studio 2005 (any edition), use its built-in XML editor; otherwise, I recommend the XML Notepad 2007 editor for working with XML code.

XML code in the Office 2007 Custom UI Editor.

```
Microsoft Office 2007 Custom UI Editor

File    Edit    Sample

Custom UI

<customUI xmlns="http://schemas.microsoft.com/office/2006/01/customui">
    <ribbon startFromScratch="false">
        <tabs>
            <tab id="dbCustomTab"
                label="List Fields"
                visible="true">
                <group id="dbListingOptionsGroup"
                    label="Listing Options">
                    <button id="btnListTableFields"
                        label="List Table Fields"
                        enabled="true"
                        imageMso="Table"
                        size="normal"
                        onAction="ListTableFields"/>
                    <button id="btnListQueryFields"
                        label="List Query Fields"
                        enabled="true"
                        imageMso="AccessNewQueryDesign"
                        size="normal"
                        onAction="ListQueryFields"/>
                </group>
            </tab>
        </tabs>
    </ribbon>
</customUI>

No document is currently opened...                          Ln 25  Col 12
```

Customizing the Ribbon in an Access Database

If you want to add tabs, groups, or controls to the Ribbon in an Access database, you have to write XML and (optionally) VBA code — unlike customizing toolbars and menus, you can't just drag a command to a location on any toolbar or menu, as in previous versions of Access. The only manual customization available in Access 2007 is adding commands to the Quick Access Toolbar. In a major change from previous versions of Office, you can't programmatically add commands to standard Ribbon groups, or remove standard commands from groups, although you can hide tabs completely, and add new groups containing custom commands.

Patrick Schmid on Access 2007 Ribbon Customizability

The best discussion of Access 2007 Ribbon customizability (or the lack thereof) is from the October 18, 2006 entry on MVP Patrick Schmid's blog:

If you ask me about the customizability of the new Ribbon UI in Office 2007, my answer would be: too little, too difficult. Compared to previous Office versions, especially Office 2003, 2007 simply has a serious customization deficiency. In fact, most users will probably conclude that the Ribbon cannot be customized at all.

In contrast, Office 2003 is the most customizable Office ever. You can locate your menus and toolbars anywhere you want on the screen, create your own menus and toolbars, change icons and labels, modify toolbars and menus, and so on. There is almost no limit as to what components of the UI a user can alter. Customizing Office 2003 is also easy to do, as alteration can be achieved with a few mouse clicks.

The Ribbon UI of Office 2007 though is a completely different story. Static with very limited customizability is probably the description most users would give this new UI. Most users probably only discover the Quick Access Toolbar (QAT) and then conclude that this must be it. Is that really all there is? How did we end up with such a lack of customization?

Why Office 2007 has a customization deficiency

Microsoft had to create the Ribbon UI completely from scratch. If you have read through some of the Office UI Bible, you can get an idea of the huge amount of resources that went into creating this new UI. However, even at Microsoft resources are limited. Therefore, the need for every feature of the new UI had to be justified. Real customizability was unfortunately a feature that didn't make the cut.

As the Office UI Bible explains, the UI team could not make the case for customizability, if only ~1.9% of the Office 2003 sessions of roughly one hundred million users were with customization. The case is even weaker, as 85% of those customizations involve four or fewer buttons. Therefore, Microsoft decided to support the case encountered by 99.7% of all users: no customization or four or fewer buttons. That left the remaining 0.3% in the rain. Those 0.3% represent around 1.35 million people, as there are 450 million paid Office customers, and are also the ones who are most likely to participate in the Office development process, e.g., through participation in the beta. My opinion about this approach can be found in my designing with statistics post.

In addition to this argument, a highly customizable UI unfortunately presents a massive support issue. You can see this, if you try to remember how many times you accidentally moved a menu or toolbar in Office 2003, or customized it otherwise by accident. You probably know how to undo your accident, but many, many users do not.

Why do I keep calling it a customization deficiency?

Microsoft decided that in order to make those 99.7% of all users happy, one toolbar was enough. In order to prevent accidental customization and make sure users always have that toolbar accessible, it became non-floatable. Born therefore was the Quick Access Toolbar. That is not the end of the customization story though. There is also one Ribbon tab that you can hide or show, namely the Developer tab. You can also customize the status bar fully. Toolbars and menus created in a previous Office version and by legacy (meaning non-Office 2007) add-ins can also be used, but not created, in 2007. Last, but not least, galleries can be customized. Some "customize" themselves automatically, e.g. the recent document list or the shapes gallery. Others can be manually customized, especially in Word. For example, the galleries for page numbers, headers and footers can be customized by the user.

But that's it. Seriously, that is it. Everything else, especially the vast majority of the Ribbon, is static and cannot be customized. Therefore, describing Office 2007 as having a "customization deficiency" or complaining about the lack of customization in it, reflects appropriately the state of affairs in 2007.

Although you can't customize the standard Ribbon tabs and groups, you can add new tabs and groups to the Ribbon, though the technique is completely different than writing VBA code to work with CommandBars, as in past versions of Access. There are several steps to customizing the Ribbon in an Access database:

1. Write XML code to define the Ribbon customizations.
2. Create a table in the Access database to store the Ribbon names and their XML code.
3. (Optional) Write VBA callback procedures to run from custom Ribbon command buttons.
4. Close the database, then reopen it, to load the Ribbon(s) from the table.
5. Select the Ribbon to load into the database.
6. Close and reopen the database to load the Ribbon.

In addition to creating the XML code, VBA code (if needed), and table, you also have to close and reopen the database twice to get the Ribbon customizations to appear — once to load the Ribbon, and again after selecting the Ribbon to use in the database. The next few sections guide you through customizing the Ribbon in an Access database.

 The sample database for this section is Test Ribbon.accdb.

Creating the XML Code

Table 15.1 lists some of the most commonly used XML elements for customizing an Access 2007 Ribbon.

TABLE 15.1

XML Elements for Use in Customizing the Ribbon

Element Name	Usage	Comments
customUI	The top-level element for a custom Ribbon	
ribbon	The Ribbon definition	Set the startFromScratch attribute to "true" to create a new, blank Ribbon. (The quotes are needed, a difference from VBA code with its True and False keywords.) If set to "false" or omitted, the customizations are applied to the standard Ribbon.
tab	Creates or references a Ribbon tab	
group	Creates or references a group on a tab	
id	Unique name of a custom control	
idMso	Name of a standard control	
label	Text displayed on a control	
button	A command button on a Ribbon	The onAction attribute specifies the name of a function to run when the button is clicked.
dropDown	A drop-down list	Automatically limited to list selections.
comboBox	A drop-down list that allows manual entries	Users can enter selections or select from the list.
imageMso	The image to use for the control	Set with the name of a built-in Ribbon control (or a custom image you have created).
size	The size of the control	The choices are "normal" and "large".
supertip	The text to display in the pop-up that appears when your mouse hovers over a control	
visible	Whether the control is visible or not	The choices are "true" or "false".
enabled	Whether the control is enabled or not	The choices are "true" or "false".

> **NOTE** Element names in XML use camel-casing notation; the first letter of the element name is lowercase, and other components have their first letter capitalized (giving the appearance of a camel's hump). Example: dropDown.

You can start by creating a table to hold the Ribbon XML code, or create the XML code first, as you prefer. If you have just one table of Ribbon code, the convention is to call it USysRibbons, with the USys prefix indicating that it is a user-created system table. The table has three fields, as described in Table 15.2.

TABLE 15.2

The USysRibbons Table

Field Name	Data Type	Usage
ID	AutoNumber	Unique ID field
RibbonName	Text, 255	Name of the custom Ribbon
RibbonXML	Memo	The XML code with Ribbon settings

Viewing the USysRibbons Table

The USysRibbons table is a system table, so you won't see it unless you turn on display of system tables by opening the Access Options screen from the Office menu:

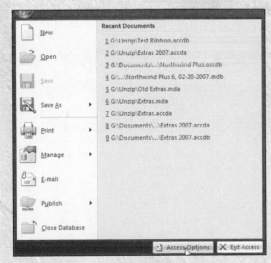

Opening the Access Options screen.

continued

continued

And then select the Current Database page and click the Navigation Options button:

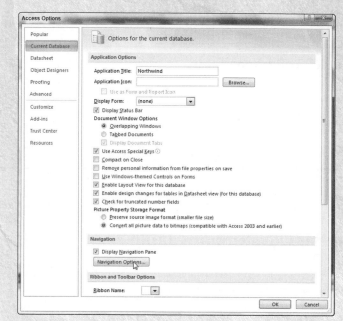

Opening the Navigation Options dialog.

On the Navigation Options dialog, check the "Show System Objects" checkbox:

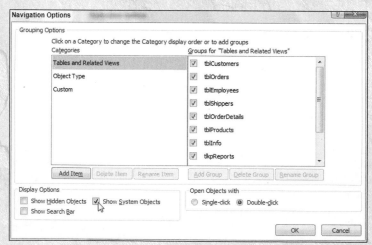

Turning on display of system objects in the Navigation Options dialog.

The following screen shot shows the USysRibbons table in datasheet view, with the record for the ListFields Ribbon visible:

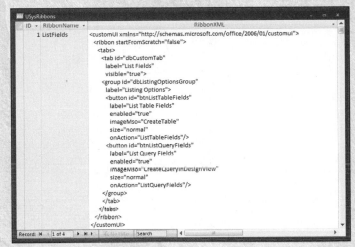

The USysDBRibbons table in datasheet view.

CROSS-REF For more exhaustive coverage of XML, see Wrox's *Beginning XML*.

Although you can edit the XML code directly in the Access USysRibbons table (use Ctrl+Enter to go to a new line), it's a lot easier working with it in an XML editor, such as the one in VB 2005 (standard or Express), or the XML Notepad 2007 utility. Figure 15.4 shows what the same code looks like in the XML Notepad 2007 editor, after opening the code saved as Ribbon.xml.

NOTE IntelliSense doesn't work for Access Ribbon XML code in Visual Basic 2005 Express, but it does work in Visual Studio 2005.

It is much easier to work with XML code in the XML Notepad 2007 or the Visual Studio 2005 editor. In the XML Notepad 2007 editor, you have a TreeView pane on the left, and each attribute is shown with its matching value in the right pane; in the Visual Studio 2005 editor, the components are color-coded and you have IntelliSense to aid in creating code. Bracket matching (see the shaded `<tabs>` and `</tabs>` names in the figure) also helps, in case you started a bracketed code segment and forgot to end it. For XML code in the Visual Studio 2005 editor, the colors have the meanings listed in Table 15.3.

FIGURE 15.4

XML code in the XML Notepad 2007 editor.

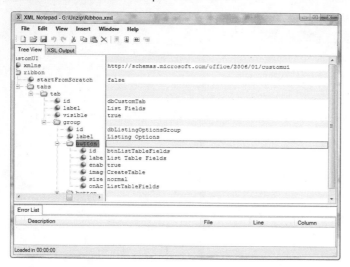

TABLE 15.3

Color-Coding for XML Code in the VB 2005 XML Editor

Color	Code Component(s)
Red	Attribute Name
Blue	Attribute Value Delimiter Keyword
Green	Comment
Brown	Name
Grey	Doc Tag Processing Instruction
Black	Text
Aqua	XSLT Keyword

NOTE   In order for XML documents to be able to use elements and attributes that have the same name but come from different sources, there must be a way to differentiate between different sources of markup elements. In XML, a namespace is a collection of names, identified by a URL reference, that are used as element types and attribute names in XML documents.

The XML code starts with specifying the namespace as `http://schemas.microsoft.com/office/2006/01/customui`. This is the only XML namespace used for Office 2007 Ribbons.

Next, the Ribbon's `startFromScratch` attribute is set to "false" (for VBA programmers, note that in XML code, the syntax is "false", with the quotes, not just False, as in VBA code). This setting means that you are modifying the standard toolbar, as opposed to creating a Ribbon from scratch.

The next sections show how to customize the Ribbon in various ways.

Adding a New Tab, Group, and Controls to the Ribbon

To create a custom tab for the Ribbon, under the <tabs> section of the XML code, add a tab line and set its id and label attributes as desired. The `id` attribute is a unique identifier for a custom Ribbon control that can be used elsewhere in XML code to reference the tab, and the `label` attribute is set with the caption text to display on the tab. Set the tab's visible attribute to "true" to display it. Next, create one or more groups for the custom tab, setting their id and label attributes with the names and captions of the groups. Finally, add one or more controls to a group (or several groups) on the tab; for the sample XML code I created two buttons, each of which runs a callback function.

CROSS-REF   See Table 15.1 for a list of the most commonly used elements for creating tabs, groups, and controls on the Ribbon.

Controls have (minimally) id and label attributes, and also an `enabled` attribute (usually set to `"true"`). They typically display an image, which is usually set with `imageMso` argument, using a value corresponding to the standard Ribbon button that has the image you want to display.

NOTE   You can't remove a control from a standard Ribbon group, or add a control to a standard group; see the sidebar earlier in this chapter for Patrick Schmid's illuminating commentary on this issue. For Microsoft's justification of this policy, see the Developer Overview of the User Interface for the 2007 Microsoft Office System article (`http://msdn2.microsoft.com/en-us/library/aa338198.aspx`). It boils down to something like "We made the Ribbon perfect, so users don't need to customize it." Needless to say, I (and many other developers and power users) disagree. The Ribbon is indeed a great improvement over command bars and menus, but I would really like to be able to drag a button I need to a standard group, or remove one that I never use.

To use the Form image on a custom control, use `"CreateForm"` as the imageMso argument value when defining the button in XML code.

The control's size attribute has only two selections: "large" and "normal". Lastly, for a command button, set the onAction attribute with the name of a function to run when the button is clicked.

Finding Control Names for Use in XML Code

If you want to assign a familiar Access image to a button on the Ribbon, you need to know the name of the standard Access control that uses this image, so you can set the `imageMso` argument for the button with that name. You can download an Excel worksheet (AccessRibbonControls.xls) with this information from `http://www.microsoft.com/downloads/details.aspx?familyid=4329d9e9-4d11-46a5-898d-23e4f331e9ae&displaylang=en` on the Microsoft web site.

> **CAUTION** Even though Office 2007 has been released, the latest worksheets of control names were prepared during the beta (November 2006), and they are not entirely accurate for the release version of Access, especially for tab names. Hopefully an updated set of worksheets will be posted soon.

However, there is another, more convenient method that works fine for many controls: Open the Access Options screen from the Office menu, and click the Customization page. This page is intended for customizing the Quick Access Toolbar, but it is also very useful for finding out control names for use in XML code. To find a control name, first select the Ribbon tab from the "Choose command from" drop-down list, then select the control in the list. As you hover the mouse over the control, its name appears in parentheses after the friendly name:

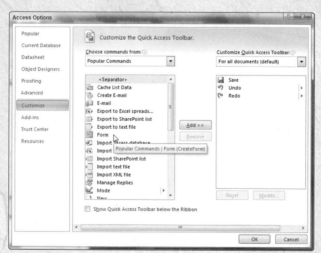

Getting the control name for use in assigning an image to a control on the Ribbon.

Removing a Tab or Group from the Ribbon

To remove one of the standard tabs or groups from the Ribbon (in reality, you are hiding it, not deleting it), set its visible attribute to "false", using idMso instead of id to indicate that you are referencing a built-in Ribbon tab or group. The following line of XML code turns off the standard Create tab:

```
<tab idMso="TabCreate" visible="false"/>
```

To remove a built-in tab or group from the Ribbon, you need to know its name. The AccessRibbonControls.xls worksheet is useful for finding the names of tabs or groups: just sort the worksheet by Control Type, and look at the tab or group rows. To save time, the names of the standard tabs are listed in Table 15.4.

TABLE 15.4

Built-in Access Ribbon Tab Names

TabAddIns	TabPivotChartDesign
TabAdpDiagramDesign	TabPivotTableDesign
TabAdpFunctionAndViewToolsDesign	TabPrintPreviewAccess
TabAdpSqlStatementDesign	TabQueryToolsDesign
TabAdpStoredProcedureToolsDesign	TabRelationshipToolsDesign
TabControlLayout	TabReportToolsAlignment
TabCreate	TabReportToolsDesign
TabDatabaseTools	TabReportToolsFormatting
TabExternalData	TabReportToolsLayout
TabFormToolsDesign	TabReportToolsPageSetupDesign
TabFormToolsFormatting	TabReportToolsPageSetupLayout
TabFormToolsLayout	TabSourceControl
TabHomeAccess	TabTableToolsDatasheet
TabMacroToolsDesign	TabTableToolsDesignAccess

Table 15.5 lists the standard group names.

TABLE 15.5

Built-in Access Ribbon Group Names

FileManageMenu	GroupAdpOutputOperations
FilePrintMenu	GroupAdpQueryTools
FileSaveAsMenuAccess	GroupAdpQueryType
FileServerMenu	GroupAdpSqlStatementDesignTools
GroupAdminister	GroupAnalyze
GroupAdpDiagramLayout	GroupAutoFormatAccess
GroupAdpDiagramShowHide	GroupClipboard

continued

529

TABLE 15.5 *(continued)*

GroupCollectData	GroupMacro
GroupControlAlignment	GroupMacroClose
GroupControlAlignmentLayout	GroupMacroRows
GroupControlPositionLayout	GroupMacroShowHide
GroupControlsAccess	GroupMacroTools
GroupControlSize	GroupMarginsAndPadding
GroupCreateForms	GroupMarginsAndPaddingControlLayout
GroupCreateOther	GroupMoveData
GroupCreateReports	GroupPageLayoutAccess
GroupCreateTables	GroupPivotChartActiveFieldAccess
GroupDatabaseSourceControl	GroupPivotChartDataAccess
GroupDatabaseTools	GroupPivotChartFilterAndSort
GroupDatasheetRelationships	GroupPivotChartShowHide
GroupDataTypeAndFormatting	GroupPivotChartTools
GroupDesignGridlines	GroupPivotTableActiveFieldAccess
GroupExport	GroupPivotTableDataAccess
GroupFieldsAndColumns	GroupPivotTableFilterAndSort
GroupFieldsTools	GroupPivotTableSelections
GroupFindAccess	GroupPivotTableShowHideAccess
GroupFontAccess	GroupPivotTableToolsAccess
GroupFormatting	GroupPosition
GroupFormattingControls	GroupPositionLayout
GroupFormattingGridlines	GroupPrintPreviewClosePreview
GroupGroupingAndTotals	GroupPrintPreviewData
GroupImport	GroupPrintPreviewPrintAccess
GroupLayoutShowHide	

Table 15.6 lists the standard control names.

TABLE 15.6	
Built-in Access Ribbon Control Names	
AccessRelinkLists	AdpOutputOperationsSortDescending
AddInsMenu	AdpOutputOperationsTableRemove
AdpConstraints	AdpPrimaryKey
AdpDiagramAddRelatedTables	AdpStoredProcedureEditSql
AdpDiagramAddTable	AdpStoredProcedureQueryAppend
AdpDiagramArrangeSelection	AdpStoredProcedureQueryAppendValues
AdpDiagramArrangeTables	AdpStoredProcedureQueryDelete
AdpDiagramAutosizeSelectedTables	AdpStoredProcedureQueryMakeTable
AdpDiagramColumnNames	AdpStoredProcedureQuerySelect
AdpDiagramColumnProperties	AdpStoredProcedureQueryUpdate
AdpDiagramCustomView	AdpVerifySqlSyntax
AdpDiagramDeleteTable	AdpViewDiagramPane
AdpDiagramHideTable	AdpViewGridPane
AdpDiagramIndexesKeys	AdpViewSqlPane
AdpDiagramKeys	AdvertisePublishAs
AdpDiagramModifyCustomView	AlignCenter
AdpDiagramNameOnly	AlignLeft
AdpDiagramNewLabel	AlignLeftToRightMenu
AdpDiagramNewTable	AlignRight
AdpDiagramRecalculatePageBreaks	ApplyCommaFormat
AdpDiagramRelationships	ApplyCurrencyFormat
AdpDiagramShowRelationshipLabels	ApplyFilter
AdpDiagramTableModesMenu	ApplyPercentageFormat
AdpDiagramViewPageBreaks	AutoFormatGallery
AdpManageIndexes	AutoFormatWizard
AdpOutputOperationsAddToOutput	AutoSumAverage
AdpOutputOperationsGroupBy	AutoSumCount
AdpOutputOperationsSortAscending	AutoSumMax

continued

TABLE 15.6   *(continued)*

AutoSumMin	ControlSpecialEffectMenu
Bold	ControlSpecialEffectRaised
Bullets	ControlSpecialEffectShadowed
BusinessFormWizard	ControlSpecialEffectSunken
CacheListData	ControlSubFormReport
ClearGrid	ControlTabControl
ClearMenuAccess	ControlTitle
CloseDocument	ControlToggleButton
ColumnWidth	ControlUnboundObjectFrame
ComAddInsDialog	ControlWizards
ControlActiveX	ConvertDatabaseFormat
ControlAlignToGrid	Copy
ControlAttachment	CreateClassModule
ControlBoundObjectFrame	CreateDiagram
ControlChart	CreateEmail
ControlImage	CreateForm
ControlLayoutRemove	CreateFormBlankForm
ControlLayoutStacked	CreateFormInDesignView
ControlLayoutTabular	CreateFormMoreFormsGallery
ControlLine	CreateFormPivotChart
ControlLineColorPicker	CreateFormSplitForm
ControlLineThicknessGallery	CreateFormWithMultipleItems
ControlLineTypeGallery	CreateLabels
ControlLogo	CreateMacro
ControlMarginsGallery	CreateModule
ControlPaddingGallery	CreateOtherObjectsMenu
ControlPage	CreateQueryFromWizard
ControlRectangle	CreateQueryInDesignView
ControlSetControlDefaults	CreateReport
ControlSnapToGrid	CreateReportBlankReport
ControlSpecialEffectChiseled	CreateReportFromWizard
ControlSpecialEffectEtched	CreateReportInDesignView
ControlSpecialEffectFlat	CreateShortcutMenuFromMacro

CreateStoredProcedure	Delete
CreateTable	DeleteTab
CreateTableInDesignView	DrillInto
CreateTableTemplatesGallery	DrillOut
CreateTableUsingSharePointListsGallery	ExportAccess
CustomizeHide	ExportDBase
Cut	ExportExcel
DatabaseAccessBackEnd	ExportHtmlDocument
DatabaseAnalyzePerformance	ExportLotus
DatabaseAnalyzeTable	ExportMoreMenu
DatabaseCopyDatabaseFile	ExportOdbcDatabase
DatabaseDocumenter	ExportParadox
DatabaseEncodeDecode	ExportSavedExports
DatabaseLinedTableManager	ExportSharePointList
DatabaseMakeMdeFile	ExportSnapshot
DatabaseMoveToSharePoint	ExportTextFile
DatabaseObjectDependencies	ExportWord
DatabasePartialReplica	ExportXmlFile
DatabasePermissions	FieldList
DatabasePermissionsMenu	FileBackupDatabase
DatabaseRelationships	FileBackUpSqlDatabase
DatabaseSetLogonSecurity	FileCloseDatabase
DatabaseSqlServer	FileCompactAndRepairDatabase
DatabaseSwitchboardManager	FileDatabaseProperties
DatabaseUserAndGroupAccounts	FileDropSqlDatabase
DatabaseUserLevelSecurityWizard	FileManageMenu
DataRefreshAll	FileNewDatabase
DatasheetColumnDelete	FileOpenDatabase
DatasheetColumnLookup	FilePackageAndSign
DatasheetColumnRename	FilePrintMenu
DatasheetNewField	FilePrintPreview
DateAndTimeInsert	FilePrintQuick
DefaultView	FilePublishToSharePoint

continued

TABLE 15.6	*(continued)*
FileSave	FindDialog
FileSaveAs	FindNext
FileSaveAsAccess2000	First10RecordsPreview
FileSaveAsAccess2002_2003	Font
FileSaveAsAccess2007	FontAlternateFillBackColorPicker
FileSaveAsMenuAccess	FontColorPicker
FileSaveAsPdfOrXps	FontConditionalFormatting
FileSendAsAttachment	FontFillBackColorPicker
FileServerLinkTables	FontSize
FileServerMenu	FormatCellsDialog
FileServerTransferDatabase	FormatPainter
FilterAdvancedByForm	FormattingDataType
FilterAdvancedMenu	FormattingDecreaseDecimals
FilterAfterSelection	FormattingFormat
FilterBeforeSelection	FormattingIncreaseDecimals
FilterBeginsWithSelection	FormattingRequiredField
FilterBetween	FormattingUnique
FilterBySelection	FormControlButton
FilterClearAllFilters	FormControlCheckBox
FilterContainsSelection	FormControlComboBox
FilterDoesNotBeginsWithSelection	FormControlEditBox
FilterDoesNotContainSelection	FormControlGroupBox
FilterDoesNotEndWithSelection	FormControlLabel
FilterEndsWithSelection	FormControlListBox
FilterEqualsSelection	FormControlRadioButton
FilterExcludingSelection	FormHeaderOrFooterShowHide
FilterIsNotSelected	GoToMenuAccess
FilterIsSelected	GoToNewRecord
FilterLargerThanSelection	GridlinesColorPicker
FilterNotEqualsSelection	GridlinesGallery
FilterSmallerThanSelection	GridlinesStyleGallery
FiltersMenu	GridlinesWidthGallery
FilterToggleFilter	GridShowHide

GroupAddInsCustomToolbars	GroupFormattingControls
GroupAddInsMenuCommands	GroupFormattingGridlines
GroupAddInsToolbarCommands	GroupGroupingAndTotals
GroupAdminister	GroupImport
GroupAdpDiagramLayout	Grouping
GroupAdpDiagramShowHide	GroupLayoutShowHide
GroupAdpOutputOperations	GroupMacro
GroupAdpQueryTools	GroupMacroClose
GroupAdpQueryType	GroupMacroRows
GroupAdpSqlStatementDesignTools	GroupMacroShowHide
GroupAnalyze	GroupMacroTools
GroupAutoFormatAccess	GroupMarginsAndPadding
GroupClipboard	GroupMarginsAndPaddingControlLayout
GroupCollectData	GroupMoveData
GroupControlAlignment	GroupPageLayoutAccess
GroupControlAlignmentLayout	GroupPivotChartActiveFieldAccess
GroupControlPositionLayout	GroupPivotChartDataAccess
GroupControlsAccess	GroupPivotChartFilterAndSort
GroupControlSize	GroupPivotChartShowHide
GroupCreateForms	GroupPivotChartTools
GroupCreateOther	GroupPivotChartType
GroupCreateReports	GroupPivotTableActiveFieldAccess
GroupCreateTables	GroupPivotTableDataAccess
GroupDatabaseSourceControl	GroupPivotTableFilterAndSort
GroupDatabaseTools	GroupPivotTableSelections
GroupDatasheetRelationships	GroupPivotTableShowHideAccess
GroupDataTypeAndFormatting	GroupPivotTableToolsAccess
GroupDesignGridlines	GroupPosition
GroupExport	GroupPositionLayout
GroupFieldsAndColumns	GroupPrintPreviewClosePreview
GroupFieldsTools	GroupPrintPreviewData
GroupFontAccess	GroupPrintPreviewPrintAccess
GroupFormatting	GroupQueryClose

continued

TABLE 15.6 *(continued)*

GroupQueryResults	ImportLotus
GroupQuerySetup	ImportMoreMenu
GroupQueryShowHide	ImportOdbcDatabase
GroupQueryType	ImportOutlook
GroupRecords	ImportParadox
GroupRelationships	ImportSavedImports
GroupRelationshipsTools	ImportSharePointList
GroupRichText	ImportTextFile
GroupSchemaTools	ImportXmlFile
GroupSharePointList	IndentDecrease
GroupSharepointLists	IndentIncrease
GroupSizeAndPosition	Italic
GroupSortAndFilter	LabelFontDialog
GroupSourceControlManage	LoadFromQuery
GroupSourceControlShow	MacroArguments
GroupTableDesignShowHide	MacroConditions
GroupTableDesignTools	MacroConvertMacrosToVisualBasic
GroupTextFormatting	MacroNames
GroupToolsAccess	MacroRun
GroupViews	MacroShowAllActions
GroupViewsShowHide	MacroSingleStep
GroupWindowAccess	MailMergeGoToFirstRecord
GroupZoom	MailMergeGoToNextRecord
HeaderFooterPageNumberInsert	MailMergeGoToPreviousRecord
HideDetails	MailMergeGotToLastRecord
HorizontalSpacingDecrease	ManageReplies
HorizontalSpacingIncrease	MasterViewClose
HorizontalSpacingMakeEqual	MenuPublish
HyperlinkInsert	MergeToWord
ImportAccess	Numbering
ImportDBase	ObjectBringToFront
ImportExcel	ObjectGallery
ImportHtmlDocument	ObjectsAlignBottom

ObjectsAlignLeft	PivotChartMultipleUnified
ObjectsAlignRight	PivotChartSortByTotalAscending
ObjectsAlignTop	PivotChartSortByTotalDescending
ObjectSendToBack	PivotChartSortByTotalMenu
ObjectsGroup	PivotChartType
ObjectsSelect	PivotClearCustomOrdering
ObjectsUngroup	PivotCollapseFieldAccess
OleDdeLinks	PivotCollapseFieldAccess
PageBreakInsertOrRemove	PivotCreateCalculatedTotal
PageHeaderOrFooterShowHide	PivotCreateCalulatedField
PageMarginsGallery	PivotDropAreas
PageOrientationLandscape	PivotExpandField
PageOrientationPortrait	PivotExpandIndicators
PageSetupDialog	PivotExportToExcel
PageSizeGallery	PivotFieldList
Paste	PivotFilterBySelection
PasteAppend	PivotFormulasMenu
PasteDuplicate	PivotGroupItems
PasteSpecial	PivotHideDetails
PasteSpecialDialog	PivotMoveField
PivotAutoCalcAverage	PivotMoveToColumnArea
PivotAutoCalcCount	PivotMoveToDetailArea
PivotAutoCalcMax	PivotMoveToFieldArea
PivotAutoCalcMenu	PivotMoveToFilterArea
PivotAutoCalcMin	PivotRefresh
PivotAutoCalcStandardDeviation	PivotRemoveField
PivotAutoCalcStandardDeviationPopulation	PivotShowAll
PivotAutoCalcSum	PivotShowAsMenu
PivotAutoCalcVariance	PivotShowAsNormal
PivotAutoCalcVariancePopulation	PivotShowAsPercentOfColumnTotal
PivotAutoFilter	PivotShowAsPercentOfGrandTotal
PivotChartLegendShowHide	PivotShowAsPercentOfParentColumnItem
PivotChartMultiplePlots	PivotShowAsPercentOfParentRowItem

continued

TABLE 15.6   *(continued)*

PivotShowAsPercentOfRowTotal	QueryCrosstab
PivotShowDetails	QueryDataDefinition
PivotShowOnlyTheBottomMenu	QueryDelete
PivotShowOnlyTheTopMenu	QueryInsertColumn
PivotShowTopAndBottomItemsMenu	QueryInsertColumns
PivotSubtotal	QueryMakeTable
PivotSwitchRowColumn	QueryParameters
PivotUngroupItems	QueryReturnGallery
PositionAnchoringGallery	QueryRunQuery
PositionFitToWindow	QuerySelectQueryType
PostcardWizard	QueryShowTable
PrintColumns	QuerySqlPassThroughQuery
PrintDataOnly	QueryTableNamesShowHide
PrintDialogAccess	QueryTotalsShowHide
PrintPreviewClose	QueryUnionQuery
PrintPreviewEightPages	QueryUpdate
PrintPreviewFourPages	QuickAccessToolbarCustomization
PrintPreviewMultiplePagesMenu	RecordsAddFromOutlook
PrintPreviewTwelvePages	RecordsCollapseAllSubdatasheets
PrintPreviewZoom10	RecordsDeleteColumn
PrintPreviewZoom1000	RecordsDeleteRecord
PrintPreviewZoom150	RecordsExpandAllSubdatasheets
PrintPreviewZoom200	RecordsFreezeColumns
PrintPreviewZoom25	RecordsHideColumns
PrintPreviewZoom50	RecordsInsertSubdatasheet
PrintPreviewZoom500	RecordsMoreRecordsMenu
PrintPreviewZoom75	RecordsRefreshMenu
PrintPreviewZoomMenu	RecordsRefreshRecords
PrintPreviewZoomTwoPages	RecordsRemoveSubdatasheet
PropertySheet	RecordsSaveAsOutlookContact
PublishToPdfOrEdoc	RecordsSaveRecord
QueryAppend	RecordsSubdatasheetMenu
QueryBuilder	RecordsTotals

RecordsUnfreeze	SharePointListsWorkOffline
RecordsUnhideColumns	ShowClipboard
Redo	ShowMargins
RelationshipDesignAllRelationships	SizeToFit
RelationshipsClearLayout	SizeToFitAccess
RelationshipsDirectRelationships	SizeToGridAccess
RelationshipsEditRelationships	SizeToNarrowest
RelationshipsHideTable	SizeToShortest
RelationshipsReport	SizeToTallest
ReplaceDialog	SizeToWidest
ReplicationCreateReplica	SortAndFilterAdvanced
ReplicationOptionsMenu	SortDown
ReplicationRecoverDesignMaster	SortRemoveAllSorts
ReplicationResolveConflicts	SortSelectionMenu
ReplicationSynchronizeNow	SortUp
Revert	SourceControlAddDatabase
RowHeight	SourceControlAddObjects
RulerShowHide	SourceControlCheckIn
SaveAsQuery	SourceControlCheckOut
SaveObjectAs	SourceControlCreateDatabaseFromProject
SelectAllAccess	SourceControlGetLatestVersion
SelectAllRecords	SourceControlOptions
SelectMenuAccess	SourceControlProperties
SelectRecord	SourceControlRefreshStatus
ServerConnection	SourceControlRun
ServerFilterApply	SourceControlShareObjects
ServerFilterByForm	SourceControlShowDifferences
ServerProperties	SourceControlShowHistory
ServerRestoreSqlDatabase	SourceControlUndoCheckOut
SetDatabasePassword	SpellingAccess
SharePointListsDiscardAllChanges	SubformInNewWindow
SharePointListsDiscardAllChangesAndRefresh	SubformMenu
SharePointListsDiscardChangesMenu	SynchronizeData

continued

TABLE 15.6   *(continued)*

TabAddIns	TabReportToolsFormatting
TabAdpDiagramDesign	TabReportToolsLayout
TabAdpFunctionAndViewToolsDesign	TabReportToolsPageSetupDesign
TabAdpSqlStatementDesign	TabReportToolsPageSetupLayout
TabAdpStoredProcedureToolsDesign	TabSetAdpDiagram
TabControlLayout	TabSetAdpFunctionAndViewTools
TabCreate	TabSetAdpSqlStatement
TabDatabaseTools	TabSetAdpStoredProcedure
TabExternalData	TabSetFormReportExtensibility
TabFormToolsDesign	TabSetFormTools
TabFormToolsFormatting	TabSetFormToolsLayout
TabFormToolsLayout	TabSetMacroTools
TabHomeAccess	TabSetPivotChartAccess
TableColumnsDelete	TabSetPivotTableAccess
TableDesign	TabSetQueryTools
TableIndexes	TabSetRelationshipTools
TableListAlertMe	TabSetReportTools
TableListPermissions	TabSetReportToolsLayout
TableRowsDelete	TabSetTableToolsDatasheet
TableRowsInsertWord	TabSetTableToolsDesign
TableSharePointListsModifyColumnsAndSettings	TabSourceControl
TableSharePointListsModifyWorkflow	TabTableToolsDatasheet
TableSharePointListsRefreshList	TabTableToolsDesignAccess
TableTestValidationRules	TextDirectionLeftToRight
TabMacroToolsDesign	TextDirectionRightToLeft
TabOrder	TextHighlightColorPicker
TabPivotChartDesign	TotalsCountRecords
TabPivotTableDesign	TotalsMenu
TabPrintPreviewAccess	TotalsStandardDeviation
TabQueryToolsDesign	TotalsSum
TabRelationshipToolsDesign	TotalsVariance
TabReportToolsAlignment	Underline
TabReportToolsDesign	Undo

VerticalSpacingDecrease	ViewVisualBasicCodeAccess
VerticalSpacingIncrease	VisualBasic
VerticalSpacingMakeEqual	WindowMoreWindowsDialog
ViewMessageBar	WindowNameGoesHere
ViewsAdpDiagramPrintPreview	WindowsArrangeIcons
ViewsAdpDiagramSqlView	WindowsCascade
ViewsDatasheetView	WindowsDataEntry
ViewsDesignView	WindowSplit
ViewsFormView	WindowsSwitch
ViewsLayoutView	WindowsTileHorizontally
ViewsModeMenu	WindowsTileVertically
ViewsModeMenu	WindowUnhide
ViewsPivotChartView	Zoom100
ViewsPivotChartView	ZoomFitToWindow
ViewsPivotTableView	ZoomOnePage
ViewsReportView	ZoomPrintPreviewExcel
ViewsSwitchToDefaultView	

The XML code listed next (the Ribbon name is TurnOff) turns off the standard Home tab, and removes the Export group from the External Data tab:

```
<customUI xmlns=
"http://schemas.microsoft.com/office/2006/01/customui">
    <ribbon startFromScratch="false">
        <tabs>
          <tab idMso="TabHomeAccess"
             visible="false">
          </tab>
          <tab idMso="TabExternalData"
             visible="true">
             <group idMso="GroupExport"
                visible="false">
             </group>
          </tab>
        </tabs>
    </ribbon>
</customUI>
```

NOTE In order to see this (or any) custom Ribbon in an Access database, you need to select it in the "Ribbon Name" drop-down list in the Access Options dialog, as shown in Figure 15.8.

Figure 15.5 shows the External Data tab, without the Export group.

FIGURE 15.5

The External Data tab without the Export group.

VBA Code

 **TIP**   To open the References dialog, select References from the Tools menu in the Visual Basic window.

To run commands from controls on your customized Ribbon, you need to write a callback procedure for each Ribbon command button. First, set a reference to the Office 12.0 object library in the References dialog (see Figure 15.6); it is needed to support various Ribbon-related objects in the code.

FIGURE 15.6

Setting a reference to the Office 12.0 object library.

The sample Test Ribbon database contains two procedures to be run from Ribbon buttons on the List Fields custom Ribbon; note the `ByVal control As IRibbonControl` argument, which links the procedure to the control:

```
Public Sub ListTableFields(ByVal control As IRibbonControl)

On Error Resume Next
```

First, clear data from the old table of table and field names:

```
strTable = "zstblTableAndFieldNames"
strReport = "zsrptTableAndFieldNames"
DoCmd.SetWarnings False
strSQL = "DELETE * FROM " & strTable
DoCmd.RunSQL strSQL
```

Fill the table with table and field names, iterating through the database's TableDefs collection:

```
Set dbs = CurrentDb
Set rst = dbs.OpenRecordset(strTable, dbOpenTable)

For Each tdf In dbs.TableDefs
    strTable = tdf.Name
    If Left(strTable, 4) <> "MSys" Then
        Set flds = tdf.Fields
        For Each fld In flds
            strFieldName = fld.Name
            With rst
                .AddNew
                !TableName = strTable
                !FieldName = strFieldName
                !DataType = fld.Type
                !ValidationRule = fld.ValidationRule
                !Required = fld.Required
                .Update
            End With
        Next fld
    End If
Next tdf

rst.Close

DoCmd.OpenTable strTable

strTitle = "Table filled"
strPrompt = "Print report now?"
intReturn = MsgBox(strPrompt, vbQuestion + vbYesNo, _
    strTitle)
If intReturn = vbYes Then
    strReport = "zsrptTableAndFieldNames"
    DoCmd.OpenReport strReport
End If

ErrorHandlerExit:
    Exit Sub
```

```
ErrorHandler:
   MsgBox "Error No: " & err.Number _
      & "; Description: " & err.Description
   Resume ErrorHandlerExit

End Sub

Public Sub ListQueryFields(ByVal control As IRibbonControl)

On Error Resume Next

   Dim strQueryName As String
   Dim qdf As DAO.QueryDef
```

First, clear data from the old table of query and field names:

```
   strTable = "zstblQueryAndFieldNames"
   strReport = "zsrptQueryAndFieldNames"
   DoCmd.SetWarnings False
   strSQL = "DELETE * FROM " & strTable
   DoCmd.RunSQL strSQL
```

Fill the table with query and field names, iterating through the database's QueryDefs collection (only select queries will have their fields listed):

```
   Set dbs = CurrentDb
   Set rst = dbs.OpenRecordset(strTable, dbOpenTable)

   For Each qdf In dbs.QueryDefs
      strQueryName = qdf.Name
      Debug.Print "Query name: " & strQueryName
      If Left(strQueryName, 4) <> "MSys" Then
         Set flds = qdf.Fields
         For Each fld In flds
            strFieldName = fld.Name
            With rst
               .AddNew
               !QueryName = strQueryName
               !FieldName = strFieldName
               !DataType = fld.Type
               !Required = fld.Required
               .Update
            End With
         Next fld
      End If
   Next qdf

   rst.Close

   DoCmd.OpenTable strTable
```

```
      strTitle = "Table filled"
      strPrompt = "Print report now?"
      intReturn = MsgBox(strPrompt, vbQuestion + vbYesNo, _
         strTitle)
      If intReturn = vbYes Then
         strReport = "zsrptTableAndFieldNames"
         DoCmd.OpenReport strReport
      End If

ErrorHandlerExit:
   Exit Sub

ErrorHandler:
   MsgBox "Error No: " & err.Number _
      & "; Description: " & err.Description
   Resume ErrorHandlerExit

End Sub
```

Once you have created the XML code and stored it in the USysRibbons table, and written any needed callback procedures to run from command buttons on the Ribbon, you need to close the database and reopen it, to load the customized Ribbon(s). Then you have to select the Ribbon you want to use in the database, as described here:

1. Close the database, then reopen it.

2. Click the Office button, then the Access Options button (Figure 15.7).

FIGURE 15.7

Opening the Access Options screen.

545

3. Select the Current Database page and select the Ribbon you want to load from the Ribbon Name drop-down list, as shown in Figure 15.8.

FIGURE 15.8

Selecting the Ribbon to load into a database.

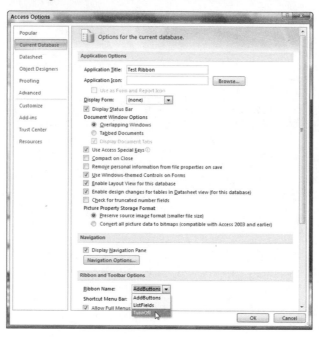

4. Close the database and reopen it, and, as in Figure 15.9, now you should see the Ribbon customization.

FIGURE 15.9

The Listing Options tab created by the ListFields custom Ribbon.

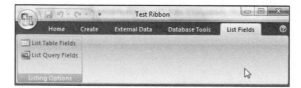

5. To load another Ribbon, select it from the Ribbon Name drop-down list, and close and reopen the database.

> **NOTE** You may get an error message like the one shown in Figure 15.10 when reopening a database after creating or editing XML code. Note the line and column reference, which should help in figuring out what the problem is, even if the error description isn't much help. Sometimes it is as simple as a missing bracket.

FIGURE 15.10

An informative error message when loading Ribbon customization XML code.

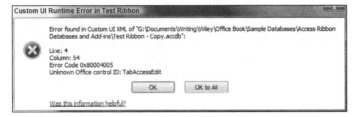

Form Ribbons

You can also make form Ribbons, to replace or customize the built-in Ribbons. The Test Ribbon database has a sample form Ribbon, AddButtons. This Ribbon displays for a specific form, after selecting it in the Current Database page of the Access Options screen, and in the form's property sheet. The XML for the AddButtons Ribbon is shown in Figure 15.11.

FIGURE 15.11

The XML code for the custom AddButtons form Ribbon.

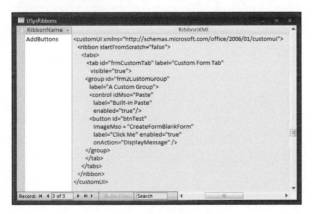

This code adds a custom tab called Custom Form Tab, with a single group and two command buttons. The Built-in Paste button runs the default Paste command (if there is something in the Clipboard to paste); the Click Me button pops up a simple message box. To display a custom Ribbon on a form, you need to select the Ribbon name in the form's RibbonName property, as shown in Figure 15.12.

FIGURE 15.12

Selecting a Ribbon for a form.

The custom tab is shown in Figure 15.13.

FIGURE 15.13

A form custom Ribbon with two buttons, and the message box popped up by the Click Me button.

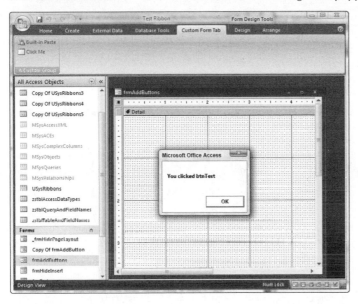

Customizing the Ribbon with an Access Add-in

Because Access add-ins (in previous versions of Access) didn't add buttons to command bars (menus or toolbars), you can't replace old code referencing CommandBars with new code referencing the Ribbon. However, you can replace a set of menu add-ins with a single menu add-in to load a custom Ribbon, and place the rest of your add-in's commands on the Ribbon. As an example, I made a version of my Extras 2007.accda add-in (the sample database for Chapter 14) and modified it to load a custom Ribbon.

NOTE The sample library database for this section is Extras (Ribbon).accda,

CAUTION If you are attempting to install an add-in in Access 2007 running on Windows Vista, you may get the security warning shown in Figure 15.14. Some special techniques are needed to get Access Ribbon add-ins to work in Vista; see the "Getting Your Add-ins to Work in Vista" sidebar for details. This is not a problem when installing add-ins for Access 2007 running on Windows XP.

FIGURE 15.14

A security warning when attempting to install an Access add-in for Access 2007 running on Windows Vista.

CROSS-REF See *PC Magazine Windows Vista Security Solutions* (Wiley, 2007) for more information on dealing with Vista security issues.

NOTE In Windows Vista, callback functions won't run from Ribbon buttons unless you include the name of the add-in database project before the function name, as I have done in the XML code listed below.

The technique for creating the Ribbon XML and storing it in a table is the same as for a regular Access 2007 database, as described in the previous section. The Extras (Ribbon) library database has only one add-in with three records in its USysRegInfo table, to load the ExtrasRibbon from the USysRibbons table. Its XML code is listed next:

```
<customUI
xmlns="http://schemas.microsoft.com/office/2006/01/customui">
    <ribbon startFromScratch="false">
        <tabs>
            <tab id="dbCustomTab"
                label="Extras"
                visible="true">
            <group id="dbListingGroup"
                label="Listing Fields">
              <button id="btnListTableFields"
                  label="List Table Fields"
                  enabled="true"
                  imageMso="CreateTable"
                  size="normal"
                  onAction="Extras(Ribbon).ListTableFields"/>
              <button id="btnListQueryFields"
                  label="List Query Fields"
                  enabled="true"
                  imageMso="CreateQueryInDesignView"
                  size="normal"
                  onAction="Extras(Ribbon).ListQueryFields"/>
              <button id="btnOpenOptionsDialog"
                  label="Select Options"
                  enabled="true"
                  imageMso="CreateFormBlankForm"
                  size="normal"
                  onAction="Extras(Ribbon).ExtrasOptions"/>
```

```
        </group>
        <group id="dbBackupGroup"
           label="Database Backup">
          <button id="btnBackupFrontEnd"
              label="Back up current database"
              enabled="true"
              imageMso="Copy"
              size="normal"
              onAction="Extras(Ribbon).BackupFrontEndDB"/>
          <button id="btnBackupBackEnd"
              label="Back up back-end database"
              enabled="true"
              imageMso="Copy" size="normal"
              onAction="Extras(Ribbon).BackupBackEndDB"/>
        </group>
      </tab>
    </tabs>
  </ribbon>
</customUI>
```

The USysRegInfo table with the Enable Extras Tab menu add-in records is shown in Figure 15.15.

FIGURE 15.15

The USysRegInfo table with a set of records for a single menu add-in.

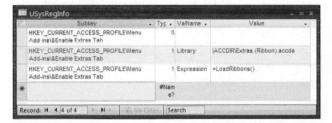

Getting Your Add-ins to Work in Vista

Because of Vista's new security features, you need to take a few more steps when creating and installing an Access 2007 add-in to get it to install and work in Vista. The first step is to run Access as an administrator. Right-click the MSACCESS.EXE file in the Office 12 subfolder under the Microsoft Office folder, and select "Run as administrator":

continued

continued

Figure SB-6. Running Access as an administrator

Open the add-in from the Access window, open the UsysRegInfo table and (if necessary) change the capitalization of "Menu Add-ins" to "Menu Add-Ins" (capitalizing the I). This is only necessary for running add-ins in Vista; "Menu Add-ins" works fine for Access 97 through 2003.

One extra step may also be needed: If your Access 2007 add-in creates a Ribbon, and its buttons have callback functions, you also need to include the VBA project's name before the callback function name in each `onaction` argument in the USysRibbons table. Instead of just

```
onAction="ListQueryFields"
```

you need

```
onAction="Extras (Ribbon).ListQueryFields"/>
```

After making the above changes to the add-in's system tables, compile the add-in's code, and save and close it. Now you should be able to install the add-in and run its menu add-in(s), and its Ribbon buttons should work.

The Extras (Ribbon) add-in has only a single menu add-in: Enable Extras Tab, which runs a procedure (listed next) that copies the USysRibbons table into the calling database, and attempts to load the table.

CAUTION Loading a table programmatically with the LoadCustumUI function doesn't always work; if the table is not automatically loaded, you can load it manually, as described earlier in this chapter (see Figure 15.8).

The basExtrasRibbon module also contains several callback procedures, which are the same as those in the standard Extras 2007.accda add-in, except for the `ByVal control As IRibbonControl` argument (plus one new procedure, for backing up a back end database).

TIP How did I find the GUID for Office 12's object library? I found the path from the References dialog, then searched for it in the Registry, using the RegEdit utility; the GUID is on the line above the one listing the path.

```
Public Function LoadRibbons()
'Must be a function so it can be run from USysRegInfo table.

On Error Resume Next

    Dim i As Integer
    Dim strRibbonName As String
    Dim strRibbonXML As String

    Set dbsCode = CodeDb
    Set dbsCalling = CurrentDb
```

Add a reference to the Office 12 object library (if there isn't one already).

```
    Application.References.AddFromGuid _
        "{000C0126-0000-0000-C000-000000000046}", 1, 0
```

Copy the USysRibbons table to the calling database, after deleting any existing table of that name, if there is one.

```
    Set dbsCalling = CurrentDb
    strCallingDb = CurrentDb.Name
    Set tdfsCalling = dbsCalling.TableDefs
    strTable = "USysRibbons"
    Set tdfCalling = tdfsCalling(strTable)
    DoCmd.SetWarnings False
    If tdfCalling Is Nothing Then
        Debug.Print strTable & " not found; about to copy it"
        DoCmd.CopyObject destinationdatabase:=strCallingDb, _
            newname:=strTable, _
            sourceobjectType:=acTable, _
            sourceobjectname:=strTable
    Else
```

Table found; delete it and then copy current version.

```
            tdfsCalling.Delete (strTable)
            DoCmd.CopyObject destinationdatabase:=strCallingDb, _
                newname:=strTable, _
                sourceobjectType:=acTable, _
                sourceobjectname:=strTable
            Debug.Print " Old "; strTable _
                & "deleted; about to copy current version"
        End If

        Set rst = dbsCalling.OpenRecordset(strTable)
        rst.MoveFirst
        Do While Not rst.EOF
            strRibbonName = rst![RibbonName]
            strRibbonXML = rst![RibbonXML]
```

Load the Ribbon from the table record (if it has not already been loaded).

```
            Application.LoadCustomUI _
                customuiname:=strRibbonName, _
                customuixml:=strRibbonXML
        rst.MoveNext
    Loop

    dbsCalling.Close
    Set dbsCalling = Nothing

ErrorHandlerExit:
    Exit Function

ErrorHandler:
    MsgBox "Error No: " & Err.Number _
        & "; Description: " & Err.Description
    Resume ErrorHandlerExit
End Function
```

Once the add-in has been loaded, you can select Enable Extras Tab from the Add-ins menu on the Database Tools tab of the Ribbon, as shown in Figure 15.16.

Selecting a menu add-in to load a custom Ribbon from an Access add-in.

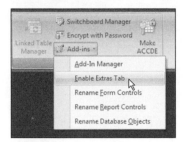

CROSS-REF See Chapter 14 for information on installing an Access add-in.

Close and reopen the database. If the ExtrasRibbon was not automatically loaded, select it manually, then close and reopen the database again; you should now see the Extras tab, as shown in Figure 15.17.

The Extras tab loaded from an Access add-in.

The "Select Options" button opens the dialog where various options can be selected; the other buttons run functions to list table or query fields, or back up the current database or its back end.

Figure 15.18 shows the Select Options dialog:

FIGURE 15.18

The Select Options dialog for selecting a backup folder and entering prefixes to exclude.

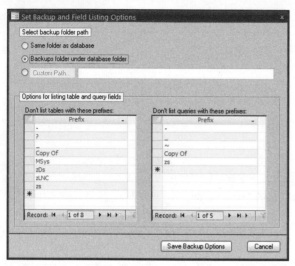

CAUTION   The Ribbon is a new feature for Office, and (not surprisingly) even in the release version of Access 2007 it is not entirely stable, especially when the buttons run procedures from an add-in. You may find that you have to repeatedly uninstall and reinstall an add-in, unload and reload a Ribbon, and (most of all!) repeatedly close and reopen a database to get a Ribbon that calls add-in procedures to work. Hopefully this instability will clear up in an upcoming patch or service release of Office 2007.

If you select the List Table Fields command, a table is filled with the names of tables and their fields, and a message box asks if you want to print the report bound to the table now, as shown in Figure 15.19:

FIGURE 15.19

A table filled with names of tables and their fields.

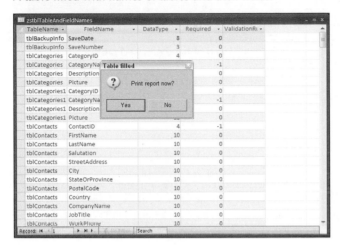

Selecting the "Back up back end database" command extracts the name of the back end database from the Connect string of a linked table, and presents an InputBox with a proposed save name, which can be edited as desired. The InputBox is shown in Figure 15.20

FIGURE 15.20

An InputBox with a proposed save name for a back-end database.

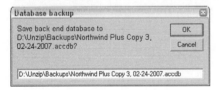

If you run this command in a database that has no linked tables, you will instead get the message shown in Figure 15.21:

FIGURE 15.21

A message when attempting to back up the back end for a database that has no linked tables.

The procedures for the "List Table Fields", "List Query Fields", "Select Options", "Back up current database", and "Back up back end database" buttons are similar to those in the Extras 2007.accda add-in, except that they use the ByVal control As IRibbonControl argument that is needed to run them from Ribbon buttons; their code is not listed here.

Summary

Although at first it may appear that the new Ribbon is not customizable, you can in fact customize it, at least by adding new tabs and groups, with controls to run your code. This chapter covered writing XML code to load a custom Ribbon, and VBA code for procedures to run from the custom Ribbon buttons, both in regular Access 2007 databases and in library databases for Access 2007 add-ins. The next chapter describes how to write Shared add-ins working with the Access Ribbon in Visual Basic 2005.

Chapter 16

Customizing the Access Ribbon with a Visual Studio 2005 Shared Add-in

I n Chapter 13, I described creating a VB 6 COM add-in to add extra
functionality to Access. VB 6 (though still supported by Microsoft) is not
the latest version of Visual Basic; if you want to use the latest version,
that is VB 2005, included in Visual Studio 2005, available in several editions.
There are significant differences between these versions of VB and some compatibility problems with Office 2007, but you can create Visual Studio 2005
add-ins that work with Access, though at present the job is much harder than
it should be, and their functionality is limited, because the Visual Studio Tools
for Office add-in does not yet include an Access add-in template.

This chapter describes creating a simple Visual Studio Shared add-in for
Access that will run in both Windows XP and Windows Vista.

Preparing to Write a Visual Studio Add-in

Before you start writing a Visual Studio add-in, there are several preliminary
steps you need to take. The first is to check that.NET support is enabled for
Office, to support the Access interoperability component needed to work
with Access.

Adding .NET Support to Office

Since your installation of Office 2007 may not have .NET support enabled,
you need to check that this feature has been selected; it is required in order
to create Shared add-ins. To check whether.NET support is enabled, you

need to run Office install. In Windows Vista, first select Programs in the Control Panel, then Programs and Features, then select the Microsoft Office item, as shown in Figure 16.1. If you are running Windows XP, start by selecting the Add or Remove Programs applet in the Control Panel, then the Microsoft Office 2007 item.

FIGURE 16.1

Changing the Office 2007 installation in Windows Vista.

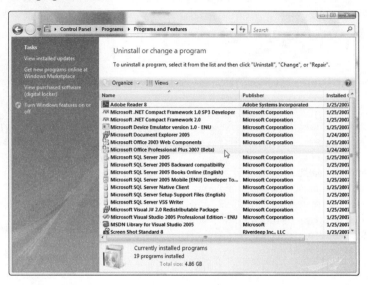

On the next screen, shown in Figure 16.2, select the Change option, then "Add or Remove Features" for Vista, or the "Add or Remove Features" option for Windows XP.

In the Installation Options dialog, drop down the Microsoft Office Access list; if the .NET Programmability Support item has a big red X, that means that it is not installed. To install it, drop down its list and select the "Run from My Computer" item (see Figure 16.3).

FIGURE 16.2

Selecting the "Add or Remove Features" option for changing Office in Windows XP.

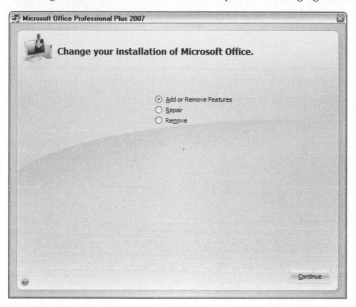

FIGURE 16.3

Selecting the "Run from My Computer" option for .NET programmability support.

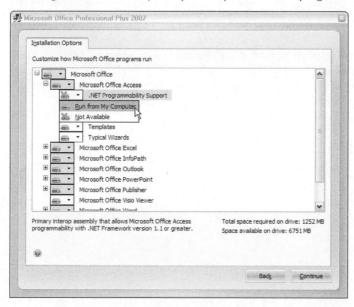

If you want to create add-ins for any other Office components, select "Run from My Computer" for their .NET Programmability Support components as well. After clicking Continue, Office installs the new features, and when it is done, you will get a success screen, depicted in Figure 16.4; click Close on this screen, and then close the Add/Remove Program applet.

FIGURE 16.4

The success screen after changing the Office configuration.

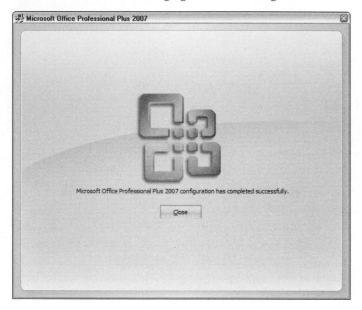

Although VB 2005 Express has an Upgrade Wizard, it isn't helpful in upgrading a VB 6 COM add-in to VB 2005 because the Express edition of VB 2005 doesn't support creating add-ins. If you attempt to upgrade a VB 6 COM add-in with this wizard (or the similar wizard in Visual Studio 2005), all the project components will be upgraded except the critical Access Designer, and you will get a message "Activex Designer AccessDesigner.Dsr was not upgraded" in the Upgrade Report, as shown in Figure 16.5.

FIGURE 16.5

The Upgrade Report for a VB 6 COM add-in, showing that the Access Designer was not upgraded.

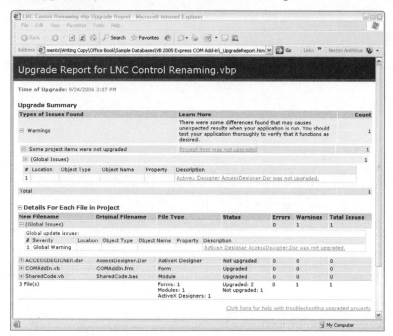

CROSS-REF The VB 6 COM add-in was the topic of Chapter 13.

You might think that Visual Studio Tools for Office 2005 (VSTO) would be an appropriate tool for creating Access add-ins, when supplemented with the downloadable upgrade that supports Office 2007 — after all, Access is part of Office. But this is not so. Though you can create add-ins for all the other major Office 2007 components, and some minor ones as well (see Figure 16.6), you can't create an Access add-in with VSTO, and therefore in this section I use Visual Studio 2005 for creating a Shared add-in (this is the new name for what was previously called a COM add-in).

To create a Shared add-in that adds capability to Access, start by running Visual Studio 2005 and selecting File ⇨ New Project. In the New Project dialog, select the Extensibility selection under the Other Project Types category, then select the Shared Add-in template. Enter the add-in's name and solution name; you can either accept the default location for the add-in's files or browse for a custom location, as I did in Figure 16.7.

FIGURE 16.6

The VSTO New Project Office screen, showing that Access add-in creation is not supported.

FIGURE 16.7

Creating a Shared add-in in Visual Studio 2005.

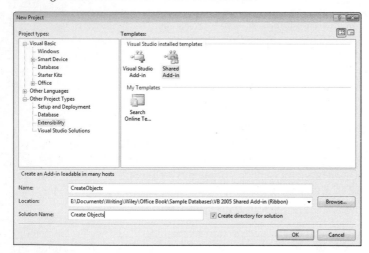

CAUTION The add-in's name can't contain spaces or punctuation marks—just letters and numbers. However, the solution name can contain spaces or punctuation marks.

After clicking OK, you will get a "Welcome to the Add-in Wizard" screen, as seen in Figure 16.8.

FIGURE 16.8

The first screen of the Shared Add-in Wizard.

Running Visual Studio 2005 in Windows Vista

In order to run Visual Studio 2005 on Windows Vista, you need to install a Service Pack and then a hotfix. The first download to install is the Visual Studio 2005 Service Pack 1, which can be downloaded from `http://msdn2.microsoft.com/en-us/vstudio/bb265237.aspx` (in various versions depending on the edition of Visual Studio). The hotfix is called the Visual Studio 2005 Service Pack 1 Update for Windows Vista Beta; it can be downloaded at `http://www.microsoft.com/downloads/details`
`.aspx?familyid=fb6bb56a-10b7-4c05-b81c-5863284503cf&displaylang=en`.

After installing the service pack and hotfix, when you run Visual Studio 2005, you will probably get this message:

continued

continued

If you click on the link, you will get a Web page with more links to pages with information about running Visual Studio 2005 on Vista:

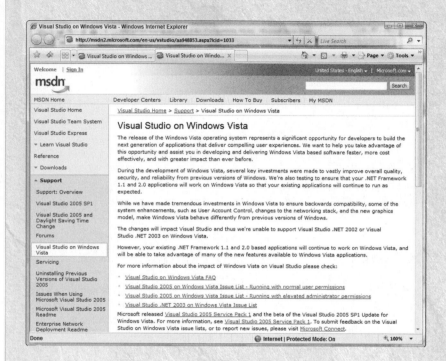

For running Visual Studio 2005 on Vista, the link you need is the third one, "Running with elevated administrator permissions." There is a lot of information on this page, but basically you only need one thing: when running Visual Studio in Vista, right-click its icon and select "Run as administrator" from its context menu:

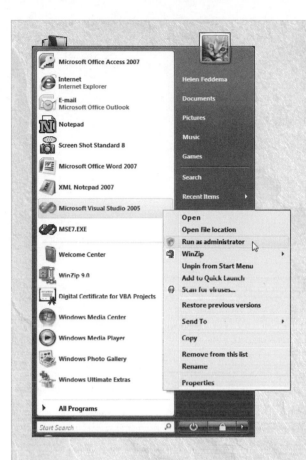

Now you can create new projects or open existing projects, and work with them as in Windows XP, and your Visual Studio add-in Ribbons (and other customizations) will work in Access 2007 databases.

On the screen depicted in Figure 16.9, select Visual Basic as the programming language to use (it may be the only choice, depending on the language support you selected when installing Visual Studio).

FIGURE 16.9

Selecting a programming language for the add-in.

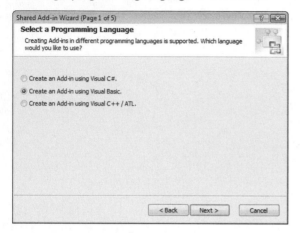

On the next screen, shown in Figure 16.10, select Microsoft Access as the application host.

FIGURE 16.10

Selecting an application host for the add-in.

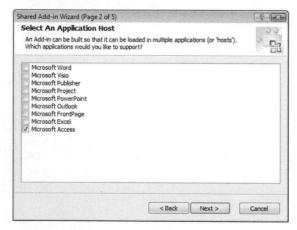

On screen 3 of the wizard (see Figure 16.11), enter the add-in's name and description (not the same as the project name and solution name entered on the first screen).

FIGURE 16.11

Giving the add-in a name and description.

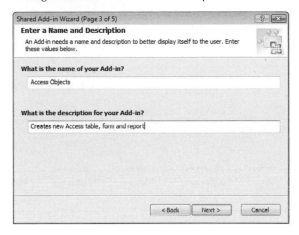

Next, as depicted in Figure 16.12, select add-in options — during development, it's best to check only the first checkbox, so only you (the developer) can work with the add-in.

FIGURE 16.12

Selecting add-in options.

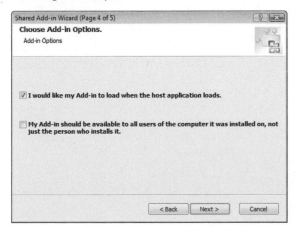

The final page of the Shared Add-in Wizard (see Figure 16.13) gives a summary of the selected options.

FIGURE 16.13

The Summary page of the Shared Add-in Wizard.

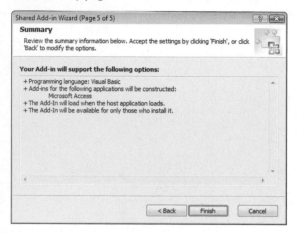

On clicking Finish, the new add-in project is created, with all the necessary components, and the Connect class (the Connect.vb module) is displayed, as shown in Figure 16.14 (note the similarity to the Access Designer in the VB 6 COM add-in). To work with the references more easily, select Project ➪ Show All Files, and expand the References folder in the Solution Explorer at the right of the screen.

 If you don't see the References folder in the Solution Explorer, select Show All Files from the Project menu to make the folder visible.

FIGURE 16.14

The new Shared add-in project.

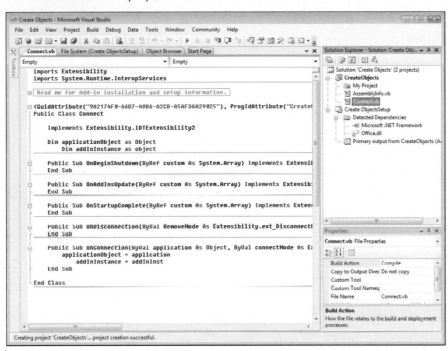

Next, add a reference to the Access Interoperability item. To add references, right-click the References folder and select Add Reference, then select the .NET tab, select "Microsoft.Office.Interop.Access" (as in Figure 16.15), and click OK.

Figure 16.16 shows the solution's references in the Solution Explorer.

FIGURE 16.15

Adding a reference to the Interop.Access item.

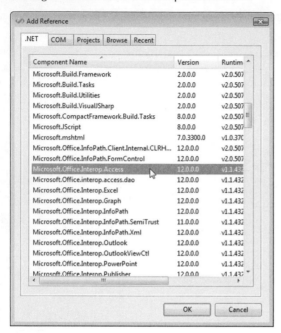

FIGURE 16.16

The Access Interoperability reference, and standard references.

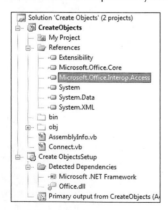

The next step is to add some Imports statements under the two default statements in the Declarations section of the class module, using IntelliSense (see Figure 16.17):

```
Imports Extensibility
Imports System.Runtime.InteropServices
Imports Microsoft.Office.Core
Imports Access = Microsoft.Office.Interop.Access
```

FIGURE 16.17

Using IntelliSense to add an Imports statement to the Connect class module.

Next, replace the class-level variables (applicationObject and addInInstance), both declared as Object, with typed references, replacing Dim with Private (I also gave the applicationObject variable a more application-specific name, appAccess):

```
Private appAccess As Microsoft.Office.Interop.Access.Application
Private addInInstance As Microsoft.Office.Core.COMAddIn
```

After adding statements and modifying the variables, there are some more modifications to be made to the code in the Connect class module. These changes are described in the next section.

Modifying the Connect Class Module Code

If you were (for example) creating an Excel 2007 add-in using VSTO 2005 with the 2007 upgrade, you could add Ribbon support to your add-in by simply adding a Ribbon Support item to your project. Visual Studio 2005 lacks a Ribbon Support item, and VSTO doesn't support creating Access add-ins, so this step requires extensive manual modification of the Connect class module, to support working with Access and the Ribbon.

In the `OnConnection` method, modify the rows that set the application (Access) and add-in variables as follows:

```
appAccess = DirectCast(application, _
    Microsoft.Office.Interop.Access.Application)
addInInstance = DirectCast(addInInst, _
    Microsoft.Office.Core.COMAddIn)
```

Next, modify the two lines that set the Access and add-in variables as follows:

```
appAccess = DirectCast(application, Access.Application)
addInInstance = DirectCast(application, Core.COMAddIn)
```

Add another `Implements` statement to the Connect class as follows:

```
Implements Extensibility.IDTExtensibility2
Implements IRibbonExtensibility
```

NOTE   If all this manual modification of the Shared add-in code is getting tedious, hopefully the next version (v. 3) of VSTO will include an Access template that will eliminate most of the hand-coding for support of Access Shared add-ins and the Ribbon.

After adding the `Implements IRibbonExtensibility` line, a new function stub should appear in the Connect class module, `GetCustomUI`.

NOTE   If you don't see the function stub, try doing a Save All. If it still doesn't appear, just type in the whole function.

Add a line of code to this function, as listed next:

```
Public Function GetCustomUI(ByVal RibbonID As String) As String _
    Implements Microsoft.Office.Core.IRibbonExtensibility.GetCustomUI
    Return My.Resources.Ribbon
End Function
```

Finally, open the Assembly.vb class from the Solution Explorer and add information about the add-in (you don't have to fill in all the information), as shown in Figure 16.18.

This completes the general changes to the Connect class module; now you need to add code for your add-in's specific functionality.

Adding Assembly information to the add-in.

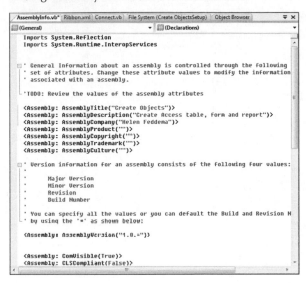

Adding Functionality to the Shared Add-in

For the Visual Studio add-in I used components of the Access object model to create a table, form, or report programmatically, adding fields to the table and controls to the form or report. To implement this functionality, I needed to write the custom Ribbon's XML code, three button functions, and some supporting code.

To create the Ribbon XML and embed it within the project, first create an XML File item by selecting Project ⇨ Add New Item, and then the XML File item in the Add New Item dialog (give the file the name Ribbon.xml), as shown in Figure 16.19.

FIGURE 16.19

Creating an XML File item for Ribbon support.

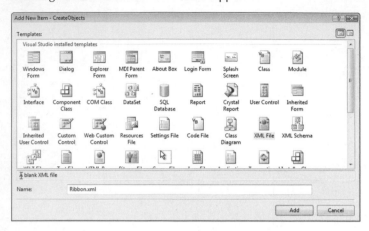

The XML code for the Ribbon in this add-in is listed here (see Chapter 15 for more detailed information on creating Ribbon XML code):

```xml
<?xml version="1.0" encoding="utf-8" ?>
<customUI
xmlns="http://schemas.microsoft.com/office/2006/01/customui">
  <ribbon startFromScratch="false">
    <tabs>
      <tab id="dbDemoTab"
         label="Visual Studio Add-in"
         visible="true">
        <group id="dbAccessObjectsGroup"
           label="Create Access Objects">
          <button id="btnCreateTable"
             label="Create New Table"
             enabled="true"
             imageMso="Table"
             size="normal"
             onAction="CreateTableInDesignView"/>
          <button id="btnCreateForm"
             label="Create New Form"
             enabled="true"
             imageMso="CreateFormInDesignView"
             size="normal"
             onAction="CreateNewForm"/>
          <button id="btnCreateReport"
             label="Create New Report"
             enabled="true"
```

```
              imageMso="CreateReportInDesignView"
              size="normal"
              onAction="CreateNewReport"/>
          </group>
        </tab>
      </tabs>
    </ribbon>
  </customUI>
```

Next, the XML file needs to be treated as a resource within the project, so you don't have to deal with a separate text file. To do this, select Ribbon.xml in the Solution Explorer, and select Embedded Resource as the value for the Build Action property in its properties sheet (see Figure 16.20).

FIGURE 16.20

Selecting Embedded Resource as the Build Action property of the Ribbon.xml file.

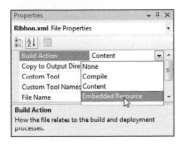

Next, select "CreateObjects Properties" from the bottom of the Project menu (if you are working with a different project, its name appears instead of CreateObjects). Click the Resources tab; if you have not already created a resources file, all you will see is the link shown in Figure 16.21.

FIGURE 16.21

A link to add a resource to a project.

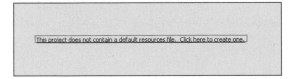

Click the link to create a resources file; a datasheet appears, with columns for Name, Value, and Comment. Drag the Ribbon.xml file from the Solution Explorer to the Resources pane; now, as in Figure 16.22, you will see an icon for the Ribbon.xml file.

FIGURE 16.22

The Ribbon.xml file added to the project's resources file.

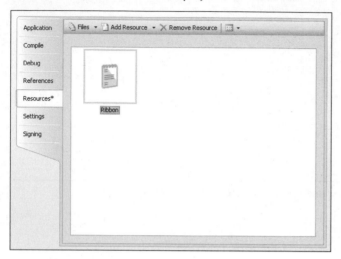

Each of the buttons in the Ribbon XML code needs its own procedure; the three button procedures, plus a standard add-in error handler (same as in the VB 6 COM add-in) are listed next:

```
Public Sub CreateNewTable(ByVal control As _
Microsoft.Office.Core.IRibbonControl)

On Error GoTo ErrorHandler

Dim strSQL As String
Dim strTable As String
Dim obj As AccessObject

strTable = "tblTest"
strSQL = "CREATE TABLE " & strTable & " (FileDate DATE, " _
  & "FileNumber LONG, FileName TEXT (100), " _
  & "Current YESNO);"
Debug.Print("SQL Statement: " & strSQL)
```

Create table if it doesn't already exist.

```
For Each obj In appAccess.CurrentData.AllTables
    If obj.Name = strTable Then
      'Table already exists
      GoTo ErrorHandlerExit
    End If
  Next
```

Create the table.

```
appAccess.DoCmd.RunSQL(strSQL)

ErrorHandlerExit:
  Exit Sub

ErrorHandler:
  AddInErr(Err)
  Resume ErrorHandlerExit

End Sub

Public Sub CreateNewForm(ByVal control As _
  Microsoft.Office.Core.IRibbonControl)

On Error GoTo ErrorHandler

Dim frm As Microsoft.Office.Interop.Access.Form
Dim txt As Microsoft.Office.Interop.Access.TextBox
Dim lbl As Microsoft.Office.Interop.Access.Label
Dim cbo As Microsoft.Office.Interop.Access.ComboBox
Dim lst As Microsoft.Office.Interop.Access.ListBox
Dim chk As Microsoft.Office.Interop.Access.CheckBox
```

Create a new form.

```
frm = appAccess.CreateForm()
frm.RecordSource = "tblTest"
txt = appAccess.CreateControl(FormName:=frm.Name, _
 ControlType:=Microsoft.Office.Interop.Access.AcControlType.acTextBox, _
  Section:=Microsoft.Office.Interop.Access.AcSection.acDetail, _
  Left:=0, Top:=0, Width:=2500, Height:=400)

lbl = appAccess.CreateControl(FormName:=frm.Name, _
  ControlType:=Microsoft.Office.Interop.Access.AcControlType.acLabel, _
  Section:=Microsoft.Office.Interop.Access.AcSection.acDetail, _
  Left:=0, Top:=1000, Width:=2500, Height:=400)

cbo = appAccess.CreateControl(FormName:=frm.Name, _
ControlType:=Microsoft.Office.Interop.Access.AcControlType.acComboBox, _
  Section:=Microsoft.Office.Interop.Access.AcSection.acDetail, _
  Left:=0, Top:=2000, Width:=2500, Height:=400)


lst = appAccess.CreateControl(FormName:=frm.Name, _
ControlType:=Microsoft.Office.Interop.Access.AcControlType.acListBox, _
  Section:=Microsoft.Office.Interop.Access.AcSection.acDetail, _
  Left:=0, Top:=3000, Width:=2500, Height:=400)
```

```
chk = appAccess.CreateControl(FormName:=frm.Name, _
ControlType:=Microsoft.Office.Interop.Access.AcControlType.acCheckBox, _
  Section:=Microsoft.Office.Interop.Access.AcSection.acDetail, _
  Left:=0, Top:=4000, Width:=2500, Height:=400)

ErrorHandlerExit:
Exit Sub

ErrorHandler:
  AddInErr(Err)
  Resume ErrorHandlerExit

End Sub

Public Sub CreateNewReport(ByVal control As _
  Microsoft.Office.Core.IRibbonControl)

On Error GoTo ErrorHandler

Dim rpt As Microsoft.Office.Interop.Access.Report
Dim txt As Microsoft.Office.Interop.Access.TextBox
Dim lbl As Microsoft.Office.Interop.Access.Label
Dim cbo As Microsoft.Office.Interop.Access.ComboBox
Dim lst As Microsoft.Office.Interop.Access.ListBox
Dim chk As Microsoft.Office.Interop.Access.CheckBox
```

Create a new report.

```
rpt = appAccess.CreateReport()
rpt.RecordSource = "tblTest"
txt = appAccess.CreateReportControl(ReportName:=rpt.Name, _
ControlType:=Microsoft.Office.Interop.Access.AcControlType.acTextBox, _
  Section:=Microsoft.Office.Interop.Access.AcSection.acDetail, _
  Left:=0, Top:=0, Width:=2500, Height:=400)

lbl = appAccess.CreateReportControl(ReportName:=rpt.Name, _
  ControlType:=Microsoft.Office.Interop.Access.AcControlType.acLabel, _
  Section:=Microsoft.Office.Interop.Access.AcSection.acDetail, _
  Left:=0, Top:=1000, Width:=2500, Height:=400)

cbo = appAccess.CreateReportControl(ReportName:=rpt.Name, _
ControlType:=Microsoft.Office.Interop.Access.AcControlType.acComboBox, _
  Section:=Microsoft.Office.Interop.Access.AcSection.acDetail, _
  Left:=0, Top:=2000, Width:=2500, Height:=400)

lst = appAccess.CreateReportControl(ReportName:=rpt.Name, _
ControlType:=Microsoft.Office.Interop.Access.AcControlType.acListBox, _
  Section:=Microsoft.Office.Interop.Access.AcSection.acDetail, _
  Left:=0, Top:=3000, Width:=2500, Height:=400)
```

```
chk = appAccess.CreateReportControl(ReportName:=rpt.Name, _
ControlType:=Microsoft.Office.Interop.Access.AcControlType.acCheckBox, _
  Section:=Microsoft.Office.Interop.Access.AcSection.acDetail, _
  Left:=0, Top:=4000, Width:=2500, Height:=400)

ErrorHandlerExit:
  Exit Sub

ErrorHandler:
  AddInErr(Err)
  Resume ErrorHandlerExit

End Sub

Public Sub AddInErr(ByVal errX As ErrObject)
```

Displays a message box with error information.

```
Dim strMsg As String

strMsg = _
  "An error occurred in the Extras add-in" _
  & Microsoft.VisualBasic.Constants.vbCrLf _
  & "Error #:" & errX.Number _
  & Microsoft.VisualBasic.Constants.vbCrLf _
  & "Description: " & errX.Description
MsgBox(strMsg, MsgBoxStyle.Critical, "Error!")

End Sub
```

> **NOTE** The syntax for named constants is much more verbose in Visual Studio 2005 than in Access VBA or VB 6: Instead of (for example) `acControlType`, you need the full enum reference, `Microsoft.Office.Interop.Access.acControlType`.

If you turn on the Error List pane (View ➪ Error List), you will see a number of warnings about implicit conversion of a variable from Access control to a specific Access control type (see Figure 16.23).

In general, you can clear up conversion warnings by using a conversion function in the code, but Visual Studio 2005 doesn't have any conversion functions for Access controls, so you just have to live with the warnings (the code will run fine).

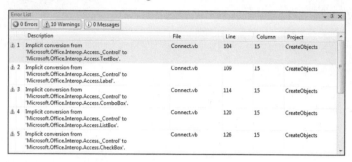

FIGURE 16.23

Implicit conversion warnings in the Error List.

If you are very skilled at writing code, and very lucky, at this point you could install and test the code, and everything would work perfectly. But it's more realistic to expect that there will be some bugs in the code that will prevent the add-in from working, so it's a good idea to do some debugging at this point, to save the time you would spend going through the installation and then finding that the add-in doesn't work as expected.

Debugging the Add-in

The Error List pane (mentioned in the previous section) helps you to locate any errors in your code; you can double-click an item to go to the line of code that caused the error. When working with an add-in, you can use the "Start Debugging" selection on the Debug menu to step through the code — but first you have to select Access as the application to start when debugging. To do this, select "CreateObjects Properties" from the bottom of the Project menu (if you are working with a different project, its name appears instead of CreateObjects). Click the Debug tab and select Access as the "Start external program" option selection. (Figure 16.24 shows the Select File dialog that appears when you click the Browse button to the right of the "Start external program" option.)

Now you can set breakpoints in your code (using the F9 function key), as with Access VBA, and when you select Start Debugging on the Debug menu, Access will open automatically. Select (or create) a new database, and then click the add-in's buttons to run and debug the code; it will stop at the breakpoints you have set so you can step through the code with the F8 function key.

Selecting Access as the program to start when debugging.

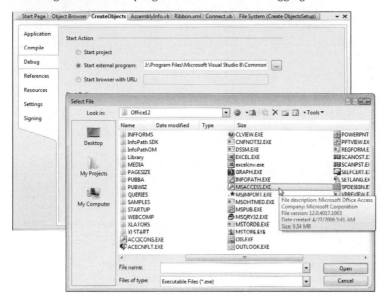

Building and Installing the Add-in

After finding and correcting any errors in the add-in's code, you are ready to build the add-in; to do this, click the Save All button, and then select Build from the context menu of the "Create ObjectsSetup" item in the Solution Explorer (the name is your add-in's name plus "Setup"), as shown in Figure 16.25.

When "Build succeeded" appears in the lower-left corner of the status bar, you can then install the solution by selecting Install from the same context menu.

 If the Install selection is disabled after a successful first build, select Rebuild; after that, Install should be enabled.

FIGURE 16.25

Building the solution.

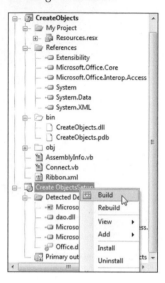

Selecting Install starts the awkwardly named Create ObjectsSetup Setup Wizard (see Figure 16.26).

FIGURE 16.26

The first screen of the Setup Wizard.

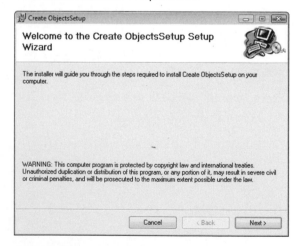

Clicking Next gets you the Select Installation Folder screen (see Figure 16.27), where you can either accept the default location or browse for another location, and select whether the add-in is available to all users or just you.

FIGURE 16.27

Selecting the installation folder for the solution.

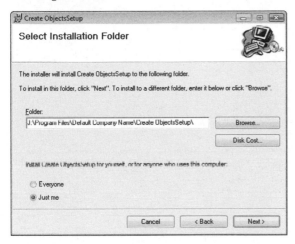

On the Confirm Installation screen of the Setup Wizard shown in Figure 16.28, click Next to start the installation.

FIGURE 16.28

The Confirm Installation screen of the Setup Wizard.

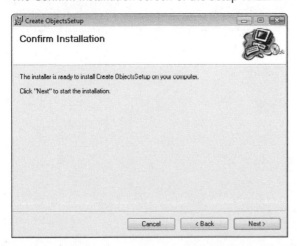

The next screen, omitted here, shows a progress bar while the solution is being installed.

When the installation is complete, you will get the Installation Complete screen, depicted in Figure 16.29.

The final screen of the Setup Wizard.

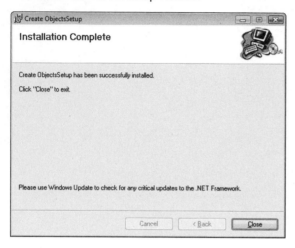

Generally speaking, after clicking Close on the last wizard screen, the add-in is installed automatically; however, if you don't see the custom Ribbon that the add-in should create in an Access 2007 database, you can install it manually. Open the Access Options dialog from the Office menu, and select the Add-ins page. At the bottom of the page click the Go button to the right of the COM Add-ins drop-down, as shown in Figure 16.30.

The COM Add-ins dialog (shown in Figure 16.31) looks the same as in older versions of Access. If you see the add-in listed, just check it; otherwise, you can browse for it.

FIGURE 16.30

Opening the COM Add-ins dialog from the Add-ins page of the Access Options dialog.

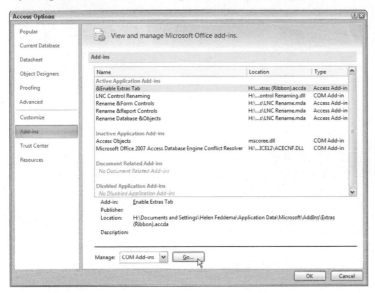

FIGURE 16.31

Installing a COM add-in in the COM Add-ins dialog.

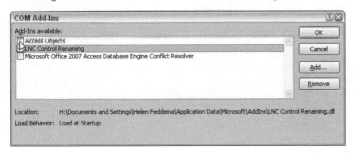

Using the Add-in

To test the add-in, open any Access 2007 database (or create a new database). As in Figure 16.32, you should see a new Visual Studio Add-in tab on the Ribbon with a group called "Create Access Objects" containing three buttons. There is no need to manually add the Ribbon, or even to close and reopen the database; the Ribbon appears immediately (a refreshing change from the struggle you have to go through in order to get a custom Ribbon to appear from an Access add-in).

FIGURE 16.32

A new tab and group created by the add-in.

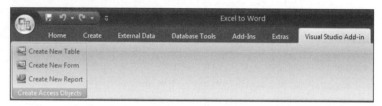

Clicking the "Create New Table" button creates a new table with several fields of different data types, the "Create New Form" button creates a new form with the new table as its record source and several controls of different types, and the "Create New Report" button creates a new report, also with the new table as its record source and several controls of different types. Figure 16.33 shows the new table in design view.

FIGURE 16.33

A new table created by the add-in.

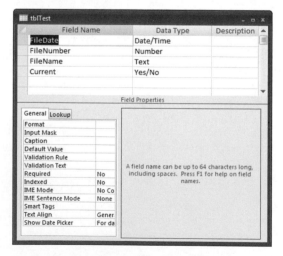

Figure 16.34 shows the new form; the new report is similar.

A form created by the add-in.

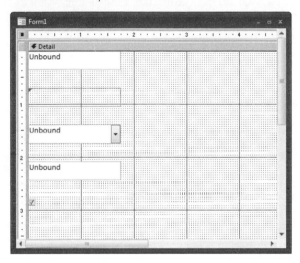

NOTE The form is called Form1 (or another number); it can't be renamed in code, either in the Visual Studio add-in or directly in Access VBA, because the `Name` property of the `Form` object is read-only when the form is created using the `CreateForm` method (and similarly for the `CreateReport` method).

Summary

After working with all three add-in types (Access, VB 6, and Visual Studio 2005), my conclusion is that Access add-ins have advantages over both VB 6 and Visual Studio 2005 add-ins, at least if you are running Windows XP. One of the most significant advantages of Access add-ins is that they are themselves Access databases, and this allows you to copy database objects from the code database to the calling database. If you need forms in a VB or Visual Studio add-in, you have to create them from scratch as VB or Windows forms; reports (in some versions of VB), can only be created using Crystal Reports. Another advantage of Access add-ins is that only an Access add-in can create a wizard or builder. And finally, Access add-ins use VBA code, so you don't need to learn a new programming dialect, just a few special techniques.

However, if you want your Access add-ins to create custom Ribbons, there are some roadblocks at present. Getting the custom Ribbon to display, and to run add-in code, may require so much time spent in uninstalling and reinstalling the add-in, unloading and reloading the table, and closing and reopening the database numerous times, that you get totally frustrated in trying to get the add-in's custom Ribbon to display (and its buttons to work). By contrast, Access add-ins that create menu add-ins and property builders work just fine once they are installed, and so do Ribbons and buttons created by VB 6 and Visual Studio add-ins.

When you need to put a button somewhere other than on the Add-Ins tab, and you don't want to fiddle with getting Ribbon buttons to work from Access add-ins, you can create a VB or Visual Studio add-in — both work very well with Ribbons.

Another special consideration is running add-ins on Windows Vista — at present, Access add-ins have problems with Vista security, while (at least if you have installed the hotfix mentioned in the "Running Visual Studio 2005 in Windows Vista" sidebar — Visual Studio add-ins run fine in Vista. Hopefully, v. 3 of VSTO should (at long last!) include an Access template, which should greatly simplify the process of creating Shared add-ins for Access.

Chapter 17

Creating Standalone Scripts with Windows Script Host

F or many versions now, Windows has had its own scripting language, Windows Script Host, a dialect of Visual Basic Script (VBS). Windows Script Host (WSH) scripts can be run from the command line (for those versions of Windows that have a command line, click Start ➪ Run), by double-clicking the script file in an Explorer window, and also from the Windows Vista Task Scheduler, which is handy if you want to run a script automatically, on a regular schedule.

One use for a WSH script is to create a database backup at regular intervals; another is to copy Word or Excel templates, or other supporting files, to the appropriate folder, as part of an Office application setup, when you don't want (or need) to create a full Install package. WSH scripts are also useful for working with files in a folder, doing tasks such as deleting or renaming files containing a certain prefix, suffix, or extension. This chapter describes how to create and modify WSH scripts, including sample scripts for some common uses.

IN THIS CHAPTER

Writing Windows Script Host scripts

Using the Microsoft Script Editor and the VBS Help file

Differences between VBS and VBA code

Scripts for working with Office documents

Scripts for working with files

Using the Windows Vista Task Scheduler to run a backup script

Tools for Working with Windows Script Host Scripts

Though you can create and edit WSH scripts with Notepad, it is a lot easier to work with them in the Microsoft Script Editor (MSE), using the VBScript downloadable Help file for reference. Curiously, neither the MSE nor the VBScript Help file appears as part of the interface when you work with a WSH script; you have to locate (and possibly download) these files and set them up manually to provide a more functional working environment. The next sections tell you how to obtain and use these tools for working with WSH scripts.

The Microsoft Script Editor

The Microsoft Script Editor (MSE) has been part of Office for several versions now, but you might not be aware of its existence. It doesn't appear in either the Microsoft Office or Microsoft Office Tools program group, nor is it one of the Open With selections on the right-click menu of a VBS file.

The MSE executable is located in the following path for Office 2007: C:\Program Files\Common Files\Microsoft Shared\OFFICE12\MSE7.EXE, as shown in Figure 17.1.

FIGURE 17.1

The Microsoft Script Editor executable (MSE7.EXE).

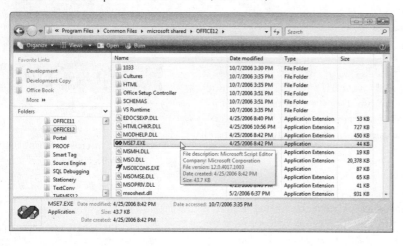

You can open the MSE directly by double-clicking the MSE7.EXE file, and then open a script to edit from its File ➪ Open menu, but for convenience you may wish to pin the executable file to the Start menu, as shown in Figure 17.2.

For even greater convenience, you can select the MSE as the program to use when opening VBS files. To do this, right-click a file with the .vbs extension in an Explorer pane, and select the Choose Default Program command (see Figure 17.3).

FIGURE 17.2

Pinning the MSE executable to the Windows Vista Start menu.

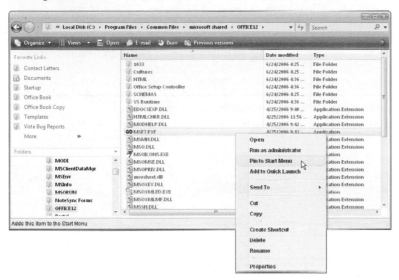

FIGURE 17.3

Choosing the MSE as the default program to use with VBS files.

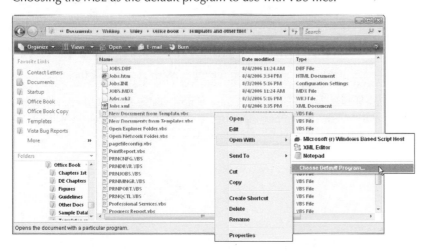

 The "Microsoft (r) Windows Based Script Host" entry in the Recommended Programs group on the Open With dialog runs the script, rather than opening it for editing.

Curiously, the MSE is not shown in either the Recommended Programs or Other Programs group in the Open With dialog (shown in Figure 17.4), so you need to browse for it in the C:\Program Files\Common Files\Microsoft Shared\OFFICE12\ folder.

FIGURE 17.4

The Open With dialog for selecting the program to use when opening a VBS file.

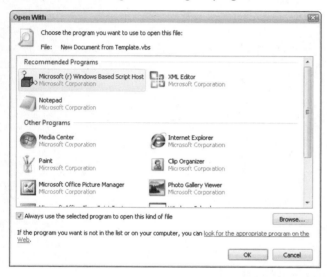

Figure 17.5 shows the MSE executable being selected in the Open With . . . Browse dialog.

Back on the main Open With dialog, Microsoft Script Editor is now visible in the Other Programs group, and you can select it and click OK to open the script in the MSE. After selecting MSE7.EXE as the file to use when opening a VBS file, you will see the MSE as a selection on the Open With menu (Figure 17.6).

FIGURE 17.5

Selecting the MSE executable as the file to use when opening VBS files.

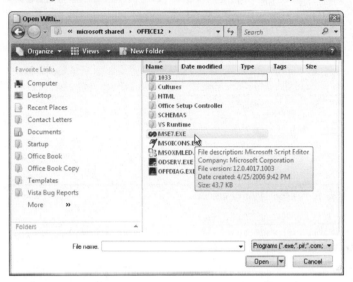

FIGURE 17.6

Selecting the MSE for use in opening VBS files.

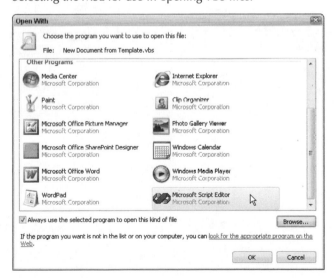

If you leave the "Always use the selected program to open this kind of file" checkbox checked when opening the script file, then double-clicking a VBS file will open MSE, and you will need to select "Microsoft (r) Windows Based Script Host" from the Open With menu to run the script; leaving this checkbox unchecked means that double-clicking the VBS script file will run the script, and you can select the MSE to edit the script from the Open With menu. I generally leave it unchecked, to make it easier to run scripts.

> **TIP**   If you want to run scripts by double-clicking them, select "Microsoft (r) Windows Based Script Host" as the program to use when opening VBS files, and check the "Always use the selected program to open this kind of file" checkbox.

Figure 17.7 shows the new MSE entry on the Open With menu of a VBS file.

FIGURE 17.7

The Microsoft Script Editor selection on a VBS file's Open With menu.

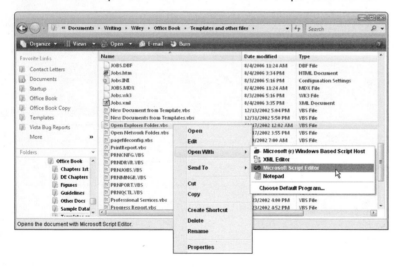

> **NOTE**   If you have Visual Studio 2005 installed, you will see that program on the Open With menu, and you can open a script in Visual Studio; however, the Visual Studio editor (for VBScripts) is basically just a text editor with some color-coding, so I recommend using the MSE instead.

The MSE window (shown in Figure 17.8) has some similarities to the Visual Basic module window for an Access (or another Office program), and to the VB 6 editor.

FIGURE 17.8

A WSH file open in the Microsoft Script Editor.

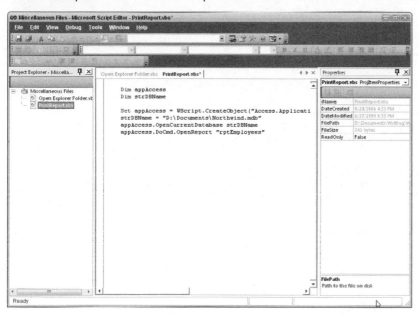

For full details on using the MSE, open Help from the MSE menu, and select Microsoft Script Editor Help. There are several Help topics related to using the MSE, as shown in Figure 17.9.

WARNING The MSE's Help file is web-based, so it is only available if you are connected to the Internet.

The VBScript Help File

As mentioned in Chapter 9, Microsoft has provided a Help file for VBScript that is a model of good design and usefulness (unlike the Help files for Office 2007); to get this Help file, download the Microsoft Windows Script 5.6 Documentation file from the Microsoft Web site at http://www.microsoft.com/downloads/details.aspx?familyid=01592C48-207D-4BE1-8A76-1C4099D7BBB9&displaylang=en.

The Help file (script56.chm) is a compiled HTML Help file, which can be opened in both Windows XP and Windows Vista. Unlike the MSE's own Help file, the script56.chm file is available whether or not you are connected to the Internet, although you do have to have a connection to download the file.

For working with WSH scripts, the VBScript Language Reference and Windows Script Host Help books are of the most use; they are shown opened in the Help file in Figure 17.9, with the Windows Script Host Object Model Help topic selected.

The Windows Scripting Technologies Help file.

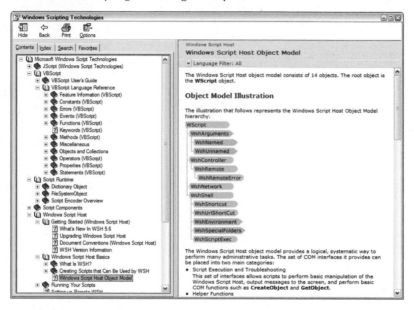

For help on using the MSE itself, open its Help file from the Help button on the editor's menu, then select "Microsoft Script Editor Help" to open a page of MSE-related Help topic selections, as shown in Figure 17.10.

There is a good deal of overlap between the Help file available from the MSE and the one down-loaded from the Scripting web page, but in my opinion the downloaded Help file is much easier to use, because of the hierarchical tree-type topic list, so if you have the option of opening this Help file in Windows XP, I recommend you use it; otherwise, if you are connected to the Internet, you can use the MSE Help file.

FIGURE 17.10

The Microsoft Script Editor Help topics.

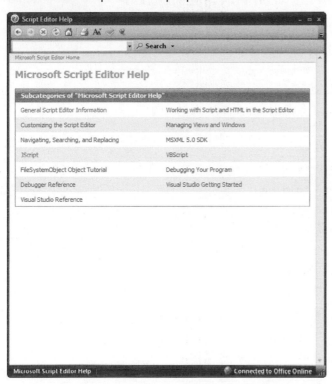

Differences between VBA and VBScript Code

If you are used to writing VBA (or VB) code, you will find that VBScript (VBS) lacks some of the features you are used to. Table 17.1 (taken from the "Visual Basic for Applications Features not in VBScript" topic in the VBS Help file) lists all the VBA features not supported in VBS code.

TABLE 17.1

Syntax Differences between VBA and VBS Code

Category	Omitted Feature/Keyword
Array Handling	Option Base Declaring arrays with lower bound <> 0
Collection	Add, Count, Item, Remove Access to collections using ! character
Conditional Compilation	#Const #If...Then...#Else
Control Flow	DoEvents GoSub...Return, GoTo On Error GoTo On...GoSub, On...GoTo Line numbers, Line labels
Conversion	CVar, CVDate Str, Val
Data Types	All intrinsic data types except Variant Type...End Type
Date/Time	Date statement, Time statement
DDE	LinkExecute, LinkPoke, LinkRequest, LinkSend
Debugging	Debug.Print End, Stop
Declaration	Declare (for declaring DLLs) Optional ParamArray Static
Error Handling	Erl Error Resume, Resume Next
File Input/Output	All traditional Basic file I/O
Financial	All financial functions
Object Manipulation	TypeOf
Objects	Clipboard Collection
Operators	Like
Options	Deftype Option Base Option Compare Option Private Module
Select Case	Expressions containing Is keyword or any comparison operators Expressions containing a range of values using the To keyword.
Strings	Fixed-length strings LSet, RSet Mid Statement StrConv
Using Objects	Collection access using !

Though this table is useful, it doesn't cover all the differences between VBA and VBS code, nor does it identify the ones that are most likely to cause trouble when converting VBA code to VBS. When working with both Outlook VBS and WSH scripts I have found a number of differences between the two dialects of VB that need to be taken into account when writing VBS code (especially when converting VBA code to VBS). These differences are listed in Table 17.2.

TABLE 17.2

Programming Technique Differences between VBA and VBS Code

VBA Feature	VBS Feature
All named constants can be used as arguments, or for setting values.	Only a very limited number of basic named constants are supported. Use the Object Browser opened from a VBA module window to locate the numeric equivalent of a named constant (in Figure 17.11 you can see that 40 is the numeric equivalent of the `olContact` named constant).
Variables can (and should) be declared as specific data types, for example `Dim appOutlook As Outlook.Application`.	Data typing of variables is not supported. Remove all data typing of declarations when converting code from VBA to VBS — for example, instead of `Dim appOutlook As Outlook.Application`, in VBS the declaration is just `Dim appOutlook`.
Full error handling is supported, typically using `On Error GoTo ErrorHandler` with a section specifying the error handling to be done.	Only very limited error handling is supported, using `On Error Resume Next`. However, you can use various methods of the FileSystemObject to determine whether files exist before performing operations on them, as an alternative to VBA-type error handling for file operations. You can also determine whether or not an object has been set by checking whether it is equal to `Nothing` (for example, `fil Is Nothing`).
You can use `Debug.Print` statements to write data from variables to the Immediate window as the code is executing, for debugging purposes.	`Debug.Print` is not supported; you must use `MsgBox` statements instead, which hold up code execution until you click OK (after the script is running correctly, comment out the `MsgBox` statements).
In a `For Each . . . Next` statement, use the variable in the `Next` line (for example, `Next fil`).	In a `For Each . . . Next` statement, omit the variable in the `Next` line (for example, `Next`).
The `Nz` function is supported (in Access VBA code, or other VBA code if there is a reference to the Access object library).	The `Nz` function is not supported, use the `IsNull` function, or check that a value is equal to `""`, as substitutes.
To comment out a multi-line code statement using the underscore line continuation character, you only need to put an apostrophe at the beginning of the first line.	To comment out a set of lines using the line continuation character, you must put an apostrophe at the beginning of each line.

601

Using GetObject and CreateObject in VBS

In VBA code, you can use `GetObject` to set a reference to an existing instance of an application, such as Word or Excel, to avoid creating numerous instances running in the background (you can see several WINWORD.EXE processes in the Task Manager in the following figure). Typically, an error handler detects whether `GetObject` set the reference, and if not, `CreateObject` is used instead. Although the `GetObject` function worked correctly in earlier versions of Windows, unfortunately, this technique doesn't work when you run VBS scripts in Windows Vista. Whether you use `GetObject` (with a slightly different syntax), or `CreateObject`, and whether or not there is a running instance of an application, a new instance is created every time the script is run.

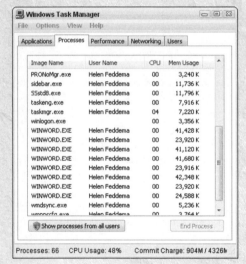

Multiple instances of Word in the Task Manager.

FIGURE 17.11

Viewing the numeric equivalents of named constants in the `OlObjectClass` Outlook enum in the Object Browser.

Useful Scripts

You can use WSH scripts for a number of different purposes, which are described in the following sections.

Setup Scripts

The CopyTemplateUser.vbs script copies a template called Test.dot from the current folder (the folder where the script file is located) to the default User Templates folder; the CopyTemplateWorkgroup.vbs script copies Test.dot from the current folder to the Workgroup Templates folder (if one has been selected). Each one puts up informative message boxes as the code runs. (The `MsgBox` lines can be commented out after verifying that the script works correctly.)

Setting the User Templates and Workgroup Templates Paths

To view (or set) the User Templates and Workgroup Templates path, click the Office button in any Word document and click the Word Options button:

Opening the Word Options dialog.

On the Word Options dialog, select the Advanced page, scroll down to the bottom of the page, and click the File Locations button:

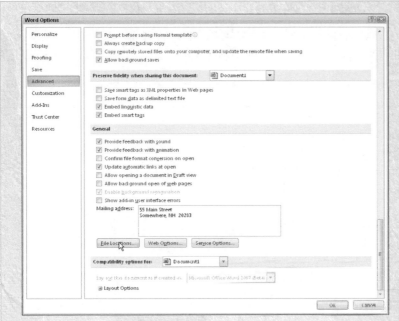

The Advanced page of the Word Options dialog.

The File Locations dialog opens, where you can view and set the User Templates and/or Workgroup Templates folder paths. To set a folder path, simply select the appropriate selection (User templates or Workgroup templates) in the File types list, click the Modify button, and browse to the desired folder location:

The File Locations dialog, where you can set the template paths.

To test one of these scripts, copy the Test.dot template to the same folder as the script (you can also copy any Word template, and rename it "Test.dot.") Right-click the CopyTemplateUser.vbs file in an Explorer window and select "Microsoft (r) Windows Based Script Host" from the Open With menu, as shown in Figure 17.12.

FIGURE 17.12

Running a WSH script.

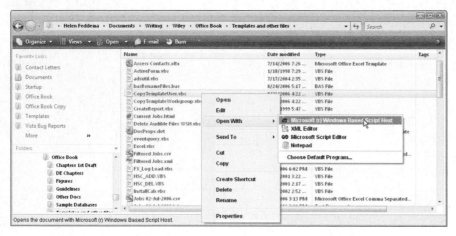

If you have not commented out this message box, you will first see a message listing the template name and current path (Figure 17.13).

FIGURE 17.13

A message box listing the template name and path for copying a Word template.

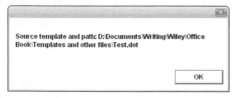

Next, if the copy is successful, you will get the message (the path may be different on your system) shown in Figure 17.14.

FIGURE 17.14

A success message after copying the template to the User Templates path.

If the copy could not be done, because Test.dot could not be located in the current folder, you will instead get the message shown in Figure 17.15.

FIGURE 17.15

A message indicating that the template to be copied could not be found.

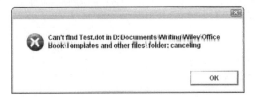

NOTE When you open the MSE, you may see a script open in the code pane, and other scripts listed in the Project Explorer; these are the scripts that were recently opened. If you see the script you want to edit in the Project Explorer, just select it.

The text of CopyTemplateUser.vbs is listed next. There are several commented-out MsgBox statements in this script; if you want to display these message boxes, uncomment these lines by removing the apostrophe at the beginning of the line:

```
Dim strTemplate
Dim strUserTemplatePath
Dim appWord
Dim fso
Dim strScriptPath
Dim strScriptName
Dim strScriptNameAndPath
Dim fil
Dim strPrompt
Dim strTemplatePath

strScriptName = WScript.ScriptName
```

Get the path of the current script, extracting it from the `ScriptFullName` property:

```
strScriptNameAndPath = WScript.ScriptFullName
strScriptPath = Mid(strScriptNameAndPath, 1, _
   Len(strScriptNameAndPath) - Len(strScriptName))
strTemplate = "Test.dot"
```

Get the User Templates path from the Word Options dialog, using the `DefaultFilePath` property with the argument 2 (most named constants can't be used in VBS):

```
Set appWord = WScript.CreateObject("Word.Application")
strUserTemplatePath = appWord.Options.DefaultFilePath(2) _
   & "\"
'MsgBox "User templates path: " & strUserTemplatePath
If strUserTemplatePath <> "\" Then
   Set fso = _
      WScript.CreateObject("Scripting.FileSystemObject")
   strTemplatePath = strScriptPath & strTemplate
   'MsgBox "Source template and path: " & strTemplatePath
```

Try to locate the template file, using the FileSystemObject's `GetFile` method; quit if it is not found:

```
Set fil = fso.GetFile(strTemplatePath)
If fil Is Nothing Then
   strPrompt = "Can't find " & strTemplate & _
      " in " & strScriptPath & " folder; canceling"
   MsgBox strPrompt, vbCritical + vbOKOnly
   Quit
Else
```

Copy the template to the User Templates folder, using the `Copy` method of the `File` object:

```
      fil.Copy strUserTemplatePath, True
      MsgBox strTemplate & " copied to " _
         & strUserTemplatePath
   End If
Else
   strPrompt = _
      "User template path not selected; canceling"
   MsgBox strPrompt, vbCritical + vbOKOnly
End If
```

The CopyTemplateWorkgroup.vbs is similar, but it has some more error handling, to deal with the situation where the Workgroup Templates path has not been selected in Word:

```
Dim strTemplate
Dim strWorkgroupTemplatePath
Dim appWord
Dim fso
```

```
Dim strScriptPath
Dim strScriptName
Dim strScriptNameAndPath
Dim fil
Dim strPrompt
Dim strTemplatePath
Dim strCurrentPath

strScriptName = WScript.ScriptName
```

Get the path of the current script, extracting it from the `ScriptFullName` property:

```
strScriptNameAndPath = WScript.ScriptFullName
strScriptPath = Mid(strScriptNameAndPath, 1, _
   Len(strScriptNameAndPath) - Len(strScriptName))
strTemplate = "Test.dot"
strCurrentPath = strScriptPath & strTemplate
```

Get the User Templates path from the Word Options dialog, using the `DefaultFilePath` property with the argument 2 (most named constants can't be used in VBS):

```
Set appWord = WScript.CreateObject("Word.Application")
strWorkgroupTemplatePath = _
   appWord.Options.DefaultFilePath(3) & "\"
If strWorkgroupTemplatePath <> "\" Then
  Set fso = _
   WScript.CreateObject("Scripting.FileSystemObject")
strTemplatePath = strScriptPath & strTemplate
'MsgBox "Source template and path: " & strTemplatePath
```

Try to locate the template file, using the FileSystemObject's `GetFile` method; quit if it is not found:

```
Set fil = fso.GetFile(strTemplatePath)
If fil Is Nothing Then
   strPrompt = "Can't find " & strTemplate & _
      " in " & strScriptPath & " folder; canceling"
   MsgBox strPrompt, vbCritical + vbOKOnly
   Quit
Else
```

Copy the template to the Workgroup Templates folder, using the `Copy` method of the `File` object:

```
   fso.CopyFile strCurrentPath, _
      strWorkgroupTemplatePath, True
   MsgBox strTemplate & " copied from " & _
   strCurrentPath & " to " _
      & strWorkgroupTemplatePath
End If
```

```
Else
   strPrompt = _
      "Workgroup template path not selected; canceling"
   MsgBox strPrompt, vbCritical + vbOKOnly
End If
```

One or the other of these files (with the appropriate template name replacing "Test.dot") would be useful as part of an Office application that includes one or more Word templates; all the user needs to do to install the template(s) in the right location is to run the script.

If you need to copy a set of templates to the User Templates or Workgroup Templates folder, you don't need to hard-code the template names, so long as the templates you want to copy are the only templates in the current folder. The CopyAllTemplates.vbs script listed next copies all the Word 2007 (*.dotx) templates in the current folder to the User Templates folder:

```
Dim strTemplate
Dim strUserTemplatePath
Dim appWord
Dim fso
Dim strScriptPath
Dim strScriptName
Dim strScriptNameAndPath
Dim fil
Dim filTemplate
Dim strPrompt
Dim strTemplatePath

strScriptName = WScript.ScriptName
strScriptNameAndPath = WScript.ScriptFullName
```

Get the path of the current script:

```
strScriptPath = Mid(strScriptNameAndPath, 1, _
   Len(strScriptNameAndPath) - Len(strScriptName))
```

Get the User Templates path from the Word Options dialog, using the `DefaultFilePath` property with the 2 argument:

```
Set appWord = WScript.CreateObject("Word.Application")
strUserTemplatePath = appWord.Options.DefaultFilePath(2) _
   & "\"
'MsgBox "User templates path: " & strUserTemplatePath
If strUserTemplatePath <> "\" Then
   Set fso = _
      WScript.CreateObject("Scripting.FileSystemObject")
   Set fld = fso.GetFolder(strScriptPath)
```

610

Copy all Word 2007 (*.dotx) templates from the current folder to User Templates folder, with a message box for each one (comment out the MsgBox line to suppress these messages):

```
lngCount = 0
For Each fil In fld.Files
   If Right(fil.Name, 4) = "dotx" Then
      strTemplate = fil.Name
      fil.Copy strUserTemplatePath, True
      MsgBox strTemplate & " copied to " _
         & strUserTemplatePath
      lngCount = lngCount + 1
   End If
Next
Else
   strPrompt = _
      "User template path not selected; canceling"
   MsgBox strPrompt, vbCritical + vbOKOnly
End If
```

> **NOTE** The sample database for this chapter is Northwind.accdb. This is a version of the sample Northwind database, with its tables renamed according to the Leszynski Naming Convention.

Office Scripts

PrintReport.vbs demonstrates another use of scripts; it prints a report from Northwind.accdb, without the need to open the database. This could be handy if you need to print out labels on a regular basis. The code for this script is listed as follows:

```
Dim appAccess
Dim strDBName

Set appAccess = _
   WScript.CreateObject("Access.Application")
Set fso = _
   WScript.CreateObject("Scripting.FileSystemObject")
```

Modify the hard-coded file path as needed for your system:

```
strDBName = "D:\Documents\Northwind.accdb"

On Error Resume Next
   appAccess.OpenCurrentDatabase strDBName

Set fil = fso.GetFile(strDBName)
If fil Is Nothing Then
   strPrompt = "Can't find " & strDBName & _
      "; canceling"
   MsgBox strPrompt, vbCritical + vbOKOnly
   Quit
```

```
Else
    'Print report
    appAccess.DoCmd.OpenReport "rptCustomerLabels"
End If

Set appAccess = Nothing
```

> **TIP** If the MSE is already open, you can open a new script for editing by dragging the script file from an Explorer pane into the MSE window.

Northwind.accdb has a form for selecting an invoice to print by order number. But you might want to be able to quickly print an invoice without opening the database; the PrintInvoice.vbs script listed next does just this:

```
Dim appAccess
Dim strDBName
Dim lngInvoiceNo
Dim strTitle
Dim strPrompt

Set appAccess = _
    WScript.CreateObject("Access.Application")
Set fso = _
    WScript.CreateObject("Scripting.FileSystemObject")
strDBName = "D:\Documents\Northwind.accdb"

On Error Resume Next
    appAccess.OpenCurrentDatabase strDBName

    Set fil = fso.GetFile(strDBName)
    If fil Is Nothing Then
        strPrompt = "Can't find " & strDBName & _
            "; canceling"
        MsgBox strPrompt, vbCritical + vbOKOnly
        Quit
    Else
        strTitle = "Select invoice"
        strPrompt = "Select an invoice to print (10248 - 11077)"
        lngInvoiceNo = CLng(InputBox(strPrompt, strTitle))
        'MsgBox "Invoice No.: " & lngInvoiceNo
```

Run a lengthy SQL statement to create a table for use as a report record source:

```
strSQL = "SELECT DISTINCT qryInvoices.OrderID, " _
    & "qryInvoices.ShipName, qryInvoices.ShipAddress, " _
    & "qryInvoices.ShipCityStateZip, " _
```

```
      & "qryInvoices.ShipCountry, " _
      & "qryInvoices.CustomerID, qryInvoices.CompanyName, " _
      & "qryInvoices.BillToAddress, " _
      & "qryInvoices.BillToCityStateZip, " _
      & "qryInvoices.BillToCountry, " _
      & "qryInvoices.Salesperson, " _
      & "qryInvoices.OrderDate, qryInvoices.RequiredDate, " _
      & "qryInvoices.ShippedDate, qryInvoices.Shipper, " _
      & "qtotInvoiceDetails.SumOfExtendedPrice " _
      & "AS Subtotal, " _
      & "qryInvoices.Freight, [SumOfExtendedPrice] " _
      & "+ [Freight] " _
      & "AS Total INTO tmakInvoice " _
      & "FROM qryInvoices " _
      & "INNER JOIN qtotInvoiceDetails " _
      & "ON qryInvoices.OrderID = " _
      & "qtotInvoiceDetails.OrderID " _
      & "WHERE qryInvoices.OrderID = " & lngInvoiceNo
    appAccess.DoCmd.SetWarnings False
    appAccess.DoCmd.RunSQL strSQL
    appAccess.DoCmd.OpenReport "rptSingleInvoice"
End If

Set appAccess = Nothing
```

When this script is run, an input box pops up where you can enter an invoice number, as shown in Figure 17.16.

FIGURE 17.16

An input box popped up from a WSH script.

After you enter the invoice number and click OK, a SQL statement is run to create a make-table query that is part of the record source of rptSingleInvoice, and that report is printed. The report is shown in Figure 17.17.

FIGURE 17.17

An Access report printed from a WSH script.

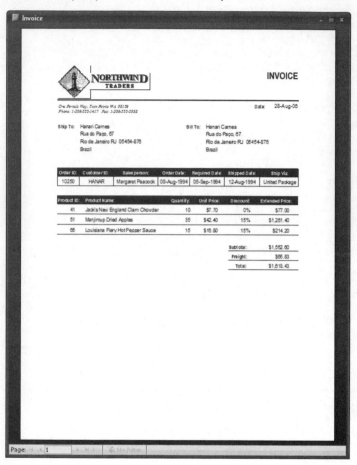

As a quick alternative to opening Word or Excel and selecting the correct template, you can also use a WSH script to create a new Word document or Excel worksheet based on a template. This technique can be useful when users have problems selecting the correct template to use when creating a new Word document or Excel worksheet. The New Document from Template.vbs script listed next opens a new Word document based on a Word 97-2003 template located in the main User Templates folder:

```
Dim appWord
Dim strTemplatePath
Dim strUserTemplatePath
Dim strTemplate
Dim docs
```

```
strTemplate = "Test Letter.dot"
Set appWord = WScript.CreateObject("Word.Application")
```

Get the User Templates path from the Word Options dialog, using the `DefaultFilePath` property with the argument:

```
strUserTemplatePath = appWord.Options.DefaultFilePath(2) _
    & "\"
'MsgBox "User templates path: " & strUserTemplatePath
If strUserTemplatePath <> "\" Then
Set fso = _
WScript.CreateObject("Scripting.FileSystemObject")
strTemplatePath = strUserTemplatePath & strTemplate
MsgBox "Source template and path: " & strTemplatePath

On Error Resume Next
    Set fil = fso.GetFile(strTemplatePath)
        If fil Is Nothing Then
            strPrompt = "Can't find " & strTemplate & _
                " in " & strTemplatePath & " folder; canceling"
                MsgBox strPrompt, vbCritical + vbOKOnly
            Quit
        Else
        Set appWord = WScript.CreateObject("Word.Application")
        appWord.Visible = true
        Set docs = appWord.Documents
        docs.Add(strTemplate)
        End If

    Else
        strPrompt = _
            "User template path not selected; canceling"
        MsgBox strPrompt, vbCritical + vbOKOnly
    End If
```

The New Worksheet from Template.vbs script listed next opens a new Excel worksheet based on an Excel 2007 template located in the main User Templates folder:

```
Dim appExcel
Dim strTemplatePath
Dim strTemplate
Dim bks
Dim wkb
Dim wks

    strTemplate = "Access Contacts.xltx"
```

Get the User Templates path from the Word Options dialog.

```
Set appWord = WScript.CreateObject("Word.Application")
strUserTemplatePath = appWord.Options.DefaultFilePath(2) _
  & "\"
Set fso = _
  WScript.CreateObject("Scripting.FileSystemObject")
strTemplatePath = strUserTemplatePath & strTemplate
MsgBox "Source template and path: " & strTemplatePath

On Error Resume Next

Set fil = fso.GetFile(strTemplatePath)
If fil Is Nothing Then
  strPrompt = "Can't find " & strTemplate & _
    " in " & strScriptPath & " folder; canceling"
  MsgBox strPrompt, vbCritical + vbOKOnly
  Quit
Else
  Set appExcel = WScript.CreateObject("Excel.Application")
  appExcel.Visible = True
  Set bks = appExcel.Workbooks
  Set wkb = bks.Add(strTemplatePath)
  Set wks = wkb.Sheets(1)
  wks.Activate
End If
```

Miscellaneous Scripts

The next script is one I made to automate the process of deleting temporary files from Audible.com downloads. These files are sometimes not automatically deleted and have to be deleted manually, which is a nuisance; the Delete Audible Files.vbs script is listed as follows:

```
Dim fso
Dim strPath
Dim strFile
Dim strFilePath
Dim blnFound

    Set fso = CreateObject("Scripting.FileSystemObject")
    blnFound = False

    strPath = "E:\Audible\Bin\"
    strFile = "Debug.log"
    strFilePath = strPath & strFile
    If fso.FileExists(strFilePath) Then
        fso.DeleteFile strFilePath
        blnFound = True
    End If
```

```
strFile = "aadownload.log"
strFilePath = strPath & strFile
If fso.FileExists(strFilePath) Then
    fso.DeleteFile strFilePath
    blnFound = True
End If

strFile = "aaschedule.log"
strFilePath = strPath & strFile
If fso.FileExists(strFilePath) Then
    fso.DeleteFile strFilePath
    blnFound = True
End If

strFile = "aasubsschedule.log"
strFilePath = strPath & strFile
If fso.FileExists(strFilePath) Then
    fso.DeleteFile strFilePath
    blnFound = True
End If

If blnFound = True Then
 MsgBox "Deleted Audible temp files"
Else
    MsgBox "No Audible temp files found"
End If
```

The script first sets a blnFound variable to False (it would be a Boolean variable, if variables could be declared with data types in VBS). Then the script uses the FileExists method of the FileSystemObject to determine whether a file exists, and delete it if so, setting blnFound to True. At the end of the code, depending on whether the blnFound variable is True or False, a message box appears saying either "Deleted Audible temp files" or "No Audible temp files found."

You probably don't need the Delete Audible Files.vbs script, but you may find the Delete Temp Files.vbs script useful. This script uses the GetSpecialFolder method of the FileSystemObject, with the 2 argument, to set a fldTemp variable to the Temp file folder, and puts up a message box that asks if you want to delete all files in it; if you click the Yes button, the script attempts to delete all the files in that folder (the On Error Resume Next statement goes to the next file if a file can't be deleted, because it is in use):

```
Dim fso
Dim fldTemp
Dim fil
Dim n
Dim intResult
Dim strPrompt
```

```
        Set fso = CreateObject("Scripting.FileSystemObject")
        Set fldTemp = fso.GetSpecialFolder(2)
        strPrompt = "Delete all files in " & fldTemp & "?"
        intResult = MsgBox (strPrompt, vbQuestion + vbYesNo)
        If intResult = 6 Then

    On Error Resume Next
        n = 0

      For Each fil in fld.Files
        fil.Delete
        n = n + 1
      Next

      MsgBox "Approximately " & n _
          & " temp files deleted from " & fldTemp
    End If
```

The next script, Rename Files.vbs, renames figure files in a folder in a specific manner; the strNewFileName = Mid(fil.Name, 9) line of the script can be modified to rename files as needed:

```
        Dim fld
        Dim lngCount
        Dim fso
        Dim strScriptPath
        Dim strScriptName
        Dim strScriptNameAndPath
        Dim fil
        Dim strPrompt

        strScriptName = WScript.ScriptName
```

Get the path of the current script, using the ScriptFullName property:

```
        strScriptNameAndPath = WScript.ScriptFullName
        strScriptPath = Mid(strScriptNameAndPath, 1, _
          Len(strScriptNameAndPath) - Len(strScriptName))

    On Error Resume Next
        lngCount = 0
        Set fso = CreateObject("Scripting.FileSystemObject")
        Set fld = fso.GetFolder(strScriptPath)

        For Each fil In fld.Files
```

Check the first character and extension (modify as needed for your requirements):

```
        If Left(fil.Name, 1) = "-" And _
           Right(fil.Name, 3) = "tif" Then
```

Modify the following line as needed for your requirements:

```
        strNewFileName = Mid(fil.Name, 9)
        fil.Name = strNewFileName
        lngCount = lngCount + 1
    End If
Next

strTitle = "Files renamed"
strPrompt = lngCount & " files in " _
    & strScriptPath & " renamed"
MsgBox strPrompt, vbInformation, strTitle
```

Scheduling a Backup Script with the Windows Vista Task Scheduler

If you want to run a script automatically at a regular interval, you can schedule it as a task in the Windows Vista Task Scheduler. One such use is to make a backup copy of a database every day at a specific time. The DailyDatabaseBackup.vbs script makes a dated backup copy of the sample Northwind.mdb database every day at the specified time.

WARNING A VBS script run from the Windows Explorer can have spaces in its name, but if you intend to run a script from the Task Scheduler, its name can't contain spaces. You won't get an error when selecting the script, but when the Task Scheduler attempts to run it, you will get an error and it won't run.

```
Dim fso
Dim fil
Dim strPrompt
Dim strDBPath
Dim strDBName
Dim strDBNameAndPath
Dim strDBNameBackup
Dim strScriptName
Dim strScriptNameAndPath
Dim strBackupNameAndPath

strScriptName = WScript.ScriptName
strScriptNameAndPath = WScript.ScriptFullName
```

Modify the hard-coded path as needed for your system:

```
strDBPath = "E:\Documents\"
strDBName = "Northwind.mdb"
strDBNameAndPath = strDBPath & strDBName
MsgBox "Database name and path: " & strDBNameAndPath
```

```
        strDBNameBackup = Left(strDBName, Len(strDBName) - 4) _
            & " Backup for " & FormatDateTime(Date(), 1) _
            & ".mdb"
    MsgBox "Backup name: " & strDBNameBackup
    strBackupNameAndPath = strDBPath & strDBNameBackup
```

Check that the database is in the specified folder, and quit if it is not found:

```
    On Error Resume Next
    Set fso = _
        WScript.CreateObject("Scripting.FileSystemObject")
    Set fil = fso.GetFile(strDBNameAndPath)
    'MsgBox "Error #: " & Err

    If fil Is Nothing Then
        strPrompt = "Can't find " & strDBName & _
            " in " & strDBPath & " folder; canceling"
        MsgBox strPrompt, vbCritical + vbOKOnly
        Quit
    Else
```

Copy the database to a backup:

```
        fso.CopyFile strDBNameAndPath, strBackupNameAndPath, _
            True
        MsgBox strDBName & " copied to " _
            & strDBPath & " as " & strDBNameBackup
    End If
```

You can run this script manually, but for assurance that a backup will be made every day, you can schedule the script to run from the Windows Task Scheduler. To open the Task Scheduler, first open the Control Panel, and select the Administrative Tools program group (Figure 17.18).

In the Administrative Tools program group, select the Task Scheduler, as shown in Figure 17.19. If you get a UAC message, click Continue.

FIGURE 17.18

Opening the Administrative Tools program group in the Control Panel.

FIGURE 17.19

Selecting the Task Scheduler in the Administrative Tools program group.

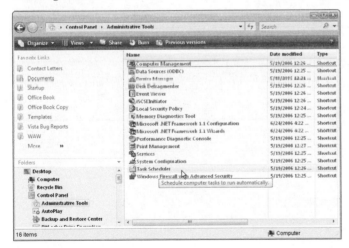

In the Task Scheduler window, select Create Basic Task (Figure 17.20).

FIGURE 17.20

Creating a Basic Task in the Task Scheduler.

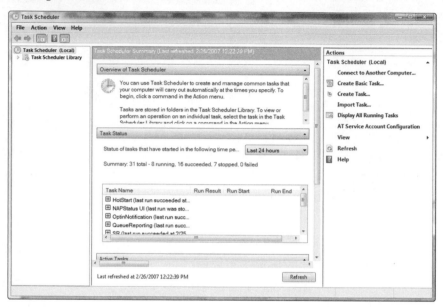

Next, as displayed in Figure 17.21, enter the name and description of the task.

FIGURE 17.21

Entering the task's name and description.

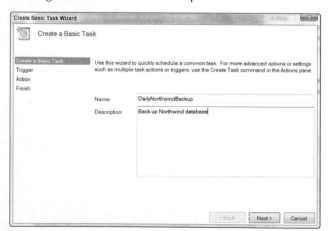

On the next screen (Figure 17.22), make a selection for when the task should be run (choose Daily to run it every day).

FIGURE 17.22

Specifying that the task should be run daily.

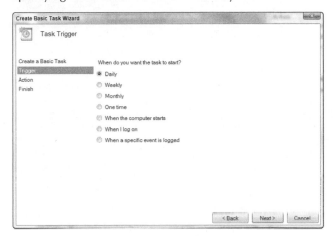

On the screen shown in Figure 17.23, enter the time to run the script.

FIGURE 17.23

Specifying the time to run the script.

Next, specify an action to run at the specified time. Selecting "Start a program" runs a script (see Figure 17.24).

FIGURE 17.24

Selecting the "Start a program" option to run a script.

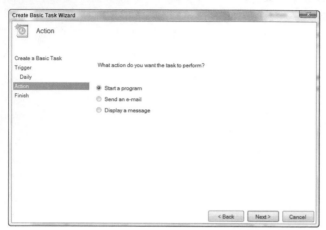

On the Start a Program screen, depicted in Figure 17.25, browse for the script to run.

FIGURE 17.25

Selecting a script for the Task Scheduler to run.

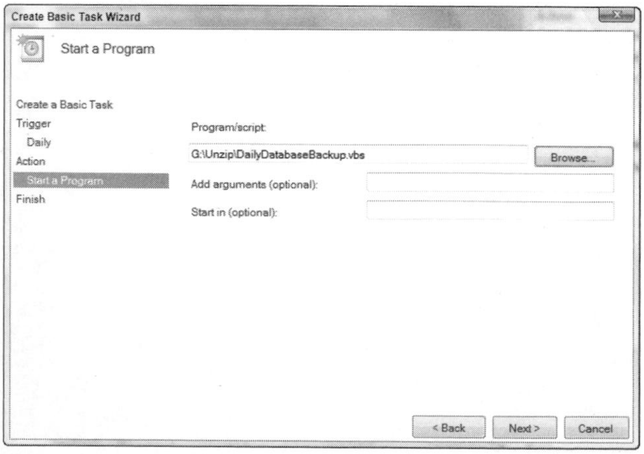

The final screen of the Task Scheduler Wizard displays a success message, shown in Figure 17.26.

FIGURE 17.26

The final success message indicating that a task has been scheduled.

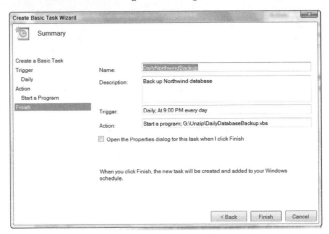

Now the Daily Database Backup.vbs script will be run at 9 PM every day without user intervention. When it is run, you will get several messages showing the name of the database to be copied, the name of the copy of the database (shown in Figure 17.27), and a final message showing where the copy was made. You will probably want to comment out these message boxes after verifying that the script runs.

FIGURE 17.27

A message from a VBS script run from the Task Scheduler.

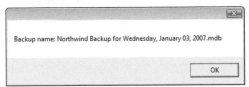

Summary

Although not part of Office, WSH scripts are a useful addition to VBA code running from within Office applications, for tasks such as running daily backups, ensuring that users make documents and worksheets from the right templates, and copying setup files to the right folder. Because these scripts use a dialect of VBScript that will run in the last few versions of Windows as well as Vista, they are very useful when you need to perform an action, or a series of actions, in different boot partitions or on different computers, running different versions of Windows.

Chapter 18

Working with SQL Server Data

Y̶ou can store data directly in an Access database, but Access also has the capability of storing and retrieving data using other database engines, including Microsoft SQL Server. Storing data directly in an Access database works fine for most database applications that would be used by individuals or small businesses. However, an organization that needs to store gigabytes of data (say, data on the entire population of the U.S. for marketing purposes or scientific data from thousands of studies) needs to use a SQL Server back end, rather than storing data in an Access database. Additionally, any organization concerned about keeping its data secure can benefit from the extra security features that SQL Server provides. But storing your data in SQL Server doesn't mean that you have to abandon the familiar Access interface: even when you use SQL Server for data storage, you can still use Access to develop the application's interface.

IN THIS CHAPTER

SQL Server 2005 versus SQL Server 2005 Express

Configuring SQL Server 2005

Preparing an Access database for upsizing

Using the Upsizing Wizard to upsize an Access database to SQL Server 2005

Linking an Access front end to data in a SQL Server database

NOTE The sample databases for this chapter are:

- **AdventureWorks SQL.accdb** (Access front end to SQL Server tables)
- **Basic Northwind v 1 (linked SQL Server tables).accdb** (Access front end to SQL Server tables)
- **Basic Northwind.accdb** (Access database for upsizing)
- **Basic Northwind CS.adp** (Access project front end for SQL Server tables)

In Windows Vista and Office 2007, it isn't easy to connect an Access front-end database to a SQL Server back end. In Office 2003 running on Windows XP, using the Upsizing Wizard to convert an Access database to a SQL Server back end was easy — even trivial. This task is now a major chore because you need to work through a long list of SQL Server settings and then

Windows security settings just to be able to connect to SQL Server before you even attempt to connect Access to SQL Server or upsize an Access database.

This chapter helps you navigate through the SQL Server and Windows settings you need to do several SQL Server-related tasks:

- Convert an Access database to SQL Server for use as a back end (this is known as upsizing the database)

- Create a client/server application with a SQL Server back end and an Access project front end

- Link an Access database to tables in a SQL Server database

Getting SQL Server 2005

If you have installed Visual Studio 2005, you should already have SQL Server 2005, as it is installed by default as part of the Visual Studio installation. To check this, open the Control Panel and select the Programs and Features applet; note that the Installed On date is the same for Microsoft SQL Server 2005 and Microsoft Visual Studio 2005 Professional Edition (see Figure 18.1).

FIGURE 18.1

Microsoft SQL Server 2005 listed in Programs and Features.

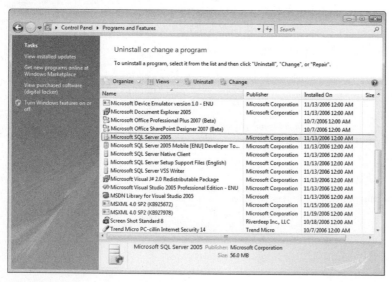

If you don't have SQL Server 2005 installed, you can download the Express version free, from `http://msdn.microsoft.com/vstudio/express/sql/`.

Compared to the full version, SQL Server 2005 Express (SSE) has a number of limitations, but it is fine for experimenting with SQL Server as a back end, or developing small applications. SSE includes all the core database features of SQL Server 2005, but it lacks support for enterprise features. If you need to create an enterprise application, you will need one of the other editions of SQL Server 2005, but for individual or small business use, SSE is very suitable.

> **NOTE** For a full comparison of the features of the five editions of SQL Server 2005, see the tables here: **www.microsoft.com/sql/prodinfo/features/compare-features.mspx.**

SSE is an upgrade to the Microsoft Database Engine (MSDE), which was included in the higher-end editions of previous Office versions. Compared to MSDE, SSE has several enhancements:

- The maximum database size has doubled, from 2GB to 4GB.

- MSDE's limitation on the number of concurrent users to five (with performance degrading significantly if there were more users) has been removed.

- The SQL Server Management Studio (included with SSE) gives you a user-friendly interface for working with saved queries and stored procedures, as well as various administrative tasks.

- The new XCopy deployment feature allows you to copy a database file to another computer, even if the database is not open. Other users can then connect to the database copy using the AttachDBFileName connection string argument.

> **NOTE** SQL Server 2005 must be upgraded to Service Pack 2 to work with Access 2007. If you have an earlier version, when you first run SQL Server 2005, or attempt to connect to it, you will get a message advising you of the need to upgrade, with a reference to a web page with the SP2 upgrade links for both SQL Server 2005 and SSE.

Preparing an Access Database for Upsizing to SQL Server

To convert an Access database (or just its tables) to SQL Server (this is known as upsizing), you need to run the Upsizing Wizard, as described in the "Using the Upsizing Wizard" section later in this chapter. However, before you run the Upsizing Wizard to upsize an Access database to SQL Server 2005 or SSE, you need to make some preparations in your database:

- Make sure that each table has a unique index, because a SQL Server can't update a table that lacks a unique index.

- Make any hidden tables visible (see sidebar that follows), because the Upsizing Wizard can't upsize hidden tables.

- Compile all the code, and correct any errors.

Making Hidden Tables Visible

To make hidden tables visible, click File ⇨ Access Options, select the Current Database page, and click the Navigation Options button:

The Navigation Options button on the Current Database page of the Access Options dialog.

On the Navigation Options dialog, check the "Show Hidden Options" checkbox:

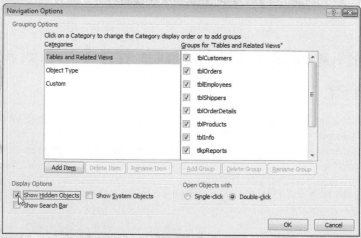

Making hidden objects visible in the Navigation Options dialog.

You may have code in an Access database that was originally created many versions ago, but you haven't upgraded it because it still runs. Before upsizing to SQL Server, you should make sure that all your code is up to date, because SQL Server is much less forgiving than Access.

I made a sample database for this chapter, Basic Northwind.accdb, based on the old Northwind sample database that came with several previous versions of Access. Because Northwind was originally created many versions ago, and has only been minimally upgraded over Access versions, there is a good deal of old code in this database — some of it very old code indeed: Access 95 or earlier. Before upsizing, I took the opportunity to update all the code to the current syntax.

For example, the old Northwind code uses the `IsLoaded` function, provided in a module. Many versions of Access ago, this function was needed, but since Access 2000, you don't need a special function to check whether a form is loaded — just use the `IsLoaded` property of the form, as an item in the AllForms collection. Here is some typical code for returning to the main menu, as used in a standard `Form_Close` event procedure:

```
Dim prj As Object

Set prj = Application.CurrentProject

If prj.AllForms("fmnuMain").IsLoaded = True Then
    Forms![fmnuMain].Visible = True
Else
    DoCmd.OpenForm "fmnuMain"
End If
```

Some features that are supported in Access applications won't survive upsizing, unfortunately. Functions called from calculated expressions in queries are not supported in SQL Server, so when you upsize a query that uses functions in calculated field expressions, you will get an error. I recommend removing the functions from query calculated expressions before upsizing; after the database is upsized, you can modify the corresponding stored procedure or user-defined function as needed in a way that will work in SQL Server.

Configuring SQL Server 2005 for Data Access

In Access 2003, you didn't need to do any special SQL Server setup before upsizing an Access database to SQL Server using the Microsoft Database Engine (MSDE), the predecessor to SQL Server 2005 Express. But the situation in Office 2007 is very different. In addition to preparing your Access database, you also have a considerable number of setup chores to do to make SQL

SQL Server Books Online

You can download a set of books on SQL Server 2005 from www.microsoft.com/technet/prodtechnol/sql/2005/downloads/books.mspx.

Once downloaded and installed, you can open the SQL Server Books Online from the newly created Documentation and Tutorials group under the Microsoft SQL Server 2005 program group:

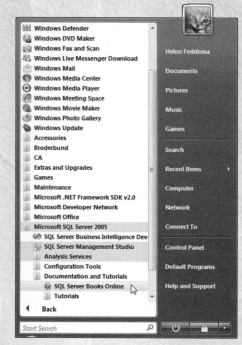

Opening SQL Server Books Online Help.

The books include documentation for both the regular version of SQL Server 2005 and SSE:

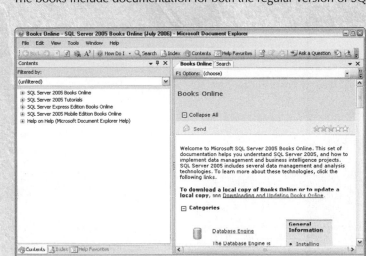

The Contents page of SQL Server Books Online.

If you have upgraded SQL Server 2005 to Service Pack 2, make sure to also download the equivalent upgrade for SQL Server Books Online (available from the same web page as the SP2 patch for SQL Server, www.microsoft.com/sql/ctp.mspx), so the documentation will reflect the SP2 changes.

Server (or SSE) available as a back end for Access. By default, when SQL Server (or SSE) is installed, it may not be set to run on startup. To ensure that SQL Server is running and available, follow these steps:

1. Open the SQL Server Configuration Manager from the SQL Server (or SSE) group on the Start menu, as shown in Figure 18.2.

2. Select SQL Server 2005 Services in the left pane of the SQL Server Configuration Manager (Figure 18.3). In Vista, you may get a User Account Control (UAC) message. If so, just click Continue.

FIGURE 18.2

Selecting the SQL Server Configuration Manager item on the Start menu.

FIGURE 18.3

Selecting the SQL Server 2005 Services page in the SQL Server Configuration Manager.

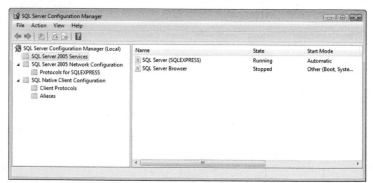

3. As depicted in Figure 18.4, right-click the SQL Server (SQLEXPRESS) row and select Properties.

FIGURE 18.4

Opening the SQL Server (SQLEXPRESS) properties sheet.

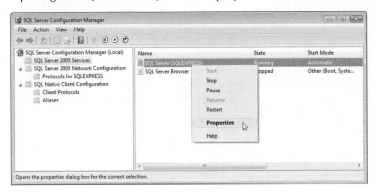

4. Select the Service tab in the properties sheet.

5. If the start mode is not automatic, drop down the Start Mode list and select Automatic, as in Figure 18.5.

FIGURE 18.5

Selecting the Automatic start mode for SQL Server.

6. Click OK. Next, right-click the SQL Server Browser row and select Properties.

7. Click the Service tab and set the Start Mode attribute to Automatic if needed, similar to step 5.

8. If you had to set the start mode to Automatic, and the state of the Browser was stopped, start it manually by right-clicking the SQL Server Browser row and selecting Start (Figure 18.6).

FIGURE 18.6

Manually starting the SQL Server Browser.

9. You will get a progress bar (see Figure 18.7) as the SQL Server service is started.

FIGURE 18.7

Starting the SQL Server service.

Next, you must enable network access — this is required even if you are connecting to SQL Server on the same computer.

1. Start by expanding the SQL Server 2005 Network Configuration folder in the left pane of the SQL Server Configuration Manager, and select the Protocols for SQLEXPRESS folder under it.

2. Enable the TCP/IP protocol from its right-click menu (Figure 18.8).

FIGURE 18.8

Enabling the TCP/IP protocol.

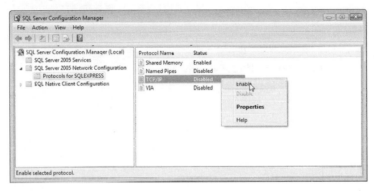

3. You will get a message, shown in Figure 18.9, that you have to stop and restart the service. You can do this by right-clicking SQL Server (SQLEXPRESS) in the SQL Server 2005 Services folder and selecting Restart, or by shutting down and restarting Windows.

FIGURE 18.9

A warning after enabling a protocol.

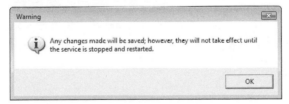

4. If your connection makes use of the Named Pipes protocol, you can enable it in a similar fashion.

Next, you have to configure SQL Server to allow remote connections (for some reason, this is necessary even if you have installed SQL Server on the same computer as Access):

1. Select SQL Server Surface Area Configuration (see Figure 18.10) from the Configuration Tools group in the Microsoft SQL Server 2005 program group. If you are running Vista, you may get a message that the program has known compatibility issues. If so, you need to install the SP2 service pack for SQL Server 2005.

FIGURE 18.10

The SQL Server 2005 Surface Area Configuration dialog.

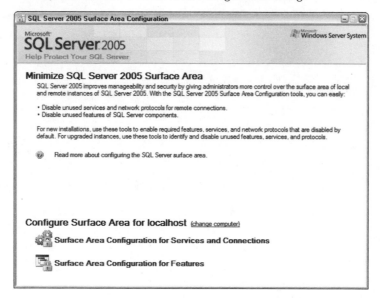

2. Click the Surface Area Configuration for Services and Connections item (see Figure 18.10).

3. Expand the Database Engine item (if necessary) and click Remote Connections.

4. Select Local and Remote connections, and select the appropriate protocol, usually "Using TCP/IP only" (Figure 18.11).

FIGURE 18.11

Surface area configuration for SQL Server.

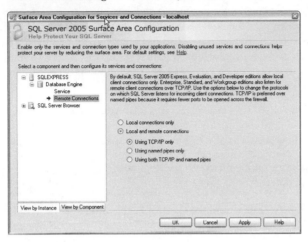

5. When you close this dialog, you will be back on the SQL Server 2005 Surface Area Configuration dialog. If needed, click the other link ("Surface Area Configuration for Features") and enable any features you plan to use (Figure 18.12).

FIGURE 18.12

Enabling SQL Server features.

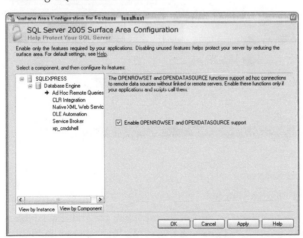

6. Restart SQL Server by selecting Restart from the right-click menu for "SQL Server (SQL-EXPRESS)" in the SQL Server 2005 Services folder.

Getting through the Firewall

After working your way through the SQL Server settings, SQL Server should be started and running. At this point, if you open an Access database and start the Upsizing Wizard in an attempt to upsize the database, you will see the SQL Server instance in the Upsizing Wizard's second screen — but that doesn't mean you can connect to it. Most likely access will be blocked by the Windows firewall. To prevent this problem, you will need to first set up the Windows firewall to allow connections to SQL Server and the SQL Server Browser. The following sections explain how to get through the Windows XP and Windows Vista firewalls, respectively.

Windows XP

Follow these steps to allow access to SQL Server through the Windows XP firewall:

 If you are using another firewall, the steps needed to allow access to SQL Server will be somewhat different.

1. Open the Security Center from the Control Panel, and click the Windows Firewall item (see Figure 18.13).

The Windows XP Security Center.

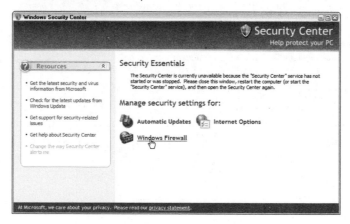

2. Click the Exceptions tab.
3. Click the Add Programs button.
4. SQL Server will probably not appear on the list of programs available for selection on the Add a Program screen, so click the Browse button, as shown in Figure 18.14.

FIGURE 18.14

The Add a Program dialog for selecting an exception to the Windows XP firewall.

5. First, browse for the SQL Server file sqlservr.exe, which is probably located in C:\Program Files\Microsoft SQL Server\MSSQL.1\MSSQL\Binn (Figure 18.15).

FIGURE 18.15

Selecting the SQL Server executable for exclusion from the Windows XP firewall.

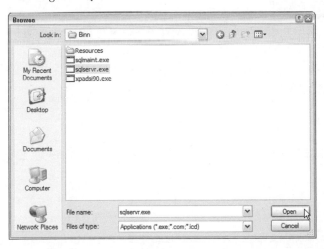

6. After clicking Open, sqlserver.exe will be listed in the Add a Program dialog, as seen in Figure 18.16.

FIGURE 18.16

The SQL Server executable in the Add a Program dialog.

7. Click OK, and you should see sqlserver.exe in the List of Exceptions.

8. Next, browse for the SQL Server Browser service, file name sqlbrowser.exe, probably located in C:\Program Files\Microsoft SQL Server\90\Shared, and click OK to add it to the List of Exceptions (Figure 18.17).

FIGURE 18.17

The SQL Server executable and browser in the list of firewall exceptions.

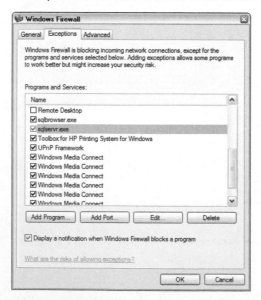

Windows Vista

For the Windows Vista firewall, the steps are somewhat different:

1. Start by opening the Control Panel and clicking the "Allow a program through Windows Firewall" link under the main Security link (Figure 18.18).

FIGURE 18.18

Opening the Windows Vista "Allow a program through Windows Firewall" Security window.

2. Alternately, you can click the Security link, and then click the "Allow a program through Windows Firewall" link in the Security window (Figure 18.19).

3. If you get a User Account Control warning, click Continue to proceed.

4. The Windows Firewall Settings dialog opens (Figure 18.20); it is substantially similar to the Windows Firewall dialog in Windows XP.

FIGURE 18.19

Clicking the "Allow a program through Windows Firewall" link in the Security window.

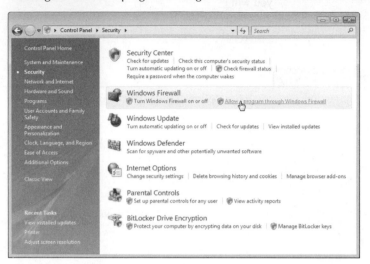

FIGURE 18.20

The Windows Firewall Settings dialog.

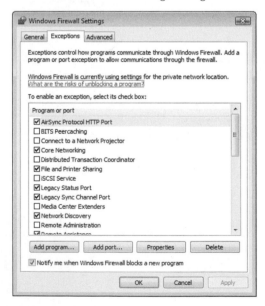

5. Click the "Add program" button to open the Add a Program dialog (Figure 18.21). Some SQL Server utilities are listed in the Programs list, but not SQL Server itself, or the SQL Server Browser, so you will need to browse for them.

6. First browse for the SQL Server file sqlservr.exe, which is probably located in C:\Program Files\Microsoft SQL Server\MSSQL.1\MSSQL\Binn (see Figure 18.22).

FIGURE 18.21

The Add a Program dialog.

FIGURE 18.22

Selecting the SQL Server executable for exclusion from the Windows Vista firewall.

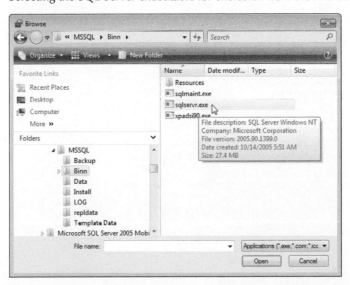

7. After clicking Open, sqlserver.exe will be listed in the Add a Program dialog, as shown in Figure 18.23.

The SQL Server executable in the Add a Program dialog.

8. Click OK, and you should see sqlserver.exe in the list of Exceptions.

9. Next, browse for the SQL Server Browser service, file name sqlbrowser.exe, probably located in C:\Program Files\Microsoft SQL Server\90\Shared, and click OK to add it to the list of exceptions (Figure 18.24).

FIGURE 18.24

The SQL Server executable and browser in the list of firewall exceptions.

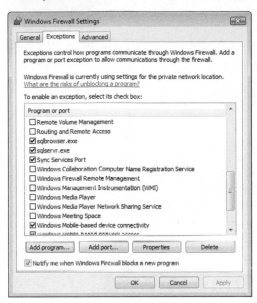

Other Security Roadblocks

Depending on what security software you have installed, you may have to deal with one or more other security warnings when attempting to connect to SQL Server. On my system, when attempting to connect to SQL Server in my Windows XP partition I get a message (Figure 18.25) from the Symantec Internet Worm Protection component of Norton Antivirus (even when connecting to SQL Server on the same computer!), and I have to click OK to proceed with the connection.

If your front-end database needs to connect to SQL Server running on another computer on the same network (a common scenario), this warning pops up on the server machine — this may be a show-stopper, unless the client and server machines are side by side on your desktop. Otherwise, you may not be able to rush over to the server computer in time to click OK on the security alert before the connection attempt times out, and thus you won't be able to connect to SQL Server on the client machine.

FIGURE 18.25

The Norton Internet Worm Protection warning.

Using the Upsizing Wizard

Access 2007 includes a handy tool for converting Access tables to SQL Server tables and (if desired) some Access queries to SQL Server stored procedures: the Upsizing Wizard. You can take a minimalist approach, and just convert your Access tables to SQL Server tables linked to the Access database, using the familiar Access interface as a front end; or you can convert the interface portion of the database to a project with a SQL Server back end. Converting just the tables is fine if you intend to use your Access forms, queries, and reports in an Access front end, and you just want to store your data in a SQL Server back end.

If you want to convert your Access database to an Access project front end with a SQL Server back end so that you can make design changes to SQL Server tables and views and work with SQL Server objects such as database diagrams, stored procedures, and user-defined functions, then you should convert the interface objects as well as the data tables, selecting the Client/Server option when upsizing the database.

The following sections illustrate both upsizing approaches.

NOTE The sample database to be upgraded is Basic Northwind.accdb, a version of Northwind with a naming convention applied to all objects, and a limited number of queries, forms, and reports.

Converting Access Tables to SQL Server Tables

To start the Upsizing Wizard, from the Ribbon's Database Tools tab, click the SQL Server command from the Move Data group, as shown in Figure 18.26.

FIGURE 18.26

Starting the SQL Server Upsizing Wizard.

The first screen of the Wizard (Figure 18.27; just like the one in Access 2003) offers a choice to use the existing database or create a new one. Generally, it is a good idea to create a new database.

> **CAUTION** The Help button on the wizard screen shown in Figure 18.27 doesn't open context-specific Help, as you might expect. Instead of getting a topic with information that would help with the decision to use the existing database or create a new one, you get the main Access Help screen, with a Table of Contents and a Search box. This is not an improvement over previous versions of Access, where context-specific Help was generally available in wizards. In Access 2003, for example, if you run the Upsizing Wizard and click the Help button on the first screen, you will get a "Use the Upsizing Wizard" Help topic, with pertinent information for each screen of the wizard.

FIGURE 18.27

The first screen of the Upsizing Wizard.

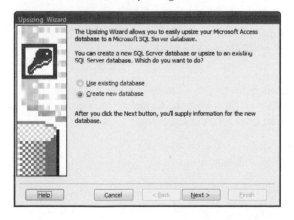

 After clicking Next, you may be required to provide the name of your computer. To find the name of your computer, follow the steps below, depending on your Windows version:

- For Windows Vista, first select the System and Maintenance link in the Control Panel.
- On the System and Maintenance page, click the "See the name of this computer" link under the main System link. The full computer name is located in the "Computer name, domain, and workgroup settings" group, as shown in Figure 18.28.

FIGURE 18.28

Finding out the full computer name in Windows Vista for use in the SQL Server connection syntax.

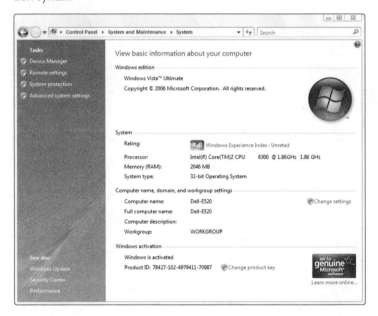

- For Windows XP, open the properties sheet for the My Computer icon on your desktop (or the System shortcut in the Control Panel), and click the Computer Name tab (Figure 18.29); the full computer name (with an extra terminating period) is listed in the middle of the page.

FIGURE 18.29

Finding out the full computer name in Windows XP for use in the SQL Server connection syntax.

On the second screen of the wizard, shown in Figure 18.30, select the running instance of SQL Server, using a name composed of the name of your computer followed by a backslash and SQLEXPRESS, check the Use Trusted Connection checkbox, and edit the proposed database name as desired.

CAUTION If you are running Windows XP, most likely the default selection in the SQL Server box will be "(local)". Help for the Upsizing Wizard (and various documents in SQL Server Books Online) recommends using this selection, but I have found that it doesn't work; the only syntax that works on my system is DELL_DIMEN_8300\SQLEXPRESS, where the portion before the backslash is my computer name (this is the default syntax if you are running Windows Vista). I found this syntax using Google; as usual, Google has proved to be of more help in finding information on using Access 2007 than Microsoft's own Help resources. However, you may find that the "(local)" selection works, or perhaps some other syntax, such as the name you gave SQL Server when you installed it.

FIGURE 18.30

Selecting the SQL Server instance to use for upsizing.

If you get the rather formidable error message shown in Figure 18.31 when clicking Next on the second screen of the Upsizing Wizard, review your SQL Server settings; you may have missed one or more of the setup steps required for Access to connect to SQL Server.

FIGURE 18.31

An error message when trying to connect to SQL Server.

 **If you get the Norton Internet Worm Protection warning (shown in Figure 18.25), click OK on it before clicking Next on the second screen of the Upsizing Wizard.**

If you don't run into one or another roadblock, you will get the third screen of the Upsizing Wizard, shown in Figure 18.32, listing the tables in the Access database for selection.

FIGURE 18.32

Selecting Access tables for upsizing to SQL Server.

I selected all the tables with data (leaving out tblBackupInfo and some lookup tables). After select-ing the data tables to upsize, on the next screen (Figure 18.33) you can select various attributes to export.

FIGURE 18.33

Table attributes to export.

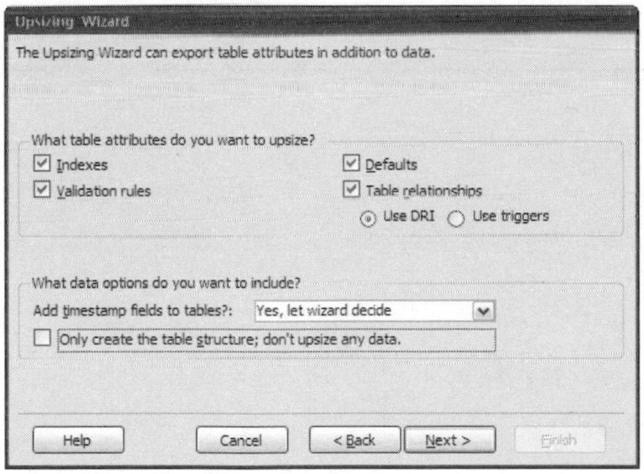

Next, you can select to create a new Access client/server application, or link the new SQL Server tables to the existing Access front end. For this section, to convert just the tables, I chose the link option (see Figure 18.34).

FIGURE 18.34

Selecting the Link option for connecting to SQL Server.

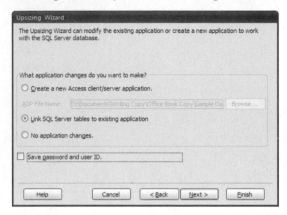

Finally, the Upsizing Wizard success screen appears (Figure 18.35); click Finish to proceed to do the upsizing using the selected choices.

FIGURE 18.35

The last screen of the Upsizing Wizard.

You will get a dialog, shown in Figure 18.36, with a progress bar listing each table in turn.

A progress bar as tables are upsized.

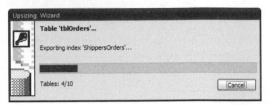

Finally, an Upsizing Wizard report is created and opened in Print Preview; you can print this report to get detailed information about the upsizing process, with lists of table fields for the tables that were successfully upsized, and a report on the error that prevented upsizing for any tables that could not be upsized. Figure 18.37 shows the page for the tblCategories table, listing the Access and SQL Server fields in two columns for comparison.

The Upsizing Wizard report.

The new SQL Server database is created in the SQL Server data folder, typically C:\Program Files\Microsoft SQL Server\MSSQL.1\MSSQL\Data. The database has the .mdf extension, and there is also a matching transaction log file with the .ldf extension. The Access front end now has two sets of tables: the original (pre-upsizing) Access tables, renamed with the suffix _local, and the linked SQL server tables, as shown in Figure 18.38. The SQL Server tables are indicated by the arrow and globe icon.

FIGURE 18.38

Linked SQL Server tables in the upsized Access database.

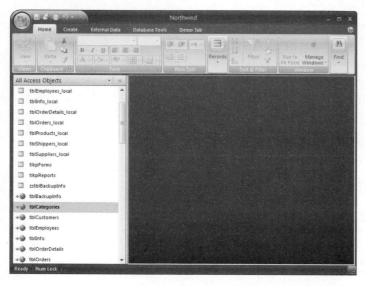

In the Access front-end database, forms and reports should work as with local Access tables. The Orders form is shown in Figure 18.39, displaying data from the linked SQL Server tblOrders.

Two of my original reports, however, wouldn't open, with Error 3219: Invalid operation. This turned out to be because the reports (or their data source queries) used the `FromDate()` and `ToDate()` functions. I made copies of the queries and reports without these functions; you can compare rptInvoices and rptInvoicesDateRange, and rptEmployeeSalesByCountry and rptEmployeeSalesByCountryDateRange, in the Basic Northwind.accdb database.

FIGURE 18.39

An Access form displaying data from a linked SQL Server table.

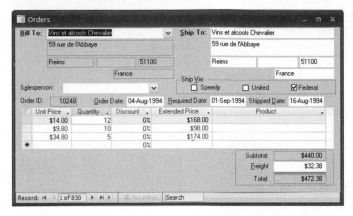

Creating a Client/Server Application

Compared with just converting the tables to SQL Server tables, and linking the Access database to them as a front end, creating an Access Project as a front end has several advantages: You can make design changes to SQL Server tables and views, some of which can't be edited from an Access front end. You can also create, edit, and use other SQL Server objects, such as database diagrams, stored procedures, and user-defined functions. In a linked Access front end, by contrast, you can't make design changes to any SQL Server objects, and you can only link to SQL Server tables and views.

To create a client/server application from an Access database, with an Access Project (.adp) as the front end to the SQL Server back end, proceed as in the previous section until you reach the screen offering a choice between creating a client/server application or linking to the SQL Server back end (this screen is shown in Figure 18.40); in this case, select the client/server application option, and edit the name of the new project as desired.

FIGURE 18.40

Selecting the client/server option for upsizing an Access database.

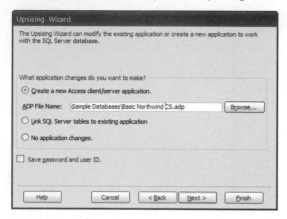

On the next screen, shown in Figure 18.41, you can choose whether to open the new ADP file, or keep the old Access database open.

FIGURE 18.41

Choosing to open the project or database.

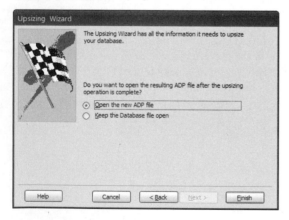

Next, you will get a dialog with a progress bar while the database objects are upsized (Figure 18.42).

The Upsizing Wizard progress bar dialog.

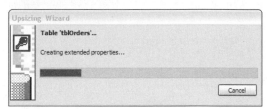

The Upsizing Wizard report opens in Print Preview; with the client/server option selected, queries and forms (and other database objects, if present) will be upsized as well as tables. The report shows which queries were upsized, and which were not, with the reasons (see Figure 18.43).

The Upsizing Wizard report.

Forms based on tables, or queries that were successfully upsized, will look the same in the project as in the original database (see Figure 18.44).

A form in an Access project displaying data from a SQL Server table.

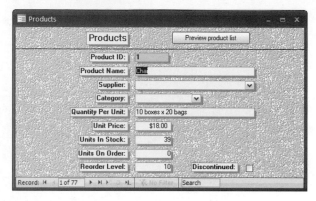

If you attempt to upsize queries as well as tables, you will find that some query types don't upsize at all, because they don't match up with views or stored procedures in SQL Server. Crosstab queries, for example, can't be upsized at all, nor can any query that uses a function in a calculated field expression. If a query isn't upsized, you need to re-create it as a SQL Server object of the appropriate type (view or stored procedure).

CROSS-REF   See the *SQL Server 2005 Bible* (Wiley, 2006) for more information about working with SQL Server features such as stored procedures and user-defined functions.

Figure 18.45 shows the four queries in the original Basic Northwind.mdb database that were successfully upgraded to SQL Server.

The first two queries were converted to views and the third and fourth to user-defined functions, as indicated by their distinctive icons. Figure 18.46 shows the qryOrderSubtotals view in design view, and Figure 18.47 shows the qryCurrentProductList user-defined function in SQL view.

You now have a client/server application consisting of an Access project front end and a SQL Server back end; from this point on you will need to use SQL Server techniques to work with the project and the back-end tables.

FIGURE 18.45

Four upsized queries in an Access project.

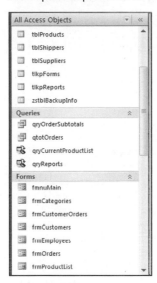

FIGURE 18.46

A SQL Server view created from an Access query.

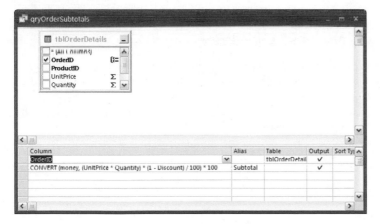

FIGURE 18.47

A user-defined function created from an Access query.

```
qryCurrentProductList                                          _  □  x
ALTER FUNCTION dbo.qryCurrentProductList
()
RETURNS TABLE
AS
RETURN ( SELECT    TOP 100 PERCENT ProductID, ProductName
FROM        dbo.tblProducts
WHERE    (Discontinued = 0)
ORDER BY ProductName )
```

Linking to Data in SQL Server Tables

You may need to connect to SQL Server databases for a company, university, or other organization that stores its data in SQL Server. If you need to link an Access database to data in existing SQL Server tables, or create a new Access front end for SQL Server tables, the process is different.

NOTE   The SQL Server database I connect to in this section is AdventureWorks, one of the sample databases you can download from the SQL Server 2005 Samples and Sample Databases (February 2007) page on the Microsoft web site, at this link: www.microsoft.com/downloads/details.aspx?FamilyID=e719ecf7-9f46-4312-af89-6ad8702e4e6e&DisplayLang=en#filelist (or possibly a page with a later date). Make sure that any sample databases you download are compatible with Access 2007. Those on the December 2006 page are compatible with Access 2007; other sample databases posted earlier are not.

Download the AdventureWorksDB.msi file, and install it by double-clicking it. This will create the SQL Server database AdventureWorks_Data.mdf in your SQL Server data folder, usually C:\Program Files\Microsoft SQL Server\MSSQL.1\MSSQL\Data.

Next, create a new, blank Access 2007 database by selecting New from the File menu. On the dialog that opens next (Figure 18.48), select the Blank Database selection, and enter the name for the new front-end database.

Close the default table (Table1) that is automatically created.

To link to the SQL Server database, follow these steps:

  1. Drop down the More list on the Import group on the External Data tab, and select the ODBC Database item, as shown in Figure 18.49.

FIGURE 18.48

Creating the new blank database.

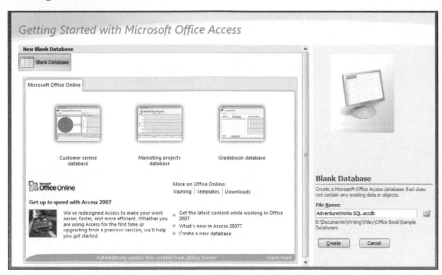

FIGURE 18.49

Starting the process of linking to a SQL Server database.

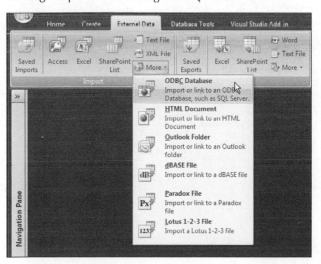

2. On the Get External Data screen (Figure 18.50), select the Link option.

FIGURE 18.50

Choosing to link to the data source.

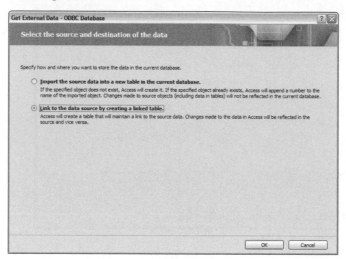

3. On the Select Data Source screen (Figure 18.51), type a name for the data source and click New to create a new DSN name.

FIGURE 18.51

Adding a new DSN name.

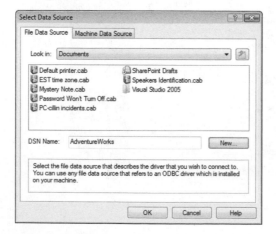

4. Select the SQL Server driver on the Create New Data Source screen (Figure 18.52) and click Next.

FIGURE 18.52

Selecting the SQL Server driver.

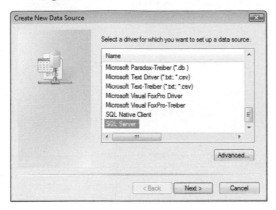

5. Type a name for the DSN file on the next screen, shown in Figure 18.53, and click Next.

FIGURE 18.53

Naming the DSN file.

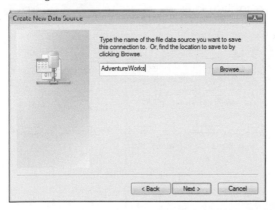

6. The Finish screen (Figure 18.54) lists the DSN name and driver you selected. (This is only the end of the DSN portion of this wizard.)

The Finish screen of the DSN Wizard.

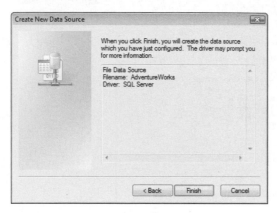

7. The next phase of the wizard starts with a screen (Figure 18.55) where you enter the description of the data source, and select a SQL Server to connect to.

Selecting a SQL Server to connect to.

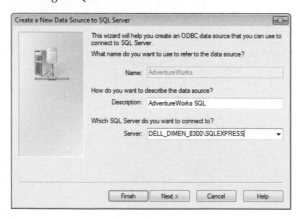

8. On the Authentication screen (Figure 18.56), generally you can accept the default selection of Windows NT authentication.

FIGURE 18.56

Selecting the authentication type.

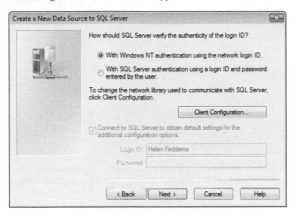

9. On the next screen, depicted in Figure 18.57, check the "Change the default database to" checkbox, and select the SQL Server database you want to connect to.

FIGURE 18.57

Selecting the SQL Server database.

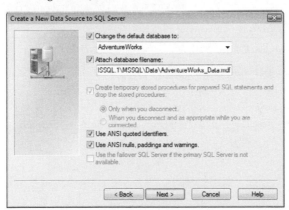

> **TIP**   If the database you want to connect to doesn't appear in the "Change the default database to" drop-down list, type in the database name, check the "Attach database filename" checkbox, and type in the full file path and name for the database .mdf file in the "Attach database filename" textbox.

10. The settings on the screen shown in Figure 18.58 can generally be left at their defaults.

FIGURE 18.58

Various SQL Server settings.

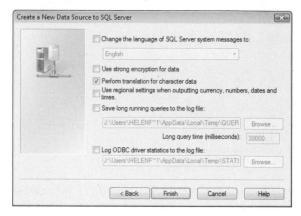

11. Click Finish to get a screen listing the ODBC data source configuration; click Test Data Source to test the connection to the database (see Figure 18.59).

FIGURE 18.59

The final screen of the ODBC SQL Server Setup Wizard.

12. You should get the success screen depicted in Figure 18.60.

FIGURE 18.60

A success message on getting a connection to a SQL Server database.

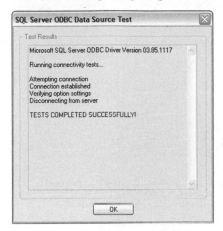

13. Click OK on the test message and then on the ODBC Microsoft SQL Server Setup screen, then click OK on the Select Data Source screen (Figure 18.61) with the newly created DSN selected.

FIGURE 18.61

Selecting the newly created DSN.

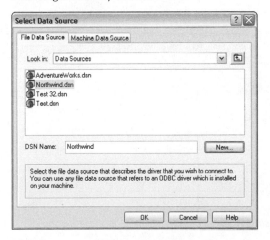

14. On clicking OK, you will get the Link Tables screen, shown in Figure 18.62, where you can select the tables to link to the Access front end.

FIGURE 18.62

Selecting SQL Server tables to link.

15. If one or more of the tables lacks a unique index, you will get the Select Unique Record Identifier message (Figure 18.63). Select one or more fields to create a unique index and click OK to proceed.

FIGURE 18.63

Selecting fields for a unique record identifier index.

16. Now, as in Figure 18.64, you can see the linked SQL Server tables in the Access database window.

FIGURE 18.64

Linked SQL Server tables in an Access front-end database.

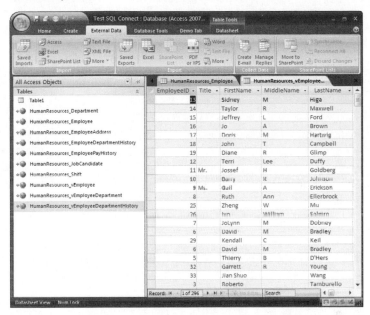

With the tables linked, you can proceed to create the Access front end for working with the SQL Server data.

The SQL Server Migration Assistant for Access

There is an alternative to using the Upsizing Wizard: the SQL Server Migration Assistant for Access (SSMA), a free Microsoft download, at www.microsoft.com/sql/solutions/migration/access/default.mspx.

Compared with the Upsizing Wizard, SSMA has a more modern look and includes a number of extra features, but as far as the basics are concerned, it should accomplish the same task: converting Access tables to SQL Server tables. However, at this time the SSMA does not support the new Access 2007 .accdb database format, so if you attempt to use this utility to upsize an Access database to SQL Server, you will just get a message saying "Unrecognized database format."

Using Access as a front end to SQL Server is a topic worthy of a complete book on its own, but the Upsizing Wizard will at least help with the first steps toward creating a client-server application: moving your data from Access tables to SQL Server tables.

Summary

Because of new security features in Office and Windows, it is much more difficult to connect an Access database to a back-end SQL Server database. With the information in this chapter, you should be able to negotiate the security settings that allow you to connect an Access database to a back-end SQL Server database, allowing you to use an Access database (or project) front end to data stored in SQL Server tables.

Index

SYMBOLS

' (apostrophe), 366
\ (backslash), 267, 268

A

.accda file format, 472, 473, 505, 511. *See also* add-ins, Access
.accdb file format, 471, 473, 482, 511, 671
Access
    backing up databases, 277–282
    calendar pop-up, 52, 53, 320
    comparing add-ins with COM add-ins, 469
    comparing contact data with Outlook contact data, 359–390
    concatenating data for export, 143–144
    CopyAccessAttsToAccess procedure, 394–395
    CopyAccessAttsToOutlook procedure, 391–392
    CopyAccessContactsToOutlook procedure, 390
    CopyAllOutlookContactsToAccess procedure, 390
    CopyOutlookAttsToAccess procedure, 392–393
    CreateProjectAppts procedure, 245–247
    CreateProjectTasks procedure, 253–254
    creating client/server applications, 657–662
    creating databases from templates, 225–229
    creating denormalized tables from linked tables, 352–359
    creating e-mails from tables, 81–85
    creating form letter reports, 8–10
    creating worksheet-type reports, 11–25
    DAO support, 90, 91–96

ExportAccountSummary function, 195–200
ExportAppointmentsToOutlook function, 241–243
ExportContactsToExcel function, 191–195
ExportFlatFileContactsToOutlook procedure, 255–258
exporting appointment data to Outlook, 72–78, 241–243
exporting contact data to Outlook, 255–258
exporting data to Excel, 184–187
exporting data to Outlook items, 220–233
exporting data to unformatted Excel worksheets, 50–52
exporting data to Word documents, 135–138
exporting data to Word using Automation code, 138–182
exporting mainframe data as Outlook Journal items, 79–81
exporting queries to Excel, 184–187
exporting task data to Outlook, 72–78, 247–249
ExportTasksToOutlook function, 247–249
filling Word documents with Access data by using TypeText method, 27–30
Help overview, 272–277
history of data transfer techniques, 4
ImportApptsFromOutlook function, 243–245
ImportContactsFromOutlook function, 259–262
importing Outlook appointment data from, 243–245
importing Outlook contacts to, 259–262
ImportTasksFromOutlook function, 250–251
Layout view, 134–135
methods for merging data to Word, 145–182
new templates in Access 2007, 230–233
Object Browser, 94

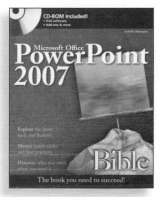
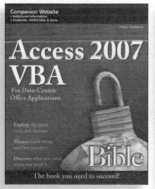

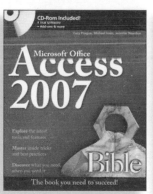